Dissenting Bodies

Dissenting Bodies

CORPOREALITIES IN
EARLY NEW ENGLAND

Martha L. Finch

COLUMBIA UNIVERSITY PRESS   NEW YORK

COLUMBIA UNIVERSITY PRESS
Publishers Since 1893
NEW YORK   CHICHESTER, WEST SUSSEX

Copyright © 2010 Columbia University Press

All rights reserved

Library of Congress Cataloging-in-Publication Data

Finch, Martha L.
    Dissecting bodies : corporealities in early New England / Martha Finch.
        p. cm.
    Includes bibliographical references and index.
    ISBN 978-0-231-13946-5 (cloth : alk. paper)—ISBN 978-0-231-51138-4 (e-book)
    1. Human body—Social aspects—Massachusetts—History—17th century.   2. Human
body—Massachusetts—Religious aspects—History—17th century.   3. Pilgrims
(New Plymouth Colony)—Social life and customs.   4. British Americans—
Massachusetts—History—17th century.   5. Protestants—Massachusetts—
History—17th century.   6. Community life—Massachusetts—History—17th
century.   7. Massachusetts—History—New Plymouth, 1620–1691.   8. Massachusetts—
Social life and customs—17th century.   9. Massachusetts—Religious life and
customs.   10. Massachusetts—Race relations—History—17th century.   I. Title.

GT497.M4F56 2010
974.4'02—dc22

2009017741

∞

Columbia University Press books are printed on permanent and durable acid-free paper.

This book is printed on paper with recycled content.

Printed in the United States of America

c 10 9 8 7 6 5 4 3 2 1

References to Internet Web sites (URLs) were accurate at the time of writing. Neither
the author nor Columbia University Press is responsible for URLs that may have expired
or changed since the manuscript was prepared.

For Hylah and Abby

CONTENTS

THIS IS A BOOK ABOUT THE HUMAN BODY—THE BODY as a conceptual idea shot through with theological, scientific, metaphorical, and other cultural meanings and implications—at a particular intellectual moment in Anglo-Protestant history. It is also a book about living human bodies—bodies that starved, ate, slept, dressed, engaged in sexual relations, became ill and recovered, were whipped, branded, hanged, murdered, and beheaded, sang, prayed, preached, and were baptized—in a particular place and time: Plymouth Colony in New England during the seventeenth century. The two bodies—one imagined, the other lived—came together in individuals' daily activities, as the dissenting Protestant separatists who colonized Plymouth engaged a "new world" and its native inhabitants and strove to shape selves and communities that thoroughly embodied their understandings of godly principles. Through such activities their physical existence and how they understood it changed, as they first labored to survive and then became healthier than in England, first struggled to create churches that embodied Christ and then established orderly church bodies, first depended upon "common affections" among members to build exclusive, cohesive communities and then enacted civil laws to regulate individuals' behaviors. Throughout, those who endeavored to make visible in the world what they believed to be God's divine will always found their ideas and practices challenged by other dissenters—those who embodied different meanings and activities.

I became interested in early New England and the bodies of those who lived there when I was a graduate student in religious studies at the University of California, Santa Barbara. I intended to study the ways people generate meanings through religious practice, especially rituals, but I did not yet have a particular religious community in mind. A single book, assigned for a seminar, inspired the direction I needed. In David D. Hall's *Worlds of Wonder, Days of Judgment: Popular Religious Belief in Early New England* I discovered to my surprise (and delight) that those Calvinist, "antiritual" early New Englanders actually engaged in an entire complex of ritual activities, with which they intended to shape their religious lives in particular ways. As I investigated further I became convinced that, despite their emphasis on intentionality and rationality, the human body was, in fact, at the center of the English Protestant dissenters' theology. I also began to see how broader early modern shifts in Anglo-European conceptions of corporeality—ideas about physiology and medicine, environment, self-presentation, and "civilization," for example—also influenced these religious nonconformists, contributing to their distinct understandings and practices. Both theological and early modern ideas about the body had everything to do with how those who colonized Plymouth understood themselves and their relationships with God, each other, and others and with how they shaped their social discourses—both words and practices—in America.

Thus, my decision to investigate corporealities in early New England was not arbitrary. Among the Calvinist Protestants who criticized the Church of England during the latter half of the sixteenth century, Plymouth's founders had gone further than most dissenters, popularly called puritans. Plymouth's founders were separatists, whose understandings of godly purity impelled them to reject the "corrupt" Anglican Church and form independent church communities. Persecuted in England for their nonconformity, they migrated to the Netherlands in 1608, where their pastor, John Robinson, developed what I call his "theology of the body," which produced an "embodied theology." For Robinson and the members of his community who established "Plimoth Plantation" in 1620, the body—both imagined and lived—was the axis upon which all religious and other cultural and social meanings turned. Robinson derived his views from English Calvinist theology, giving it a separatist spin that more forcefully grounded godliness in one's body and behavior, the visible sign that one was a "saint" and among the elect. Plymouth's leaders encoded in civil legislation and church discipline Robinson's ideas about properly embodied moral and social values, intending these prescriptions to produce individuals who enacted visible sainthood in their daily lives. Their expectations, needless to say, did not go unchallenged. Encounters with New England native people—Wampanoags, Massachusetts, and others—confronted colonists with bodies displaying radically different ideas and practices, and numerous colonists themselves, such as Thomas Morton of Ma-re Mount, Quakers, and others who challenged separatist orthodoxy, presented colonial leadership with troubling alternatives. Over time these encounters, coupled with changes in Plymouth's social demographics and eventual absorption into the Massachusetts Bay Colony in 1691, altered the ways these New Englanders thought about and experienced their bodies.

During the years spent researching and writing this book I have accumulated many debts. I owe immense gratitude for the financial and intellectual support of several institutions: the Department of Religious Studies at the University of California, Santa Barbara; the Pew Program in Religion and American History at Yale University; the Young Scholars in American Religion Program at Indiana University-Purdue University Indianapolis; and the Center for the Study of Religion at Princeton University. I also want to thank Carolyn Travers and Jill Hall at Plimoth Plantation, Jeremy Bangs at Pilgrim Hall Museum, and the staffs at the American Antiquarian Society, Massachusetts Historical Society, Beineke Library, and William Andrews Clark Memorial Library.

My interest in religious studies began when I was an undergraduate at Syracuse University; I am especially grateful to one of my professors there at the time, Amanda Porterfield, who continues to provide encouragement. Words can never adequately express appreciation for the time and energy graduate advisors invest in a student's labors. I thank Charles Long for his insights about religion and colonial encounters; Wade Clark Roof for his Southern hospitality, marvelous sense of humor, and helping me think about bodies and embodiment; Ann Marie Plane for suggesting I focus on Plymouth Colony, introducing me to New England native people's history, exploring late twentieth-century southern New England with me, and reading numerous early drafts; and especially Catherine L. Albanese, for her persistent support of my work, her always rigorous and creative thinking, and her generous, extraordinarily detailed attention to my writing. My friends and colleagues from UCSB continue to provoke stimulating conversation and offer unending support, especially Sarah McFarland

Taylor, to whom I am indebted for suggesting the title of this book, and Stephen Berkwitz, who helped with manuscript preparation.

The Pew Program at Yale provided an initial arena in which to share early drafts with others who also were thinking about colonial America; I thank Harry Stout, Jon Butler, Jane Kamensky, and especially Amy DeRogatis, who read the entire manuscript and provided insightful suggestions. Philip Goff and Becky Vasko of the Young Scholars Program at IUPUI brought together eleven early-career scholars of American religion over a two-year period to engage in sustained conversations about our work; each member of this remarkable group contributed helpful insights to my project, especially Rachel Wheeler, Kristen Schwain, and our mentors Ann Taves and Steve Prothero, but I am most indebted to Doug Winiarski, who went above and beyond the call of duty to provide his remarkable expertise, insights, and resources. The book came to fruition while I was a visiting research fellow at Princeton's Center for the Study of Religion, where I received the generous support of Robert Wuthnow, Anita Kline, Jenny Wiley Legath, and Marie Griffith; Chris Garces and Tammy Brown provided thoughtful readings of chapter 1. I thank the Department of Religious Studies at Missouri State University for granting me time off from teaching and other duties while I resided at Princeton. Many of those already named read and commented on chapter drafts or portions that have been published as articles; others are John Corrigan, Janet Lindman, Michele Tarter, Etta Madden, and several anonymous readers. Those who responded to drafts presented at professional meetings and colloquia are too numerous to mention by name, but I thank them nevertheless. I am grateful to Melissa Hutchens, MD, who provided helpful insights into Massasoit's medical condition in chapter 1. I also appreciate my students who have asked good questions and taught me much, especially my graduate assistant Jonathan Olson, who researched the book's illustrations. I am indebted to Randall Balmer, who believed in my manuscript. Wendy Lochner at Columbia University Press has been unfailingly patient and supportive.

I am deeply thankful for friends and family members who provided moral, practical, and other kinds of crucial support at various times throughout this project. Although he would deny it, without Dennis Palumbo's profound insights and unflagging encouragement this book would not exist. Finally, my greatest debt is to my daughters, Hylah Hedgepeth and Abigail McGill, who somehow survived growing up with this project to become remarkable young women; they are my shining stars.

Dissenting Bodies

Embodying Godliness

J OHN ROBINSON, PASTOR OF AN ENGLISH SEPARATIST
congregation living in exile in the Netherlands during the early decades
of the seventeenth century, was deeply concerned about the bodies and
souls of the men and women who were members of his church, many of
whom soon would establish Plymouth Colony in New England. Believing
that puritan reforms of the Church of England were insufficient for achieving purity in polity and worship, Robinson's congregation refused to conform to the mandates of English church and civil authorities. Its members
had separated themselves from the national church and, threatened with
imprisonment and execution in England, emigrated to Amsterdam and
then Leiden, where they hoped to form the true body of Christ, a community of "visible saints" committed to reproducing godliness in the world.
Their pastor understood the church community, as well as individuals' relationships with each other and with God, in what he considered "concrete"
terms, explicitly grounding his theology in human embodiment. For nonconforming and dissenting English Protestants like the members of Robinson's separatist community, divine grace entered a person's soul through
the physical senses, and inner grace, in turn, motivated one's actions in the
world. One's hidden spiritual state meant nothing unless it was manifested
visibly through one's work, dress, speech, sexual activities, food consump-

tion, and every other aspect of behavior. Salvation began and ended in the body, and those who eventually left the Netherlands for New England attempted to structure families, churches, and towns in ways that promoted their fundamentally corporeal understanding of Christian faith and experience. The following chapters explore Robinson's and other dissenting ministers' theology of the body and the ways it played out in the "everyday theologies"—the mutable, often conflicting understandings of the proper Christian life that people develop as they "think about and share collective knowledge about right and wrong, godly and sinful, natural and unnatural, and healthy and sick"—and activities of the inhabitants of Plymouth Colony during the seventeenth century.[1]

Robinson described the relationship between the individual and one's social world in ways that, remarkably, seemed to anticipate more recent views developed by sociologists of knowledge like Pierre Bourdieu.[2] For Robinson, a godly individual was produced by a particular *habitus* (to use Bourdieu's terminology), or sociocultural environment, that imparted its values through one's physical senses. Reacting to the sensuous excesses of late Renaissance culture against which Robinson and other dissenters took a stand, separatists wanted to engender a different kind of human being, one who exhibited modesty and moderation—what William Bradford, the second governor of Plymouth Colony, encapsulated in the adjective *plain*. "Outward" plainness, they believed, both produced and demonstrated "inward" godliness. Bourdieu explained the social processes of creating such a "new man" as "deculturation" and "reculturation." By reconfiguring the "seemingly most insignificant details of *dress, bearing*, physical and verbal *manners*," he wrote, the fundamental values of a newly formed society are "given body, *made* body by the transubstantiation achieved by the hidden persuasion of an implicit pedagogy, capable of instilling a whole cosmology, an ethic, a metaphysic."[3]

Robinson recognized that for his implicit pedagogy to be persuasive and effective in instilling a new, comprehensive way of imagining and living in the world, it must be applied from the moment of birth. He believed an infant entered a familial *habitus* that insinuated itself into the child's mind and heart through the physical senses, shaping his or her awareness of self and world with particular kinds of human touch, food, clothing, gestures, and speech that intentionally molded a young person into a moral individual. Ideally, the child internalized this corporeal shaping, over time and with persistence developing self-imposed constraints on personal conduct, constraints that produced the good behavior sustaining the "common affections" of a harmonious, godly society. As infants "sucked [their mothers'] milk," Robinson wrote, they sucked "their [mothers'] manners also, by being continually with them, and receiving their first impressions from them." It was essential that children be able to ingest "the greater benefit of good mothers," that is, "godly" mothers, who recognized that divine grace was not imparted "by natural generation"—through the mother's or father's "seed"—but must be learned through "godly education."[4]

When children grew older, fathers, with their "greater wisdom and authority," were to take over educational duties: "Good fathers are more behoveful for [children's] forming in virtue and good manners," because fathers, "by their severity," could correct mothers' (and grandparents') natural indulgences, more forcefully inscribing godly education on the child's body in order to mold his or her soul properly. Because children had inherited Adam's original sin, they had "a stubbornness, and stoutness of mind arising from natural pride, which must, in the first place, be broken and beaten down" in order to produce a foundation of "humility and tractableness" upon which other virtues could be built. Wielding "severity of discipline" and "the rod of correction," a father rendered his child's body and heart "tender" to receive divine grace. Expressing pride and willfulness in numerous physical ways, especially through the voice, children should not be allowed to realize "that they have a will of their own, but in their parents' keeping: neither should these words be heard from them, save by way of consent, 'I will' or 'I will not.'" Parents also must wean their children from pride through "plain and homely diet and apparel," attendance at school, and engagement in some kind of labor "in which they may be exercised diligently." When parents did not physically restrain and repress willfulness in their son or daughter, the child grew into an "unbroken youth"—a rowdy teenager—led by his or her "lusts" and, finally, into an adult with "a kind of unwieldiness, inflexibility and obstinacy" that undermined an orderly society, making "uncomfortable" those who attempted to "converse with them."[5]

Robinson's principles of human development—the implicit pedagogy derived from his theology of the body—generated a *habitus* located first in the home and then in the public world. Godly values and their correspondent manners became embodied knowledge, physically ingested with mother's milk and simple foods and shaped by the disciplining rod and homely apparel. By adulthood this godly knowledge ideally had become second nature, displayed in daily life through, among other behaviors, diligent labor at one's calling and pleasant social relations with one's neighbors. From infancy through adulthood, one's body required specific kinds of disciplining that would tame the inner flesh and tenderize the heart, opening it to God's grace; the regenerated will, in turn, provoked godly actions as the physical, public signs that one had received that saving grace. Such a person was now a visible saint, a person who embodied sainthood. Believing themselves divinely called to wean themselves from the world and its corrupt luxuries and live as God's elect, Robinson's congregation attempted to build "pure" church congregations in England and the Netherlands. Later, in New England, they attempted to create entire civil communities of visible saints.

Over forty years ago Edmund S. Morgan familiarized historians of early New England with the term *visible saints*, describing them as "those who appeared to be saved, . . . those who could demonstrate by their lives, their beliefs, and their religious experiences that they apparently (to a charitable judgment) had received saving faith," and he discussed the ways the doctrine of visible sainthood contributed to separatist principles of church formation.[6] Yet few, including Morgan, have recognized or investigated the immediate correspondence between soul and body that English separatists, puritans, and other nonconformists espoused—what I am calling their theology of the body. Nor have they explored or delineated the complex and often contradictory everyday meanings and practices of the body generated by that theology. Before Morgan wrote about visible sainthood, Perry Miller had noted the puritan belief that "the presence of grace could be verified by external symptoms, . . . that faith was recognizable" in the "outward evidences" of one's behavior, and he described the principle of *eupraxia*—good practices, or right conduct—as a reflection of the English Calvinist "shift of emphasis in theology and philosophy from contemplation to action, from beatitude to utility."[7] Nevertheless, as Amanda Porterfield has shown more recently, Miller posited a "complete separation . . . between supernatural grace and all its natural simulacra. Puritanism," he claimed, "could exist only on condition that it maintain the distinction, and when we shall find the division closing up, we shall perceive the dwindling of piety."[8]

Miller's view that New England's "Augustinian strain of piety" depended upon a radical split between grace and its physical manifestations, between the spiritual and the material, overlooks the central importance of corporeality in nonconformists' philosophical, theological, and practical understandings of God, world, and self and the critical linkage between body and soul, between the "outward act," as puritan William Ames put it, and the "inward act," at the heart of their personal and social ethics. Dissenting ministers viewed subjective intentionality and objective behavior as so closely interwoven that the "outer body"—one's conduct—immediately and accurately displayed the truth of the "inner heart"—one's godly or sinful character; the internal willing and the external action were, in fact, "two phases of the same act" producing "one act in manner."[9] Only God could see into a person's soul and know his or her true motivations; thus, internal motivations required externalization in behavior, making publicly visible one's private moral state, assuring oneself and others that one was, indeed, a saint. "Faith," Robinson succinctly wrote, "if it be not fruitful in all good works . . . is dead." One must conjoin the "bodily hand" of works with the "spiritual hand" of faith; "in truth of affection and in deed of action" one "must love [goodness and piety] *in the concrete*, where both the person, and good in him, are *visible*."[10] Robinson's embodied theology articulated the "remarkably visceral doctrine of salvation" described by Porterfield, which "reflected [English Calvinists'] basic acceptance of the body as the basis of religious life." Imagining each person as an integrated moral being and locating sanctity in the moral governance of the body, they closed the medieval gap between soul and body.[11]

Furthermore, dissenting Protestants often viewed their corporeal existence more positively than Miller thought. In spite of his important revelation that New England puritans "live[d] the life of the senses" and viewed "all that supports life, preserves or restores health, [and] feeds natural hungers" as good and enjoyable in moderation, Miller also argued that puritans denigrated the body and its sensual desires. Even when a person had been infused with divine grace, "corruption . . . still adheres to physical being."[12] Miller's contradictory representations of the puritan body and its senses, like his conflicting arguments about the puritan relationship between soul and body, perhaps reflect the complexities and complications dissenting divines encountered when they attempted to formulate their understandings of the human body. At least three interrelated intellectual developments contributed to the development of their embodied theology: John Calvin's anthropology, the Protestant iconoclastic impulse, and Petrus Ramus's epistemology.

Calvin, from whom English dissenters took their doctrinal cues, had offered a shifting, kaleidoscopic view of the body.[13] When observed from one angle, human corporeality was inherently and fundamentally good: God had created human beings in the divine image, and a person could "find

God a hundred times both in his body and his soul."[14] Likewise, Calvin's intellectual offspring in England believed the human body was a "natural good thing," the highest of all God's physical creations; the divine image shone through "a grace and majesty in the person, especially in the face of man."[15] Yet Calvin knew that people often experienced their physical existence in far less elevated terms; when he viewed the body from a second perspective, the difficulties of corporeal life came into focus. Having inherited Adam's sin, one's body became ill and felt pain, it aged; while it was the beautiful temple of the soul and spirit, the body was also a "frail lodging" and a "hut of mud." Puritan Thomas Cartwright explained that God had formed Adam's body "of the very dust of the earth" so that "man" would "vnderstand of what base matter his body was framed, that so hee might have occasion to bee lowly, and humble in his owne sight" and realize "the absolute authority that God hath ouer man." Original sin introduced a distinction between soul and body, placing the body in a subordinate position requiring direction by the soul; yet, as Mary Potter Engel has argued, even here Calvin and his followers did not "denigrate, reject, or finally separate" the body from the soul.[16]

In fact, it was not the body but the "flesh"—the soul's lust for worldly things—that was immoral and must be held in check. Flesh, Calvin wrote, was "everything which we have from [sinful human] nature"; it was the aspect of the human being that must be born again. Viewed from this third angle, body and flesh were qualitatively different entities; one's physical body, though made of dust, reflected the image of God, was by nature "good," and, unlike the flesh, did not require a rebirth.[17] Calvin, then, saw the actions of the body not as sinful in themselves but as manifestations of the state of the soul, whether "fleshly" or "spiritual." This view freed a person to enjoy the sensory pleasures given by God every day: the beauty of the natural world in the colors and scents of flowers; sculpture, painting, and music; eating and drinking all kinds of foods in merry feasts; sexual pleasures with one's spouse—all were desirable, Calvin believed, as long as one did not indulge excessively. Likewise, one should avoid extreme ascetic practices; fasting from food and abstaining from marital sex were only to be done occasionally in order to "mortify and subdue the flesh [not the body], that it may not wanton" and to humble the soul in preparation for prayer and meditation.[18] The guiding principle was moderation in all things, with the body as the morally neutral medium for persuading the soul and enacting the desires and strivings of the heart's moral or immoral intentions. Wanton overindulgence in the sensory appetites that led to idle and irresponsible behavior was a sin of the corrupting and corruptible flesh, not the body.

Calvin's views on human embodiment were complex and multifaceted, but ultimately produced a coherent and functional anthropology. For his English followers, the body was not governed by an extreme Augustinian dualism that rejected corporeal life and its sensory pleasures. Rather, dissenting divines exalted the human body-soul unity as the highest of material beings created by God and bearing God's image. Yet they problematized the body as the site of conflict between spirit and flesh; the battle occurred in the deepest recesses of the human heart but always was influenced by and expressed through one's conduct in daily life. For some Protestants, these ideas about the body provided theological support for the iconoclastic violence that raged across England during the second half of the 1500s and first half of the 1600s. Although most dissenting ministers, following Calvin's lead, did not advocate smashing, ripping, burning, or otherwise destroying crucifixes, vestments, communion silver, stained-glass windows, and other ritual objects, the iconoclastic impulse engaged radically new understandings of materiality and sacredness that reflected a new valuing of the human body itself as the site of sacred power (see figure I.1).[19] Laypeople were now visible saints, the "living icons of common plainness," as Ann Kibbey has described them, replacing the ornately decorated, "dead" statues of Mary, Jesus, and the Catholic saints.[20] Embodying the sacred, the Protestant layperson enjoyed direct access to divine knowledge and power through the Word of God. But such personal and immediate access required a system of apprehending and interpreting the Word that was accessible to the uneducated masses. As Miller and others have pointed out, the epistemological theories of rhetorician and logician Petrus Ramus fit the bill.[21]

Ramus located the human body and its sensory perceptions—taste, touch, smell, and especially hearing and sight—as the vehicles through which information about the world entered one's soul. There, the rational mind made sense of that information and, in turn, informed the will, which directed the body to behave appropriately in good conduct, or *eupraxia*. Puritan theologians adapted Ramus's epistemology to argue that grace and sin also entered the human soul by way of the five physical senses—Cartwright imagined them as the body's "windowes"—either regenerating one's heart, affections, and will and motivating one to conduct oneself as a visible saint or feeding one's fleshly desires and producing immoral behavior. John Robinson explained the connections among a

voozt belet. (Te Liere hebben sp sulcks oock
willen doen/ maer de Wet heeft hen belooft | Lepden/ Delft/ den Oziel/ ende andere
plaetsen in Hollandt.

Gens effræna armis quid quæſo lædis inermes
Tasne ſacrata Deo audaci ſpoliare rapinâ

Vana ſuperſtitio patrum ſimulachra ferebat.
Non furor hæc tollat; duce ſed ratione gerantur

Iaer-dicht. | waren/ dat ſp de ſelve niet af en epſchten

FIGURE I.I *The Iconoclasm of 1566.* Protestant iconoclasts stole or destroyed Roman
Catholic material culture—statues, stained glass, altars, documents, vestments, and altar
hangings—transferring divine presence from ritual objects to their own living human bodies.
(From Pieter Bor, *Nederlantsche oorloghen,* 1621–1634. Courtesy of the Library of Congress.)

person's God-given sensory perceptions, reason, and faith: when "used" rightly, they worked together not to "destroy" but to "order and perfect" each other, for "'faith comes by hearing,' at the first . . . and is nourished, and increased both by hearing, and seeing, and by the benefit of all the other senses afterwards."[22]

Separatists picked up this model of corporeality, which combined Calvin's anthropology of soul and body, the iconoclastic transference of sacred power into living human bodies, and Ramus's embodied epistemology, and ran with it, carrying it to its logical, practical conclusion in their radical views on church formation. The Calvinist doctrine of predestination differentiated between the "invisible" church, a spiritual community composed only of those elect, godly members who had been chosen by God for salvation, and the "visible" church, the physical community of people, both the elect and those destined for damnation, who gathered for worship. Because salvation occurred in one's heart and was invisible to the human eye, most puritans believed it was impossible to determine with certainty the members of the invisible church. Thus, they accepted that the visible church—the Church of England—must embrace everyone to guarantee that the elect were included. Robinson, however, countered this inclusive view in the era's most complete statement of English Protestant separatism, *A Justification of Separation from the Church of England*, published in Amsterdam in 1610. Previously a more radical separatist, Robinson reflected his move in *A Justification* to a more moderate stance on church polity, a move that was provoked by his frequent conversations with non-separatist William Ames in Leiden and would have great influence on the establishment of congregationalism across New England.[23] Yet because of his full commitment to the English Calvinist theology of the body developed by Ames and other nonconforming divines, including himself, which propounded that the elect could, in fact, be distinguished visibly from the damned by their moral behavior, Robinson insisted on separatism: the exclusive, voluntary gathering of visible saints—those who believed they had received God's grace and demonstrated it in their actions—for mutual edification and "true" worship.

Although he acknowledged with nonseparating divines that some of the chosen could be found within the Church of England, Robinson believed the church was also full of "atheists and ungodly persons" and could not be "purified" by reforming its liturgical ceremonies. Membership within the corrupt church, he feared, made one's body and soul vulnerable to corruption, thus "we take ourselves rather bound to show our obedience [to

God and Scripture] in departing from [the church], than our valor in purging it."[24] Furthermore, Robinson argued, a person's soul and body could not be severed from each other, but this was what nonseparating doctrines attempted to do: they located a faithful person's soul in one church—the true, invisible one—and one's body in another—the corrupt, visible one.[25] Yet God had "ennobled the *whole* man soul and body with His image and joined them together in one person: the soul to inform, and quicken the body, and the body to be quickened, and used by it, as an active, and lively instrument for her operations, and work." Only death could dissolve "so great a work of God and of the habitation of his own image" as the human body-soul unity.[26] Thus, "we must rank our bodies also under the regimen he hath established for the well ordering and preservation of his kingdom for ever," that is, "pure" churches containing only members who were saints both invisibly through the godliness of one's inner soul and visibly through the godly actions of one's outer body. Intentionally leaving a corrupt institution to form a physically and emotionally intimate covenanted community gave God's kingdom concrete existence in the world.[27]

Robinson's theology of the body informed his principles of separatism, providing his congregation's members with their self-identification as a distinct community physically removed from the Church of England and with the doctrinal foundation upon which they built their church polity and social organization. They believed the creation of "new men"—visible saints—and a new society—the true body of Christ—was best accomplished by physically isolating themselves from the contagion of a prideful and profligate world. Escaping persecution for their radical religious nonconformity in England, Robinson and his congregation emigrated to Amsterdam in 1608, but finding the separatist church there torn by internal conflicts, they moved to Leiden the following year, where they were initially relatively free to form their religious society and practice their godly values as they wished.[28]

In Leiden their pastor's "love was great towards them, and his care was always bent for their best good, both for soul and body." They flourished communally and spiritually, "coming as near the primitive pattern of the first churches," William Bradford believed, "as any other church of these later times have done." Yet their material conditions left something to be desired. They worked hard for little economic profit, which caused many adults to age physically before their time. But they were concerned especially about their children, whose heavy labors caused "their bodies [to] bow under the weight of the same, and bec[o]me decrepit in their early youth, the vigour of nature consumed in the very bud as it were." They also observed Dutch social culture undermining parental authority: their children were being drawn away by "the great licentiousness of youth in that country . . . into extravagant and dangerous courses, getting the reins off their necks and departing from their parents . . . so that they saw their posterity would be in danger to degenerate and be corrupted." As well, the truce between Holland and Spain had ended and the countries were preparing for war; the exiled community feared the purported cruelty of the Spanish and the "famine and pestilence" war would bring. Given the dangers remaining in Leiden posed to their physical and moral constitutions, they decided to remove themselves to a place where they believed they would be free to build a society whose members were tightly bound by common affections and untouched by the corruptions of the world, where they could raise their children according to specific godly values and practices as their Pastor Robinson had outlined, where they might exert not only ecclesiastical but also civil authority that precisely determined how human bodies and souls—and the corporate social body they constituted—would be shaped.[29]

Although Robinson, despite his best intentions, was never to set foot on American soil, he had taught his congregation well. When the company of saints aboard the *Mayflower* arrived in New England in late 1620 to colonize the area they named "Plimouth Plantation," their pastor's theological ideas about the body and godly behavior were explicit, conscious principles, at least in the minds of company leaders like William Bradford, William Brewster, and Edward Winslow. Yet the Plymouth saints also carried with them from England other models of embodiment that permeated popular understandings of human corporeality: early modern ideas about public self-presentation and ancient humoral-faculty theories about the body and soul. Widespread and commonplace in England, such understandings often were less explicit but nevertheless thoroughly assumed by early New Englanders and equally as influential in how they went about treating bodies, their own and others'. Despite their iconoclastic rejection of the "papist" Church of England and the immoral extravagances of English social culture, the colonists were thoroughly English and wanted to remain that way. One of the primary reasons they left Holland for North America, in fact, was their concern that they would "lose our language and our name of English" and their children "would in few generations become *Dutch*, and so lose their interest in the *English* Nation."[30]

The separatist doctrine of visible sainthood nicely cohered with, indeed likely was influenced by, common early modern ideas about self-fashioning and self-presentation. These ideas were based on the principle, inherited from medieval and Renaissance theory, of a presumably direct linkage between one's private inner character and one's public outer self, "a sympathy between physical and moral qualities, . . . between outer appearance and inner reality, or between being and seeming."[31] One's dress, manners, and other outward characteristics should accurately display one's gender, level of education, economic status, social rank, occupation, and other "inward properties" in order to sustain a well-ordered, hierarchically stratified society. Thus, since the fourteenth-century English civil authorities had enacted elaborate sumptuary legislation to define and regulate an immediate correspondence between a person's outward self-presentation and his or her inward nature. Yet the late sixteenth and early seventeenth centuries saw great social and cultural upheaval in England: economic shifts brought greater wealth to some in the middling classes, while the poorer classes sank into deeper poverty; burgeoning industrialization and the enclosure of land previously available for common use prompted a population shift toward urban centers; and the Reformation encouraged individuals to reject the state-supported Church and gather their own independent churches.[32] Attempting to maintain balance on such shifting ground, early modern English developed "an increased self-consciousness about the fashioning of human identity as a manipulable, artful process." During the early seventeenth century, Stephen Greenblatt has observed,

> self-fashioning acquires a new range of meanings: it describes the practice of parents and teachers; it is linked to manners or demeanor . . . ; it may suggest hypocrisy or deception, an adherence to mere outward ceremony; it suggests representation of one's nature or intention in speech or actions. . . . It invariably crosses the boundaries between . . . the shaping of one's own identity, the experience of being molded by forces outside one's control, [and] the attempt to fashion other selves.[33]

Robinson's directives for fashioning a moral person registered his recognition that self-identity could be willfully manipulated, thus the need for parents to circumscribe and control willfulness in their children from the moment of birth. Indeed, Protestant nonconformists feared this new sense of fluid possibility in constructing alternative public personas, for it fully complicated the supposedly direct linkage between soul and body and potentially undermined in at least two ways the doctrine of visible sainthood upon which separatism rested: a person might belligerently act above his or her station in life, behaving as if one were better than one's neighbors; or a person might behave with false piety in order to disguise his or her immoral nature, deceiving others by presenting oneself publicly as a visible saint in order to hide private lusts of the flesh. Both signified a prideful heart, the greatest threat to a cohesive godly society, for pride "puffed up" self-interest, causing a person to value oneself above the common good. Pride could make people pretend to be wealthier or better educated than they actually were and look down their noses at their neighbors. But pride also, Robinson and others realized, could cause one to mask one's true inner nature with hypocritical modesty and plainness, like the extreme ascetic behavior condemned by Calvin, which seriously complicated the way visible sainthood was supposed to work. This kind of person had "put on the outside an vizard [visor; mask] of sanctity" that hid one's inner sin. Robinson felt assured that "the Lord will in due time pluck off [the mask]"; however, "in the meanwhile man's dim sight cannot pierce through it."[34]

Nonconformists seemed driven to have eyes that could read through another's body into his or her soul, that could distinguish visibly between the real and the artificial and determine whether a person were a saint or a sinner. "The capacity to tell the difference between a real and a temporary faith, a true and a hypocritical profession, was at a premium," Peter Lake has noted. "It was doubly so since puritan piety oscillated violently between the inward and the outward, the objective and the subjective, the personal and the social."[35] A true saint strove to temper such oscillations by sustaining a transparent coherence between soul and body—one's behavior should serve as a sparkling clear window onto one's heart. Nonconformists believed they could achieve such transparency with "plain" and "honest" dress, gesture, manners, speech, and other aspects of "outer" embodiment that expressed "inner" honesty, humility, and modesty, in short, moderation— neither excessively self-promoting nor overly self-denying. Indeed, Bradford extolled the founders of Plymouth Colony as having lived "a plain country life" in "plain country villages" in England; his use of "plain," Michelle Burnham explains, indicated "simple, honest, and direct forms of behavior or presentation," as well as "a social status that is ordinary, common, or lowly."[36]

The early modern self was fluid and permeable, potentially taking on alternative identities not only by willful manipulation, but also by virtue of the "natural" humoral constitution of the human body itself. The ancient

Galenic theory of the four elements and their corresponding humors and properties—fire and choler, which were hot and dry; air and blood, which were warm and moist; water and phlegm, which were cold and moist; and earth and melancholy, which were cold and dry—provided the standard scientific model for human physiology and anatomy, health and medicine, the interconnections between body and soul, and the relations between humans and other things in the material world. A complex organic being, the early modern body housed the "spirits" and humors—fluids, particles, and qualities in constant flux and flow—which it perpetually generated and burned, "concocted" and digested, mixed and separated, ingested and excreted in an ongoing creation and degeneration of matter. The embodied self was not a private, stable, or clearly bounded entity, neither internally in the permutations between spirit and matter nor externally in one's exchanges with the physical environment. Climate, weather, seasons, temperature, air, food, exercise, and social circumstances immediately and continuously altered a person's physiology and psychology. Because everything in the physical world was constituted of the same elements and humors, human beings shared qualities and characteristics with other "bodies"—stars, planets, animals, plants, rocks, lakes, and so on. All things existed along the Great Chain of Being, a hierarchical continuum of matter extending from inorganic objects, through plants, animals, and humans, to the subtle materiality of celestial beings (see figure I.2). The four humors generated the four temperaments (choleric, sanguine, phlegmatic, and melancholic), which signified a person's tendency to particular feelings and actions. The temperaments were visible in the "complexion," which consisted of one's physical constitution (height, weight, skin color, and hair type) and "carriage" or behavior (see figure I.3). Like the nonconformist ideal of plainness, modesty, and moderation in all things, the humoral ideal was for the individual to maintain balance among one's humors, known as the golden mean, in order to sustain physical and moral health.[37]

In humoral theory the soul, the animating life force of the organic body, was a single entity conceptually subdivided into a hierarchical triad of "faculties" reflecting the similarities and continuities among humans, animals, and plants along the Great Chain of Being. The vegetative soul existed in all living things—plants, animals, and humans alike—and oversaw nourishment, excretion, growth, and reproduction. The sensitive soul, possessed only by animals and humans, contained the faculties of appetite, sense, feeling, motion, and perception and evaluation of objects; it directed the body's movements toward desirable and away from undesirable objects.

FIGURE I.2 *The Great Chain of Being.* God, surrounded by his archangels, is enthroned at the top of the engraving. The chain is arranged hierarchically, moving downward from God, through lesser celestial beings, human beings, fowls, fishes, animals, vegetation, to tormented bodies and souls in hell. In the right margin angels fall from heaven, becoming demons. (From Diego Valades, *Rhetorica Christiana*, 1579. Courtesy of the Library of Congress.)

FIGURE 1.3 *The Four Humors.* One of many Renaissance representations of the humors, this engraving divides the human body into halves (male and female) and quadrants (the temperaments), illustrating the correspondences among body, humors, complexions, temperaments, planets, and astrological signs. (From Leonhard Thurneisser zum Thurn, *Quinta Essentia*, 1574. Courtesy of Yale University, Harvey Cushing/John Hay Whitney Medical Library.)

Finally, the rational soul was unique to humans, giving them their likeness to the angels and the abilities to distinguish between good and evil and to contemplate and know oneself and God.[38] Body, soul, and temperament interpenetrated, continuously exchanging spirits and qualities and fluidly shaping and reshaping each other. Thus, a person paid close attention to the ways one's physical health affected one's moral state, and vice versa. When pre-Cartesian humoral theory met Protestant theology, Michael C. Schoenfeldt has argued, they "conspire[d] to highlight the particular physiological and psychological makeup of the individual." That is, "they demand[ed] of the ethical subject . . . participation in a discourse of deeply embodied inwardness."[39] Of special concern to those, like Plymouth's colonists, who ventured into foreign lands was the idea that the humoral body was permeable to its environment—climate, air, temperature, and food continuously altered one's physiological and moral constitution—and colonial leaders feared that some among them might become "savage" like their new environment. When humans failed to use their rational, moral souls—that which differentiated them from other creatures—to control their "animal passions," there was the danger of slipping from a human to a bestial state. Godly colonists knew they must keep close watch over the ways they physically engaged the New England "wilderness" and their moral responses to that encounter.

Colonists' deeply embodied simultaneously inward- and outward-looking modes of knowing oneself and others experienced radical challenges in New England, especially when they encountered "wilderness creatures," the indigenous Algonquians. Karen Ordahl Kupperman has described the ambivalent mixture of "fear and anticipation" with which colonists approached America and its native people, an ambivalence that provoked a variety of intercultural experiences and interpretations on both sides.[40] Bradford feared the "savages" would exact cannibalistic tortures on vulnerable English bodies, but actual contact with Wampanoags and other native groups near Plymouth produced far more complicated and complex exchanges that registered the differences, and sometimes the similarities, between two distinct modes of embodiment: Indian and English. The earliest colonists were fascinated by the Indians' bodies. With limited abilities to communicate verbally, the Indians and English "read" each others' physical sizes, gestures, hairstyles, clothing, and ornamentation for information about the other. Indeed, Plymouth colonists described the Indians' bodies and behaviors in far more detail than they did their own, providing important information about early New England indigenous people and their lives. But their descriptions and interpretations of Indian bodies also reveal much about colonists' perceptions of their own bodies. Other bodies and their behaviors, in fact, offered mirrors in which visible saints saw reflected back the dangers of ungodliness and in which we can read, conversely, the forms they expected godly bodies to take. Daniel Gookin, a seventeenth-century historian of English missionary activities among New England Indians, believed that in the native people "we may see, as in a mirror, or looking glass, the woful, miserable, and deplorable estate, that sin hath reduced mankind unto naturally, and especially such as live without means of cultivating and civilizing, as these poor, brutish barbarians have done for many ages." Indians, Gookin believed, did have rational souls, yet they were "like unto the wild ass's colt, and not many degrees above beasts in matters of fact." One's environment, either savage or civilized, made all the difference: persons who were "born and bred among civilized and christian nations" should "praise God for such a mercy," for God, "in his divine providence and abundant goodness, made this distinction between them and others."[41] However, other colonists saw reflected in Indian bodies their own shortcomings; Rhode Island's Roger Williams, Plymouth's Edward Winslow, and others often held up Indians as superior to the English, both physically—they were taller, stronger, and better adapted to the environment—and morally—they were more modest and hospitable.

Recognizing the mutability of the body and its moral constitution, colonial leaders strove to mold their children into "living icons" of modest godliness; they also imposed their ideas about proper embodiment, to varying degrees of success, upon those who did not necessarily subscribe to the same principles of a properly formed body and a well-lived life: New England native people and those English colonists who resisted such impositions, like Thomas Morton of Ma-re Mount, servants, and Quakers. In fact, many, if not most, human bodies in Plymouth Colony never became thoroughly enculturated in the ways the founding settlers had envisioned. Only half of the passengers aboard the *Mayflower* were members of Robinson's congregation, and he and Bradford anticipated from the beginning that the "strangers" in their midst would create problems. Furthermore, they feared that transplantation into a "savage" wilderness environment like that of New England, where, William Bradford believed, "only savage and brutish men . . . range up and down" and there were no Christian or "civilized" social constraints on individuals, would entice many to corrupt their bodies and souls in numerous ways.[42] The colonists quickly built familiar forms of material culture—English dwellings, palisaded towns, and fenced fields—and established particular social institutions—the godly family, civil legislation and the court system, and church order—with the hopes of molding inhabitants' experiences and behaviors, and ultimately their souls, properly.

The academic turn to the human body has produced a number of sophisticated studies of embodiment in Christian history.[43] Scholars have been concerned with developing post-Cartesian approaches (which notably, as the similarities between Robinson's and Bourdieu's models indicate, echo pre-Cartesian views) that value the body itself as a source of knowledge and embodied practices as effective producers of cultural information and meanings. Such approaches also expose the mutability and contingency of the human body, previously assumed by modernists to be universal, unchanging, and essential. Michel Feher, Susan Bordo, and Anthony Fletcher, for example, have developed similar models of the critical exchanges between self and society that occur at the nonrational, embodied level. In his three-volume collection of articles *Fragments for a History of the Human Body*, Feher located the historical human body at a dialectical intersection. Here, at the interchanges between life and thought, between behavior and assumptions, the body senses, moves, and feels, it learns its own particular kind of knowledge, and enacts that knowledge in the social world. "This intersection is complex, often turbulent," Feher explains, "for the vital processes cannot fuel figures of thought without causing them to renew themselves, while concepts that attempt to reflect the living being cannot do so without constantly altering its direction." Rather than conceiving of the body as an essentialized biological organism without history or culture, Feher's histories of the body's modes of construction "turn the body into a thoroughly historicized and completely problematic issue."[44] In offering a variety of glimpses of the ways people have construed their embodiment throughout history and in many different cultural settings, Feher's collection reveals both the elusive flexibility of the human body's contours and the complex interplay between cultural understandings of the body and practices of daily life.

While Feher located historical bodies at the intersection of life and thought, Susan Bordo has proposed two kinds of bodies: the "intelligible body" and the "practical" or "useful body."[45] The former, like Feher's "thought" about the body, is a culture's ideas about corporeality: scientific, philosophical, aesthetic, and theological representations of its members' individual bodies as well as the bodies of "others," or those perceived as geographically or ideologically outside the community. These culturally contrived characteristics of the intelligible body are historically contingent and provide particular understandings about how the soul and body are related, how the body is physiologically constructed and functions, and how the body is related to the divine, natural, and human worlds. Bordo implies but does not explicitly discuss, however, a significant characteristic of the intelligible body: much of it exists below the level of conscious social discourse and personal awareness. As Bourdieu argued, people often take for granted their normative understandings of what the body *is* and how it is to behave; such implicit, cultural constructions carry the naturalizing belief that *all* human bodies are (or should be) like this.[46] A culture codifies its particular understandings of the intelligible body into what Bordo terms "rules," both explicit and implicit, that direct the body's training, shaping, dressing, feeding, healing, and disciplining and its appropriate interactions with other bodies. These rules produce the concrete, useful, practical body—Feher's embodied "life"—that daily enacts (or refuses to enact) the intelligible body and its rules; the useful, practical, lived body is informed by and in turn reproduces or resists cultural norms and power relations. Historian Anthony Fletcher, in his analysis of gender in early modern England, offers a model similar to those of Bordo and Feher. Like Bordo's intelligible and practical bodies and the rules that link the two, Fletcher writes about "ideology" that produces particular "experience" or "practice" via the "necessary link" of "prescription."[47]

Feher, Bordo, and Fletcher provide the theoretical framework on which this study of bodies in Plymouth Colony hangs as it explores the interplay among conceptual ideas about embodiment, such as humoral-faculty theory and Robinson's theology of the body, the rules implicitly derived from these conceptual ideas and often explicitly legislated or taught by civil and church authorities, and the ways living human beings actually experienced and "used" their own and others' bodies in daily life, sometimes in compliance with the rules and other times in direct resistance to them. Accessing and analyzing historical bodies that have been dust for at least three centuries is difficult, however. We cannot know firsthand how these bodies looked, what they smelled like, how they gestured; we cannot see the meaningful raise of an eyebrow—and even if we could, we might not be able to interpret it properly.[48] We cannot taste the foods they ate nor experience the effects on one's body of particular styles of clothing— sometimes the same set of clothes worn day after day. We cannot feel the humiliation and pain of a young wife accused of fornication before her marriage, tied to the public post, stripped to the waist, and whipped, her back bloodied by the lashes. Nor can we bump shoulders in the crowd of on-lookers who watched that whipping and heard her cries, or who observed a young man accused of bestiality and a mother convicted of murdering her four-year-old daughter being led to the scaffold, confessing their crimes, and being "hanged by the neck vntill their bodyes are dead." And we can-not experience the impact that confronting a foreign landscape had on the first colonists: attempting, after more than a decade of urban life in Leiden, to orient themselves in a thoroughly unfamiliar environment; surviving only on parched corn, a few clams, and water for weeks at a time; meeting with a kiss or stabbing to death with a knife other human beings—Indians, who shaped their bodies in exotically different ways than did the English. The everyday embodied, sensory experiences and activities in which the colo-nists engaged—cooking a meal of pottage over a hot fire in August, smell-ing an ear of corn for ripeness, sitting on a hard bench in a cold meeting-house in the middle of January during a two-hour sermon after fasting for the day, feeling the tightening of one's waistcoat and stays as an unwanted pregnancy progressed, emptying a chamber pot when one's child was af-flicted with the "flux," or diarrhea—were so commonplace (or vulgar) as to be unremarkable; colonists rarely considered detailing these activities in writing for any reason, especially for the consumption of future historians, a worthwhile undertaking.[49] Furthermore, no informants are available to ask questions about intentionality. The "meanings" of these experiences and activities—why one did commonplace activities in particular ways or what one thought about them—often never entered the actor's conscious awareness (as our quotidian activities and experiences usually do not for us now) and were certainly not recorded for future reference.

However, a careful reading of the extant sources reveals much informa-tion about why the self was embodied in particular ways, how that em-bodiment was to be accomplished, and in what ways it was actually done, or not done, and the consequences in seventeenth-century Plymouth. My primary sources are of three kinds: *scholarly treatises* on humoral theory and medicine, theology, church discipline, philosophy, and rhetoric, such as the extensive writings of John Robinson; *descriptive literature*, including travel narratives, journals, histories, and letters, like those written by Captain John Smith, Thomas Morton, William Bradford, and Edward Winslow; and *of-ficial documents*, such as church and court records, civil legislation, maps, and probate inventories. Granted, all of these sources were produced by one kind of person: a small group of educated European males. The voices and activities, indeed the bodies, of everyone else—women, children, Indians, servants—are mediated through the written words of English and, occasionally, Dutch men. And yet there remains extensive material about corporeality, which may be read closely in order to flesh out various kinds of bodies in Plymouth.

This study draws upon the large, varied, and sophisticated corpus of scholarship on early New England. As Gary B. Nash observed over twenty years ago, the community studies of pre-Revolutionary New England towns "make the several hundred thousand souls who lived in this region one of the most studied human populations in the annals of history."[50] It might seem that yet another discussion of colonial New England is, at best, simply a creative reworking of the familiar material or, at worst, thoroughly redundant. However, since the late 1980s David D. Hall and others have moved beyond earlier intellectual and social histories to write cultural histories that develop ever more richly detailed and nuanced insights into colonial life.[51] Some cultural historians have touched on various aspects of embodiment in early New England.[52] I draw upon these and other excellent studies, yet I beckon bodies of all kinds, Indian and English, saintly and transgressive, from the peripheries into the center. Rather than turning to the body to explicate or exemplify a particular theme or topic, such as witchcraft, colonial encounters, or female piety, or dismembering bodies into body parts, such as the tongue or hair, this book develops a sustained focus on the human body itself, both whole and in parts, figurative and literal, at the center of seventeenth-century life and thought in Plymouth Colony.[53]

I think and write as a religious studies scholar, which means I bring recent discussions among historians of American religion to bear on the New England sources. Drawing from post-Geertzian anthropological and post-structuralist historical methods, students of American religion have become comfortable at the meaning-filled site of interplay between our subjects' conceptual philosophical and theological principles and their concrete realities of everyday life—what has been called "lived religion." Historian of American Catholicism Robert Orsi has delineated four elements necessary for understanding the ways people invest their lives with religious meanings. First, the scholar must nurture an awareness of the possibilities and limitations "of what can be desired, fantasized, imagined, and felt" within a particular culture. Second, she must have an understanding of how social institutions—"marriage and kinship patterns, moral and juridical responsibilities and expectations, the allocation of valued resources, and so on"—reinforce those cultural parameters and structure an individual's experiences. Third, she must develop "a sense of what sorts of characteristic tensions erupt within these particular [social and cultural] structures." Finally and most significantly for my study, the scholar must understand "the knowledges of the body in the culture, a clear sense of what has been embodied in the corporeality of the people who participate in religious practices, what their tongues, skin, ears 'know.'"[54] This book interweaves analyses of cultural structures, social institutions, and conflict in order to disclose and interpret the ways various groups of people located their bodies as the sites at which they continuously generated meanings permeated with religious significance.

Colonial bodies—how they were disciplined toward moral behavior, how they were clothed, how they gestured during religious rituals, how Indians and English observed and interpreted each others' bodies—can be read like texts to provide a richly nuanced understanding of Plymouth social culture, in which religious and "secular" modes of thought and life so interpenetrated that one cannot be understood without considering the other. When the colonists observe and comment upon their own or others' bodies, they offer guidelines for interpreting the meanings their physical experiences and activities carried for them. Reading bodies in this way, using clues provided by the actors themselves, reveals how religious and other structures of consciousness physically and immediately functioned for these people in ways often different from what was prescribed in, for example, carefully composed sermons or treatises. Finding meanings in the dynamic exchanges between abstract, theological concepts and concrete, material life places human bodies at the center of religious culture. Historians of religion who make this move disclose the implicit power religious and other discourses carry for ordering and shaping human existence and experience. The dialectical exchange between bodies and culture allows religious directives to shape bodies and their experiences, while at the same time human agents are continuously sustaining, resisting, and reshaping the structures and meanings of their worlds through their bodily activities. To state the obvious, it is in the body that human life exists. Concrete actions, not abstract thoughts, carry the ultimate practical agency and authority both to reinforce and to undermine cultural structures.

How the godly in Plymouth represented themselves to each other and others and enacted those representations in physical interactions expressed their visions of themselves as religiously motivated people. But the same could be said for those who colonized other New England regions, which begs the question of why I have chosen to locate my study in Plymouth and not any or all of the other northern colonies. In part, I wanted to narrow my focus to attend to the distinct characteristics of bodies in a particular place. More importantly, Plymouth has been given short shrift in early New England studies, often treated as a poor, less interesting cousin of the other colonies, especially Massachusetts. Scholars tend to erase Plymouth's distinctiveness, citing from its documents when such quotes or examples support their arguments about other colonies.[55] Studies focused on Plymouth, in contrast, often have been "Pilgrim" histories—traditional narrative institutional histories often driven by genealogical interests or concerned with promoting, debunking, or otherwise responding to the Pilgrim myth.[56] One exception is John Demos's exemplary social history, now almost forty years old, on family life in Plymouth Colony, which describes dress, food, and family relations, for example, and contributes important demographic information to my own work.[57] More recently, historical archaeologist James Deetz and cultural historian Patricia Scott Deetz have explored everyday life in Plymouth in a valuable descriptive study drawn from archaeological evidence, court records, probate inventories, and a few journals.[58] Yet they, like Demos, say very little about religion, and, with a popular readership in mind, they begin with the "First Thanksgiving" and conclude with a chapter on Plimoth Plantation, the living history museum James Deetz directed in the 1960s and 1970s, thus preserving mythical views of America's earliest "founding fathers."

At least three characteristics—practical, doctrinal, and attitudinal—worked together to make Plymouth in many ways different from the other New England colonies: its demographics, its separatism, and its emphasis on modest plainness and the "common affections." Plymouth's civil and ecclesiastical leaders often seemed less concerned about regulating inhabitants' bodies than the Bay and Connecticut authorities, due in part to the fact that Plymouth was demographically more homogeneous and economically poorer than the other colonies. Thus, they had less need, for example, to establish elaborate sumptuary legislation, which regulated how people clothed their bodies in order to sustain hierarchical social stratification, than did the Bay Colony guided by Governor John Winthrop's vision of a divinely ordained social hierarchy: "some must be rich some poore, some highe and eminent in power and dignitie; others meane and in subieccion."[59] Instead, Plymouth's single sumptuary law until the 1680s disallowed all inhabitants wearing disguises, reflecting leaders' promotion of plain transparency between body and soul. Putting more weight than other nonconformists on the external visibility—the corporeality—of internal godliness distinguished Plymouth's separatists, at least early on, from puritans who settled in other parts of New England. In spite of separatism's rigorous reputation, driven by its uncompromising rejection of the established Church of England, John Robinson exhibited a moderate, loving temperament and promoted affectionate, nonhierarchical relationships among the saints, which played out not only among church members but also, remarkably, in their attitudes toward outsiders. Although Plymouth's saints experienced their fair share of social conflict and certainly exerted disciplinary force against the most disorderly among them, they tended to treat Quakers, Baptists, and other radical dissenters like Roger Williams less viciously than did Massachusetts. As well, they enjoyed friendlier relations with many of their Indian neighbors and engaged in less rigorous missionizing techniques among the Plymouth natives. Moreover, the church in the village of New Plymouth had more sporadic and generally less well-educated and theologically rigorous ministerial leadership than did other New England churches; lay leadership, coupled with Robinson's ideal of common affections among all members, seemed to produce a more democratic religious environment and more flexible views on doctrine and ritual practice.[60]

Despite these important differences between Plymouth and the other New England colonies, its inhabitants had inherited virtually the same cultural and theological principles as had their puritan neighbors in Massachusetts, Connecticut, and New Haven, and ultimately, over time, understood and treated their own and others' bodies in similar ways. Soon after the Massachusetts Bay Colony was established in 1629, Plymouth's separatism and the Bay's puritanism began to look very much like each other. Some tenuousness underlay the first decades of contact between the two colonies, but they eventually realized that for the economic survival of both, their similarities were more significant than were their differences. Maintaining minor distinctions in church polity took a back seat to the real-life exigencies of creating a godly, civilized society in America. Robinson, always very practical in his outlook, had moderated his separatist views, and the puritans who colonized the Massachusetts Bay area encountered there no Anglican Church to purify and reform. In New England both separatists and puritans found themselves isolated from much of what had provided the impetus for their particular doctrinal stances in England; together they conspired to create congregationalism. By the second half of the seventeenth century, Plymouth's churches were employing ministers who had been trained at Harvard College in Massachusetts, and there was free social and economic exchange between the two colonies. Thus, while this is specifically a study of separatist Plymouth, much of what it discovers about Plymouth might also apply to the puritan New England colonies.

The book is organized thematically, with chapters moving from broader intellectual and physical contexts, within which Plymouth's saints understood and lived their corporeality, to progressively more intimate spaces; each chapter follows a historical trajectory. The first chapter explores a cluster of related encounters between English and native people occurring early in Plymouth's history. The dynamic encounters, involving illness, healing, starvation, violence, murder, and a beheading, serve as a focusing lens through which to observe, analyze, and interpret the broader cultural, scientific, and theological models that informed the separatists' understandings about corporeality. Chapter 2 further develops these cultural models and colonial encounters by locating colonists' bodies as the sites at which English culture and New England nature met, where immediate human exchanges with the physical environment took place. A tension inhered in conceptions of the humoral body as permeable and vulnerable and the Calvinist body as sturdy and industrious. While the saints feared being consumed by wilderness "savagery"—that is, being physically and morally altered by contact with indigenous climate, soil, foods, and peoples—they also intentionally altered the landscape through physical labor, "civilizing" the wilderness according to English patterns and consuming its resources. Civilizing the landscape produced close-knit villages in which most colonists pursued their daily lives, lives that were exceedingly public in many ways. Chapter 3 investigates the public shaping of the self in Plymouth through dress, work, speech, illicit sexuality, and corporal punishment, all of which provided the means by which individuals embodied and displayed morality (and immorality) and social status and negotiated public social relations. Through the public spectacles of corporal punishment—whippings, brandings, and hangings—of those they viewed as threats to the moral order and purity of the social body, colonial authorities attempted to clarify and reinforce their understandings of proper behavior.

The saints materialized ideas about order and purity most effectively, but not uncontestedly, within their covenanted churches. Chapter 4 explores the connections between the corporate social body of the Plymouth church and the individual bodies of church members. Pastor John Robinson elaborated a model of the church as the "body of Christ," using vivid metaphors of the humoral human body to describe the workings of the church body. By ritualizing individual bodies through Sabbath worship, the sacraments of baptism and the Lord's Supper, fast and thanksgiving days, and censure and excommunication, church members practiced a ritual complex intended to "feed" the church body and "purge" it of polluting elements in order to sustain its health and purity. Despite the very public nature of early New England life in church and village, authorities recognized the home as the primary place in which godly values were to be inculcated in order to produce a godly society. Because colonists tended to write far more about Indian bodies and practices in the home than they did about their own, the concluding chapter moves between Indian and English modes of domestic life in that most intimate of spaces, the family dwelling, and the activities that took place there: marital sexuality, childrearing, sleeping, and eating.

The materials related to Plymouth use the term *body* in multiple, multifaceted ways, all of which echo and reflect each other, a single image or term implying numerous meanings. Robert Blair St. George has described this fluid accretion of the metaphorical and the literal in early New England, where the "the visual vied with the verbal for semiotic authority." And yet,

> word and thing were inextricably linked, referentially interdependent, constantly implicated in each other's ways of making meaning. . . . Implication opens to view much of what we normally term the symbolic; however, it exposes it not by reifying "meaning" in isolated events but by suggesting an open-ended skein of entangled, involved descriptive passages that loop back continually and bring normally latent tissues that tie one referent to another, and another, and another, and . . . into public view.[61]

Body, as both word and thing, functioned as a primary concrete metaphor in Plymouth Colony, moving from the physiological human body to many other kinds of bodies and body parts, gathering meanings as it spun out to the heavenly bodies and circled back to earthly animal, human, and social bodies, the ever building and thickening layers of implied meanings generating and reinforcing the body's centrality in separatist theology and life. Corporeality slipped from one layer to the next and back again, easily shifting between literalism and metaphor, and in a very real way this slippage affirmed the fundamental importance the physical human body—its composition, sensory experiences, and functions—carried in Protestant nonconformist structures of thought. The following chapters explore these multiple layers of corporeality in one particular place and time: Plymouth Colony during the seventeenth century.

CHAPTER I

Massasoit's Stool and Wituwamat's Head

Body Encounters

E
XCREMENT, SICKNESS, HEALING, MURDER, HANGINGS,
beheading, theft, whipping, starvation, sex—such was the visceral
stuff of encounters among English settlers and New England native people in March of 1623 near the young village of New Plymouth.
Three interrelated incidents—the curing of an Indian leader's illness, the
physical and moral disintegration of an English settlement to the north of
Plymouth, and the killing of another Indian leader and the impaling of his
head on Plymouth's meetinghouse-fort—and their attendant details evoke
central themes in meanings of embodiment early in the colony's history.
The company of saints who arrived in New England in 1620 to establish
Plymouth plantation brought with them complex and nuanced perspec-
tives on human corporeality, weaving together secular and religious understandings of medicine, sexuality, violence, and moral discipline. They drew
their understandings from a number of interrelated early modern models
of the human body—particular philosophical, theological, scientific, and
aesthetic understandings of its constitution and function—which provided
the basic tools for orienting themselves in the unfamiliar wilderness environment and conducting social relations.

Encountering others—in this case Indians and "ungodly" English
men—pushed the saints' experiences far beyond the familiar, however,

challenging their preconceived ideas about their own and others' corporeality. Focusing on a single set of incidents occurring within a discrete
historical moment does not afford a synchronically or diachronically broad
view of corporeality in Plymouth, but it does offer an entry into the central themes that motivated the colonists across time and space, which later
chapters pursue in further detail. The events of 1623 highlight several fundamental issues of material existence that have confronted human beings
everywhere and at all times, issues regarding body and soul, individual and
society, health and illness, life and death, sex and gender, self and other,
wholeness and dismemberment, human and animal. The colonists offer to
us their unique struggles with these issues, demonstrating how this particular group of people defined their bodies and embodied their lives within
the crucible of colonial encounters.

Plymouth Colony, March 1623

During a difficult spring, when colonists were still unsure whether their
plantation would be a providential success or a miserable failure, Governor William Bradford received word that Massasoit, chief *sachem* of the
Wampanoags and important ally of the colonists, was very ill, perhaps already dead. Three men from the plantation—Edward Winslow, a gen-
tleman visiting from London named John Hamden, and Hobbamock, a
Wampanoag who frequently traveled with the colonists as interpreter and
negotiator—journeyed forty miles west on foot to visit Massasoit in his
village, Sowams.[1] When they arrived, they discovered the sachem's house
crowded with people "in the midst of their charms for him, making . . .
a hellish noise," Winslow described, while several women were gathered
around Massasoit, rubbing his body. Winslow pushed his way to Massasoit's
side and greeted the sachem, who could no longer see and scarcely speak
but grasped Winslow's hand, expressing his pleasure that the Englishman
had come to visit him. Massasoit had not eaten or drunk anything in two
days but was able to swallow a bit of fruit preserves Winslow fed him on the
tip of a knife, although he "could scarce get [it] through his teeth." Looking into the sachem's mouth, Winslow saw that it was "exceedingly furred"
and his tongue was "swelled in such a manner, as it was not possible for
him to eat such meat as they had, his passage being stopped up." So Winslow washed his mouth and scraped his tongue, removing an "abundance
of corruption." Feeling a bit better, Massasoit ate some more preserves,
which brought on a great improvement, and his sight returned. Winslow

inquired "how he slept, and when he went to stool" and learned that Massasoit had not slept in two days and "had not had a stool in five."

The next day, although he felt inadequate to the task ("being somewhat unaccustomed and unacquainted in such businesses" of medicine), Winslow and a Wampanoag woman boiled up a broth of cornmeal, a handful of strawberry leaves, and a sliced sassafras root, which they strained through a handkerchief. Upon drinking the tonic, the sachem's sight further improved and "he had three moderate stools, and took some rest." After a temporary setback of vomiting and nosebleeds, caused by his ingesting (against Winslow's advice) a large portion of greasy duck broth, Massasoit slept for several hours and awakened cured, "his body so much altered" for the better since the colonists' arrival. Winslow "washed his face, and bathed and suppled his beard and nose with a linen cloth"; the sachem was so pleased with the results of Winslow's ministrations that he implored him to do the same for others in the village who were ill. So the Englishman willingly washed out the mouths of the sick, though the "poisonous savours" rather disgusted him.[2] Massasoit rewarded Winslow for his generosity by quietly warning him, through Hobbamock, of a plot afoot among the Massachusetts, a native group to the northeast of the Wampanoags. The Massachusetts apparently were planning an attack on English settlers at the fledgling Wessagusset colony in the Massachusetts Bay area, about twenty-seven miles north of Plymouth.[3] The sixty or so "lusty" men who lived at Wessagusset (or "Weston's colony") had arrived in New England ten months earlier to establish a fishing and trading post. Plymouth's leaders described them as an "unruly company [with] no good government over them." As would Thomas Morton and his men a few years later, the first of Weston's men to arrive immediately "set up a maypole & weare very merry." Fearing nearby Indians, however, they moved to Plymouth where they were "housed" and "victualled" and their sick members cared for until the end of summer. By then, the rest of Weston's company had arrived from England and they returned to the Bay area to establish their settlement at Wessagusset.[4]

Weston's "unjust and dishonest" men were far from being godly saints. While staying in Plymouth they had stolen from the plantation's crucial corn supply when it was still green in the fields—for which they had been admonished and "well-whipped," to no avail. Once settled at Wessagusset they refused to plant crops; instead, complained Sir Ferdinando Gorges, who had helped Thomas Weston obtain the patent for his colony, "they couzen [cheat; defraud] and abuse the Savages in trading and trafficking, selling them Salt covered with Butter in stead of so much Butter, and the like couzenages and deceipts." After "wasting" all their supplies in trading with the nearby Massachusetts, the men "fell to plain stealing, both night and day, from the Indians," at one point thinking it possible to take the Indians' corn by force, which Plymouth quickly admonished they not do, fearing the Massachusetts would attack Plymouth in revenge. Hoping to appease the natives, the Weston men hanged one of their own who had stolen corn. Even worse, Bradford heard rumors that they "kept Indian women," which Gorges confirmed: "They . . . impudently and openly l[ie] with their women." Investors in England had warned Plymouth that one of the men, Andrew Weston, brother of Thomas who had commissioned the colony, was a "heady young man and violent" and the rest of them were "unreasonable men." Another warned, "As for Mr. Weston's company, I think them so base in condition (for the most part) as in all appearance not fit for an honest man's company." They "are no men for us," a third wrote. "I fear these people will hardly deal so well with the savages as they should. I pray you therefore signify to Squanto [Tisquantum, a Patuxet who, like Hobbamock, served as Plymouth's interpreter and intermediary with local natives] that they are a distinct body from us, and we have nothing to do with them, neither must [we] be blamed [by the Indians] for their faults, much less can [we] warrant their fidelity." Thomas Weston himself admitted his men were "rude fellows," but he hoped to "reclaim them from that profaneness . . . and by degrees draw them to God."[5]

Weston's hopes for his colony proved to be unrealistic. During the winter and early spring of 1622–23, as supplies became scarce, the men sold their clothing and bedding to the Massachusetts and were "so base," in the eyes of Plymouth observers, that they became the Indians' servants, cutting their wood and "fetch[ing] them water for a capful of corn." One of them even "turned salvage [*sic*]" (went native), according to Wessagusset man Phineas Pratt, and the rest thoroughly demeaned themselves, foraging like animals in order to survive, for "at last most of them left their dwellings and scattered up and down in the woods and by the watersides, where they could find ground nuts and clams, here six and there ten." One man, weakened with hunger, became stuck in the mud while gathering shellfish and died there. The rest "were ready to starve both with cold and hunger also, because they could not endure to get victuals by reason of their nakedness," the result of trading their clothing to the Indians. Many, "being most swelled, and diseased in their bodies," died. The Massachusetts, indeed, lost all respect for Weston's men; the "boldness" of "the Indians' carriages . . . increased abundantly." They "contemned and scorned" the Englishmen and "began greatly to insult over them in a most insolent manner," snatching their food right out of the cooking pot over the fire and eating it "before their faces," holding "a knife at their breasts" if they complained, and stealing their "sorry blankets" off them as they lay sleeping, leaving them to "lie all night in the cold, so as their condition was very lamentable." Bradford attempted to explain why a group of young, strong, able-bodied men, who initially had been well provided for, could have reached such desperate straits: "It must needs be their great disorder, for they spent excessively whilst they had or could get it." According to Winslow, they "more regarded their bellies than any command or commander."[6]

Such was the situation at Wessagusset when Massasoit warned Winslow that the Massachusetts, led by their sachem Wituwamat, were planning to attack Weston's colony, presumably using the very weapons the Englishmen had traded to them. However disgusted they were by the behavior of Weston's men, the saints at Plymouth were indebted to Thomas Weston, who had been one of their plantation's London investors. They felt a moral obligation "to reskew the lives of our countrie-men, whom we thought (both by nature, and conscience) we were bound to deliver," even though it had been the "evill and deboyst [debased; morally corrupt] cariage" of the men at Wessagusset that had "so exasperated the Indians against them." They also feared the Massachusetts, with their newly acquired firearms, threatened Plymouth as well. So they commissioned their military captain Myles Standish and enough men to take on all the Indians at the Bay with an order to quell the native conspiracy. Standish was to "pretend trade" in order to "trap . . . that bloody and bold villain" Wituwamat, bringing his head back to Plymouth so "that he might be a warning and terror to all of that [same] disposition." Standish and his party of about ten men, including Hobbamock, arrived at Wessagusset to find that Weston's men had, for all intents and purposes, gone native: they "feared not the Indians, but lived and suffered them to lodge with them, not having sword or gun" and claiming they needed no protection or rescuing. Standish warned Wessagusset's overseer, John Sanders, of their intelligence from Massasoit regarding a Massachusett attack, which seemed further supported when an Indian approached Standish, allegedly for trade purposes, but Standish "saw by his eyes that he was angry in his heart." Soon Wituwamat himself and some of his men arrived in Wessagusset, where they used "insulting gestures and speeches." Wituwamat "bragged of the excellency of his knife," on whose handle a woman's face was carved, while Pecksuot, Wituwamat's *pniese*, or counselor of war, "a man of greater stature than the Captain," taunted Standish about his short height.[7]

The next day, under the pretense of discussing trade relations between Plymouth and the Massachusetts, Standish conspired to lock himself and his party in a Wessagusset house with Wituwamat, Pecksuot, Wituwamat's teenage brother, and a fourth Massachusett man. Once they all had gathered in the house, the colonists launched a surprise attack on the four Indians. Standish, piqued by the insulting stabs at his manliness delivered earlier by the pniese, snatched Pecksuot's needle-sharp knife from his neck, and the two men violently struggled until Standish got the better of the pniese and killed him with his own knife. The English also killed Wituwamat and the fourth Massachusett in the house, captured and hanged Wituwamat's brother, and quickly hunted down and destroyed three more Indians. Hobbamock admired Standish's bravado: "Yesterday Pecksuot, bragging of his own strength and stature, said, though you were a great captain, yet you were but a little man; but to-day I see you are big enough to lay him on the ground." Roused by his success, Standish's fiery temperament came into play again later in the day. He and his men exchanged musket shots and arrows with an Indian party in the woods, and then Hobbamock, himself a pniese, single-handedly chased the Indians into a swamp, where Standish attempted to "parley" with them but received "nothing but foul language" in return. The captain "dared the sachim to come out and fight like a man, showing how base and womanlike he was in tonguing it as he did." The Indians, however, quietly escaped.[8]

Having tasted the blood of victory in Plymouth's first major skirmish with New England Indians, Captain Myles Standish and his party returned home in triumph, bearing Wituwamat's head as instructed. They were "received with joy, the head being brought to the fort, and there set up."[9] Six months later Emmanuel Altham visited Plymouth and observed, "[The Indian's head] is set on the top of our fort, and instead of an ancient [a flag], we have a piece of linen cloth dyed in the same Indian's blood, which was hung out upon the fort."[10] However, John Robinson, the separatists' pastor who had remained in the Netherlands, viewed Standish's bellicose behavior with a less exuberant eye. In a letter to Governor Bradford, Robinson roundly criticized the plantation's leaders for their "killing of those poor Indians" and wished that "you had converted some before you had killed any!" Although the Indians may have "deserved it," they had been provoked by "those heathenish Christians," Weston's men. It would have been better to "punish" only one or two of the main instigators, perhaps

Wituwamat and Pecksuot, in order to put "the fear into many." Finally, Robinson was especially concerned about "the disposition of your Captain." He believed Standish to be "a man humble and meek amongst you" under ordinary conditions, but "if this be merely from an humane spirit"—because Standish was a "civilized" Englishman, rather than impelled by a godly character—"there is cause to fear that by occasion, especially of provocation, there may be wanting that tenderness of the life of man (made after God's image) which is meet [suitable; proper]." It was obvious to Robinson that Plymouth had intended to establish their superiority over the Indians through the massacre of Wituwamat and his men, and he admonished the plantation's leaders for such worldly motivations: "It is . . . a thing more glorious in men's eyes, than pleasing in God's or convenient for Christians, to be a terrour to poor barbarous people." Furthermore, "where blood is once begun to be shed, it is seldom staunched of a long time after. . . . And indeed I am afraid lest, by these occasions, others should be drawn to affect a kind of ruffling course in the world."[11]

Robinson's concerns about whether Standish's behavior reflected the image of God, Winslow's treatment of Massasoit's illness, Plymouth's complaints that Weston's men had become savages, Standish's violent massacre of the Massachusetts, and the saints' impaling of Wituwamat's head on the meetinghouse-fort—all of these materialized distinct, though clearly contested, understandings of the human body brought by the separatists to New England. They had "removed" themselves from England and the Netherlands to North America at a critical moment in philosophical and theological developments in the West: the early modern intersection of late Renaissance, Reforming Protestant, not yet Cartesian understandings of human corporeality. The saints at Plymouth attempted to follow the specific teachings of their beloved pastor, John Robinson, but they were also people of a larger historical time and cultural location, their views of this new world and their experiences in it shaped by old world structures of consciousness that were themselves in process of change. In his intellectual history of seventeenth-century New England, Perry Miller brought to light what he regarded as the formative elements in the development of the "New England mind." However, because he was, after all, interested in minds, not bodies, Miller failed to recognize the ways these and other intellectual developments gave shape to the New England body, indeed the ways they located the human body at the center of dissenting Protestant thought. Of course, just as there was no single "puritan mind," neither was there a singular "puritan body," yet divines wove together a number of conceptual threads to produce common understandings of human embodiment, which in turn provided guidelines for the behavior and treatment of living human bodies.[12]

Miller discussed three interrelated strains of early modern thought, which contributed to the Plymouth separatists' understandings of embodiment and influenced their actions and interpretations of others' actions during the events of 1623. Galenic medical physiology imagined the body as constituted of humors and faculties and linked the four elements of earth, fire, air, and water with the four bodily humors and four psychological temperaments. John Calvin's Reformed theology built upon and reworked traditional humoral-faculty principles, weaving them with a biblical anthropology that validated the body and its sensory experiences, yet problematized it as the site of conflict between the spirit and the "flesh." And logician and rhetorician Petrus Ramus promoted a practical epistemology grounded in the body—its sensory perceptions and appropriate conduct—guided by the rational mind, which English Calvinists adapted for use.[13] John Robinson conflated humoral, Ramist, and Calvinist conceptions of the body and its relationship to the soul to develop his distinct ideas about lived religious community and moral behavior, advocating a fundamentally embodied theology that located living human bodies as the sites at which critical meanings of God, the world, and self coalesced. At least two other cultural forces also shaped the saints' views of their own and others' bodies in Plymouth. The Protestant iconoclastic impulse swept across England from the mid-1500s into the seventeenth century, inciting the violent destruction of Roman Catholic material culture and relocating divine power from religious statues to the living bodies of the godly elect. In part driven by a Protestant ethos, other forces threatened to unravel the immediate connection between soul and body, between one's inner nature and outer self-presentation, promoted by Robinson; indeed, individuals might manipulate their bodies—through speech and gesture, for example—in deceptive ways. Like other attempts to come to terms with the shifting winds of early modernity, Robinson's theology of the body simultaneously reflected, resisted, and reworked these old and new models of embodiment.

To confuse matters further, in New England the saints encountered very different bodies and modes of embodiment from those they knew in their separatist community, tightly bound by common affections and lifestyle, in England and the Netherlands. In the eyes of Plymouth's leaders,

Weston's men clearly exemplified what happened when supposedly civilized Englishmen let their fleshly desires run rampant in a "wild" setting. Encounters with Wampanoags, Massachusetts, and other Indians, however, demonstrated how complicated "reading" and physically engaging "savage" American bodies—and interpreting those encounters—could be. When the first Plymouth colonists arrived, they found themselves inserted into an intricate, already existing web of native social relations, as some Indians attempted to win their favor and others threatened to run them out of the country, and colonists often found it difficult to distinguish between the two. Some native groups had established peaceful relations with each other and were united through kinship and trade; others were competing for hunting lands and trading rights; and others, like Massasoit's Wampanoags, were experiencing internal struggles for political power. All of these indigenous relations were in constant flux, an instability that had been exacerbated since the late 1500s by the arrival of Europeans, who brought new diseases causing a massive depopulation of native villages, new forms of trade relations, and new material culture, especially woolen cloth, metal tools, and firearms. Although they had anticipated they would be negotiating with Indians and brought English trade goods—beads and tools—with which to do so, on-the-ground experiences taught the Plymouth colonists just how complicated successfully participating in this complex network of social relations would be. They also quickly realized how utterly dependent their survival was on the Indians' goodwill during these early years, which blurred their preconceived distinctions between the primary categories of civilized and savage. With minimal ability to communicate verbally, they had to learn to read native bodies—their clothing and ornamentation, gestures, facial expressions, and manners—which they did, to varying degrees of success, both by peering through their own familiar cultural lenses and by gradually familiarizing themselves with Indian modes of embodiment.[14]

Thus, shifting facets of the particular historical moment in England and America conspired to generate the unstable world from which the Plymouth saints derived their notions about material existence and within which their bodies were embedded and experienced daily life, presenting unique challenges that contributed to the ongoing shaping and reshaping of the practical meanings of their own and others' bodies. Opening up the events of early 1623 allows us to unravel the various threads of corporeality the colonists explicitly and implicitly employed to negotiate their activities in a new world.

"His Body So Much Altered":
Native Healing and Humoral Medicine

Edward Winslow brought with him ancient humoral conceptions of physiology and medicine when he arrived in Sowams to attend to the very ill Massasoit. In fact, the understanding that one's physical constitution and psychological temperament were inextricably linked through the exchange of humoral qualities among body, soul, and spirit already had aided Winslow in an earlier evaluation of Massasoit's character. In 1621, during a ceremony to establish the peace treaty between the Wampanoags and Plymouth colonists, Winslow had "read" the sachem's physical appearance:

> In his person [Massasoit] is a very lusty man, in his best years, an able body, grave of countenance, and spare of speech. In his attire little or nothing differing from the rest of his followers, only in a great chain of white bone beads about his neck, and at it behind his neck hangs a little bag of tobacco, which he drank [smoked] and gave us to drink; his face was painted with a sad red like murry [brownish red], and oiled both head and face, that he looked greasily. All his followers likewise, were in their faces, in part or in whole painted, some black, some red, some yellow, and some white, some with crosses, and other antic works; some had [deer or beaver] skins on them, and some naked, all strong, tall, all men in appearance.[15]

English observers directly encountering for the first time New England native people were fascinated with Indian bodies—their physical appearance being the most immediately accessible aspect of their persons. Colonists struggled to determine the humanness of such strange wilderness creatures, highlighting those characteristics that most differentiated Indian from English. For the colonists, the Indians' "appearance was important," Karen Ordahl Kupperman has argued, "because it was the key communicator of the truth about one's character and status." In early modern England the ways a person presented oneself outwardly revealed his or her inner qualities, for a person's humoral constitution generated one's "temperament," or tendency to particular feelings and actions, which were visible in an individual's "complexion"—one's physical "countenance" and "carriage." By describing some of the Wampanoag men as "naked" Winslow meant not only that they wore simple clothing (he had earlier described Tisquantum's nakedness as "only a leather about his waist, with a fringe"). He also expressed his belief that their minimally clothed bodies communicated their inner characters: modest and simple, indicating honesty and straightforwardness. Winslow might have imagined Massasoit as sanguine, the most desirable of the four temperaments and complexions—"fleshy, ruddy, amiable, intelligent, courageous"—as he linked Massasoit's lusty, able body, his sharing of tobacco, and his controlled speech with his grave, dignified nature. These characteristics and his unique bodily ornaments all displayed Massasoit's position as sachem and reassured Plymouth leaders that he would be a trustworthy ally. In general, early English observers admired Indian males' physiques, their "lustiness," or robust vigor and strength, and their height. In fact, despite their exotic decorations— painted faces and greased heads, bone beads and animal skins—Winslow concluded, based on their tall, strong, erect bodies, that Massasoit and his followers were "all men." This acceptance of the natives' basic humanness, based on observing their bodies, allowed the Plymouth men to enter into a mutually beneficial political agreement with the Wampanoags.[16]

Two years later, that pact brought Winslow to Massasoit's sickbed. Previously of lusty and able body, the sachem was now at death's door. When he responded to Massasoit's request that his English friends at Plymouth visit him in his time of illness, Winslow, politically astute concerning the maintenance of good relations with native allies, was observing an important native social practice. He knew that "when any [Indians] are visited with sickness, their friends resort unto them for their comfort, and continue with them ofttimes till their death or recovery," and the colonists also should "observ[e] this their laudable custom."[17] Admitting he was no trained physician, educated in the arcane details of anatomy and medicine, Winslow explained his healing of Massasoit as the result of divine providential power. Yet Winslow's approach both to evaluating Massasoit's character and to diagnosing his sick body and applying healing ministrations indicated his dependence on humoral theory. When he arrived in Massasoit's village, he found the sachem's hut filled with villagers desperate to help their leader. Winslow, however, interpreted their behavior as less a "comfort" to Massasoit than a hindrance to his well-being, registering a significant difference between Indian and English understandings of the body's health and healing practices.

In order to heal those who were sick or wounded, New England Indians employed *powahs* or *powwows*, shamanic ritual specialists who called upon sacred powers, or *manitou*. Powahs worked within an inclusive social setting; the creation of an effective healing environment required the affective participation of the entire community. When great sachems became ill, for example, people often traveled from miles around to attend to them; Winslow heard that some had traveled "not less than a hundred miles" to visit Massasoit on his deathbed.[18] The weakened human body, they believed, responded to intense stimulation of all the senses simultaneously: the sight of one's friends and family gathered closely around and the powah's animated gestures; the sound of calling, chanting, bells, and drums; the smell of smoke and greased, sweating bodies; the feel of the skin being vigorously rubbed by caring women's hands; the taste of herbal remedies. People gathered around the powah and the ill person, generating an energetic sensory environment very different from the subdued atmosphere, peopled by three or four persons—the patient, the physician, a family member, and perhaps a minister—considered appropriate for the curing of English bodies. To English observers, powahs seemed to consort with the devil in order to heal those who were sick or wounded, generating a confusing assault on the senses more likely to invade the patient's body and undermine his or her health than to help.[19] The powah's "violent expression of many a hideous bellowing and groaning . . . sometimes roaring like a bear, other times groaning like a dying horse, foaming at the mouth like a chased boar, smiting on his naked breast and thighs," English visitor William Wood described, "continue[s] sometimes half a day, spending his lungs, sweating out his fat, and tormenting his body in this diabolical worship."[20] Winslow described "the office and duty of the powah" in more sober terms than did Wood, registering his understanding of healing as a religious undertaking and the healing ritual as a form of communal "worship"—indeed, Indians and English both believed spiritual forces were at work in individual's bodies, causing illness or health. While Christians called upon God to heal them, the powah called upon manitou, which appeared in animal forms. The "common people" joined with the powah "in the exercise of invocation, but do but only assent, or as we term it, say Amen to that he saith; yet sometime break out into a short musical note with him." Thus far, Winslow rendered the healing ceremony as something like a separatist church meeting, with song and an amen-like sign of agreement with the spiritual leader's prayers, but there the similarities quickly end. Indian powahs and English ministers or physicians embodied sacred power very differently: the powah "is eager and free in speech, fierce in countenance, and joineth many antic and laborious gestures with the same, over the party diseased."[21]

Although Winslow did not mention the presence of a powah in Massasoit's home, one was surely there, making "charms" for him. Upon entering the *wetu*, or wigwam, Winslow stepped into a strangely "violent" and "hideous" world—a radical assault on his English sensibilities. He "found the house so full of men, as we could scarce get in, though they used their best diligence to make way for us." In their midst lay Massasoit on a mat, surrounded by "six or eight women, who chafed his arms, legs, and thighs." Winslow feared the environment was so "hellish" and "noisey" that it would "distemper us that were well," let alone further hurting "him that was sick," for his humoral model of human physiology viewed Massasoit's (and his own) body as highly vulnerable to its surroundings. Native understandings may have been quite similar to colonists' humoral views of the body's permeability to air, temperature, sound, and other sensory stimulations; for example, Winslow recognized the women were rubbing Massasoit's body "to keep heat in him." However, whereas the Indians believed an intensely sensual environment supported their sachem's healing process, Winslow interpreted their activities as detrimental to Massasoit's health. According to separatist theology and humoral theory, human bodies required moderation and balance rather than "violent" sensory stimulation.[22]

Wanting to help his friend, Winslow called upon a lay knowledge of humoral medicine to diagnose Massasoit's illness and prescribe a remedy. English gentlemen and educated yeomen, like Winslow, tended to be particularly concerned about their health and regularly read popular medical manuals. They knew that general well-being depended on one's "natural" complexion and the climate, seasons, and stars; to generate optimum health one must manipulate a balance among the body's four humors and the external environment. Laypeople practiced preventive medicine through such means as moderating diet, exercise, and sleep, bathing, and smelling perfumes or "vapors." To cure illnesses, physicians prescribed *physicks*—medicines distilled from a variety of plant, animal, and mineral sources—according to the nature of the disease. Thus, a "hot and dry" illness required a physick believed to have cooling and moistening properties. More radical but frequently employed techniques to cleanse and purify the body of corrupting humors and restore balance involved purging by bloodletting or ingesting physicks that caused vomiting or expelled blockages of stool. Physicians closely observed how the patient's body responded—its external appearance, such as the skin's texture, and its excretions, such as the urine's color and smell—in order to judge the effects of medical applications, avoid excessive purging, and achieve humoral balance.[23]

Winslow had carried to Sowams items to use as physicks to bring Massasoit's body into humoral balance and health. A bottle of cordial had broken during the journey from Plymouth, but he still had a pot containing a "confection of comfortable conserves," a sweet preserve made by boiling mashed fruit or flowers with wine and sugar to a "thick pap" and straining it. Ingesting a confection, physicians believed, stimulated the appetite of a person whose "stomack [was] repleted with euill humours." Massasoit was able to dissolve a bit of conserve in his mouth and "swallow the juice of it," which delighted those watching, as their sachem had not been able to eat anything for two days, due to his swollen tongue and throat.[24] Winslow purged Massasoit's mouth of corrupting humors by washing it out and scraping his "furred" tongue, then Massasoit drank some water in which Winslow had dissolved more of the conserves. Within half an hour his eyesight returned and he was feeling much better. The next day the sachem asked Winslow to prepare him an "English pottage," or soup. Winslow sent a messenger back to Plymouth to get some chickens, for physicians considered chicken broth the best remedy for a swollen tongue, furry mouth, and blocked throat caused by excessive phlegm, catarrh, and rheum—evil humors distilled from the head or stomach.[25] In the meantime, Winslow prepared a broth of indigenous products at hand: cornmeal, strawberry leaves, and sassafras root. He likely knew that "corn" (any grain or legume) was considered to be the most nourishing and healthful of foods.[26] He used strawberry leaves because they were the only herb available in the early spring, but he may have known they were "good in Fevers [and] all maner of inward inflammations, . . . no enemy to the stomacke," and effective in cleansing the kidneys and urinary tract, as well as healing "sore Mouths" and removing "catarrhs." Sassafras root, which Winslow used to "relish" (make more tasty and palatable) the broth, was also "very effectual to clense the Reins [kidneys] and Bladder" and good for "Tough Flegm."[27] Winslow's close attention to Massasoit's bowel movements indicated his awareness that proper excretion was the primary sign of healthy, regular purging of used and corrupt humors. After a brief setback of vomiting and nosebleeds (apparently caused by the "lubricating" qualities of the greasy duck broth on his "weak stomach"), Massasoit's body responded to Winslow's ministrations.[28] The colonists' physician, Samuel Fuller, had remained at Plymouth but been informed of "the state of [Massasoit's] body." When Fuller sent more physicks, Winslow, not wanting to upset the sachem's return to humoral balance, dared not give them to him "because his body was so much altered."[29]

On their return to Plymouth Winslow and his traveling companion, John Hamden, stopped at Mattapuyst for the night, where Conbatant

(Corbitant), a competitor of Massasoit and previously Plymouth's "bitter enemy," asked whether the governor would send Winslow to his bedside if he too were "dangerously sick" and requested a *maskiet* (physick) from Plymouth. Winslow answered, "'Yea'; whereat he gave me many joyful thanks." In fact, as Joyce E. Chaplin also has noted, the Plymouth saints were unusual, for "nursing involved intimate bodily contact" and most New England colonists were leery of contagion, both physical and spiritual. Plymouth, however, seemed always willing to provide medical assistance to whomever needed it, including native people. In 1621, for example, after engaging some Narragansett Indians in a skirmish, the colonists apologized for wounding some of them and took a man and a woman back to Plymouth so their "surgeon [Fuller] should heal them." In 1635 the Indians who lived near Plymouth's trading outpost on the Connecticut River (near present-day Windsor) "fell sick of the small pox and died most miserably." Bradford felt compelled to detail the gruesome effects of the disease on susceptible native bodies: "the pox breaking and mattering and running one into another, their skin cleaving" to the mats they lay on, so that "when they turn them, a whole side will flay off at once, . . . and they will be all of a gore blood. . . . They were in the end not able to help one another." The English, "seeing their woeful and sad condition and hearing their pitiful cries and lamentations, . . . had compassion of them, and daily fetched them wood and water and made them fires, got them victuals whilst they lived; and buried them when they died," though they feared becoming infected themselves. "But by the marvelous goodness and providence of God, not one of the English [whose bodies, unlike natives' bodies, carried immunities] was so much as sick or in the least measure tainted with this disease," and the surviving Indians were deeply appreciative.[30]

Plymouth also helped English immigrants, saints and sinners alike. Virtually everyone who arrived on the *Mayflower* in 1620 immediately became seriously ill; those separatists who were able cared for them, including the "profane" sailors who refused to "hazard their lives" for each other. The saints, on the other hand, "had compassion" and "showed them what mercy they could," so that one, a "proud young" boatswain, proclaimed, "Oh! . . . you, I now see, show your love like Christians indeed one to another, but we let one another lie and die like dogs." Their physician Fuller, who was also a deacon in the Plymouth church, had a reputation for curing diseases by bloodletting and other means and was, apparently, extraordinarily generous with his medical expertise. When Weston's rowdy men resided in Plymouth during the summer of 1622, those who were "sick and

lame" were housed in "the best means the place could afford them" and
Fuller treated them for free. The surgeon was in great demand not only
in Plymouth; at least twice he traveled north to the Bay Colony to deal
with "infectious fevers." In the spring of 1629 he was called to the newly
founded town of Salem to battle scurvy. He spent the summer of 1630
traveling around Massachusetts attending to both the "righteous" and the
"wicked" who were experiencing the Lord's "bodily judgments" in a great
sickness. By August he was exhausted, writing to Bradford that "many are
sick, and many are dead. . . . I long to be home: I can do them no good,
for I want drugs, and things fitting to work with." In 1633 "it pleased the
Lord to visit [Plymouth] . . . with an infectious fever of which many fell
very sick and upward of 20 persons died," including Fuller himself "after he
had much helped others."[31]

Devout colonists always saw the hand of divine providence working
through sickness and healing, and Winslow made sure God's role in Massasoit's recovery not be overlooked. It seemed to surprise him, given his
admittedly limited knowledge of medicine and his unsophisticated supplies, that his ministrations to the sachem actually worked: "Never did I
see a man so low brought, recover in that measure in so short a time."
Undoubtedly this was in large part due to Massasoit's normally healthy and
strong body, but Winslow attributed to God the responsibility for his success: the sachem "had three moderate stools, and took some rest; insomuch
as we with admiration blessed God for giving his blessing to such raw and
ignorant means, making no doubt of his recovery, himself and all of them
acknowledging us the instruments of his preservation." Another sachem
at Massasoit's sickbed had tried to persuade him that the English would
not come, showing "how hollowhearted [they] were" and no "friends in
deed" but only "in show." However, when he recovered so dramatically,
Massasoit proclaimed: "Now I see the English are my friends and love me;
and whilst I live I will never forget this kindness."[32] Winslow surely heard
these words as a validation not only of his honest intentions toward Massasoit but also of the God he represented, for as a saint he hoped to embody
divine grace in the world. Underlying his motivation to help his ally was,
indeed, an impulse to prove the English God more powerful and benefi-
cent than the devilish powers behind the powah's communal authority. After curing Massasoit Winslow attended the sickbeds of many of his Indian
neighbors, where he "used the best arguments I could" to dissuade them
from their dependence on the powah's "fiend." While powahs often did
"most certainly (by the help of the Divell) worke great Cures," in separatist

cosmology it was because divine providence worked through all kinds of events in the material world.[33] Ultimately, colonists believed it was their God, working through humoral physiology, who determined whether healing of sick Indian or English bodies occurred, regardless of the rusticity or sophistication, the "hellishness" or "godliness," of the medical techniques applied.[34]

As a shamanic practitioner the powah "embodied and wielded the power of the forces of the other-than-human worlds," which often appeared in such animal forms as bears, boars, and birds, thus supporting colonists' views of (some) Indian bodies as "savage" and "beastly," like the animals that ranged the New England forests. In native cosmology the boundaries between human, animal, and spirit were fluid and permeable, and Indians embraced movement among the three realms, although they viewed it as a dangerous undertaking; only ritual specialists like powahs were capable of making those transitions successfully.[35] For the Plymouth separatists, as well, the boundaries between humans, animals, and spiritual forces were dangerously fluid, but they should not be transgressed under any circumstances. Colonists inhabited a carefully ordered hierarchical universe, inherited from medieval cosmology and humoral theory—represented by the Great Chain of Being—and Calvinist theology. Human bodies, they believed, reflected God's image as the highest beings in the created world, yet because all things were constituted of the same four elements—earth, fire, air, and water—and humors, there were interrelationships and homologies along the Chain. Higher beings shared qualities with lower beings; for example, "kings, the rulers of men, corresponded to lions, the rulers of beasts."[36]

Following Ramist and English Calvinist theories, minister John Robinson explained that what distinguished humans from lower animals was rational thought: while people shared virtually all characteristics— bodily existence and mobility, sensory experience and perception, desire and emotion—with animals, God had given humans, "the perfection of all creatures," reason, which elevated them above beasts. Just as reason gave humans the authority to "govern" the animal kingdom, so must a person utilize his or her rational mind to govern one's "animal passions." But rationality alone was not enough; one's mind and heart must be regenerated by God's grace in order to control the fleshly appetites and emotions, direct the will properly, and embody moral actions.[37] However, because all physical and soulish qualities, except rational understanding, were shared by all animate creatures along the Great Chain, there was always a danger of slippage among the levels, of humans who failed to engage their godly reason becoming, in some literal sense, beasts.

"Men Endued with Bestial . . . Affections": Weston's Colony and English Savagery

The belief that the boundaries between human and animal were danger-ously fluid and that, without care, a person might take on animal-like char-acteristics shaped the saints' attitudes toward not only Indian bodies but also English bodies and their conduct. Calvinist understandings, amplified by Robinson, of the connections among reason, will, and behavior and of the body as a site of tension between spirit and flesh underlay the language Plymouth's leaders used to describe and explain the behavior of the "rude and profane" men sent over by Thomas Weston to found the ill-fortuned colony of Wessagusset. Weston's men arrived in Plymouth during the sum-mer of 1622 accompanied by letters vilifying them as violent, dishonest, and, notably, "unreasonable"; investors also warned that Weston's men "are no men for us" and Plymouth should keep them set apart as a "dis-tinct body" and refuse to "entertain" them. From the start, then, planta-tion leaders were predisposed to expect the worst from these profane men. Yet despite their separatist ideal of building a community isolated from un-godly influences in order to sustain its physical and moral purity, they also knew firsthand the difficulties of surviving in the wilderness. Robert Cush-man, the colony's London agent, had delivered a sermon during his brief visit to Plymouth in 1621, warning against "self-love" and admonishing the saints to be quick to lend aid to those in need. When a person was reduced to begging, Cushman said, he had "lost his maiestie and the Image of that noble creature," his humanity: "What is it that makes men brazen faced, bold, bruitish, tumultuous, mutinous, but because they are pinched with want?" Perhaps the saints also remembered Robinson's teaching: God had commanded them to do good actions willingly, "at all times," toward any-one in need, and as they had the ability and resources to do so—but "with discretion."[38] Thus, Plymouth initially housed and fed these "lusty" men, although they finally drew the line at their stealing green corn from the fields and punished them with whippings. But even painful corporal pun-ishment failed to stop the headstrong scoundrels.

To make matters worse, Weston's men avoided contributing their fair share of work, which, in Plymouth's eyes, was the ultimate cause of their downfall. From Calvin through English puritans to the Plymouth saints, industrious behavior was a primary sign of godliness, for idleness was an outward manifestation of the inner flesh—that part of human nature corrupted by original sin. Human beings were composed of the "outer" body, constituted by the four elements and humors located in various bodily organs, and the "inward" soul, whose faculties also were located in different parts of the body: reason was located in the mind, at the top of the body in the head, while the will, "affections" (desires), and "passions" (emotions) were located at the center of the body, in the heart. Rational thought, feelings, intentions, and external actions, interconnected by the flow of blood and spirits throughout the body, continuously exchanged qualities and activities. Robinson's theology of the body held that Adam's sin, which all humans inherited, did not destroy "the natural powers" of the soul and body, "but only corrupteth, infecteth, and disordereth them." This corruption caused "ignorance" in the soul's rational mind and "perverseness, and disorder, with manifold lusts" in its will and affections, which then were "fulfill[ed] and execut[ed]" in the "bodily instruments." Like Calvin, Robinson argued that the human body, which reflected God's image, and the corrupt flesh were qualitatively different entities. While the physical body was "God-created" and "a natural good thing," the flesh referred to a spiritual characteristic having the power to "lead" one's affections astray. "Godly and wicked men are contraries" because they were guided by opposing "causes": godly persons were led by the spirit of God; wicked individuals were led by the flesh—their souls remained corrupted by sin and so they were ignorant and lusted after perversity, which they embodied in disorderly behavior, like "lewd and ungodly conversation." The "wisdom of the Spirit" cared for one's "spiritual state," making demands on the body that would sometimes "pinch" it—in rigorous labor and moderate food intake, for example. The "wisdom of the flesh," on the other hand, was "sure to provide for the body and outward man what may be, though with danger and prejudice of the spiritual."[39]

According to Plymouth observers, Weston's ignorant and ungodly men simply reaped the painful but just rewards of their fleshly self-indulgence. Cushman had cautioned against people immigrating to New England who "look after great riches, ease, pleasures, dainties, and jollity in this world, (except they will live by other men's sweat, or have great riches)."[40] Likewise, Robinson admonished those who were lazy and idle or who indulged the senses in frivolous pleasures, failing to exhibit self-control in their behavior. No one could "keep a good conscience before God, who makes labour but an accessary, and not a principal," he wrote. "Man is born to sore labour, in body, or mind, as the spark to fly upward." Those who were idle got into "mischief" and their bodies became "impoverished" and "weakened," while "labour brings strength to the body, and vigour to the mind."[41] Indeed, he believed, physical labor stimulated rational thought, which in turn dictated bodily control. Weston's men, on the other hand, unwilling to cultivate their own crops, "wasted" Plymouth's corn by illegally eating it when it was still green and "pleasant to taste" and frivolously spent the supplies they had brought with them on sexual and other pleasures. They "boasted of their strength . . . and what they would do and bring to pass in comparison of the people here [at Plymouth], who had many women and children and weak ones amongst them," yet their actions failed to materialize their verbal bravado.[42] Clearly, at least in Plymouth's eyes, they were lazy and disorderly, their bodies ruled by their animal appetites rather than godly reason.

After Weston's men established the Wessagusset colony in the fall of 1622 and their situation worsened, Plymouth began to see them as thoroughly fallen into evil, beastly ways. The passions and appetites, which humans shared with animals, always threatened to engulf the rational and volitional powers that made human beings human. Robinson knew it was possible for "men, though remaining, in nature, reasonable creatures, [to] perform acts plainly unreasonable and brutish, through ignorance, or appetite." Rationality must be embodied in reasonable actions, that is, not living brutishly from day to day on the fruits of other men's labors but working industriously to take care of one's bodily needs. Otherwise, one was no better than a beast—and a nasty one, at that: "He that without his own labour either of body or mind, eats the labour of other men's hands only, and lives by their sweat, is but like unto lice, and such other vermin." To the godly saints, Weston's men had become vermin, dissolving the boundaries between human and animal, civility and savagery, godliness and evil. Gorges agreed: "In their manners and behaviour they are worse than the very Savages." They engaged in illicit sexual activity, joining their bodies with those of native women, until they had nothing more to trade for sex. Then they bartered their own bodies to the Indians, cutting wood and fetching water for a "capful of corn." The Wessagusset company, never as clearly structured, rationally ordered, or emotionally bonded as separatist Plymouth, further disintegrated as some men dispersed into the wilderness and lived like animals, desperately ranging the forests and shorelines for food and sleeping in the woods. Others remained at Wessagusset but allowed Indians to mingle with them there, a dangerous move considering the Massachusetts had lost all respect for them and both groups stole freely from each other. One colonist had, indeed, "turned salvage," a term signifying a radically altered body: shedding English clothing and going "naked" like the Indians, wearing animal skins, perhaps painting and greasing his body and letting his hair grow long.[43]

When the rational mind and godly heart were abandoned and the animal passions and appetites ruled, humans took on the physical characteristics and moral qualities of beasts. Winslow complained vigorously about Weston's men, who were "rather the image of men endued with bestial, yea, diabolical affections, than the image of God, endued with reason, understanding, and holiness." They were "inhumane and intollerable," "profane men, who being but seeming Christians, have made Christ and Christianity stink in the nostrils of the poor infidels [the Indians], and so laid a stumbling-block before them." Rather than "giving good example to the poor savage heathen amongst whom they live," as properly "manner[ed]" English men should do, Weston's men demeaned themselves, earning the Indians' scornful derision. Visible examples, Winslow believed, were the embodiment of moral values and thus served as powerful motivators. Those in superior positions were to watch the kinds of examples they set for their inferiors, Robinson warned, for they were responsible for their inferiors' actions: "Examples of superiors are strong cords to draw on others, either to good or evil." One's conduct, good or bad, was "contagious," provoking righteous or evil behavior in others, and a superior who "falls from aloft, may easily bruise others besides himself, with his fall." God had endowed the English with civility, making them superior to the Indians, still mired in savage ways. Colonists should conduct themselves accordingly, serving as examples to draw the Indians to more civilized behavior, as did Plymouth, according to Dutch visitor Isaack de Rasieres: "The tribes in their neighborhood . . . are better conducted than ours [in New Amsterdam], because the English give them the example of better ordinances [laws] and a better life." Weston's men, in contrast, succumbed to their fleshly appetites, "teaching [Indian] Men to drinke drunke, to sweare and blaspheme the Name of *GOD*, and in their drunken humour to fall together by the eares [fight], thereby giving them occasion to seek revenge." Indeed, Weston's men were corporeal examples of what became of Englishmen who let their passions run wild, rather than pursuing lives that embodied the glorious image of God as did, apparently, the industrious saints.[44]

After housing and feeding them for a few months, Plymouth had purged their village of Weston's men. But within the separatist colony itself there were men who, some believed, failed to embody God's image and endangered the community's moral and physical stability and safety.[45] Robinson's theology of the body led him to express serious concerns regarding Myles Standish and his attack on Wituwamat and the other "poor Indians." Recognizing that Standish was not a visible saint—a member of the separatist church—Robinson suggested that godly self-control would have allowed him to avoid such a violent response to Pecksuot's taunts about his short stature. Robinson feared Standish failed to embody "that tenderness of the life of man (made after God's image)." Of the four humoral temperaments, Standish exhibited a choleric complexion, for he was quick to anger at perceived insults. Anger, according to Robinson, was "the strongest of all affections" and so it might accomplish great things, like "the driving away and dispelling of . . . evil." But a person who had fallen into a "fit of anger" lost all self-control and behaved like a "madman," for angry passions thoroughly altered a person's physiology, turning him into a rabid beast: "If a wrathful man saw himself in a glass, when his fit is upon him; his eyes burning, his lips fumbling, his face pale, his teeth gnashing, his mouth foaming, and other parts of his body trembling, and shaking; or but some of these deformities: he would, and worthily, loathe himself."[46]

Robinson used humoral theory to explain why "anger in the heart is so vehement in a choleric body," causing people to experience excessive "stirring and indignation at injuries offered": "The natural [cause] is the abundance of hot choler boiling in their veins, by which the blood and spirits are attenuated, and so apt to be inordinately stirred, and inflamed, upon apprehension of wrong done." Such an overabundance of choler, the "hot" and "dry" humor whose element was fire, was "helped by natural means and medicines" that cooled the blood. Then a person like Standish could engage "true wisdome and [self-]government, which represseth all inordinate motions in the mind," temper his responses to insult, and moderate his tendency to lash out in physical violence.[47] The other cause of choleric overreactions to taunts and other provocations, according to Robinson, was the flesh: "pride and self-love." Men who thought too much of themselves believed that "if they be a little wronged, some great and heinous offence is committed," justifying their "high indignation." With remarkable psychological insight Robinson noted that to such people an injury seems so great "because they seem great to themselves." Perhaps not wanting to antagonize Standish further, he avoided explicitly suggesting the captain was overcompensating for his short height by thinking himself "great," thus making him overly sensitive to Pecksuot's tauntings. But Robinson clearly believed that Standish's choleric temperament, combined with an insufficiency of godly tenderness and an overabundance of pride, situated the captain himself dangerously close to the animal kingdom. Cushman put it more succinctly: "A mercilesse man . . . is . . . (as it were) transformed into a beast-like humor; for, what is a man if he be not sociable, kinde, affable, free-hearted, liberall; He is a beast in the shape of a man."[48] Although he may have presented himself as "meek and humble" most of the time, when Standish was provoked by Pecksuot his "true" nature became visible, writ large upon his raging body and in his merciless actions.

Puritan William Ames argued that, although many acts, such as killing another human being, generally were unlawful, under certain circumstances they could be seen as morally good, such as "slay[ing] the guilty justly." The intentions of the actor and the circumstances of an act determined the action's moral character.[49] Robinson, however, debated such issues with Ames, believing that violent bloodshed, like all sin, was contagious, and he feared that Standish's attack on the Massachusetts would entice others in the separatist community, as well as the Indians themselves, to follow suit, causing the dissolution of the godly plantation. Robinson discussed the choleric complexion more than any other temperament, registering his view that pride and self-love, which could cause angry passions, lack of self-control, and violent behavior toward others, were the greatest threats to a godly community's bonds of affection and moral health and, in New England's "savage wilderness," its physical survival. Indeed, he feared that shedding the Massachusetts' blood surely would provoke the Indians to avenge themselves in return on the colonists. Robinson undoubtedly struggled with the fact that Plymouth depended upon Standish and other members of the community who had not joined the church—the "strangers" at the plantation. He realized the colony's survival required a modification of his firm stance regarding the physical separation and isolation of visible saints from the rest of society. And yet he always worried that this intermixing would pollute the godly character of the social body. The saints, he believed, must work that much harder to embody godly examples.[50] The bestial behavior of Weston's men and disintegration of the settlement at Wessagusset, as well as Standish's violent behavior, demonstrated what happened when colonists failed to maintain strict vigilance over individuals' actions and their community's physical and moral order.

"A Terrour to Poor Barbarous People":
Reading Indian Bodies and Body Parts

In fact, Plymouth colonists and New England Indians were similar in many ways, although Robinson surely would not have condoned a particular style of social discourse shared by Standish, Wituwamat, and Pecksuot: taunting and deceptive speech and gestures. As the Indians and English attempted to communicate nonverbally, at best through a native interpreter, during the early years of contact, they used speech styles, facial expressions, and gestures both to display and to hide their intentions, as they strove to read each others' bodies for clues. Dissembling—pretending to mean one thing when one actually intends something else—was seen as a serious problem in early modern England, and godly separatists promoted "plain truth" and kind words, rather than deceiving or demeaning others, in order to create a transparent society in which people behaved honestly and with affection.[51] One's body, they believed, should visibly display one's heart intentions accurately. Indeed, visual perception was a primary means of accessing truth in both Catholicism and Protestantism. In medieval Christianity, laypeople engaged divine knowledge and power through their eyes; statues, stained-glass windows, and other imagery served as "books" for the illiterate laity, who viewed and "read" them for sacred meanings. In spite of their iconoclastic rejection of the Roman Church and emphasis on the written and spoken Word, Protestant separatists also located meanings in the visible and viewed self-presentation and public display as powerful, thoroughly embodied modes of social discourse.[52] After all, they considered themselves visible saints, who publicly embodied God's grace in their hearts through their moral actions.[53] In New England, they drew upon the corporeal and visible nature of meanings to communicate nonverbally and verbally, to read Indian bodies and "savage" body parts.

Their bloody encounter in the Wessagussett house was not the first time Standish, Wituwamat, and Pecksuot had met. Relations between the Massachusetts and Plymouth had not always been so conflicted; they had established trade relations, and Bradford and others had visited Massachusett villages, where they were "kindly" entertained. But in late 1622, when Weston's men moved to Wessagusset and began engaging in close relations with the Indians, "a great sickness" like "the plague"—no doubt a European disease brought by the colonists, to which the Indians had no immunities—came among the Massachusetts, which drastically weakened their political and military power, surely eliciting sorrow, suspicion, and fear—and anger—in Wituwamat and his people.[54] Very early in the spring of 1623 Standish sailed around Cape Cod to Manomet, an Indian village about six miles southeast of Plymouth as the crow flies, to pick up a store of corn Bradford had purchased earlier. While Standish was visiting with the sachem, Canacum, in his home, in walked two Massachusett men. One was Wituwamat, "a notable insulting villain" who "oft boasted of his own valour" and laughed at the "weakness" of English men whose blood he had shed because they "died crying, making sour faces, more like children than men"; the other was probably his pniese Pecksuot. Wituwamat presented a dagger, acquired from Weston's men, to Canacum and made a long speech. Standish was unable to follow Wituwamat at the time but later, when he received Massasoit's message regarding the Massachusetts' intended attack on Weston's colony, assumed the speech delivered information about the conspiracy. Wituwamat was so bold as (allegedly) to tell Canacum in front of Standish that the Massachusetts had determined to "ruinate" Weston's colony but were waiting for reinforcements to arrive so they could attack Plymouth at the same time. Standish sensed Wituwamat's speech altered Canacum's attitude, for he "entertained" the two Massachusetts with food and drink more liberally than he had the English.[55]

Hearing the speech also seemed to alter the attitude of a Pamet Indian who up to this point had been a friend of Plymouth, always "demean[ing] himself very well toward us, being in his general carriage very affable, courteous, and loving," especially toward Standish. Now, however, Standish believed, he "entered into confederacy" with the other Indians, though "to avoid suspicion, [he] made many signs of his continued affections," offering to "help carry some of the corn" and inviting the captain and his party to spend the night with him at Pamet on Cape Cod on their return to Plymouth. How Standish knew, or thought he knew, that this man now was dissembling, attempting to deceive the colonists with his fawning gestures and generous offers of help, is unclear. Perhaps Standish believed, as when the Indian approached him with furs and "pretended" trade in Weston's colony, he could see beyond the Pamet's gestures to read the truth in his eyes: he was "angry in his heart." Or perhaps, as Kupperman has argued about English colonists in general, Standish read hidden treachery in friendly Indian behavior because he was so likely to employ deceit himself in order to gain the upper hand. In fact, the captain secretly determined to kill the Indian while they rendezvoused with him at Pamet. Standish, however, was unable to sleep that night—it was very cold, but also, given his choleric temperament, he was surely a bit irked at Wituwamet's and

Canacum's supposed expressions of disdain toward him earlier that day. His agitation kept the Indian awake as well, so the captain "missed his opportunity" to murder him.[56]

When they caught wind that Wituwamat was conspiring against them, Plymouth did not hesitate also to use treacherous tactics in return. Even the godly Winslow, who generally valued straightforward honesty, admitted that the colonists had determined "to take [the Massachusetts] in such traps as they lay for others" by "pretend[ing] trade, as at other times." Hobbamock, who praised Standish for his impressive valour, nevertheless believed the captain and his men had "demeaned themselves in this action." Another colonist, Thomas Morton, shed further light on the events at Wessagusset, emphasizing Plymouth's deception and the Indians' innocence. Describing the attack as a "Massacre" of the Indians, Morton claimed that when Standish, whom Morton dubbed "Captain Shrimp" to parody his short stature, and his party arrived in Weston's colony, they "pretended to feast the Salvages of those partes, bringing with them Porke, and thinges for the purpose, which they sett before the Salvages." The hungry, disease-weakened Massachusetts ate the food "without suspition of any mischiefe." But suddenly, "upon a watchword given," the captain and his men attacked the Indians, who, "with their owne knives (hanging about their neckes), were by the Plimmoth planters stabd and slaine." After the "slaughter," Morton noted, one of the murdered Indians (that is, his head) was "hanged up there" at Plymouth. Morton blamed Plymouth for the dissolution of Weston's colony, for, he claimed, the remaining men fled the area because they feared revenge from the Massachusetts. After the attack, the surviving Massachusetts deliberated about what name to call the "English Planters" and decided on "Wotawquenange, which in their language signifieth stabbers or Cutthroates," suggesting both the colonists' bloody attack and their treachery. For anyone who failed to recognize how "sharp-witted" Plymouth's godly men were, Morton clarified: "the Brethren could dissemble."[57]

Standish not only deployed deceptive strategies against the Massachusetts; when his choleric temperament was riled up he also scorned and taunted them, grounding his insults in early modern understandings of gendered bodies. The human body, containing hot and cold, moist and dry, humors, was a "one-sex" body, and that normative, superior body was male. Female genitalia were simply inverted male genitalia, which remained inside the body due to women's inadequate body heat. There was the very real threat that an imbalance of the humors could cause slippage between male and female, like the slippage between human and animal: gender "seemed dangerously fluid and indeterminate"; "the physical body was seen as vulnerable to the pressures of a blurred gender system." Thus, men, in particular, strove to define masculine and feminine characteristics in order to differentiate between men and women and stabilize their roles.[58] Robinson recognized the need for strict gendering of the body in order to avoid men becoming women. Men were women's "perfection," so it made some sense that women might want to imitate men "in apparel, gesture and the like" and become, "after a sort, masculine." But "men's effeminate and degenerate imitation of women" was not to be borne; it was "usually by riot and wantonness, men are transformed into women, and made feminine."[59] Men's humoral heat made them "stout of courage, fierce, testy, crafty, subtle, industrious, and politic." Women, being colder, were fatter, softer, and lazier, as well as vain, fearful, and weaker in intellect, will, and morality. Women were most likely to threaten male social order when they attempted to assert their authority over men through insubordinate, "wanton" speech; motivated by their natural vanity and pride, their unruly tongues "babbling," women tormented men to distraction with endless empty nagging.[60]

The diminutive and choleric Standish, roused by Wituwamat's and Pecksuot's taunts—and perhaps by their "incredible" bravery at "how many wounds these two pnieses received before they died, not making any fearful noise," as apparently the English did during the attack, "but catching at their weapons and striving to the last"—felt driven to prove himself a courageous, fierce, and crafty man among men. Thus, even after killing seven, he cornered more Indians in the nearby swamp and, his intentions to reach them frustrated, employed one of the most offensive insults available to him. Shouting through the shrubbery, though probably not understanding each other, the English and Indian men hurled abusive words back and forth. Standish, whose abundantly masculine complexion was ruled by the fire element, "dared the sachem to come out and fight like man," for the Indian showed "how base and womanlike he was in tonguing it as he did." The Indians fled, in the captain's eyes further embodying their fearful, "womannish" characters: all talk and no action.[61]

Despite the tactical commonalities between Standish and his Massachusett foes, Plymouth viewed the conflict at Wessagusset as a violent confrontation between two very different categories of bodies—Indian and English—with their overlays of opposing meanings; it was a "holy" battle between civilized and savage, godliness and evil, divine providence and

the devil. Colonists read Indian bodies as ciphers, communicating meanings often opaque and misleading, and they strove to clarify, delineate, and
contain those meanings. The saints consistently invested their physical en-
gagements with native people with providential import in order to explain
and justify the ways they viewed, interpreted, and treated the bodies of
various Indians. Just as Winslow imagined that God had guided his healing of Massasoit, forging a stronger bond of friendship between Sowams
and Plymouth and, therefore, greater safety for the colonists, Plymouth
viewed Standish's killing of the Massachusett Indians as a divine undertaking. God, they believed, in spite (or perhaps because) of their use of deception, had allowed the colonists to quell the Indian conspiracy successfully,
another sign of providential support for their mission in New England. But
even the saints were not in agreement about this. Robinson, although he
may have seen things differently if he had been present in Plymouth, criticized the way Plymouth handled the Massachusetts; killing so many in such
an underhanded way in order to strike fear in the Indians' hearts was *not*
pleasing to God, nor appropriate for Christians.

Indian bodies were at the centers of both events, but two very different
kinds of native bodies, according to the colonists. Wampanoags and Massachusetts appeared very similar; they both painted and greased their bodies,
which were either "naked" or clothed with animal skins, placing them all on
the unstable border between human and beast. But in colonists' eyes there
were critical corporeal differences between the two, and it was crucial to be
able to distinguish between them: in contrast to Massasoit's "grave countenance," "spare" and honest speech, and loving gestures, Wituwamat and
Pecksuot used deceptive and insulting speech and gestures. Colonists imagined that, like powah healers, pnieses like Pecksuot were in contact with
evil forces; the devil, they believed, appeared "familiarly" to pnieses and
made a "covenant" with them "to preserve them from death by wounds
with arrows, knives, hatchets, &c." Warriors like Wituwamat and Pecksuot,
"known for their courage and boldness, . . . disfigure[d] themselves" before
going into battle, and their scantily clad bodies, disguised with paint and
other "heathenish" decorations, presented a frighteningly savage appearance to their English foes.[62] Indian bodies, like English bodies, could slip
from humane civility to savage deviltry, justifying their godly destruction.

Ann Kibbey has explained how colonists used divine providence to
justify violence fourteen years later, during the Pequot War of 1637. New
England puritans, she writes, whose history of iconoclasm in England had
replaced "dead" Roman Catholic images with themselves as "the true and

living images of God," transferred that iconoclastic impulse into America. During the colonial massacre of the Pequots, "the recipients of iconoclastic violence were not merely symbolic objects, statues or paintings representing people." They were "real people who had become for the Puritans the living images of opposition to the New England Puritan living images of grace."[63] Likewise, Plymouth colonists employed iconoclastic rhetoric to invest their attack on the Massachusetts at Wessagusset with sacramental meanings. The triumphant impalement of Wituwamat's head on their fort, which they had built on the top of the hill overlooking the village when they learned of the Massachusetts' plan to attack the plantation, suggests the erection of a powerful icon of English superiority. The saints expected this savage body part to be viewed and read by all as "a warning and a terror," although Robinson criticized Plymouth's leaders for intentionally terrifying the "poor barbarous people" in order to "glorify" themselves. Significantly, the fort on which Wituwamat's head was displayed also served as the meetinghouse in which the community of saints gathered to spend the Sabbath day in praying, singing, and preaching to the glory of God. Bradford, perhaps smarting from Robinson's criticisms, made no mention of the head in his official history of the Plymouth plantation; he merely recorded that Standish and his party had "cut off some few of the [Massachusetts'] chief conspirators." But in a letter written six months after the event to their investors in London, Bradford and his assistant, Isaac Allerton, exulted that "we kil[le]d seven of the cheife of them, and the head of one of them stands still on our forte for a terror unto others." They wittily claimed that it was "by the good providence of god" that the Indians' "wickedness came upon their owne pate [top of the head]." Likewise, Emmanuel Altham stated that it was "by God's goodness" that "our chief enemy" was killed. And Winslow speculated that God, who "determined to preserve us from these intended treacheries, undoubtedly ordained this as a special means to advantage us and discourage our adversaries."[64] The saints fully believed God condoned their iconoclastic attack on the Massachusetts and public display of the leader's head in Plymouth village.

Wituwamat was not the only Indian to lose his head by colonists' hands. In July of 1676 the Plymouth General Court convicted Keeweename of instigating the "bloody murder" of Sarah Clarke and determined that "his head . . . shalbe seuered from his body, which was immediately accordingly executed."[65] Considered even more dangerous was another "crafty" Indian's body and body parts. In August of 1677 Metacom's Rebellion (King Philip's War) culminated with the death of Metacom (Philip) himself, sachem of the Wampanoags and son of Massasoit. Colonists described and treated Metacom's dead body in highly symbolic—both iconic and iconoclastic—terms: after being shot "through his Venomous and Murderous Heart" (the seat of his "bloody" passions, affections, and intentions), his corpse was dragged through the swampy mud to dry land, where it looked like "a doleful, great, naked, dirty beast." Because the sachem "had caused many an Englishman's body to be unburied, and to rot above ground," Captain Benjamin Church ordered "not one of his bones should be buried." An executioner beheaded and quartered Metacom's body on site and gave one of his hands, being "very remarkable" because it was "much scarred," to the Indian who had killed him, who later "got many a penny" by showing it to Boston gentlemen. English soldiers hung the body's quarters in the woods and carried the head into Plymouth where it was put on public display.[66] John Cotton Jr., pastor of the Plymouth church, excitedly wove together literal and metaphorical meanings of "head," coloring them with providential import, in his record of the event:

> The Head of all the mischeife, Philip, was slaine, & the Governour [of Plymouth, Josias Winslow] & magistrates the week before his death sent an order to all our ch[urch]es to keep August, 12: as a day of publick Thanksgiving for the beginning of revenge upon the enemy, & on that very day, soone after the publick worship was ended, his Head was brought into Plymouth in great triumph, he being slaine 2 or 3 days before, soe that in the day of our praises our eyes saw the salvation of God, a strong engagement to us to be carefull to pay our vowes made to the most High in the days of distre[ss].[67]

Metacom, the ultimate embodiment of violent savagery, served as a potent multivalent sign for the colonists. Previously "skulking" through the wilderness forests, wreaking havoc on English homesteads and villages, he now lay dead, his body's naked beastliness fully exposed. Philip's body, whole and in parts—"hewed in pieces before the Lord," Boston's Increase Mather described—became a commodity invested with numerous kinds of value: the slain body represented the superiority of "civilized" English military order over "savage" Indian guerilla tactics; the quartered torso with its dangling arms and legs, "hanged up as a monument of revenging Justice," compensated for the numerous English bodies Metacom had desecrated; the hand carried monetary value for the Indian who had shot him; and the severed head displayed the victory of the saints' God over the Indians' devil to those who lined the main street of the village as it was carried into Plymouth. God "brake the head of that Leviathan" and, on the day of joyful thanksgiving, "gave it to be meet [as proper vengeance] to the people inhabiting the wilderness."[68] For many years, apparently, Metacom's head sat on a pike in the center of the town of New Plymouth, an icon of English military and religious power—"a remarkable testimony of divine favor [to] the colony of Plimouth," William Hubbard exulted—and a warning reminder of the covenant between God and his people.[69]

Wituwamat's head remained on Plymouth's meetinghouse-fort for at least six months in 1623 and probably much longer, publicly displayed for people to observe the deterioration of its skin and flesh until only the skull remained to terrify.[70] "A detached head is a sign that we privilege," Regina Janes explains about beheadings. "As a sign, it can enter into a variety of discourses, and its meanings will derive from the discourse(s) of which it forms a part."[71] In Plymouth the dynamic act of seeing and reading, the sensory engagement and exchange between viewer and head, continuously generated and perpetuated multiple meanings. Wituwamat's body was dead, but his head—his face (his distinct identity), his "pate" (the seat of intellect and reason), and his power to evoke a passionate response—lived on in the day-to-day lives of Plymouth's inhabitants and visitors. Likewise, Metacom's head continued to "speak" long after it had been severed from its body. Several years after Metacom's death Boston minister Cotton Mather visited Plymouth. Standing before the severed head, he reached up with his hand and wrenched "the Jaw from the exposed *Skull* of that blasp[h]emous *Leviathan*." Mather performed such a gruesome act in order "to shut Philip up," Jill Lepore surmises, to "put an end to Philip's blasphemy."[72]

The Reformation with its attendant iconoclastic impulse marked a major shift in ideas about the physical senses, from the superiority of sight and image to the superiority of hearing and the spoken word. Yet the display of the heads of Wituwamat and Metacom in Plymouth indicates the persistence throughout the seventeenth century of Protestants communicating and accessing meanings through visual perception. Corporeal images, displayed in particular ways and invested with particular meanings, still sometimes carried more power than did words to reach out and evoke a visceral response from the viewer, as had medieval images of Mary and Jesus. For Catholics sacred statues were living icons of divine inspiration; for Protestant iconoclasts they were "dead" and "empty," yet also alive in their thorough saturation with meanings that must be eradicated. For Plymouth's saints, Indians' severed heads—safely dead yet animated with vital meanings—functioned as visible icons of God's goodness and sovereign authority. Indians, in contrast, read them as warning "books." An Indian prisoner who was made to view Wituwamat's head "looked piteously" upon it and immediately confessed in detail to a Massachusett plot to avenge Wituwamat's slaying. By the time Altham visited in September, he connected the display of Wituwamat's head with the natives' submission: "The Indians are most of them fled from us, but they now seek to us to make peace."[73] Likewise, the death of Metacom and display of his head marked the end of his rebellion, yet the head continued to speak to colonists, reminding them of savagery's threat.

The Plymouth saints read their exchanges with Massasoit, the Massachusetts, and Weston's men as examples of God's presence in the world materialized in the actions of their own bodies. The process of translating various medical, theological, philosophical, and aesthetic understandings of the body into actual lived experience often occurred at a subtle, implicit level but always resulted in explicit and effective activity in the material world. These inherited models of corporeality shaped and directed their interpretations of their own and others' behavior, while allowing for subtlety in those interpretations. Initially reading all Indians as "savages," for example, the colonists soon realized that their survival depended upon learning to differentiate among them. Combining their own views about character, comportment, and deception with such learned factors as native body decorations, social etiquette, and the like, Plymouth's leaders distinguished between "good" and "bad" Indians—that is, those who were likely either to aid or to hinder them in furthering their colonial enterprise—in order to engage native people appropriately, at least from the colonists' perspective. Likewise, they read Englishmen's bodies for their inner characters, but because colonists were expected to behave in a more "civilized" and godly manner than Indians, the saints also imposed theological categories of corporeality upon the English. Thus, Weston's men and even Plymouth's captain, Myles Standish, were vulnerable to criticism when their behaviors failed to match the ideal expectations.

The separatists' inherited models of embodiment were complex, sometimes overlapping and reinforcing each other and at other times creating conflicting interpretations of various kinds of bodies and their activities and treatment. Together, however, they produced a more or less coherent conception of corporeality that generated certain kinds of human behavior and provided standards for the evaluation of behavior. But this ideal body was a mutable, problematic one, for it carried potentials for health and sickness, human and beast, divine and evil, industry and idleness, pleasure and frugality, hunger and satisfaction, honesty and treachery, and ultimately life and death. The saints knew their own bodies were vulnerable to all of these possibilities, but in these particular incidents more vulnerable were those of Massasoit, Wituwamat, the Wessagusset men, and Myles Standish. While Standish's choleric constitution caused him to fall short of embodying the image of God, his conduct served a useful role in the establishment of Plymouth's authority among its neighbors. The bodies of Weston's men, however, threatened by disorderliness and starvation, fully slipped into diabolical, animal-like behavior. The body of Massasoit, which colonists viewed as more civil even than those of some Englishmen, bore the potential for healing, which in turn solidified social bonds between himself and his healer. Wituwamat's savage body, in contrast, needed to be destroyed in order to be transformed into an icon of both exultation and terror. Plymouth inscribed colonial relations of power on the bodies of Massasoit and Wituwamat; Winslow's power to heal Massasoit indebted the Wampanoags to him, while Standish's power to kill Wituwamat and impale his head on the meetinghouse-fort solidified the colonists' superiority over the Massachusetts. By healing one Indian body and raising up the severed head of another, the saints promoted themselves and their God in the hierarchy of New England social relations. An English Protestant corporeality began to inscribe itself on the American landscape and its bodies. Yet the separatists' struggle to maintain their sense of distinct communal identity in an unfamiliar "wilderness" environment that threatened bodily survival and social solidarity was not over.

CHAPTER 2

A Banquet in the Wilderness

Bodies and the Environment

T HE FIRST COMPANY OF ENGLISH SEPARATISTS SAILED within sight of Cape Cod on a cold day in November 1620, after a grueling transatlantic voyage aboard the *Mayflower*. Upon their initial glimpse of the sandy, wooded shoreline, William Bradford reported, "they fell upon their knees and blessed the God of Heaven" for their safe arrival in a "new world." Having endured two months of stormy ocean passage during which most had become ill and two people had died, they were "not a little joyful" to be able again "to set their feet on the firm and stable earth, their proper element." Although they sensed this foreign "wilderness" must finally be their proper home, its "hideous and desolate" appearance discouraged them. With "no friends to welcome them nor inns to entertain or refresh their weatherbeaten bodies; no houses or much less towns to repair to, to seek for succour," New England gazed upon them with its "weatherbeaten face." The separatists saw themselves, chilled and exhausted, reflected in the land's gray winter visage. To turn away from that face engendered no hope, for "if they looked behind them, there was the mighty ocean," barring them "from all the civil parts of the world." Before them lay a land filled with the unfamiliar and unknown—"woods and thickets," "wild beasts," and "savage and brutish men"—which the settlers would have to face. They set to carving out "a place of habitation" for themselves.[1]

Bradford wrote his description of the birth of Plymouth Colony ten years after the fact, and he presented the saints' initial experiences of New England in a particular way for a particular purpose. He intended his history to emphasize the dangers of the North American wilderness and the advances the English settlers and their God had made upon it since those meager and tenuous beginnings. Bradford's account of the *Mayflower's* landing articulated a fundamental conflict between "civilized" and "savage" that was familiar to his readers and shaped much of the English rhetoric about New England. However, an earlier account, *A Relation or Iournall of the beginning and proceedings of the English Plantation setled at* Plimoth *in New England*, familiarly known as "Mourt's Relation" but probably written by Edward Winslow, was composed within a year or two of their landing. The *Relation* provides a more complex and ambivalent rendering of the event and a more concrete account of the immigrants' initial contacts with the New England landscape that describes colonists' immediate physical engagement with the environment. Winslow's *Relation* offers little in the way of rhetorical gloss, instead representing the first days in America as intensely physical, as English senses encountered new sights, smells, sounds, and tastes and their bodies responded accordingly. Rather than Bradford's dark and threatening vision of New England, according to Winslow the saints' initial sighting of the coastline "much comforted us, especially seeing so goodly a land, and wooded to the brink of the sea. It caused us to rejoice together." After anchoring in the "pleasant bay" the weary travelers waded to shore and "relieved ourselves with wood and water, and refreshed our people." Unable to catch fish they found fat mussels, which unfortunately caused them "to cast and scour [vomit and have diarrhea]," but Winslow maintained his cheery outlook, for "we were soon well again."[2]

In the following days and weeks the English actively engaged the land in numerous ways and responded with both fear and ebullience. They repeatedly waded three-quarters of a mile between anchored ship and rocky shore through chilly surf, the sea spray freezing on their coats "as if they had been glazed, . . . which caused many to get colds and coughs." A reconnoitering party discovered "excellent black earth," woods that were open and easily traversed due to regular burnings by the Indians, and juniper, "which smelled very sweet and strong and of which we burnt." Meanwhile, the women went on shore "to wash [clothing], as they had great need."[3] Another party of sixteen heavily armed men set out to penetrate further inland and find a site on which to settle. During this three-day expedition through the forest they glimpsed five or six Indians, who ran away as the Englishmen followed them (during a later excursion they would be frightened upon hearing some Indians' "great and strange cry," which was "dreadful," and arrows and musket shots would be vigorously exchanged). In their pursuit of the Indians, the party "marched through boughs and bushes . . . which tore our very armor to pieces," and thirst drove them to drink "our first New England water with as much delight as ever we drunk drink in all our lives," for this water "was now in great thirst as pleasant unto them as wine or beer had been in foretimes." They discovered Indian graves and winter stores of maize buried in the ground, and they loaded themselves with as much corn as they could carry, given that they were also "laden" with heavy armor. They grew fatigued walking in sand along the shoreline and so moved inland again, finding cultivated land, strawberry plants, walnut trees, and canoes.[4]

On the third day, as they turned back toward their ship, the party lost its way in the woods, a perpetual danger that would take several English lives throughout the seventeenth century. Bradford, who was walking in the rear of the single-file line, was caught by a leg and jerked into the air by "a very pretty device, made with a rope of [the Indians'] own making and having a noose as artificially [artfully] made as any roper in England can make, and as like ours as can be." After releasing Bradford from the snare they finally "marched" their way out of the woods and returned to the ship.[5] Within days, colder weather set in, which, coupled with inadequate food supplies, constant drenching from the freezing surf, and the rigorous labor required to investigate the coastline and inland reaches for a place to settle for the winter, caused many members of the English party to become ill. Those physically able decided to take advantage of the cleared and cultivated site of a deserted Indian village, Patuxet, and set about constructing shelters there.[6] Although they knew they were "but strangers as yet at Patuxet," they soon found themselves adapting to the new environment as they learned native land cultivation and fishing practices from Tisquantum, whom the English also called Squanto, the only surviving member of the original Patuxets.[7]

The separatists had been urban artisans—weavers, tailors, printers, and so on—during their twelve-year tenure in Leiden in the Netherlands and, although many had descended from yeoman farming backgrounds in England, they initially were unprepared for the harsh realities of the wintry New England wilderness.[8] Leiden was a densely populated city rich in Eu-

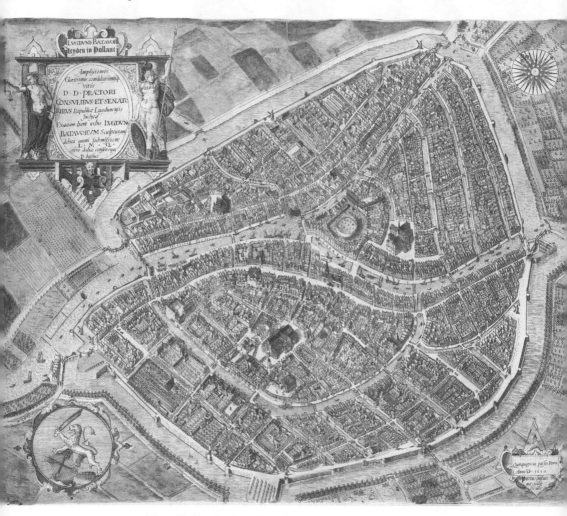

FIGURE 2.1   *Plan of Leiden*, by Peter Bast, 1600. The map shows the densely populated urban neighborhood of Pieterskerk (the church is the large building at lower center), where John Robinson and his congregation lived. (Courtesy of Regional Archives, Leiden.)

ropean intellectual and material culture (see figure 2.1); the New England coastline presented a radically different kind of environment (see figure 2.2). Confronted with a multitude of unfamiliar but often exhilarating experiences and the perceived and real dangers of Indians, wolves, cold weather, disorientation in the woods, lack of nourishment, unfamiliar foods, and illness, Winslow developed a narrative of their first months in New England that tracks a thoroughly visceral engagement with what they saw as a "wilderness"—the terrain, climate, vegetation, animal life, and human

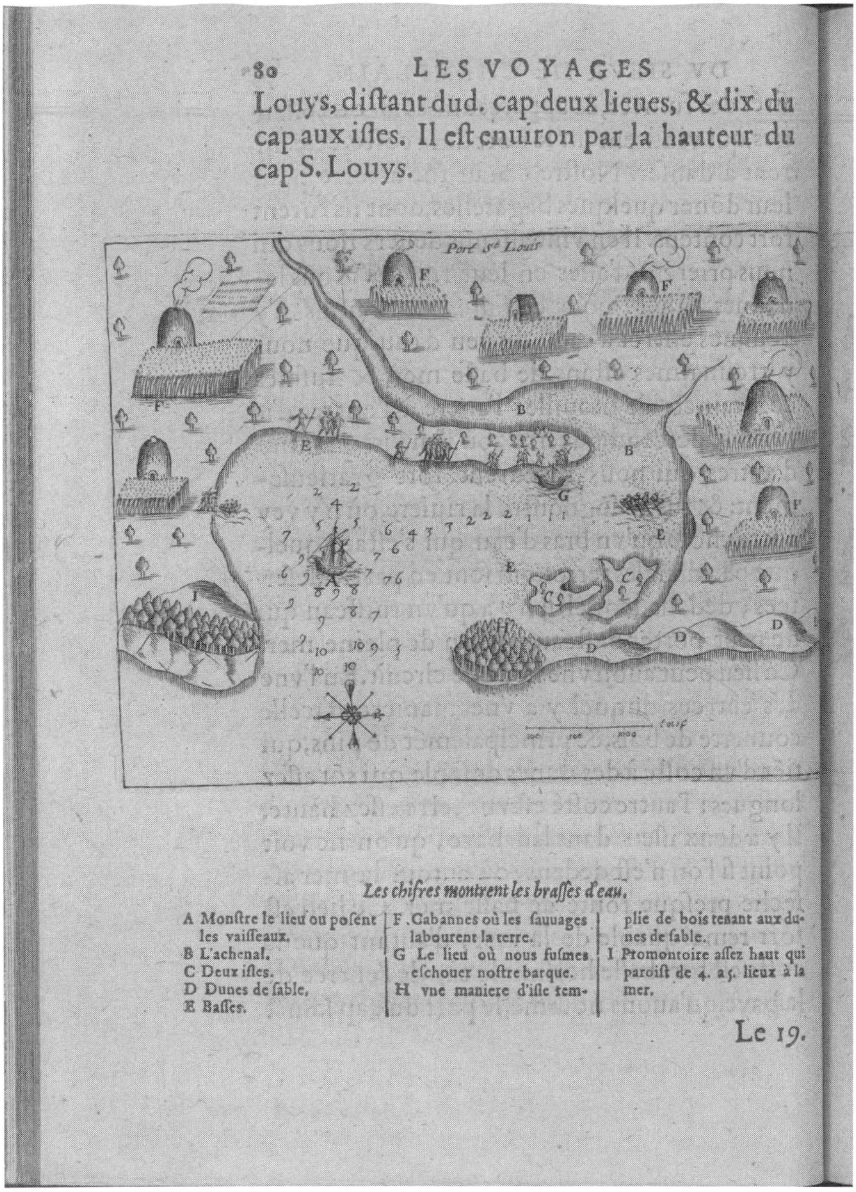

Louys, diſtant dud. cap deux lieues, & dix du
cap aux iſles. Il eſt enuiron par la hauteur du
cap S. Louys.

Port S.t Lovis

Les chifres montrent les braſſes d'eau.

A Monſtre le lieu ou poſent
les vaiſſeaux.
B L'achenal.
C Deux iſles.
D Dunes de ſable.
E Baſſes.

F. Cabannes où les ſauuages
labourent la terre.
G Le lieu où nous fuſmes
eſchouer noſtre barque.
H vne maniere d'iſle tem-

plie de bois tenant aux dunes de ſable.
I Ptomontoire aſſez haut qui
paroiſt de 4. a5. lieux à la
mer.

Le 19.

FIGURE 2.2 *Sketch of Port of St. Louis* [Patuxet]. When Champlain arrived in what would later be named Plymouth Harbor, he encountered the thriving Wampanoag village of Patuxet on its shores. Disease completely destroyed Patuxet's population between 1615 and 1617, except for Tisquantum who was in England at the time, opening the site for the *Mayflower* company to establish the village of New Plymouth. (From Samuel de Champlain, *Les Voyages de Samuel de Champlain*, 1605. Courtesy of the Library of Congress.)

inhabitants. The struggle to survive and learn to manipulate this new world operated in the immediate contact between human bodies and physical environment, dialectical moments that would alter English physiology and New England landscape.

Exchanges between body and environment are always saturated with particular cultural concerns, expectations, and interpretations. Images of New England as both wilderness and garden provided biblical metaphors for what godly colonists believed to be their divinely ordained mission to transform untamed, chaotic, raw space into familiar, civilized, productive farms and villages.[9] The polarized categories of wilderness and garden corresponded to other dichotomies—savage and civilized, nature and culture—that collapsed in lived experience, as colonists went about organizing the new world. "The source of people's ability to intervene in the world comes not from prevailing forms of discourse or social classifications," Chris Shilling writes, "but from the body's own material relationship to its environment." Humans apprehend their immediate surroundings through the physical senses and orient themselves according to basic body postures: up and down, front and back, left and right.[10] Thus, Bradford, perched at the edge of a new continent and a new life, literally and metaphorically faced the wilderness, with England at his back: "Which way soever they turned their eyes (save upward to the heavens), they could have little solace or content in respect of any outward objects."[11] Lacking outward bodily comforts, the saints would have to look "upward" to God and inward to their own moral constitutions. Bradford located his body as the site where the material and spiritual worlds met and where old and new, English culture and American nature, civilized and savage interpenetrated. The human body, Bryan S. Turner explains, is "simultaneously an environment (part of nature) and a medium of the self (part of culture). The body is crucially at the conjuncture of human labour on nature . . . and thus critically at the conjuncture of the human species between the natural order of the world and the cultural ordering of the world."[12] The colonists' activities as they made their first tentative steps into New England produced increasingly complex and enmeshed relations with the new environment.

Human bodies, Arnold Berleant argues, are "dynamic and fluid," engaged in continuous "transaction with the field they inhabit." As it "ingests" and "exploits" its immediate environment, one's body, in turn, is received into and shaped by it: "The very forms our bodies take are themselves the product of . . . environment."[13] Plymouth saints used words like "appetite," "devour," and "consumption" to describe this mutual ingestion between themselves and New England. They employed two basic understandings about their corporeal relationship to the environment that joined forces to produce a distinctive interplay of meanings and activities around consuming and being consumed. The first they derived from Protestant nonconformists' theology of the body promoted by their pastor John Robinson, the second from ancient theories of the humors and faculties. From the former, separatists had inherited the idea of sainthood's visibility in "godly industry," which they interpreted as hard physical labor to convert the savage wilderness into a civilized landscape. Combining godly industry with the driving colonial motif of "possession," they identified their distinctive "English physiology as their nation's peculiar asset in the project of colonization."[14] The separatists voyaged to New England to "plant" themselves in the wilderness: acquiring land, domesticating it according their ideas of godly civilization, and exploiting its natural resources for profit—in effect, consuming the environment. During the first months, however, the wilderness threatened to possess them, to swallow them whole: Mary Allerton gave birth to a stillborn boy, Bradford's wife Dorothy fell overboard—or jumped in despair—and drowned while the *Mayflower* was anchored in Provincetown Harbor, and one after another became seriously ill until half their original party of 102 members had died.[15] William Wood blamed environmental elements unfamiliar to English bodies weakened by the ocean crossing: "The searching sharpness of that purer climate creeping in at the crannies of their crazed bodies caused death and sickness."[16]

Wood's notion that the climate literally insinuated itself into their bodies reflected common ideas about human physiology and its relationship to its material surroundings. Because humans shared humoral qualities with all other things, the boundaries between soul, body, and environment were unstable and permeable; there was a "unity between the environment and the intimate self."[17] Climate, weather, seasonal variations, temperature, air, food, and physical exercise continuously altered one's physiology and moral character. While debating in Leiden their potential move to New England, the saints worried that "the miseries of the land which they should be exposed unto, would be too hard to be borne and likely, some or all of them together, *to consume and utterly to ruinate them*."[18] They anticipated that inclement weather, rugged terrain, and unfamiliar foodstuffs might cause ill health and even death. Furthermore, humoral-faculty theory taught that living in a new land, if it did not kill them outright, inevitably would cause their bodies and souls to take on qualities of the new environment;

without vigilance, they could, in fact, become wilderness creatures, their civil godliness consumed by the environment and replaced with a "savage" character.

The saints' theology of the body countered their humorally based concern that their bodies and souls might be perilously consumed by their surroundings. Rigorous, intentional labor as a true sign of divine chosenness, they hoped, would negate the undesirable effects of the environment's savage influence. By closely monitoring individuals' behavior and promoting "industry" to clear trees, build fences, roads, and houses, and cultivate fields, transforming the landscape into an English garden, the saints believed they could resist dangerous physical and moral mutations. God's economic reward would come as they progressively possessed more land and commodified more natural resources, such as furs, fish, and timber.[19] Although the New England environment confronted them with an inescapable material presence that threatened to absorb them, body and soul, into its savage bosom, it also enticed them with the possibility of increased physical health and material gain as they ingested New England air, foodstuffs, land, and resources. The malleable humoral and industrious godly body was the site of mutual exchange—consuming and being consumed—between the physical environment and cultural ideas about that environment, producing distinctive human bodies in Plymouth Colony.

"Satan Hath More Power in These Heathen Lands": The Consuming Wilderness

It was especially during the first years of colonization that Plymouth's saints felt the wilderness's potential to consume them utterly, body and soul. In a humoral economy, physical and moral health depended upon a balance or harmony between one's constitution and the surrounding environment. For John Robinson all material things were "bodies," created by God's providential power, and "the heavenly bodies, the sun, moon, and stars" had direct "influence, . . . operation, . . . power, and effects upon the bodies here below." The "position and disposition of the stars and celestial bodies" caused "the least and suddenest natural change in the air, water, or other elementary bodies [earth and fire]," thus continuously altering "all things [plants, animals, and humans] framed and compounded of them." As the creator and governor of all things, God worked through this natural humoral economy to "order both the being and [the] motions of all creatures," including the constitutions and activities of human bodies.[20]

With such interdependent correspondences and relations among humans, their earthly environments, and the celestial and divine realms, English travelers speculated about the effects of foreign climates on their humoral constitutions as they explored new lands and came into contact with new cultures and peoples in America. John Josselyn, who visited New England in 1638 and 1663, contended that some people could not easily live in places other than where they had grown up, "for the certain agreement of nature . . . is between the place and the thing bred in that place." When people migrated to new lands they took on new characteristics, like plants that absorbed the qualities of the soils in which they were rooted. Colonists employed the organic theme of transplantation in multiple ways as they uprooted and replanted themselves into new environments; labeling the English settlements in America, such as that at Plymouth, "plantations" indicated both a figurative and a literal transplantation of Anglo people, plants, animals, and culture. Yet they feared the effects transplanting themselves into a new world might have, for "the original stamp given by climate can be changed only by effort . . . victory is tenuous and ramparts must always [be] watched."[21]

The exchange of humors between human beings and the New England wilderness potentially endangered colonists, who might become physically ill or take on "savage" qualities, both physical and moral, before they were able to domesticate the land. Thus, promotional writers like John Smith assured their readers that New England was "a most excellent place, both for health and fertility." In 1630 puritan Francis Higginson organized his description of New England according to the four elements because, he asserted, God had ordained that "the life and wel-fare of euerie Creature here below . . . doth depend . . . vpon the temperature and disposition of the foure Elements, Earth, Water, Aire, and Fire." He proceeded to prove "that there is hardly a more healthfull place to be found in the world that agreeth better with our English Bodyes." Thomas Morton found New England to be superior to England in every way—its soil more fertile, air healthier, wildlife more fecund, winds less violent, and rain more moderate. For Wood the country was colder in the winter and in summer "hotter than is suitable to an ordinary English constitution," and yet "both men and women keep their natural complexions . . . fresh and ruddy" and "not very many [are] troubled with inflammations or such diseases as are increased by too much heat."[22] Despite his concerns, Josselyn thrilled at the country's healthfulness and ability to purify and refine one's body.[23] Even those who had not actually set foot in New England felt comfortable echoing the well-circulated opinions of those who had; John White proclaimed, "No Countrey yields a more propitious ayre for our [English] tempor, then *New-England.*"[24]

The American wilderness, then, appeared to offer an agreeable setting for a transplantation of the "English vine." However, for a separatist sensibility, the fear persisted that settlers might become physically and morally contaminated by a savage land, subsumed by a foreign environment. The Plymouth saints expected to be exposed to "famine and nakedness and the want, in a manner, of all things" and believed that "the change of air, diet and drinking of water would infect their bodies with sore sicknesses and grievous diseases." (In fact, they originally intended to plant themselves in northern Virginia rather than even further south, because they knew that "such hot countries are subject to grievous diseases and many noisome impediments which other more temperate places are freer from, and would not so well agree with our English bodies.")[25] Bradford imagined in visceral detail cannibalistic tortures the "savage people, who are cruel, barbarous and most treacherous" might inflict on vulnerable English bodies: "flaying some [of us] alive with the shells of fishes, cutting off the members and joints of others by piecemeal and broiling on the coals, eat[ing] the collops of their flesh in their sight whilst they live, with other cruelties horrible to be related." Even "the very hearing of these things could not but move the very bowels of men to grate within them and make the weak to quake and tremble."[26] Although Bradford's fear that the Indians might devour their English flesh proved to be unfounded, the saints' ocean crossing and first years in New England did present numerous physical challenges that at least for a time kept the question open as to which side—savage or civilized—would consume the other.

Fears of being devoured, body and soul, by the entire experience of migration and transplantation consumed the separatists even before they set sail on the *Mayflower.* They knew the transatlantic voyage would be fraught with physical discomforts. Some detractors in the Leiden congregation argued against emigrating, contending that "the length of the voyage was such as the weak bodies of women and other persons worn out with age and travail (as many of them were) could never be able to endure." Robert Cushman quipped that "poor William Ring and myself do strive who shall be meat first for the fishes." In fact, halfway across the Atlantic, one of the sailors died of "a grievous disease" and his body was thrown overboard; as they approached the coast, William Butten, servant boy to the company's physician Samuel Fuller, also died. Experienced seaman John Smith imagined the miseries aboard the *Mayflower.* "Being pestred nine weeks in this leaking vnwholesome ship, lying wet in their cabbins, most of them grew very weake, and weary of the sea."[27] The trip was, indeed, physically and mentally grueling; Bradford grumbled that they "endur[ed] a long imprisonment as it were in the ships at sea."[28] Tightly "compact together on one ship," they encountered several storms, during which "the winds were . . . fierce and the seas . . . high" and bodies were thrown about as the ship violently pitched from side to side. During one raging tempest "a lusty young man called John Howland" was thrown overboard, "but it pleased God that he caught hold of the topsail halyards." Dragged along "sundry fathoms under water," he nevertheless held on until he could be hauled up into the ship "and his life saved."[29] The stormy environment so completely engaged the physical senses that the rational mind was unable to control the body and emotions as it should: "The ears lay so sensible to the terrible cries and murmurs of the winds," recorded a Virginia-bound passenger in 1609, that "this constant roaring din worketh upon the whole frame of the body" so it "gives not the mind any free and quiet time to use her judgment and empire."[30] Spoiled foods and fetid water further undermined passengers' sense of well-being. Wood believed the reason so many *Mayflower* passengers died during their first months in New England was "not because the country was unhealthful but because their bodies were corrupted with sea-diet, which was naught—the beef and pork being tainted, their butter and cheese corrupted, their fish rotten."[31]

More serious than a poor diet were such illnesses as scurvy, typhus, and smallpox, which quickly spread among passengers during the *Mayflower*'s and later voyages to Plymouth. Winslow advised a common remedy: "Bring juice of lemons, and take it fasting; it is of good use."[32] Those who became ill brought their diseases to Plymouth; in 1630 a shipload of more saints from Leiden carried an "infection that [had grown] among the passengers at sea; it spread also among them ashore, of which many died, some of the scurvy, others of an infectious fever which continued some time amongst them." Virtually everyone at least experienced seasickness, and to make matters worse they had to bear the tauntings of the ship's crew, like the "lusty" and "profane" sailor who harassed the sick but whom God eventually smote with a fatal disease. The grueling nature of the sea voyage operated on vulnerable bodies and minds in devastating ways. When the saints on board the *Mayflower* finally arrived in New England, the physical and mental toll exacted by the ocean passage was compounded by the fact that they arrived during the winter months with meager food supplies and no shelter from the elements: "They landed their people, many of them weake and feeble through the length of the Navigation, the leakinesse of the ship, and want of many other necessaries such undertakings required," Sir Ferdinando Gorges described. Their bodies weakened and minds disoriented by the transatlantic passage, the wilderness environment would consume half of them within the first few months.[33]

It would take several years, in fact, for the colonists to feel they had more than a tenuous grip on their survival. Settlers arriving in 1623 were "daunted and dismayed . . . [and] full of sadness" when they saw the effects of wilderness life on the first settlers. Each reacted differently according to their "diverse humors": some wanted to return immediately to England, "others fell a-weeping," and still others "pit[ied] the distress they saw their friends had been long in, and still were under." With barely enough clothing to keep warm or food—"a lobster or a piece of fish without bread or anything else but a cup of fair spring water"—to stay alive during the previous two and a half years, Bradford somewhat exaggerated, "the freshness of the[ir] former complexions" had much "abated."[34] Even as the English over time became physically acclimated to the wilderness, as they learned to navigate its woods and waters, it still threatened, sometimes literally, to devour them. Throughout the seventeenth century forty deaths—over half of those deaths investigated by Plymouth's coroner juries—were caused by environmental factors: being exposed to inclement weather, falling through ice or from rocks, drowning in rivers, ponds, or the ocean, being crushed by falling trees, or being struck by lightening. The juries closely inspected each dead body, reading it for clues about its demise. When James Peirse was struck by lightening in June of 1660, for example, the jury reported, "Wee did view his corpes" and determined Peirse had died of "thunder and lightening, which appeereth by these cleare demonstrations: his body was burnt on the right side downe to the calfe of his legg, as alsoe his shirt burnt on his stomache and other partes of it, his wastcoate being la[c]ed cloase with a fishing line, and not burnt, saue only scorched in the inside next to his shirt."[35]

Natural bodies of water were serious dangers; more colonists met their deaths by drowning than by any other environmental threat. Nathaniel West, for example, walked "vpon the iyce, it brake, and hee fell in and was drowned" in March 1658/9.[36] In May 1679 James Colbey went fishing on the Patucket River, slipped or fell in, and drowned. Three years later four men were out in a canoe when the wind rose and "caused a great sea," capsizing the canoe and drowning two of them. People also frequently became lost in the wilderness. John Billington "lost himself in the woods" for five days in 1621, "living on berries and what he could find" until he wandered into the native village of Manomet, where the Indians helped him return home. In February 1651 nine-year-old John Slocum was not so fortunate; out gathering cranberries with a group of friends, he "strayed in the woods" and never returned. Not until the following January did someone stumble upon his skull and "some other partes of the corpse, . . . with parte of his clothes torne into smale peeces, and dispersed into diuers places," as well as "certaine bones" and "some part . . . of his bowels not quite consumed." Apparently young John had wandered around until, "being spent with weariness and cold, [he] perished among the brushy shrubs," where "ravenous creatures" tore and "devoured" his body, scattering parts of the carcass.[37]

Devoured by wild creatures, "overcome by the violence of the weather," "drownded in a boate wracke," losing the "right path to gitt home again," being "killed by the cold"—all were serious environmental threats. But interwoven with bodily survival concerns—indeed, seen as even more critical—was the danger of persons' souls becoming corrupted by the savage wilderness, of the physical environment consuming not simply one's physical body but one's moral soul. If a person did not take care, godly colonists feared, degenerate activities would be "a natural consequence of transplantation into a wilderness environment."[38] They imagined the human body as a plant, which became rooted in the soil and absorbed the elements from its surrounding environment—air, water, sunlight—in order to grow and mature. Unhealthy elements produced a sickly plant, while healthy plants required unflagging attention to their cultivation. Likewise, savage wilderness qualities could produce a savage human being, thus a person must closely monitor one's own and others' proclivities and activities. Weston's men at Wessagusset exemplified what happened when supposedly civil, Christian men allowed their fleshly desires to run rampant in the wilderness. Even more degenerate in Plymouth's eyes was Thomas Morton of Ma-re Mount, who, according to Bradford, thoroughly demonstrated the evil effects of the seductive wilderness on English men. Morton, indeed, imagined New England as "a faire virgin, longing to . . . meete her lover in a Nuptiall bed"—and himself as her lover.[39] Morton had arrived five years after the *Mayflower* and settled in the area of Mount Wollaston, which he named Ma-re Mount.[40] From the outset Bradford was disgusted with the uncontrollable Englishman, who had "more craft than honesty" and been "a kind of pettifogger" in London. Like Weston's men, Morton and his party arrived as traders intending to make their fortunes from the riches of the country, not as families living in disciplined, godly households, answering to civil and ecclesiastical authorities. While Plymouth palisaded its village against wilderness dangers, as we shall see, and bore an innate suspicion and fear of the "skulking savages" (despite their good relations with and utter dependence upon many Indians), Ma-re Mount was open to the surrounding woods, for Morton reveled in "the bewty of the Country with her naturall indowements" and freely pursued economic and social exchanges with local native people. These radically different understandings of the body, the environment, and their effects on each other first collided when Plymouth discovered Morton was trading guns to the Indians for furs, and other conflicts soon followed.[41]

Indians "better fitted and furnished [with firearms] than the English themselves," Bradford feared, made for more dangerous Indians. Historians have debated whether English firearms were actually more efficient and effective than native bows and arrows, but the colonists certainly believed they were.[42] With the weapons acquired from Morton, native men became more adept at using English firearms than were Plymouth's farmers and craftsmen—a skill colonists thought were a direct result of Indians' innate physiological abilities derived from their wilderness life. Plymouth's Nathaniel Morton observed that after Thomas Morton taught them how to shoot, Indians became "more active . . . than any of the English" at hunting and fowling "by reason of their swiftness of foot, and nimbleness of body, being also quicksighted, and by continual exercise, well knowing the haunts of all sorts of game." Bradford complained, "The natives . . . can use [the guns acquired from Morton] with great dexterity, excelling our English therein," and he dreaded the Indians might employ their newfound weaponry and skills against Plymouth, "beating" the colonists "with [their] own arms." An English tool of civilizing power in the hands of an Indian became a tool of savagery; Indian bodies were now "full of pieces all over, both fowling pieces, muskets, pistols, etc.," and "swords, rapiers, and javelins," while the separatists "live but at the Indians' mercy." When colonists came upon "Indians in the woods armed with guns, it was a terror unto them."[43]

Bradford directly linked the physical threat of armed savages skulking through the forest with the moral threat of Englishmen who allowed themselves to run amok in the uncivilized wilderness; he worried that "decent" people "stand in more fear of their lives and goods in short time from this [Morton's] wicked and debased crew than from the savages themselves." Except for their own small plantation, Bradford saw the New England "woods and thickets" as not yet domesticated; the wilderness was a dangerous, chaotic "wasteland," void of (civilized) human habitation, and thus the ideal environment for the release of "fleshly" indulgences normally controlled by society's rules and regulations. The "lawless" Morton had attracted "all the scum of the country or any discontents" to Ma-re Mount (spelled "Merry-mount" by an offended Bradford), where they "fell to great licentiousness and led a dissolute life, pouring out themselves into all profaneness." Morton "became Lord of Misrule" and erected an eighty-foot-tall maypole with deer antlers affixed at the top. His men spent what they earned through trade with Indians on "quaffing and drinking, both wine and strong waters in great excess," and dancing hand-in-hand with fellow Indian carousers around the "idle or idol maypole," "like so many fairies, or furies." To Bradford it appeared "as if they had anew revived and celebrated the feasts of Roman goddess Flora, or the beastly practices of the mad Bacchanalians." In fact, Morton did intend their festivities to be "Revels & merriment after the old English custom" of May Day, which echoed ancient pagan fertility rites that tapped into the sacred powers of the natural world. Rather than fearing the wilderness, Morton imagined it as a voluptuous womanly body, awaiting consummation with Englishmen's "art & industry," symbolized by the phallic maypole thrust into the earth, to bring forth her fruits. To Bradford, such un-Christian, erotically charged activities embodied the licentious slip into barbarism, "the demonic descent into primitivity" the savage environment exerted on those who failed to control their animal passions.[44]

Plymouth was convinced these unregulated male bodies engaged in even "worse practices," acting out their symbolic maypole festivities in actual sexual liaisons with Indian women, whom Bradford claimed Morton invited to Ma-re Mount as "consorts" and with whom he and his men "frisked together." Whether Morton and his men actually "abused the Indian women most filthily," as Bradford imagined, is unclear.[45] On all points Morton confirmed and even elaborated on Bradford's description of Ma-re Mount's maypole festivities, except for the presence of women. Bradford's fantasies, however, exposed his fear of a fundamental commingling of the categories of civilized and savage. The most intimate joining of two kinds of bodies in sexual consummation dissolved the barrier he believed was absolutely critical to maintain. The separatists had inherited a "deep-rooted and long-standing English fear," David D. Smits argues, "that, through biological amalgamation, English men would adopt the manners, customs, and language of colonized regions inhabited by 'savage' peoples." They believed that sexual liaisons with Indian women promoted the disintegration of civilized social order and godly moral order.[46] However, such beliefs did not stop Indian women and English men from enjoying intimate contact throughout the seventeenth century—and sometimes appearing in Plymouth's court on charges of engaging in sexual activities with each other.[47] Neal Salisbury believes that "such carryings on would have been entirely out of character for the Indians." But native social structure, unlike that of English separatists, allowed sexual encounters before marriage, and Smits notes, "There is some evidence to indicate that Algonquian women found English males quite appealing" for their "possession of food, . . . alluring trade goods, . . . [and the] indulgent affection that English husbands [allegedly] bestowed on their wives." For the godly saints, however, despite their much-admired modesty Indian women served as a corporate symbol of "wilderness temptations."[48] Feminized wilderness savagery consumed vulnerable masculine civilization, they imagined, when Indian women lured English men into their bodies.

Like the Wessagusset colonist who "turned salvage," some Englishmen were so seduced by the liberalities of wilderness life that they fully turned their backs on colonial society to live among Indians and acquire their lifestyle. In 1629 Plymouth's investors sent one Edward Ashley to manage their trading post at Penobscot, on the coast about 240 miles north of Plymouth, but plantation leaders were "not a little trouble[d]" about him.[49] Ashley's English body, according to Bradford, had become "savage" and his morals "very profane." He lived with the Indians, adopting their "manners," going "naked," speaking their language, and, worst of all, "commit[ing] uncleanness with Indian women." Plymouth leaders knew that Ashley, already consumed by wilderness life, was not to be trusted living so far from the influence of civil society. Although the investors in England had recommended him, Bradford believed they knew nothing of wilderness physical and moral temptations. Ashley promised he would do "better," but Plymouth "feared he might still run into evil courses . . . and God would not prosper his ways," so they decided to send with Ashley one of their own, Thomas Willet, a godly, "discreet" young man, whom they thought would be able to keep "Ashley in some good measure within bounds." Willet, however, was unsuccessful, for Ashley, "a crafty pate," the following year sent all the beaver furs he had received from the Penobscot Indians back to England without reimbursing Plymouth for the supplies and trade goods they had provided him. He was finally "taken in a trap" and arrested, for he, like Morton, had committed an unpardonable offense: "trading powder and shot with the Indians." Undoubtedly, Plymouth imagined Ashley received his just reward, for the ship on which he was returning imprisoned to England foundered and he "was cast away at sea." With an almost audible sigh of relief Bradford concluded, "This was his end."[50]

Despite the colonial authorities' attempts to restrain people from escaping the controlled confines of the village to homestead deep in the wilderness, many did so throughout the seventeenth century. They tended to be poorer and of lower social classes, usually not affiliated with a church body, and thus inherently suspect in the eyes of Plymouth's church and civil elite and, like Weston's men, Morton, and Ashley, identified with heathen savagery.[51] In 1675, for example, John Arther, Mathew Boomer, and John Leyton, who lived with or near Indians, were hauled into court for "liueing lonely and in a heathenish way from good societie"; they were ordered to attend regular public worship services and "liue otherwise orderly," or they would be expelled from the colony. Ten years earlier Arther had appeared in court for "abusiue speeches" and for "entertaining" the wives of two men. Mathew Boomer's son apparently fulfilled the court's expectations that living in the wilderness, far from "good society," provoked barbarous behavior. In early 1686 John Brandon brought complaints against Mathew Jr. claiming that Boomer had beaten Brandon and made threatening speeches against him and had attempted to rape Brandon's wife, Mary. Boomer was found guilty of both accusations, as well as of allowing his Indian servants to hunt on the Sabbath.[52] The lures of the wilderness environment—freedom from the constraints of civil, godly society, commodities that could enrich a young, unlanded Englishman, and allegedly generous native women—were powerful seductions for those ruled by the flesh, Bradford knew only too well. He blamed Thomas Morton for "inveigling" away from Plymouth young men who were enticed by a less constricted lifestyle and for arming the surrounding Indians so that the village and its outlying farms "expect[ed] daily to be overrun and spoiled by the savages." But these uncivilized Englishmen and Indians did their dirty deeds outside of Plymouth. Even more threatening than such external forces was the danger of the environment's savagery creeping inside the plantation itself and inciting physical and moral impurity among its inhabitants. After Plymouth's experiences with Weston's men, when other "bad" or "helpless" men—that is, those whom plantation leaders thought susceptible to the wilderness's dissolute moral effects—arrived, Plymouth did its best to send them packing before their corrupt behavior could take root in the community.[53]

However, there were colonists who initially appeared acceptable but quickly changed when transplanted into wilderness soil. Within a month of arriving in New England in 1630 John Winthrop complained to his wife, Margaret: "I thinke there are some persons who never shewed so much wickednesse in England as they have doon heer." In 1642 a crop of sexual sins—adultery, incest, sodomy, and bestiality—flourished at Plymouth, and Bradford connected these heinous acts with the environment: "Things fearful to name have broke forth in this land oftener than once." He dreaded that, although their community had been planted in the wilderness by "religious men . . . and they came for religion's sake," the country's seductive powers could undermine their best intentions and nurture seeds of wickedness that bore fruit in the colonists' bodies. However, not relishing the notion that "Satan hath more power in these heathen lands, as some have thought," Bradford preferred to imagine that "the Devil may carry a greater spite against the churches of Christ and the gospel here" because of how diligently "they endeavour to preserve holiness and purity amongst them." In other words, if Satan truly held sway in New England, if there were something inherently evil about the environment itself, "any transplantation of civility and Christianity" would be "frustrate[d]," John Canup explains, and the separatist project ultimately doomed. But even if, as Bradford hoped, the wilderness were not finally Satan's domain, the saints still must watch each other closely, lest "one wicked person may infect many" and sin—both moral and physical—thrive in the heathen soil. "As was the human body," Rhys Isaac notes, the body politic was "thought to be as subject to aging, infirmity, and decay." Like physical contagion and disease, with which the colonists were all too familiar, spiritual disease could spread quickly from person to person, always through physical bodies and their actions, and consume the entire community.[54]

Despite Bradford's and others' fears regarding the physical and spiritual threats posed by uncontrolled interaction with the environment, colonists eventually discovered that New England actually offered an exceptionally healthy and prosperous climate for English bodies, and over time most gave themselves over to the virtues of the wilderness. Concerns that ingesting indigenous foods and breathing wilderness air would affect their humoral bodies negatively proved unfounded as the Plymouth colonists adapted to wilderness life and thrived. Gorges, putting an initially overly positive but ultimately accurate spin on their experiences, wrote that the *Mayflower* passengers "were not many daies a shoar before they hadd gotten both health and strength, through the comfort of the Ayr, the store of fish and fowle, with plenty of wholsome rootes and hearbs the Country affoarded." Indian corn, or maize, which natives taught them how to cultivate successfully, quickly became their "staff of life," according to Winslow, "without which they cannot long preserve health and strength." In 1638 John Wiswall described the "pleasant country" of New England, noting that "it is a fine land, good for corn, especially Indian, which is a very precious grain for divers uses besides bread." John Winthrop Jr. penned a glowing treatise on Indian corn in 1662, describing its general health-giving qualities, especially for kidney stones and scurvy, and its cultivation, both native practices and later English modifications of them "by the helpe of the Plough," though many English farmers still used the "good husbandry" learned from the Indians. Over time, the colonists became seasoned maize cultivators. Winthrop displayed an intimate knowledge of the cultivation of Indian corn and its beneficial effects on the human body, exemplifying the physical adaptations to the environment colonists made as they struggled to survive and later thrived in wilderness soil.[55] They first intentionally mimicked native practices of corn cultivation and then implemented them as second nature, developing a dynamic exchange between indigenous land and foods and English bodies. As they learned to cultivate squash, beans, and corn, gather fruits and nuts, and hunt deer, fish, and fowl, the environment, in a sense, absorbed them into itself, as they, in turn, ingested its products.

Colonists, in fact, felt they lived with more "physical vigor" than their English counterparts. Wood, like many others, boasted that he had been chronically ill in England but "being planted in that new soil and healthful air [of New England], which was more correspondent to my nature . . . , scarce did I know what belonged to a day's sickness."[56] They also grew taller, due to a higher consumption of meat and dairy products, than in England. The average height of the first English men in Plymouth was approximately five feet, six inches; women averaged five feet in height. They probably were, in fact, shorter than the New England Indians, whose bodies they frequently described as tall.[57] By the mid-1700s American-born men and women of Anglo descent averaged two to three inches taller than their English counterparts.[58] And colonists lived longer: men who survived childhood in England lived to about sixty-nine years of age, women to fifty-six; Plymouth men could expect to live into their seventies and women into their sixties or seventies.[59] Some allowed that New England's healthful and agreeable climate stimulated women to be more fertile and produce more twins. The lower ratio of female to male colonists caused women to marry at a younger age (twenty to twenty-two years) and have larger families (seven to ten children), and infant mortality rates were lower (approximately one in five children died before age twenty-one), than in England.[60] Thomas Morton linked the fecundity of the environment with human fertility: New England, that "happy land," was "apt . . . for the increase of Minerals, Vegetables, and sensible Creatures [animals]," as well as "reasonable Creatures, Children." In 1651 George Gardyner claimed that in New England "the English people are well coloured and have many children, which thrive well." Wood believed that there were "more double births [twins] than in England, and the women likewise hav[e] a more speedy recovery and gathering of strength after their delivery than in England." Winslow, writing from Plymouth in 1624, summarized: when compared with "other parts of America, I cannot conceive of any to agree better with the constitution of the English, not being oppressed with extremity of heat, nor nipped by biting cold; by which means, blessed be God, we enjoy our health, notwithstanding those difficulties we have undergone, in such a measure as would have been admired if we had lived in England with the like means."[61]

Looking back on their first decades in America, Bradford marveled at the saints' ability to thrive in the face of adversity. Regardless of the dangers of the ocean crossing and wilderness life to the stability and integrity of their bodies and souls, and the fears they might be consumed by the environment and transformed into fundamentally different kinds of creatures, New England provided, he believed, the raw materials and experiences that had enabled them to become healthier and thus more godly people than any could be in England. "It is not by good and dainty fare, by peace and rest and heart's ease in enjoying contentments and good things of this world only that preserves health and prolongs life," he asserted. Rather, it was *because* they had experienced many "enemies to health"—"change of air, famine or unwholesome food, much drinking of water, sorrows and troubles," all of which were normally "causes of many diseases, consumers of natural vigour and the bodies of men, and shorteners of life"—that God had supported them and allowed them to prosper. Of anyone at Plymouth, Bradford seemed most inclined to feel anxious about the saints' rejection of England and transplantation in the New England wilderness, which he attempted to justify by mingling ideas about the health and spiritual benefits of living in America and holding up rigorous life in New England as morally and physiologically superior to the "civilized" world of those who still languished in England.[62]

Over time, Plymouth colonists became thoroughly invested in New England, given over to what they construed as the often threatening but ultimately invigorating actions of the land's climate and natural resources upon their physical and moral beings. The humoral understanding of the body—a body that engaged its material surroundings in a continuous exchange of qualities—meant that human beings could not remain unchanged by new environments. As the saints planted themselves in New England, becoming "rooted" there and making it their home, their bodies absorbed wilderness resources and practices and were, in turn, absorbed by them, their physiological, mental, and moral structures altered from those they had been in England or Holland.[63] Mostly for the better, they believed, colonists were consumed by wilderness culture. Admittedly, as Bradford argued, thriving in the environment, rejecting its savagery but acquiring the godly character it could instill, required hard physical labor and a determination to withstand difficulties in the "weatherbeaten face" of adversity. Successfully working the land and gaining a visceral sense of its character stifled the colonists' fears of the dangerous power the wilderness might exert on them. Despite their original intentions, within the first few years settlers began to push outside the palisaded town, claiming new land for themselves.

"A Pleasant Banquet Is Prepared": Consuming the Wilderness

In 1620, after twelve years of exile in the Netherlands, where "they found worse air and diet than that they came from [in England]," the saints determined to remove themselves to America. They wanted the opportunity to pursue freely their particular understanding of godly worship and hoped to advance the gospel of Christ "in those remote parts of the world" or at least be "stepping-stones unto others for the performing of so great a work."[64] However, beneath such religious rhetoric lay another motivation at least as powerful, if not more so—"the consumption of space."[65] The Plymouth saints were from the lower end of the English "middling" class and saw the North American continent and its much advertised natural resources as an opportunity provided by God for the furtherance of worldly enterprise. Plymouth's Robert Cushman argued for the colonists' legal rights to the land, contending that not only had James I claimed English possession of New England by royal decree, but God had rendered the land itself "spacious and void," "a vast and empty chaos"—a wilderness.[66] In fact, European diseases had decimated the native population in New England during the late sixteenth and early seventeenth centuries, "emptying" the wilderness of most of its human inhabitants and facilitating English land consumption.[67] Pestilence had consumed the Indian village of Patuxet and its two thousand members in 1617, opening the site for the town of New Plymouth and eliciting Bradford's claim that New England was a "vast and unpeopled countr[y] . . . , devoid of all civil inhabitants, where there are only savage and brutish men which range up and down, little otherwise than the wild beasts of the same." It would be dependent upon English settlers, by rigorous labor and "godly industry," to plant themselves in this "empty" land in order to transform the savage wilderness into a cultivated garden.[68]

Regardless of the apparently dehumanized wilderness the saints encountered when they arrived on November 11, 1621, however, Indians had intentionally created a particular New England landscape. The colonists' exploratory party discovered "one place where the savages had burnt the space of five miles in length, which is a fine champaign [open] country, and even." Indians' twice yearly burnings of the undergrowth kept forests cleared of shrubbery, creating "park-like" environments where game animals were more easily hunted and herbaceous and berry plants could thrive. The Indians also cleared and planted irregularly shaped gardens, "small, unfenced, and multicropped" with tree stumps left in the fields as supports for beans and squash vines. To English observers' untrained eyes, however, the landscape appeared wilder and less domesticated than was comfortable.[69] To avoid physical and moral consumption by this savage environment, they believed, they must begin immediately the hard labor of Anglicizing the country to establish familiar boundaries and order, to transpose the wilderness into a safe and livable garden, to civilize the savage land. First, they required shelters and erected rustic "rendezvous," or small "open wooden barricades of three sides" that provided little protection.[70] By December 25 they had chosen the site of Patuxet for their village because it was "on high ground" with a good harbor and "a very sweet brook run[ning] under the hill side, and many delicate springs of as good water as can be drunk," and the Patuxets had cleared the land—in fact, their cornfields were still producing. Besides taking advantage of the Indians' previous labor, the colonists chose this site because "in one field is a great hill on which we point to make a platform and plant our ordnance, which will command all round about." From the hill, on which they would build their meetinghouse-fort with rooftop cannons, they could survey the countryside.

Grouping themselves into nineteen "families" in order to limit the number of houses they must erect, they began inscribing an English town onto formerly Indian land. They measured and "staked out" the village, each person receiving an area about eight by fifty feet, allotting larger plots to larger families. The first structure raised was a common building, twenty feet square, with wattle and daub siding and a thatch roof, in which they put all the beds for those who were ill. In January, when the building was filled with the sick and dying, the thatching caught fire and the roof burned, but no one was hurt and the structure survived; a significant initial environmental threat was rebuffed.[71] By the end of the first year seven families had erected houses, and four more structures had been built for plantation use. These were all one-room cottages, probably made of palisades standing side-by-side with daubing in between, thatched roofs, and wooden chimneys, in each of which several families lived. In the summer of 1622 with "all hands willing" they built their meetinghouse-fort on the hill overlooking the village. The fort had a "Watch-tower" and was "well built of stone, lome, and wood" with "their Ordnance well mounted." From this high point, they expected, "a few might easily secure the town from any assault the Indians can make," and they hoped "it would utterly discourage the savages from having any hopes or thoughts of rising against us." They completely enclosed the village with a protective palisade of eight- to ten-foot vertical poles, sharpened at their tops, "with gates to shut, which were every night locked, and a watch kept." In 1623 there were twenty houses, "four or five of which are very fair and pleasant," inside the enclosure.[72]

By 1627, according to visitor Isaack de Rasieres, there were three large gates in the palisade walls, clapboard houses stood along two crossing streets, and gardens were enclosed with clapboard: "Their houses and their courtyards are arranged in very good order." With his home an extension of his social identity, Governor Bradford's house occupied the position of highest status and greatest safety, at the center of the town where the streets crossed. Six cannons were mounted on the flat roof of the meetinghouse-fort at the top of the hill. Ordering the environment with a layout of buildings, palisade, fences, and fields in clearly defined, familiar, "civilized" patterns of social status, religious authority, military might, and domestic safety physically oriented colonists and ensured their sense of order, power, and well-being. Even John Smith, despite his peevishness that the *Mayflower* company had not hired him as their guide—and not a little smugness that their lack of "experience" initially caused them to spend "six or seven weekes in wandring up and downe in frost and snow, wind and raine, among the woods, cricks, and swamps" so that "forty of them died and threescore were left in most miserable estate"—could acknowledge that they were "living so well they desire nothing but more company."[73]

With these tenuous but ultimately successful beginnings, the colonists made their marks upon the land. Orienting their bodies in the new environment and developing a "visceral sense" of the climate, the change of seasons and weather, and how to work the land, they imposed upon the wilderness English modes of ordering the natural world, and they began to extend their influence further afield.[74] From its heart, the palisaded town, Plymouth Colony reached fingers into the wilderness as the settlers gained confidence, discovered the "savages" were friendly or subduable, plowed more fields, and established farms outside the palisade walls. Evolving principles of land ownership shaped the physical, cognitive, and emotional relations between colonist and gradually Anglicized environment. The original economic structure of the plantation was a form of communism—together inhabitants held and cultivated property equally for the "common good" and to pay off the plantation's debts to its investors. But individuals soon began to complain that some were working harder than others and yet all were reaping the benefits, grounding their arguments in corporeal aspects: physical capability, age, social status, and gender. The young men, who "were most able and fit for labour and service," complained that, if they had to "spend their time and strength to work for other men's wives and children," they should receive more "victuals and clothes than he that was weak and not able to do a quarter the other could." "Aged and graver" men, in contrast, considered it an "indignity and disrespect" to have to work as hard as or eat less food than did "the meaner and younger sort." Women also entered the fray, complaining it was "a kind of slavery" to have "to do service for other men, as dressing their meat [preparing their meals], washing their clothes, etc."[75]

The conflicts diminished "mutual respect" among inhabitants and led to the decision in 1623 that each family man should be responsible for his own parcel of land, the size determined by the number of his dependents (wife, children, and servants) and unattached young men who lived and worked with the family. The results of private property ownership were highly satisfactory, encouraging everyone to work harder: "It made all hands very industrious, so as much more corn was planted than otherwise would have been by any means the Governor or any other could use, and saved him a great deal of trouble." Women, who previously had claimed "weakness and inability" and considered it a "great tyranny and oppression" to leave their homes, now "went willingly" to work in their fields, taking their children with them.[76] This political restructuring, which allowed individuals to possess private property, transplanted traditional English yeoman farmer sensibilities into the New England wilderness.[77] The shift from communal to individual property ownership, however, undercut the founders' original intent to create a communal body whose members were tightly bound by common affections; it also gave colonists license to satisfy their hunger for more land.

Property sizes were limited by physiological constraints—that is, the time it took to walk from buildings to fields or from village to village.[78] Yeoman farmers knew their lands well, for they trudged across them daily. Approximately two-thirds of Plymouth's town records deal with the distribution of property, the boundaries of which were defined in exceptionally concrete, immediate, sensory terms and recorded as if one were hiking over the terrain (as, indeed, those appointed to determine the layout of properties did). Using such natural objects as unusual rock formations, creeks, and large trees and such human-produced markers as fields, buildings, and "heapes of stones," town planners structured and familiarized the landscape.[79] An intimate physical relationship with the environment developed as farmers "husbanded" the land: they felt and smelled the soil; toiled to plow, plant, and harvest their fields; and learned to read the weather. Thomas Morton explicitly envisioned the wilderness as a female body, but implicitly so did Plymouth farmers, who were the "husbandmen" of the feminine land. Like a woman's body, property was "broken and plowed," "brought into good culture," and "dressed," the wilderness tamed.[80] Women tended their gardens of English vegetables and herbs, their families ingesting the fruits of their labor and of the soil. While Indian corn, squash, and beans and American fish and game were staples during the first years of settlement, domesticating the wilderness required the transplantation of English fruits, vegetables, grains, grasses, and livestock. A dynamic melding of English culture and New England nature occurred in the transplanted bodies of the settlers as they became rooted in the land and consumed its products; the environment, to use Michel de Certeau's terminology, became "encysted" in their bodies.[81]

As their experiences multiplied into a familiar, embodied sense of place, Winslow could boast of Plymouth's accomplishments in fishing, hunting, and Indian relations, as well as their knowledge of wild fruits and shellfish, just a year after settlement. "We . . . walk as peaceably and safely in the wood as in the highways in England," he concluded. Yet "the country wanteth only industrous men to employ, for it would grieve your hearts if, as I, you had seen so many miles together by goodly rivers uninhabited." He believed that God had given New England as an "inheritance" to England, "and great pity it were that it should long lie in so desolate [uncultivated] a state, considering it agreeth so well with the constitution of our bodies, being both fertile, and so temperate for heat and cold, as in that respect one can scarce distinguish New England from Old."[82] Colonial possession, for Plymouth leaders, lay in physical *habitation* of the land—English bodies must live and work there, building houses and fences and cultivating property in order to realize the symbolic and literal transformation of "savage wilderness" into "civilized garden." Unlike the Indians, who roamed the land like the "wild beasts" of the forest, the separatists were to plant themselves in the soil and labor industriously there.

Colonists exposed their fundamental beliefs about the categories of "civilized" and "savage" in their rhetoric about "industrous" English settlers and "idle" Indians, which reflected conflicting conceptions of the human-environment relationship and human corporeality. Despite the critical support provided by Hobbamock, Massasoit, and Tisquantum during the first years of colonization, Cushman claimed that the native inhabitants lacked industriousness and had neither "skill [n]or faculty to use either the land or the commodities of it," and so it was an "undressed country," "marred for want of manuring, gathering, ordering, etc."[83] For the English, land was empty and available if it were not cultivated and harvested in the Anglo-European pattern of land "improvement" that entailed building permanent structures, enclosing property with fences, plowing fields, and planting English crops, as well as mining for metals and minerals and harvesting timber, fish, and furs for economic gain.[84] The Plymouth saints energized this principle with their theology of the body, which dictated a moral polemic against "idleness." Robinson, as we know, advocated "sore labour," especially husbandry, for it strengthened both body and mind: God had determined that "man" must "labour . . . in dressing the garden; and . . . eat bread by the sweat of his brow . . . . Art and industry must supply nature's defects."[85] Plymouth colonists believed God had given them the raw material of New England; to make it "useful" they must employ "art and industry," that is, English agricultural techniques and hard physical labor. Only a rigorously disciplined physical body, with its technological extensions of iron hoe, plow, and oxen, reaped the fruits of the earth.[86] To plant themselves and establish communities they must learn to exploit the land for daily subsistence: "their very survival required that they manipulate the environment."[87]

Initially dazzled by reports of the riches of indigenous fish, game, and vegetation that made New England appear to be more fertile and temperate than England, colonists soon realized the difficulties of exploiting the abundant resources. Winslow warned those in England who would come to New England expecting to consume its products easily, expecting that "the fountains should stream forth wine or beer, or the woods and rivers be like butchers' shops, or fishmongers' stalls, where they might have things taken to their hands [i.e., easily obtained]." Survival required knowledge of the environment, the means by which to procure its products, a willingness to drink plain water and eat coarse foods—and to labor diligently even for this rustic fare: "A proud heart, a dainty tooth, a beggar's purse, and an idle hand, be here intolerable."[88] Indeed, Plymouth colonists found their region's soil vastly different from that in England—it was drier and rockier and required extensive clearing of forests in order to establish enclosed, single-crop fields. Rasieres observed in 1627, "Their farms are not so good as ours [at New Amsterdam], because they are more stony, and consequently not so suitable for the plow." Physician Robert Child noted the same in 1645: compared with other parts of New England "the land [at Plymouth] is barren, the people very poore."[89]

Within the first couple of years Plymouth's leaders realized they had not chosen the most productive region. They complained to their investors in London, who advised that, although they had discovered more fertile land elsewhere, the Plymouth area was what God had given them and as long as "the land afford you bread and the sea yield you fish" they should remain there. In fact, they reasoned, staying in Plymouth meant the godly saints would be "the less envied and encroached upon; and such as are earthly minded will not settle too near your border."[90] However, in 1624 the investors wrote again, this time questioning Plymouth's leaders regarding complaints from the colony's "particulars"—those "earthly minded" who had come to Plymouth only for personal economic gain and not religious pursuits. Many of the particulars' complaints concerned bodily discomforts: unwholesome water, soil that required hard labor to cultivate, and mosquitoes. This time Bradford and others defended their region, locating the problem not in the environment but in those who complained about it. Regarding the accusation that "the water is not wholesome" they responded, "If they mean it is not so wholesome as the good beer and wine in London (which they so dearly love), we will not dispute with them; but else for water it is as good as any in the world (for aught we know) and it is wholesome enough to us that can be content therewith." Answering the complaint that "the ground is barren and doth bear no grass" they claimed: "It is here, as in all places, some better and some worse; and if they well consider their woods in England, they shall not find such grass in them as in their fields and meadows. The cattle find grass, for they are as fat as need be." Finally, leaders answered those who were "much annoyed with mosquitoes": people who "cannot endure the bite of a mosquito . . . are too delicate and unfit to begin new plantations and colonies," sarcastically adding, "we would wish such to keep at home till at least they be mosquito-proof." Nevertheless, as more "land is tilled, and the woods cut down" there would be fewer mosquitoes, until "in the end scarce any at all"—as English industry consumed New England resources, one environmental pest would be eradicated. All these complaints, Bradford summarized, were "ridiculous to all here which see and know the contrary."[91]

Colonists committed to the plantation's religious and economic project persisted in the argument that a life of ease engendered depraved bodies and souls, while the hard work and bodily discomforts demanded of Plymouth farmers produced godly people. In 1621 Cushman had advised against those coming who "look after great riches, ease, pleasures, dainties, and jollity in this world," for "the country is yet raw; the land untilled; the cities not builded; the cattle not settled." For the saints the ideal New England body was one not dissipated with sensory pleasures and a frivolous lifestyle. It was, certainly, vulnerable to the wilderness environment, but that meant it must stand strong against the weather-beaten face of physical adversity. They had hoped to leave behind in England those who preferred bodily ease and pleasures, but in New England they believed they had found another, similar group of idle people—the native inhabitants. Although colonists survived the first winter only because they had stolen corn from buried Indian stores and Tisquantum had taught them its preparation as food and crop seed, Cushman continued his diatribe: "We are compassed about with a helpless and idle people, the natives of the country, which cannot, in any comely or comfortable manner, help themselves, much less us." This tension between immediate experience and abstract belief was not limited to those at Plymouth, but reflected a general colonial ambivalence toward Native Americans. Colonists recognized their vulnerability in an unfamiliar environment and their utter dependence on Indian hospitality in the early years of settlement. They attempted both to elide their vulnerability and to justify their acquisition of natives' lands, however, with rhetoric that represented Indians as fundamentally inferior human beings—uncivilized, hostile, "wild men"—who were unable to use the land fully as God intended and, when provoked, as they were by colonial encroachment on their lands and resources, would retaliate with savage violence. The English sense of inferiority in a strange new world and of vulnerability to Indian whim impelled colonists to buttress their beliefs in English superiority by falling back on the familiar dichotomy of "civilized" and "savage."[92]

Colonists grounded their conceptions of Indians as uncivilized, incompetent, and indolent, merely "ranging up and down" the land like "wild beasts," in a combination of observations and beliefs about natives' very different relationship to the wilderness environment. It was obvious to colonists that Indians were at home in the woods and waters of New England; therefore they must be uncivilized, like the land itself. And yet settlers admired Indians' far superior intellectual and sensory knowledge of environmental elements and their exploitation. Thomas Morton, of course, proclaimed, "These people are not (as some have thought) a dull, or slender witted people; but very ingenious and very subtile." Their sensory perceptions excelled those of any English person: Indians had "the sence of seeing . . . farre beyond any of our [English] Nation" because their eyes were "black as iett; and that coler is accounted the strongest for sight." Their sense of smell was so acute that "they will distinguish between a Spaniard and a Frenchman by the s[c]ent of the hand onely." But Winslow, too, praised the Indians for being "very ingenious and observative; they keep account of time by the moon, and winters or summers; they know divers of the stars by name . . . ; also they have many names for the winds. They will guess very well at the wind and weather beforehand, by observations in the heavens." Phineas Pratt, who arrived in Plymouth in 1623, noted that "ye wild Salvages . . . have a better scill to catch such things [Fish fowle and deare] then Einglish men haue." Tisquantum astonished Plymouth settlers with his ability to catch fat, sweet eels by "trod[ding] them out with his feet, and so [catching] them with his hands without any other instrument."[93] Colonists recognized Indians bore an enviable relationship to their environment, a relationship simultaneously cognitive and embodied in sensory perceptions and everyday skills that highlighted how inept and inexperienced the English were. Indian bodies, like all human bodies, inhabited the intersection of culture and nature—shaped by native cultural understandings, physiological requirements, and environmental exigencies—and carried a visceral sense of how to live properly in their world. It would take time for colonists to develop a similar embodied knowledge of the New England environment. However, when combined with English technological developments and religious and cultural beliefs about human manipulation of the environment, that embodied knowledge would enable them ultimately to exploit the landscape in more far-reaching ways than did the Indians.

English observers could not help but marvel at the superiority of the Indians' abilities to understand and manipulate their environment, yet it also proved, they thought, the natives' close relationship to the wilderness and thus to savagery. Colonists grounded their distinctions between "civilized" and "savage" in ideas about land utilization and agricultural technology.[94] From an English point of view, it appeared that Indians were unconcerned about "improving" the land, but rather did as little work as possible to gather only the minimal necessities for survival. Ordering the environment according to an Anglo-European agricultural model required "breaking and dressing" the land: fencing properties, plowing fields, and living in immovable structures. Indians, on the other hand, did not appear to "haue any settled places, as Townes to dwell in, nor any ground as they challenge for their owne possession, but change their habitation from place to place."[95] Native land use involved moving villages to various sites in a regular pattern throughout the year, according to fish and game migrations, the growing season, the changing fertility of the soil, and the availability of wood for fuel. The English viewed this "scattered and wild course of life" as lacking in industry, and it reminded godly colonists of European gentry who lived leisurely, idle lives of hunting and fishing. Thomas Morton, however, thought their seasonal movements gave Indians an air of civilized gentility: "After the manner of the gentry of Civilized natives, [Indians] remoove for their pleasures, some times to their hunting places where they remaine keeping good hospitality, for that season; and sometimes to their fishing places, where they abide for that season likewise."[96] Wood, on the other hand, believed that because Indian men were "fettered in the chains of idleness" and would "rather starve than work, following no employments saving such as are sweetened with more pleasures and profit than pains or care," they were unable to benefit from English ways. Indian women, however, were "very industrious."[97]

In native New England hunting and gathering societies, men provided crucial animal protein and were often away from the village for days at a time hunting and fishing, while women stayed in the village, raising crops and gathering berries, nuts, and shellfish. To colonists, however, Indian male bodies were disorderly, savage, and lazy because they "ranged the forests" for wild game, while female bodies were hard-working—thus more civilized—because they stayed at home and cultivated the fields. For the English the identifying feature of civilization was agriculture, and it was the Indian women who industriously planted, tended, and harvested their crops of corn, beans, and squash. Colonists, in fact, sometimes recognized that Indian women's methods of cultivation were more effective than their own. Although most colonists assumed their agricultural technology surely was superior to that of the uncivilized natives, Winslow acknowledged that Indians near Plymouth could plant corn for four years without fish fertilizer and still "have as good corn or better than we have that set with them [fishes]." After native women obtained iron hoes from Plymouth, which allowed them further "industry in breaking up new grounds therewith," they produced even more corn. Despite his belief that the Indians naturally lacked industry and allowed the land to "lie in so desolate [uncultivated] a state," Winslow recognized that Indian modes of corn cultivation required "good labor and diligence."[98]

More significant, however, than gendered agricultural practices in differentiating English from Indian relationships to the environment and thus differentiating between civilized and savage corporeality was the English use of domesticated animals.[99] The hoe was an effective but limited technological extension of the human body. But oxen, cows, and horses that required ever more pastureland for grazing, the "deep-cutting plow" they made possible, and the fertile manure they left behind allowed for more efficient and thus more radical extensions of English bodies deeper into the wilderness and its soil.[100] Plymouth had to wait four years to obtain livestock for plowing and fertilizing their fields, when Winslow returned from a trip to England in 1624 with "three heifers and a bull." Before the colony began receiving shipments of livestock, the intensive human labor corn required had not appealed to Winslow; he wished for "cattle to till the ground" in order to grow such English grains as wheat, rye, barley, oats, and pease. It was a pity, he complained, "to see so many goodly fields, and so well seated, without men to dress and manure the same."[101] The rigorous labor of clearing large acreages of tree stumps and "navigat[ing] a heavy plowshare behind a recalcitrant team of oxen who periodically released their 'peculiar manuerance'" assured the saints that theirs was the civilized and godly mode of land ownership, as their bodies' sweat poured into the soil.[102] But their activities through their own and their animals' labors, William Cronon explains, drastically consumed the land's resources, as "deforestation, grazing, plowing, erosion, and watershed changes all contributed to a problem that became endemic to colonial agriculture in New England: soil exhaustion."[103]

The inherently unsatisfactory nature of Plymouth's soil—its barrenness and rockiness—coupled with the declining fertility of their nutrient-depleted properties prompted farmers to penetrate ever deeper into the wilderness and claim more land, while the colony's fur trading enterprises also reached further afield, seeking new regions whose resources they might exploit.[104] Between 1630 and 1640 thousands of immigrants arrived on New England shores and new homesteads and towns multiplied within and outside of Plymouth Colony, as colonists pushed the frontier westward, expanding their territorial possessions. Native inhabitants, however, were often unwilling to allow the environment be subsumed by English activities. An Indian sachem knew very well "how far the bounds and limits of his own country extendeth; and that is his own proper inheritance," Winslow observed. They "know their own bounds or limits of land, as well as [do] the rest [of the sachems know each others' lands]."[105] As contact between Pequots and colonists increased in Connecticut during the 1630s, the Indians complained that the English were "overspread[ing] their country, and would deprive them thereof in time, if they [the colonists] were suffered to grow and increase." The massacre of the Pequots in 1637 by English and Narragansett men violently enacted a central tension between different understandings of territory and corporeality. For the English it was a tension between savage and civilized bodies and their conflicting manipulations of the environment, but it was also a religious undertaking.[106] English soldiers set fire to the Pequot compound, in which were hiding four hundred old men, women, and children who were either burned to death, met with swords and "hewed to pieces" as they attempted to escape, or hunted down through woods and swamps "like animals." "It was a fearful sight to see them thus frying in the fire and the streams of blood quenching the same, and horrible was the stink and scent thereof," Bradford described. Although such a grisly vision would have deeply dismayed John Robinson, to Bradford the scent of burning Indian flesh smelled like a "sweet sacrifice" of "victory . . . and they [the saints] gave the praise thereof to God."[107] Savage bodies, piled one on top of the other like so many slaughtered pieces of meat, became sacrificial bodies, immolated as a food offering to an apparently ravenous, vengeful God. Shrouding their own outrageous violence in sacred language, the colonists' bodies became vehicles of divine, consuming power that "emptied" the environment of its dangerous savagery and opened up new land for godly settlement. Plymouth's Nathaniel Morton concluded, "The body of this [Pequot] people were wholly subdued, and their country taken from them."[108]

The dispersal of colonists into territory emptied of Indian bodies, however, worried Bradford. The history of land ownership in Plymouth reflects an inherent, growing tension between individual bodies and the social body. Bradford viewed it as a basic conflict between differing notions of the appropriate relationship between humans and environment, which played out in a layered tension between industrious, civilizing labor for the sake of communal solidarity and that same labor for the sake of personal profit, between the social body's promotion of common affections and the individual's accretion of material goods and social status, between individual bodies living closely together in compact, safely enclosed communities and those bodies freely dispersing themselves across the wilderness landscape. Colonial leaders wanted inhabitants to live "as near the town [New Plymouth] as might be . . . that they might be kept close together, both for more safety and defense" and to nurture communal sentiments, but for many colonists the hunger for land overrode leaders' desires.[109] As "commodities grew plentiful"—Plymouth's corn and livestock were needed in the burgeoning Massachusetts Bay Colony—and land was required to produce these commodities, John Alden, Myles Standish (who by now had joined the church), and other "godly pillars" of the community left New Plymouth to settle on their properties in Duxbury, Nauset, and other parts of the colony. In 1633 the general court worried that the town "is like to be dispeopled" and decided to require individuals to give up their homes in town if they were not going to inhabit them, so that others could live there "for the maintenance and strength of society."[110]

Individuals' "appetite for land" enticed them out of New Plymouth, Bradford lamented, and caused the town, like a human body, to become "weakened" and "thin" and the church at Plymouth to be "like an ancient mother grown old and forsaken of her children, though not in their affections yet in regard of their bodily presence and personal helpfulness."[111] He conceived the disintegration of the plantation's original purposes in a providential context: the painful rending asunder of the social body and dispersal of its members "will be the ruin of New England . . . and will provoke the Lord's displeasure against them."[112] Although Bradford imagined that the lack of members' "bodily presence" threatened the integrity of Plymouth's social body, in fact those who migrated in companies to establish new towns reproduced centralized, church-based communities similar to that at New Plymouth, which strengthened the godly colonial presence throughout New England. Bradford interpreted the original argument— civilizing the wilderness required planting oneself in the soil and working it with hard physical labor—as necessarily grounded in a strong, moral community presence. Attempting to do so independently of a godly social body, as had Thomas Morton and other men, put individuals in a position dangerously vulnerable to savage wilderness influences, both physical and spiritual. Nevertheless, the English population in Plymouth, as through- out all of New England, was extremely fluid and transient, as individuals sought to acquire ever more property. Land ownership meant increased wealth and status, and after a regrouping period following Metacom's Re- bellion in the 1670s, during which thousands of Indians were destroyed or enslaved, English expansion into the "emptied" frontier followed with heightened energy.[113] Even for Bradford, consuming the environment ulti- mately proved too enticing to resist. Despite his initial fears of the harmful effects of New England air, soil, and water on English bodies and souls, Bradford later rhapsodized about the wilderness garden of delights spread before the hungry saints:

> And now with plenty their poor souls were fed,
> With better food than wheat, or angels' bread; . . .
> A pleasant banquet is prepared for these,
> Of fat things, and rich wine upon the lees;
> "Eat, O my friends, (saith Christ) and drink freely,
> Here's wine and milk, and all sweet spicery;
> The honey and its comb is here to be had,
> I myself for you have this banquet made . . .
> In this wilderness."[114]

Bradford's poetical paean to the divine feast Christ had prepared for his people in a now pastoral wilderness—no longer a dangerous, savage waste- land—conflated three potent literary representations of consumption. Us- ing imagery from the biblical Song of Songs of two lovers feeding each other exotic foods, Bradford's banqueting vision echoed colonial descriptions of the overflowing abundance of fish, game, and other natural resources awaiting English people in the wilds of America. Bradford's description of a divine wilderness picnic also echoed cookery books and banqueting manu- als elaborating the exceedingly rich, varied, and abundant foods consumed by the upper classes in England.[115] The successful consummation of New

England's fertile body with English art and industry meant a translation of "her" offspring—land, fish, furs, timber, metals, and minerals—into hard, cold cash in the pockets of Englishmen, bringing them a more luxurious lifestyle and higher social status. The extravagant variety of exotic foods on the tables of English nobility and gentry displayed a level of wealth and status to which yeoman farmers did not have access but for which many hungered. In the rapidly changing economy of early modern England, as farmers were pushed off of their lands while opportunities for industrial growth and market commerce were expanding in overseas ventures, New England offered a place where industrious Englishmen might pursue their fortunes. The seeming limitlessness of the country's geography and commodities enlarged colonial appetites; the environment became "a thing consumed for the express purpose of creating augmented wealth."[116] Resisting such overt grasping for material wealth and status, Bradford consumed New England's abundance through biblical metaphors and spiritual meanings.

The religiously motivated and economically driven Plymouth saints struggled with conflicts between communal and individual interests and between godly and worldly enterprises, which they expressed in the tension between their fear of being consumed by wilderness savagery and their insatiable drive to consume its resources, reimburse their investors, and finally improve their economic standing in the New England and European markets. The struggle played out in their bodies, where the threat of physiological and moral alteration due to environmental influences was countered by communal solidarity and hard, diligent labor to alter the land and exploit its resources. They believed God had given them this region, divine providence had ordained their transplantation into its soil, and laboring to civilize the land would engender greater godliness in their souls. Ultimately, Christ offered his industrious, God-fearing people in the wilderness both a spiritual banquet and a material feast: religious and economic rewards conflated in the corporeal metaphor of eating. Godly colonists initially based social status on "moral qualities," notes James T. Lemon, but it eventually became more dependent "on property, wealth, and commerce."[117] Individuals demonstrated such religious and economic signs of personal status through the ways they publicly fashioned their bodies and daily engaged each other in village life.

CHAPTER 3

As on a Hill

Public Bodies

B EFORE THEY STEPPED OFF THE *MAYFLOWER* INTO THE
New England landscape, male company members signed a docu-
ment, now remembered as the "Mayflower Compact," in which
they agreed to "combine ourselves together into a civil body politic." The
compact reflected John Robinson's instructions to them to "join [in] common affections truly bent upon the general good." God had endowed each
person with something to contribute, he believed, and all were to work
together to care for each other and "avoid as a deadly plague of your both
common and special comfort all retiredness of mind . . . and all singularly
affected [in] any manner of way." The social world of early modern Plymouth lacked a distinct modernist split between a public self and a private
self. The ideal of society as an organic body, with all its members tightly
knit together to produce a harmoniously functioning organism, did not
allow for excessive individualism and privacy, for any "singularity" of affections or "retiredness" of mind: "The head cannot say to the foot," wrote
Robinson, "much less the foot to the head, 'I have no need of thee.'" Each
member must "repress in himself . . . all private respects" and reach out
to others "bodily," when they were in need of practical help, and spiritually, by encouraging godly behavior. The physical and moral survival of the
colony, leaders believed, depended on it.[1]

Pride, according to dissenting Protestants, was the greatest threat to the common affections binding people together in a healthy, properly functioning social body, and proud, immoral hearts always were exposed in immodest bodies and behaviors. In 1621 Robert Cushman cautioned Plymouth against "swelling pride, selfe-love and conceitedness," which colonists manifested when they sought "their owne carnall delights and fleshly wantonesse" rather than humbly attending to the physical needs— food, clothing, housing—of all equally. God never taught that "Charitie beginneth at home," Cushman proclaimed, but rather that charitable acts should extend throughout the entire community, for "you . . . have given your names and promises one to another, and covenanted here to cleave together in the service of God, and the King," that is, as both a religious and a civil body: "As you are a body together, so hang not together by skins and gymocks [gimcracks], but labour to be ioynted together and knit by flesh and synewes." Robinson described specific ways people publicly embodied pride: "Persons are vulgarly most noted for proud by their apparel," as well as "lofty eyes, stretched-forth necks, . . . and . . . strutting gestures." Pride fractured social relationships, for it caused people to feel "contempt" for "mean persons and things," to resist being "contemned by others," attempt to be different from others, and to engage in "continual strivings and janglings with others." Humble modesty, which "adorns . . . good things in a person, as blushing doth a comely countenance," was the antidote to such proud actions, and godly honesty, sincerity, and moderation—"plain and homely uprightness"—in dress, speech, and other social behaviors engendered harmonious relationships.[2]

Robinson was fully aware of the dangerous manipulability of early modern self-fashioning; externally embodying something other than one's true inner character, he believed, not only clouded the ideally transparent correspondence between one's soul and body, but also severed honest, open social relations between self and others. It was "notably proud people" who were likely to be "great hypocrites and deep dissemblers" in "counterfeiting the good" in order to hide their secret evils from public view. "Crafty" people attempted to deceive others by masking both their sinful natures and their sinful actions; visible saints, on the other hand, strove to embody plain honesty, "to be, as they appear . . . and to appear, as they are, to the glory of God, and good of men." "What is the empty shadow to the solid body?" Robinson asked rhetorically. Ultimately, the truth would be made visible—either by conscious choice, when one willingly confessed one's sins and reformed one's behavior, or by public exposure, when one was brought before the community to answer for one's actions.[3]

Plymouth's founders, believing themselves divinely called as God's elect people, expected America to offer the ideal setting in which to live out such ideals. They strove to build a "pure" society, bound by common affections and transparent social relations displayed in plain and modest bodies. Yet they recognized that human nature was inherently prideful, making people prone to "rebel . . . against the common good" and pursue their own self-interests. Thus, "the whole body," the entire community, must constrain individual members' bodies and behaviors. According to their covenant with God and each other, documented in the "Mayflower Compact," those who refused to exhibit godliness threatened the moral and social order of the entire community, laying open all bodies and their behaviors to public scrutiny and disciplinary action.[4]

Colonists derived their models of the inherent correspondence between the individual member and the civil community and the highly public nature of the self from Robinson's teachings and from common early modern English ideas. As Plymouth's inhabitants went about their daily lives, they engaged each other in numerous ways, some that religious and civil authorities considered godly and appropriate, and others that they considered sinful and even criminal. Visibility was central—a person continuously displayed his or her godly or sinful nature through every action. People corporeally communicated social meanings through speech acts, but also through such seemingly mundane means as their clothing. Nonconformists shunned elaborately ornamented dress and excessive hairstyles and feared "disguise"—that is, masking, through pretense and dissembling, the plain and transparent link between one's inner nature and outer body. Likewise, speech should be straightforward and modest; women were especially likely to reveal their proud hearts through "wanton" speech, and men as well as women engaged in violent acts of angry, "heated" speech. Dissolute and "lascivious" behavior, especially sexual activity outside the bonds of marriage—both the "natural" acts of fornication and adultery and the "unnatural" acts of sodomy and bestiality—were forbidden. All such immoral actions undermined social order and their covenant with God, authorities believed, as they encoded their principles of godly behavior in civil legislation. Those convicted of breaking the law were punished for their crimes, their bodies disciplined in public spectacles: sitting in the stocks, wearing signs describing their offenses, or being imprisoned, branded, whipped, executed by hanging, or banished from the colony. Indeed, bodies were at the center of public village life, continuously shaped both implicitly by general early modern understandings of self-presentation and explicitly through specific legislation and disciplinary actions. Colonial leaders held up certain individuals, especially devout ministers, as examples of how one should embody godliness—and other ministers as warnings of what happened to those who embodied sin.

"Innofensiue and Innocent in His Life and Conversation": Embodying the Ministry

Among the most highly regarded and thus most public members of separatist communities was the ordained minister, for ideally he exemplified in every action how others should visibly demonstrate humble godliness. In New England he worked closely with civil leaders to promote discipline and constrain sinful behavior. He was an authoritative figure not just in church meetings but at all public events, including harvest festivals, election days, and executions, where he often delivered sermons, prayers, and blessings, and he frequently visited people in their homes, eating meals, attending the sick, and catechizing children. Indeed, Plymouth's extant sources tell us more about the ways their teaching elders and ministers properly embodied (or failed to embody) their official roles than they do colony governors or other community leaders. An extraordinarily visible member of a society that functioned in very public ways, the minister was closely watched by his flock, who were quick to evaluate his behavior—and get rid of him if he fell short. In fact, acquiring and keeping a decent pastor plagued Plymouth throughout the early and middle years of the seventeenth century, and many of their difficulties in doing so were grounded in conflicts over proper embodiment of the pastor's role. As Plymouth's saints observed their church leaders, some, like John Robinson and William Brewster, epitomized the ideal pastor; others, like John Lyford, were crafty dissemblers who threatened to undermine the entire social structure; still others, like John Cotton Jr., came from questionable pasts but publicly had confessed their sins and more or less reformed their behavior.

The pastor's duties clothed him with a distinction not always reflected in his financial status but which nevertheless invested him with great social power. John Robinson's congregation seemed to love him dearly for his modest character yet vigorous leadership. When the Leiden church made the decision to migrate to America, the members agreed their pastor would remain with the larger portion of the congregation in Holland. At their parting in 1620 he and his congregation demonstrated their love for each other in intensely emotional and physical expressions. The day before the company's departure, Robinson delivered a teaching and they filled the rest of the day "in pouring out of prayers unto the Lord, with great fervency, mixed with abundance of tears." That night was "spent with little sleep with the most, but with friendly entertainment," and the next day the entire congregation boarded the two ships, "where truly doleful was the sight of that sad and mournful parting, to hear what sighs and sobs, and prayers did sound amongst them; what tears did gush from every eye, and pithy speeches pierced each other's heart." The event was so moving that even Dutch "spectators, could not refrain from tears." At the last moment Robinson, "falling down on his knees and they all with him with watery cheeks, commended them with most fervent prayers unto the Lord and his blessing; and then with mutual embraces, and many tears, they took their leave one of another." Robinson and his congregation understood that such a dramatic public display of emotions and gestures was a "real" expression of the "true Christian love" they felt toward each other; it visibly enacted the deep pain they experienced at the physical severing of their church body in two. Apparently, Robinson, who "intirely sought [his people's] good for soule and body," thoroughly embodied his own principles concerning how pastors should behave toward their people: with warm and honest physical affection rather than with a detached, "theatrical, and affected strangeness, and stateliness, specially towards their inferiors, and equals."[5]

With their pastor left behind in Leiden the Plymouth settlers lacked an ordained minister, but they did have William Brewster, who would serve as their ruling elder until his death in 1643 at eighty-four years of age. Despite his elevated social status in England—educated at Cambridge, he had served the secretary of state in the English court—Brewster's life in Plymouth, like those of the other early colonists, was physically rigorous, but he apparently displayed true godliness, exhibited by a modest diet and hard work, throughout all hardships. He lived "Many times without bread or Corne many monthes together; haueing Many times Nothing but ffish and often wanting that alsoe; and drank Nothing but water for many yeers together . . . vntill within fiue or six yeers of his death," and he "labour[ed] with his hands in the feilds as longe as hee was Able." In his character, Brewster was wise and discreet, but in his comportment "very Cheerfull" and "very sociable and ppleasent amon[g]st his fri[e]nds"; he was modest, peaceable, tender-hearted, and compassionate toward "such as were in

Missery." "Innofensiue and Innocent in his life and Conversation," Brewster often "vundervallue[d] him selfe and his owne abillities and somtimes ouervallu[ed] others," yet he was intent on maintaining a pure and orderly community. This melding of physical and moral qualities defined the ideal church elder and community leader; eulogies abound with similar extravagant praise for other New England church and civil leaders like William Bradford, John Winthrop, and John Cotton, who served as models of the socially and spiritually devoted man. When these men were gone, the eulogistic texts themselves embodied idealized paradigms of moral character: physically and intellectually rigorous, yet compassionate and loving. When read by the devout, the exemplary conduct manifested in the written word ideally became embodied in the flesh and blood behavior of the reader.[6]

Brewster served as Plymouth's teacher for many years, but during the early years they lacked a pastor who could administer the sacraments of baptism and the Lord's Supper—important rites, or ordinances, that only an ordained minister was empowered to perform. Thus, in 1624 the colony's investors sent Plymouth a minister, who embodied a very different character than did Brewster. John Lyford, ordained in the Church of England, was, like Robinson, a man of emotionally expressive "carriage"; but, the saints soon came to believe, in truth he was a treacherous dissembler, covering his inner corruption with an outer mask of fawning acquiescence. When Lyford arrived in Plymouth, he "bowed and cringed unto them, and would have kissed their hands if they would have suffered him; yea, he wept and shed many tears, blessing God that had brought him to see their faces . . . [and] to enjoy the ordinances of God in purity among His People." After he confessed to and repented of previously "being entangled with many corruptions," Plymouth accepted Lyford into their community. But he proved to be a thorn in the colony's side, a polluting member that threatened to infect the entire communal body. Despite his public gestures of love, Lyford secretly planned to undermine Plymouth's authorities. He conspired with one John Oldham, a "factious speritted man" who already had caused problems in the settlement, to hold their own separate Anglican meetings with other "vil[e]" and "prophane" colonists. Colonial authorities confronted Lyford for ministering to those who were not among the saints, at which he "burst into tears" and confessed his sins but then again "drew a company apart and sequestered himself, and would go minister the sacraments (by his Episcopal calling) without ever speaking a word unto either magistrates or brethren." At wits end, Governor Bradford held a ceremonious trial, with the entire community attending the proceedings in the meetinghouse, and ordered Lyford and Oldham to be "expelled" from the plantation. Although the two men at first held themselves "stiff[ly] and stood resolutely," when confronted with condemning evidence Oldham "began to rage furiously." Lyford, true to form, "confessed his sin [of insubordination] publicly, . . . with tears more largely than before." His dramatic display swayed some observers, who "professed they would fall upon their knees to have his censure released," so Lyford was allowed six months to leave the colony—during which time he wrote letters complaining to investors about his shabby treatment in Plymouth.[7]

The magistrates ordered the fractious Oldham, however, to leave the colony immediately, but he returned in the spring of the following year with a "flame of great choler" and "suffered his unruly passion to run beyond the limits of all reason and modesty." He railed at everyone, embarrassing even his previous supporters, and in his "mad fury" received "a cracked Crowne . . . [and] the blood run downe about his eares." Colony authorities "committed him [to the fort] until he was tamer" and then, in a public spectacle of corporal punishment and humiliation attended by the entire community, made Oldham run the gauntlet on his way out of town: "A lane of Musketiers was made, and hee compelled in scorne to passe along betweene, & to receave a bob upon the bumme b[y] every musketeer," for "everyone was ordered to give him a thump on the breech with the butt end of his musket." The men then carried him bodily to the waterside, threw him on a ship, and "bade him go and mend his manners." In fact, when he was sailing to Virginia a year or so later, Oldham's ship came in danger of capsizing; fearing for his life, he confessed the wrongs he had done to Plymouth's people, vowing that if God spared him he would amend his ways. He survived, eventually ended up in the Bay Colony, and from that time "carried himself fairly towards them" at Plymouth, who allowed him "to go and come and converse with them at his pleasure."[8]

Lyford, on the other hand, had refused to clean up his act, so that his wife "feared that some great judgment of God would fall upon them and upon her, for her husband's cause," now that they were to be ejected from the colony. Indeed, in Ireland, before his marriage to her, Lyford had fathered an illegitimate child by a woman whom he "had overcome . . . and defiled her body." During his marriage he "meddled" with their servants, his wife periodically discovering her husband and various maids engaging in sexual intercourse as "they lay at their beds' feet." With the rape and other illicit sexual activity on his record, Lyford's wife, "a grave matron, and of good carriage," feared that if they were forced to go into the "wilderness," she would "fall into the Indians' hands and . . . be defiled by them as [her husband] had defiled other women." Expelled from Plymouth, the Lyfords moved to the Bay Colony and then Virginia, where he died, and his wife eventually returned to New England.[9]

In the eyes of Plymouth's leaders, Lyford fell far short of embodying the role of an ordained minister of the Word and colony leader. Instead, he manifested dissension and corruption, which infected those around him and threatened the moral purity and social order of the entire community. Lyford's manipulative self-fashioning in tearful and cringing humiliation was persuasive enough in the short term to deceive some observers, but his gestures ultimately proved to be false; his secret behavior, brought to light, exposed the truth of his character. Oldham as well, with his choleric humor and violent rages, could not be contained within the orderly structure of the social body. Such incorrigibly polluting persons, authorities believed, must be publicly purged. Oldham's violent behavior seemed to call for a violent ejection in return; running the gauntlet was a potent form of humiliation that not only marked a specific part of his anatomy—his "bumme"—with the ultimate authority of the communal body but also reminded all who observed the spectacle that they must submit their own bodies and wills to that authority in order to remain members of the community. The incidents that followed—Oldham's true repentance and embrace back into the fold and, on the other hand, Lyford's refusal to reform and permanent rejection by the community—materialized and reinforced the saints' commitment to their religious and civil covenant with God and with each other as a social body.

Lyford was not the only minister to arrive in New Plymouth and create problems; the saints discovered it would be difficult to find a man who embodied the idealized role of pastor in the way Robinson had. After trying out several pastors, finally, with the arrival of John Cotton Jr. in 1667, Plymouth found a minister who would serve their community for three decades. Cotton, however, was not an unproblematic figure. Son of the revered John Cotton of Boston's First Church and graduate of Harvard College in the Bay Colony, Cotton married at twenty years of age. While pastor of the church at Wethersfield, Connecticut, he earned "an apparently deserved reputation for being overly familiar with other women" and was censured in 1662 for "'sinfull Rash unpeacabell' words 'of a veary high defaming natuer.'" Two years later he was called before the members of Boston's First Church for "lascivious uncleane practises with three women and his horrid lying to hide his sinne." Like Lyford, Cotton could dissemble by attempting to disguise his corrupt secret behavior with false public speech. Although he finally spoke honest words of confession and repentance and returned to church leaders' good graces, he lost his position at Wethersfield and went to work as a missionary to the Wampanoags on Martha's Vineyard for three years before being called to New Plymouth's church.[10] Despite his reckless youthful behavior, Cotton proved to be an industrious pastor in Plymouth, taking his proper place in the colony's social culture by laboring hard at his given duties and fulfilling the expectations of his rank and status in the town. Although "ruddy-faced, short, [and] a little fat," he was "a commanding speaker" and an energetic presence, building the church membership and catechizing new members, and he seemed to have learned to control his lascivious leanings, but perhaps not his tongue, for he was frequently in civil court demanding fair reimbursement for his work as pastor of the church.[11]

Pastors, as well as civil leaders, who properly embodied their duties were recognizable in public village life. When they were laboring in the woods and fields, as Brewster did, they may have been indistinguishable from other colonists. But when they fashioned themselves for official duties, which at least by Cotton's time occurred daily for him, they marked their bodies with visible signs of their distinctive status—with their clothing. Dress in Plymouth, as in early modern English culture in general, shaped the wearer's body in specific ways and communicated important information about one's gender, economic status, profession, and character, as well as one's godliness. A person's apparel made a very public statement about his or her location within the community.

"Clad in Gray Russet": Dressing the Body

Men in positions of authority, such as ministers and magistrates, regularly wore black, "a good, grave, sad, and auncient colour" according to English moralist Phillip Stubbes. Dark clothing demonstrated a sober, trustworthy, dignified character and was modest and plain, for, unlike the colorful silk and velvet garments worn by fashionable gents, it minimized the body's shape and surfaces. Black apparel provided a transparent window through the body into the humble, godly soul. The only relief from a dark suit's grave appearance was a simple white linen band, or collar, at the neck, framing the face as it reflected the image of God's glory, and white linen cuffs at the wrists, highlighting the hands as they accomplished the Lord's work. Such simplicity in dress, separatists believed, avoided the "wily-

FIGURE 3.1 *Edward Winslow*. Unknown artist, London, 1651. Winslow wears the plain black suit and white linen band, or collar, and cuffs with a touch of lace trim appropriate for his position as Plymouth's colonial governor. He also displays some ornamentation in his metal, perhaps silver, buttons and tassel at the neck, as well as notably long hair, which puritan moralists criticized. Thirty years before this portrait was painted Winslow slept with Massasoit in his wigwam on one occasion and healed him on another. (Courtesy of Pilgrim Hall Museum, Plymouth, Mass.)

FIGURE 3.2 *Josiah Winslow*. Unknown artist, London, 1651. Like his father, Josiah wears a plain dark suit, white linen band, and, apparently, his father's silver tassel at the neck. Although he does not sport silver buttons, his hair appears to be longer than even his father's. (Courtesy of Pilgrim Hall Museum, Plymouth, Mass.)

beguiles" of high fashion's artificiality. Yet the black dye required for dark clothing was expensive—even plain, sober apparel could signify elite social status. Wealthier members of the colony, like governors Edward Winslow, his son Josiah, and Thomas Prence, could dress richly in soft black wool and "the crispest of starched linen from Holland," as the formal portraits of Edward and Josiah Winslow painted in 1651 during a visit to England illustrate (see figures 3.1 and 3.2). The Winslows allowed themselves some ornamentation in the gold tassel at the neck (it appears they shared the same tassel) beneath their fine white linen bands, and Edward wore lace cuffs and metal buttons on his jacket—a quite remarkable statement of prestige and worldliness for a serious separatist leader. When Governor Prence died in 1673 virtually all his outer garments—three cloaks, two suits, seven coats, and two pairs of breeches—were made of expensive black fabrics, including a "turkey" (tapestry) cloak of "tammy" (glazed, finely woven worsted wool). He also owned silk stockings and several linen collars and cuffs.[12]

The saints did not always agree on what constituted plain and modest dress. Looking back on the history of English separatism, Bradford remembered a controversy that had rocked the exiled church in Amsterdam, with which he, Robinson, and their congregation had resided for a year in 1608 before moving on to Leiden. The conflict revolved around the wife of the pastor, Francis Johnson, and her clothing, which, according to Francis's brother George, was far too proud and fashionable for a godly pastor's wife. Bradford, on the other hand, who met Francis's wife Thomasine some ten years after the controversy, believed her apparel simply reflected her status as a former London merchant's wife (she was a young widow when she married Francis); there was nothing excessive or immodest about it. The bitter five-year-long dispute in the Amsterdam church, which only ended when Francis excommunicated his brother George in 1599, and Bradford's notable attention to it fifty years later in Plymouth demonstrate how significant and contested the meanings of dress sometimes were among the saints.[13]

In early modern England clothing supposedly displayed the truth of one's inner nature—one's social status, gender, temperament, and moral character—yet rebellious individuals consistently wore garments that blurred gender lines or pretended a higher rank. Since the 1300s English sumptuary laws had attempted to regulate apparel and hairstyles according to one's economic status, level of education, and profession. By the latter half of the 1500s Protestant social critics were contributing their moralistic commentaries, which shaped separatists' views of public self-fashioning. Proud apparel—that is, garments made of expensive fabrics like velvet or silk, or with excessive ornamentation, such as lace, ribbons, or gold or silver thread—displayed a proud heart. Modest clothing, on the other hand, expressed a humble, godly heart, which Bradford believed Francis Johnson had exhibited in his rustic apparel: "The man was a plain countryman, clad in gray russet, without either welt or guard [decorative trims of colorful fabric], . . . and the band [collar] he wore scarce worth threepence, made of their own homespinning." Most important to Bradford was the transparent correspondence between Johnson's dress and his inner character: "He was godly and humble as he was plain."[14]

For Bradford, informed by Robinson's relatively pragmatic and moderate stance on most issues, such godly plainness and modesty charted a middle path between the two extremes of hypocritical asceticism and self-indulgent pride. He extolled Plymouth's saints as living "a plain country life" in "plain country villages," where they engaged in "the innocent trade of husbandry," their lifestyles demonstrating their ordinary, humble status. Most colonists (around 350 to four hundred in 1630, two thousand by 1650, and ten thousand by 1690) were husbandmen (farmers) and craftsmen (coopers, weavers, and so on) and throughout at least the first decades held roughly equal economic status and social rank; the colony's social culture reflected far more homogeneity than did the status-conscious, merchant-oriented societies they had left behind in England and the Netherlands or the more economically diverse Bay Colony. With a cohesive society always in mind, Robinson reminded Plymouth's founders that they were "not furnished with any persons of special eminency above the rest." They were to choose as their leaders "such persons as do entirely love and will promote the common good," and he admonished them not to be "like the foolish multitude who more honour the gay coat than either the virtuous mind of the man, or glorious ordinance of the Lord." Indeed, during the early years the colonists struggled to clothe themselves sufficiently. All new garments were supplied from the colony's common stock (provided, often rather parsimoniously, by their London investors), acquired in occasional trade with ship captains or Dutch colonists from New Amsterdam, or sent by family members in England. Bradford dramatically illustrated early colonists' modest means with clothing images: "Ragged in apparel and some little better than half naked," they had "not a sole to mend a shoe" and were glad even to receive a shipment of "some Birching Lane suits," named after the street in London where second-hand clothing was sold—"to admit to buying anything there was a mark of social inferiority."[15]

Throughout at least its first few decades the colony's poor economy and homogeneous demographics, coupled with "their equal and honest minds," as Bradford claimed, apparently enabled colonial authorities to sustain the godly value of modest plainness, at least in dress if not in conduct.[16] While the Massachusetts Bay General Court established elaborate sumptuary laws in 1634, within four years of their arrival in New England (thirty years after sumptuary legislation had been abandoned in England), and expanded them several times in later decades, Plymouth's leaders did not consider such regulations necessary until twenty-five years after the colony's founding.[17] In 1645 the Plymouth General Court passed a single sumptuary law disallowing inhabitants to "use any such disguisements, visors, strang apparel, or the like to . . . lascivious and euell ends and intents." Enacted because "some abuses have formerly broken out amongst us," the law was reiterated three times in following decades. Not until the law's final enactment in 1685, when Plymouth had become more economically and demographically diverse, did the magistrates consider it necessary to deny inhabitants "Aparrel not proper for their Sect [social class or group]"—still a very simple law compared to Massachusetts's detailed legislation.[18]

Fears that some colonists were wearing "strange" (foreign) apparel echoed the battle being waged in England against European, especially French, fabrics and styles; such foreign garments were more fashion-forward and "proud" than English clothing, and their importation undercut the English woolen industry. Plymouth's sumptuary legislation also expressed the magistrates' specific concerns that disguising one's face with a "visor" (mask), a common practice among the English upper classes, demonstrated "the possible disparity between outer appearance and inner reality, or between being and seeming" and, thus, the inability to fix a person's true identity; using such deceptive self-fashioning to seduce unsuspecting victims undermined the doctrine of visible sainthood and threatened the moral health of the civil community. Like George Johnson of the separatist church in Amsterdam, who believed his brother and sister-in-law deceived others with their masks of worldly ornamentation, artificiality, and dissembling and warned them that they served as a "light upon a hill in the eies of all men," the Plymouth General Court recognized that the linkage between soul and body, inner nature and outer expression, was tenuous, contingent, and dangerously manipulable. Thus, plain and honest transparency in public self-presentation must be intentionally pursued by colonists—or legislatively enforced. However, although godly observers viewed disguise as "suspicious deceit in someone else," a person who chose to wear a mask could use it as a distinctive mode of public self-expression and resistance to colonial authority, a useful and "clever manipulation of appearances." But, as dress historian Susan Vincent notes, it was always just that—manipulation: "The appearances of identity could be altered, but not—unless by God—its essence," one's "internal truth."[19]

Notably, however, extant records indicate that throughout the 1600s no one was ever formally charged with breaking Plymouth's minimal sumptuary legislation against disguises or apparel not appropriate to social rank. Yet the saints may have exerted social pressure, especially later in the colony's history, to ensure that inhabitants avoided excessive ornamentation and wore clothing and hairstyles appropriate to one's gender, age, type of labor, and financial means. They had learned from Robinson that a person flew the "flag of pride" in apparel that was "too costly," overly fashionable, or "curiously put on." Brewster was most offended by the *nouveaux riches* who "haughtely and proudly Carry and lift vp themselues being Risen from Nothing; and haueing little else in them but a few fine Clothes or a little Riches more then others." An orderly, civil society depended upon colonists properly embodying their social rankings and displaying appropriate signs of respect. Despite his promotion of an egalitarian community, Robinson taught that "approbation" toward those of higher status "is properly in the heart, and . . . the manifestation of approbation in outward gesture, speech, or writing," such as removing one's hat in public recognition of another's rank: "[I] uncover my head [when] I meet with some friend or other to whom I owe that civil respect." In England hats were "a simple and universally understood device for a protocol of respect" as well as indicating one's class and profession, and colonists employed such standard codes of social etiquette to sustain both a properly ordered society and the common affections among its members.[20]

Although male authority figures may have worn dark, sober clothing much of the time, many colonists, including godly saints, did not. Bradford's wife Alice owned a green gown and Katherine Fallowell a green apron, Mary Ring owned red and violet petticoats, violet and "mingled coloured" waistcoats, and blue aprons and stockings, and Margaret Howland of Marshfield owned a green gown, two red petticoats, and a red waistcoat, as well as silk garters and silver and gold lace. Josiah Winslow, John Howland, and Will Wright owned red waistcoats (Wright also had a blue coat). Wealthier colonists, like William Kemp of Duxbury and John Barnes of New Plymouth, owned silk lace and scarves, belts with silver buckles, and fine, white Holland linen or satin caps. But the poorest farmers owned only one set of clothing: shirt, waistcoat, knee-length breeches, and coat for men; smock, petticoat (skirt), waistcoat, and coat for women. Joseph Ramsden, for instance, apparently wore the same "1 shirt . . . 1 hatt . . . [and] 1 suite of Clothes" day in and day out, and though he had a pair of stockings, he owned no shoes or boots. In fact, most people, laboring in their homes and fields or at their crafts, likely wore utilitarian garments of russet—a coarse, homespun woolen cloth of a "murrey" (reddish-brown), gray, or natural color—and undyed, unbleached rough linen shirts and smocks; even wealthier colonists also owned homespun garments in "sad" colors.[21]

Between their skin and outer clothing people wore "body linen," or undergarments (shirts for men and smocks, or shifts, for women; a few men owned linen drawers), whose fabrication ranged from coarse homespun to fine imported Holland linen. To the necks of their shirts or smocks all but the poorest attached a linen band: perhaps a simple ruff in the early years or a flat collar. For formal occasions, like church meetings, a person might attach white linen cuffs, perhaps with a touch of lace or embroidery, to ornament the dark formal "Sunday suit," if he or she owned one. Women regularly laundered their families' body linen, which "helped keep body dirt from the woolen outer garments so the woolens would not have to be washed," for English people rarely, if ever, bathed their bodies, although bathing might be prescribed for a specific health problem. While Stubbes advised, "Keep thy body cleane and neat," he meant only washing one's face and hands every morning and before and after meals.[22] Having clean face and hands denoted social status as well as a purified soul, illustrated in Stubbes's prayer to recite while washing: "As the filthines and pollution of my bodie is washed and made clean by the element of water; so is my bodie and soule purified and washed from the spots and blemishes of sin, by the precious blood of Iesus Christ." Cleanliness applied only to those body parts that could be publicly seen, and nonconformists regarded an overconcern with washing, like a taste for extravagant clothing, as a display of excessive vanity and pride. Using perfumes to mask body odors also was immodest, an artificial manipulation of "nature" and God's image in the human body. Indeed, the "threshold of embarrassment and shame," as Norbert Elias has termed it, was low in Plymouth by today's standards. Colonial bodies, most of which labored hard in the fields and over the cooking fire, had extended contact with their domestic animals, and threw household refuse outside their front doors, apparently smelled—of sweat and hair oils, woodsmoke, livestock, and food odors. Reputable individuals strove at least to keep their hands and faces clean and to own enough body linen and woolen outer clothing to fashion a clean and neat appearance.[23]

Clothing shaped the body, produced sensory experiences, and demonstrated status, generating a fluid linkage between one's inner sense of self and outer social relations. The feel of rough or fine linen against the skin reminded the wearer of his or her station in life and corresponded to the kind of body it enclosed, laboring or refined. Outer garments' woolen fabrics also varied in texture and value, aligning with the wearer's social rank, vocation, and character. Coarser fabric was cheaper and regularly worn by the laboring classes. Although early on rustic dress denoted godly plainness, by the eighteenth century it identified its wearer with "coarse" or "rude personal traits," while more expensive, smoother fabrics demonstrated wealthy merchants', magistrates', and ministers' "polished" and "well-finished" characters.[24]

Women's clothing, in particular, molded their bodies and movements in distinctive ways. Tight-fitting waistcoats with bone stays constrained the torso and flattened the bust, holding the female body rigidly erect from waist to shoulders. Dress historian Jill M. Hall has discovered that garments with stays "change a woman's posture, and alter the way she moves and lifts and carries objects, . . . the ways she relates to her environment. Women depicted in seventeenth-century paintings do not bend at the waist. They bend from the hips when reaching for an object on the floor; they crouch or sit on low stools as they work in the hearth. When they fall asleep in their clothes, they sit bolt upright and support their head on one hand, their elbow resting on a table or their knee."[25] While the waistcoat produced a rigid torso whose movements were constrained in certain ways, its loosely attached sleeves allowed arms to do the rigorous domestic labor required of colonial women. Unlike the loose, knee-length breeches of men, who moved freely in the public sphere, women's petticoats were ankle-length, made of heavy layers of woolen material that hindered movement and often collected mud and caught sparks from the fire as they performed their domestic duties. Wealthier women often owned gowns, usually of silk or fine woolen damask, to wear over waistcoats and petticoats for formal occasions. By the latter decades of the seventeenth century gowns became tightly fitted and elaborately constructed, with attached bodices, stomachers, and whalebone stays and often decorated with lace and embroidery, like that of wealthy Elizabeth Paddy Wensley, who was born in Plymouth and married Boston merchant John Wensley (see figure 3.3). The gown's neckline, originally cut high, became fashionably low by the middle of the century, revealing collarbone, shoulders, and upper bosom, like those worn by Wensley and Penelope Winslow, wife of Plymouth governor Josiah Winslow (see figure 3.4). Such corporeal display, including Wensley's large earrings and her bodice's elaborate lace trim and Winslow's necklace, unbound curled hair, and pearl ornamentation on her hood, or hat (which covers far less than does Elizabeth's more modest lace coif beneath a larger hood), also reveals shifts in ideals of female modesty and godly plainness.[26]

The growing heterogeneity of Plymouth social culture produced a society more stratified, in terms of both social class and religious affiliation, than existed in the earlier part of the century; by the end of the 1600s colo-

FIGURE 3.3 *Elizabeth Paddy Wensley.* Unknown artist, America, ca. 1665. The wife of Boston merchant John Wensley, Elizabeth Wensley wears the decorative clothing appropriate for her status. Her gown displays several different fabrics and colors, primarily red, with a low-cut neckline, short puffed sleeves that reveal her lower arms, and lace embellishments on her long, whaleboned stomacher, or bodice. She also wears a ring on her finger, another mark of status, but notably covers her head quite modestly, her hair entirely concealed by a lace coif beneath a loosely tied white hood, probably of silk. (Courtesy of Pilgrim Hall Museum, Plymouth, Mass.)

FIGURE 3.4 *Penelope Winslow.* Unknown artist, London, 1651. Wife of Josiah Winslow and daughter-in-law of Governor Edward Winslow, Penelope wears a fairly low-cut, olive green gown with loose white cuffs and a reddish wrap of velvet or silk. The expensive fabrics signify her status as a future governor's wife, as do her gold bead necklace and pearl-decorated hood, or head covering. Her hood barely covers her hair, which she wears in a loose, curled style popular among wealthier women, but criticized by puritan moralists. (Courtesy of Pilgrim Hall Museum, Plymouth, Mass.)

nists' dress was more likely to display that stratification than in earlier decades. Changes in clothing styles also demonstrated changing ideas about the appropriate embodiment of sainthood in the public sphere. Dress in Plymouth often communicated quietly, allowing individuals to manipulate the constraints of economic resources, one's personal sense of godliness, and perhaps peer pressure to shape their own ideas about how their bodies exhibited plainness and modesty. While authorities feared the outright deception of mask wearing, more subtle touches—wearing a few silver buttons, slipping on a silk cap, applying a bit of lace to one's collar—seemed not to disturb the common affections binding members to each other and, in fact, contributed to the orderly embodiment of a civil society. Other kinds of social behavior, however, threatened to undo completely the saints' hopes of building a pure, properly functioning social body.

"The Tongue Is the Index of the Mind": The Speaking Body

Pastor John Cotton Jr.'s speech acts—at times deceptive, other times confessional, and still other times commanding—demonstrated various uses of a body part about which nonconformists were expressly concerned: the tongue. One's speech revealed one's inner truth but it also could lie and deceive, it might express kindness and compassion but it also could rage and demean others; one's speech was a corporeal expression of personal agency that either supported or undermined public social order and the common affections. Robinson, echoing a common trope of the day, believed that words should correspond to the ideas they signified like clothing to the body it covered; both should modestly adorn and accurately reflect their referents: "Words are like clothes, used first for necessity, after for convenient ornament, and, lastly, for wantonness. . . . As a woman over curiously trimmed, is to be suspected; so is a speech," thus one should speak with "decorum," "eloquence," and "temperance."[27] Indeed, speech acts and the gestures accompanying them were regarded as potent uses of one's body in Plymouth. The words of citizens like William Brewster and William Bradford carried the power to gather the godly community and, ideally, create social order—or, as in the case of John Lyford, to undermine that order in dangerous and insidious ways. The public spoken word—from the pulpit, in the courtroom, on the street—was, as Robert St. George has claimed, "the principal genre in which seventeenth-century individuals constructed and maintained social reality." Speech expressed both the rational mind and the affective heart, weaving individuals together in social relations. But it also could fray the fragile bonds of human society.[28]

"Man is endowed above beasts; especially with reason and with speech to utter it," wrote Robinson. "Hence the tongue is called the index of the mind: and as by the index we know what is in the book; so do we by the speech what is conceived in the heart." There was a "ready passage" between one's thoughts and feelings and one's tongue: "Great is the affinity between the heart and the mouth." The tongue was a body part invested with inordinate power in early modern culture, ordained by God and nature with the ability both to engender and to destroy "the mutual intercourse of reasonable conceptions, and preservation of human society."

This was a power too easily abused, requiring external controls imposed from the moment a child's mouth could form words. Pride and willfulness were primarily expressed through the voice, thus children must not be allowed to speak "I will" or "I will not" except in obedience to their parents' wishes. Controlling one's speech was the foundation for controlling other outward manifestations of pride and producing godly individuals who embodied modesty, industry, and their proper roles in society.[29]

The communal pressure to conform within a religiously nonconformist culture created, paradoxically, a social climate in Plymouth that encouraged dissension at the same time it attempted to restrain it, which, John Demos has noted, tended to produce "a tight cluster of anxieties about aggression." The tongue's power to create social order worked when male colonists took the oath, or formal statement of allegiance, required to become a freeman and to fill any civil service role. The freeman's oath not to "speak or doe . . . any thing . . . that doth shall or may tend to the destruccon or overthrow of this present plantacions Colonies or Corporacion of New Plymouth," nor to allow anyone else to do so, vocally bound a man to upholding the social body. Despite such promises, however, inhabitants often deployed their tongues to create disorder, and court officers struggled to control such hostile vocalizations. The first law regarding a speech act, passed in 1639, forbade profane swearing and curses, and in 1653 legislation against lying and slander was issued. Throughout the seventeenth century the general court periodically reissued such regulations, including outlawing "contemptuous speech" toward the court or its laws. In fact, the most common offense was speech that undermined colonial authority, including speaking "contemptuous words" and "wild and deriding speeches" against civil and religious leaders and refusing to take the oath of allegiance, typical of Quakers. The second most common speech crime was swearing, cursing, or other profane language, and the third was slander or lying "with entent to deceiue and abuse the people with falce newes or reports." The court ordered punishments for speech infractions according to the offender's character and social status, or "the nature and quality of the person."[30]

Undoubtedly, the incidents described in court records do not reflect the full scale of verbal conflicts that occurred among inhabitants of Plymouth. Only the most difficult cases, in which the offended parties were unable to achieve satisfaction more informally, ended up in court. Court cases reveal that people employed their tongues in remarkably earthy, direct ways, often using body metaphors or accusing others of bodily infractions, in order to assert personal agency and manipulate one's social world. Reviling words against civil and church authorities were the most dangerous for their power to undermine social order, which was probably the reason they were the most common speech infractions to appear in court. One Captain North, for example, was accused of seditious and mutinous speech against colonial authorities in 1643/4. He boasted "that if he had some of them there he would make garters of their gutts, and that as little a while as he had beene here he could haue a hundred men at his commaund, or words to the like effect, with some other vnciuille carriage." North was ordered to remove himself from the colony—in the meantime he was to carry himself inoffensively. The following year a man spoke opprobrious words against the Marshfield church, "saying they were all lyers." He refused to pay his fine and so was committed to prison for a month. Mathew Fuller criticized the general court in 1658 because he thought the law requiring all inhabitants to contribute to ministers' maintenance was a "wicked and a diuillish law, and that the diuell satt att the sterne when it was enacted." Such outright criticism of the structures established to support ministers in their speaking the Word of God understandably received a whopping fifty-shilling fine—with it Fuller could have purchased such valuable livestock as a steer, a heifer, two calves, or a hog plus twelve chickens.[31]

More revealing of the ways individuals in Plymouth's intentionally close-knit community physically bumped up against each other on a daily basis are the civil actions inhabitants brought against their closest neighbors. One incident occurred in 1635 in the home of Widow Warren between herself and Thomas Williams, her servant. The two disagreed about some unnamed issues, and she, a godly woman, "exhorted him to fear God & doe his duty." Williams, worked up into a "passion & distemper," answered her that "he neither feared God, nor the diuell." Warren hauled Williams into court for blasphemy but the officers determined that, because he had spoken in a moment of passion and humbly admitted to his offence, he was not responsible for his words. A momentary "imbalance of bodily humors" might cause a person to lose control of his tongue—a frightening notion when it could mean a court appearance and a fine or whipping, but it also allowed some people to go free with simply an admonishment. Governor Edward Winslow, however, refused to buy the humoral argument and "would have had [Williams] punished with bod[i]ly punishmente, as ye case seemed to require."[32]

In fact, although most of those found guilty of a speech infraction got off with simply a fine, the corporal punishment Winslow would have imposed on Williams was employed in some cases. In 1649, for example, Richard Berry falsely accused Teague Jones of sodomy as well as "unclean practices" with the married Sara Norman. Berry finally admitted he was lying and was whipped at the post. Richard Marshall also received a whipping in 1661/2 "for many wicked and filthy speeches and actions, as alsoe for many other practices tending to the desturbance of [the] naighbourhood." Two neighbors, Ambrose Fish and Thomas Tupper, seemed to engage in an ongoing dispute in 1684 that resulted in Fish being brought into court "for carting ouer the land and breaking downe the fence of Thomas Tupper, after warning and abusing him, by giueing him [v]ile language."[33] Resentments, arguments, false accusations, neighborhood disturbances—all involved passionate words and often violent actions, as individuals attempted to use speech acts to shape the behavior and characters of others.

Lying about another person's actions or character—slander—was particularly dangerous, for it challenged one's public reputation. There were dozens of damaging labels a slanderer could use, but to call a man a rogue—a shifty, footloose vagabond—seemed to be the worst epithet one could deploy against him. Edward Doty was fined for calling William Bennet a rogue in 1633, and in 1662 Thomas Morton's wife Rose was accused of calling Abraham Jackson a "lying rascall and rogue." Rose, however, firmly denied calling Jackson a rogue, although she admitted to calling him a rascal. The court believed she actually did call him a rogue, a worse name than simply "lying rascall," but because she claimed to be sorry and "promised to be more carefull of her words for the future" they let her go with simply an admonishment. Such slanderous speech by Rose Morton was typical of the "wanton" speech acts of which women were accused in Plymouth; of the twelve women who appeared in court for speech crimes, half were there for slander or lying. Joane Barnes "frequently slaunder[ed] and defame[d]" the children of two men, who brought her into court; she was sentenced to sit in the stocks and wear on her hat a paper proclaiming her offense in capital letters. Sarah Kerbey uttered "diverse suspicious speeches" against two men, was sentenced to be whipped, but was let off with a warning. Mary Briggs was presented for "telling of a lye"; she was cleared but admonished to avoid "vnnessesary talkeing" that might cause "others to complaine." In a noteworthy twist, the only person brought into court for *not* speaking (other than Quakers for refusing to take the oath of allegiance) was Blanch Hull, "for not crying out when shee was assaulted by John Gorum in vnseemly carriage towards her." There were, indeed, times when the tongue, normally to be kept bridled (especially by women), should be loudly employed; not to do so implied collusion in sinful acts, such as rape.[34]

Women, however, appeared in court for speech violations in far fewer numbers than did men; of the 160 cases in Plymouth, only twelve had female defendants. The discrepancy between the number of women officially accused of unbridled tongues and the general belief that women's speech was dangerously uncontrolled—a lot of "unnecessary talking"—is significant. Writing about early New England in general, St. George has speculated that, because women were "viewed as naturally more talkative than men, their words may also have been tolerated longer and had less weight attributed to them." Also, a husband was expected to have authority over his wife and may have been more willing "to be constantly scolded than to admit to his neighbors how little control he had over his spouse." Finally, women had their own gender-exclusive social forums where they negotiated their speech acts among themselves.[35]

While male English authors wrote numerous commentaries on women as scolds and gossips, who used their wanton, scathing tongues to undermine proper gender relations and social order, Robinson allowed women an unusual level of speech authority. Women's physiology admittedly relegated them to an inferior position; they were "less excellent than" men and thus ordinarily "debarred by their sex" from teaching or "any other dealing wherein they take authority over the man." But Robinson did not exclude women from all speech acts in the public assembly: they "may make profession of faith, or confession of sin, say amen to the church's prayers, sing psalms vocally, accuse a brother of sin, witness an accusation, or defend themselves being accused." Even more radical than these standard nonconformist rules regarding women's public speech, however, Robinson turned on its head the common image of the female scold and granted women the freedom to use their tongues to criticize men publicly: "In a case extraordinary, namely where no man will, I see not but a woman may reprove the church, rather than [allow] it to go on in apparent wickedness." A woman might speak out in "extraordinary prophesying" when she was "immediately" and "miraculously" inspired by the Holy Spirit to stand in the midst of the congregation and deliver words of exhortation. No one should judge this form of speech, for it was divinely inspired and thus infallible—God's voice speaking to the congregation through a female "vessel." Furthermore, women could found churches: "In the planting of churches anew, when men want, which should preach the gospel, a woman may perform that, at the first." Once she had taught men and one of them had become recognized as a leader, however, she must concede to his natural male superiority and hand over to him the leadership of the congregation.[36]

A woman's body, although it normally debarred her from authoritative speech in public, rendered her an empowered vehicle of the Holy Spirit as it bypassed her inferior intellect and immediately employed her obedient lips, tongue, and throat for its divine purposes. However, despite Robinson's support of women's radical speech in the public assembly—a use of the female tongue to construct social order rather than undermine it—there are no recorded cases at Plymouth of women functioning in this prophetic manner. But Robinson's teachings may explain why no Plymouth colonists became involved with or even mentioned in extant documents the Bay Colony's antinomian controversy in 1637, when Anne Hutchinson practiced this form of extraordinary prophesying. Hutchinson claimed to be divinely inspired, criticized male church and civil authorities, and taught her followers, mostly women but also a few men, in her home—and ultimately was ejected from the colony for such insubordinate behavior.[37] The silence of Bradford, Brewster, and other Plymouth leaders on the matter may indicate that they disagreed with the Boston church's harsh indictment of Hutchinson, or they were at least ambivalent regarding her activities and the Bay leadership's response.

The pressures of living in a close community of supposedly common affections, combined with the conflicting messages women and men received regarding their speech and its need to be both controlled and employed, created a level of tension and anxiety that broke out in unruly speech acts, which often engaged other parts of the body, as well. "Lascivious speech" typically also involved "lascivious carriage"; being known as a "frequent curser and swearer," like one Phillip Read, denoted that a person embodied a generally "viciouse life" and was "otherwise debauched."[38] The tongue, indeed, was a dangerously powerful body part, and regulating its use was a primary concern among civil and church leaders. In contrast, using their tongues' power to shape their experiential social worlds was a primary concern among inhabitants. Both forms of speech—bridled and unruly—supposedly generated further corresponding actions, embodied in either a godly or a wanton lifestyle. Like one's dress, one's speech marked the body in particular ways that revealed public information about the inner self. Disciplined conduct, including that of the tongue, reflected a disciplined heart and contributed to a disciplined society. As we have already begun to see, those who failed to embody such discipline endured its public inscription directly upon their bodies through corporal punishment.

"A Merciful Cruelty": The Punished Body

Like those whose tongues refused to comply with colonial authorities' ideas about modest and appropriate speech, there were colonists who refused in other corporeal ways to adapt to the laws regulating proper conduct, and they received corporal punishment for their crimes. Colonists engaged each other physically through various criminal acts: pursuing illicit sexual liaisons, breaking and entering, fighting, stealing, kidnapping, abusing spouses, children, or servants, murder, and so on. Those who broke the laws against serious crimes often were punished harshly for their "filthy, lascivious, and abominable" offenses. Although most criminal acts generally occurred in private, intentionally hidden from watching eyes, authorities believed such acts directly affected communal welfare and so handled them in a highly public manner that created a public spectacle of the accused's body.

Public punishment and humiliation inscribed directly upon criminals' bodies the closely interwoven relations of ideology, order, and power that lay at the heart of nonconformist sensibilities. Fusing English understandings of state authority with their scriptural notions of divine authority, Plymouth's civil and ecclesiastical leaders saw themselves as God's representatives on earth, divinely commissioned—indeed commanded—to create pure, orderly communities of male and female visible saints. One's individual identity was inextricably entwined, in a very concrete way, with that of the community. Because sin was believed to enter society through the bodies of individuals, each sinful act threatened to pollute the entire community and call down divine wrath upon it. Criminal acts were bodily crimes against self, society, and God, polluting the social body and its special relationship with the divine at the same time they polluted one's personal body. Such corporeal acts demanded the appropriate corporal punishments. Robinson believed that "by rewards and punishments societies are preserved." Rewards, of course, were "more to be desired"; however, "the execution of punishments is more diligently to be looked unto," for "vice and villainy . . . can be restrained . . . only by the fear of punishment." Thus, punishments, which could save individuals and society, were "a merciful cruelty," while leniency was "a cruel mercy . . . a foolish pity," Robinson quipped, that "spoils the city," like overly fond parental love spoiled the family.[39] Punishment of the criminal's body was a public ritual intended to purify the social body and reconstruct proper social boundaries. In England rites of corporal punishment and execution reinforced the power of the state and the king; in Plymouth God's will ideally worked directly through the state and its magistrates. Public rituals of punishment, which marked bodies, and humiliation, which molded souls, like that imposed on John Oldham as he ran the gauntlet and was expelled from the town, reinforced the power of God's civil authorities and reminded onlookers of their individual responsibilities to promote personal and communal purity.[40]

During the first decade and a half of settlement "the people of Plymouth operated under an unwritten code of moral conduct"; Governor Bradford and his assistants developed legal guidelines over time by *ad hoc* application of English law and biblical injunctions to particular cases. During this early period Weston's unruly men were whipped and one execution, to "purge the land of blood," occurred—that of John Billington for the shooting murder of John Newcomen in 1630—but no other corporal punishments were recorded. By the 1630s inhabitants were demanding a detailed compilation of their colony's laws, and in 1636 the general court outlined its first comprehensive body of legislation, based on a conflation of English common law and biblical principles.[41] Eight capital crimes "lyable to death" were listed: treason, willful murder, witchcraft or compacting with the devil, willful burning of ships and houses, adultery, sodomy, rape, and "buggery" or bestiality. The two criminal offenses were fornication (and other "uncleane carriages") and stealing ships and munitions. The court also ordered instruments of punishment for every town: "a paire of stocks and a whipping post." These later were supplemented with prisons, the first completed in 1641, and cages in 1660, although there is no mention in the court records of a cage ever being used.[42] The general court periodically drafted several more codes of law. In 1658 the capital offenses were reduced to five, with adultery placed in a nether zone; listed as a capital offense, it received only severe corporal punishment. But by 1672 and 1685, under the influence of Massachusetts's more rigorous code, Plymouth increased their capital crimes to twelve: idolatry, blasphemy, treason, murder, witchcraft, bestiality, sodomy, false witness in order to take a life, manstealing (kidnapping), cursing or smiting parents, rape, and willful burning of houses or ships.[43] All of these capital crimes occurred at various times in Plymouth, but for only two of them—bestiality and murder—were the criminals actually put to death. Indeed, considering the number of crimes committed that were legally categorized as capital offenses, executions were relatively few in Plymouth.

The sentences for capital and criminal offenses in Plymouth echoed those in England. Corporal punishments were of seven kinds: sitting in the stocks, wearing a badge or a sign on one's clothing, or being whipped, imprisoned, branded on a body part, banished from the colony, or executed by hanging. The most common penalty, after a fine, was whipping, followed by spending time in the stocks. Except for the worst crimes, the courts allowed most defendants, unless they were repeat offenders, to choose between a fine and a bodily punishment; given the choice, people generally paid the fine if they could afford it. In 1661, for example, Dinah Silvester falsely accused the wife of William Holmes of being a witch. The court offered Silvester three sentencing choices: "either bee publickly whipt or pay the summe of fiue pounds to the said William Holmes," or she could simply "make a publicke acknowlidgment of her fault." Not surprisingly, she chose the latter penalty, admitting (although she claimed not to remember doing everything witnesses had described) that she had wronged her neighbor, against whom she had "entertained hard thoughts," and begging forgiveness.[44] The court usually preferred that the criminal confess and repent of his or her crime—for it brought the person into right relationship with oneself, God, and the community—and be allowed to go with an admonishment and a fine. But the offender must visibly demonstrate one's supposedly reformed heart; the court often threatened future corporal punishment if a person were not to take heed and reform his or her "carriage." Many expressed sorrow, begged for mercy, and promised to amend their actions; several solicited others to vouch for them. Servant Charles Thurstone, for instance, was accused in 1644 of "abuseing his mistress" and sentenced to be whipped at the post, but some of Plymouth's young men submitted a petition of support and Thurston's sentence was remitted "vpon tryall of his good carryage vntill the next Court."[45]

Because speaking one's confession and repentance publicly often resulted in release without any corporal punishment or in a lesser punishment, those brought before the court often manipulated this principle to work to their benefits. Giving voice to one's sin and begging for mercy achieved lesser sentences for defendants like Dinah Silvester. Likewise, in a 1650 case the unnamed wife of Hugh Norman was discovered engaged in "leude behauiour" with another woman, Mary Hammon, "vpon a bed." Neither woman received punishment: Hammon, probably because she was unmarried but also because there were no laws regarding sexual activity between women, got off with simply an admonishment; Goodwife Norman was required to acknowledge publicly her "vnchast behauior" and to amend her ways. In 1669 Jane Hallowey was imprisoned for her "turbulent and vild" words and actions toward her husband. After "one night in close

durance, [she] manifested great pensiueness and sorrow for her said miscar-
riages and engaged to carry better for the future," so she was set at liberty.
However, her husband, now suspecting his wife of adultery, returned Jane
to court a few months later, and she received the sentence of whipping, to
be carried out at a later time because she was pregnant.[46]

Like Hallowey, some were allowed postponed, suspended, or alleviated
sentences due to pregnancy or physical or mental infirmities. Anna Bessey,
convicted of physically attacking her father-in-law in 1661/2, also had her
whipping postponed (but not suspended) because she was pregnant.[47] For
tumultuous behavior in court Thomas Ewer was sentenced in 1659 to "lye
neck and heels during the pleasure of the court," that is, to be hog-tied,
a most efficient way of thoroughly restraining and immobilizing the recalcitrant body; if the person moved his arms or legs or tried in any way to
free himself, the rope tightened around his neck, strangling him. But Ewer's punishment was suspended because he "was an infeirme man, and was
troubled with a rupture, hee himselfe alsoe saying that hee is broken," but
officers warned Ewer that if he did not "carry [himself] better in the Court
for the future and rule his tongue" he would be banished from the colony.
(The only time the court followed through on the sentence of being tied
neck and heels occurred the following year, to punish Wenlocke Christer-
son, a Quaker, for behaving "turbulently and insolently" in court.)[48] In
1679 Edward Bumpas was whipped at the post for striking and abusing
his parents. However, because Bumpas was "crasey brained" this was an
"alleviated" punishment—rebellious behavior toward one's parents was a
capital offense. Perhaps Edward's parents also begged that mercy be shown
their mentally incapacitated son.[49]

While paying a fine was by far the most common sentence in Plymouth,
whipping was second in popularity with the court for any number of serious offenses: stealing (the most common crime receiving corporal punishment), repeated drunkenness, vagrancy, fornication, adultery, breaking the
Sabbath, swearing and slander, and being a Quaker.[50] Historians of early
America are familiar with the corporal punishments, like whippings, colonial courts imposed on criminals, but they have not discussed the ways
these disciplinary techniques located the human body as the primary site
of the production and reproduction of public culture in early New England. Whippings usually took place "at the post," which was placed next to
the stocks at the most public of sites: near the meetinghouse on the town
commons. After their wrists were tied to the post and their upper bodies
stripped of clothing, the convicted were whipped before a crowd of spec-

tators, sometimes until bloody and sometimes to be repeated in another township. Such were the cases of Joseph Turner of Scituate, convicted of slander and "horrid inciuillitie in words and actions" in the presence of women and sentenced to thirty stripes, half in Plymouth and half in Scituate, and Katheren Aines, a married Irish woman who committed adultery in Taunton and was sentenced to be whipped in both Plymouth and Taunton.[51] While wealthier or higher ranking colonists who committed fornication virtually always got off with a fine, illicit sexual activities among lower-class colonists, especially servants, and between colonists and Indians or African slaves called for whippings. Hannah Bonny, convicted of fornication with John Michell as well as having a "bastard child" with Nimrod, "a negro," in 1685 was sentenced to be severely whipped, as were Michell and Nimrod, who was also ordered to pay Bonny eighteen pence per week in child support. Likewise, in 1674/5 Nathaniel Soule and an Indian woman were whipped for their sexual misconduct and Soule ordered to pay the woman ten bushels of Indian corn "towards the keeping of the child" their union produced.[52]

Variations on whipping occasionally occurred. In 1639 Mary Mendame was joined by Jane Winter, as together they were "whipt at a carts tayle through the townes streets"—Mary for her adultery with Tinsin, an Indian, and Jane for committing fornication with her husband, Christopher, before they were married. Christopher himself was whipped at the post and Tinsin received a more elaborate punishment, discussed below.[53] For "whoredom" in 1665 Sarah Ensigne also was whipped at the cartstail. This was a particularly humiliating form of corporal punishment reserved in Plymouth Colony for women. Stripped to the waist and her wrists tied to the back of a cart, the female criminal was led slowly through the streets, the constable walking behind her applying the lash. Receiving a whipping was, indeed, both painful and humiliating; most sentences called for fifteen to twenty lashes. One woman, Dorothy Temple, was sentenced in 1639 to two sets of whippings after giving birth to a "male bastard," but she fainted during the first set and so the second was remitted.[54]

Whippings likely produced scars on the recipient's back, permanently marking a person with the power of the civil state. Branding, however, intentionally inscribed symbolic letters on an individual's body that permanently marked him as "polluted" and served as a perpetual warning to all who saw him. This painful inscription of an exposed body part was reserved for criminals who presented a particular threat to the community's safety and purity. An Indian servant named Will, convicted of breaking and entering, stealing "wine, rum, and spice," and "sundry other thefts and pilfrings" in 1690, was branded on one hand with the letter *B* for burglary. In 1683 the court sentenced Imdah, an Indian and "incorrigible" thief, to be banished from the colony, and in case he later tried to return he was "brand marked, soe as hee may therby be knowne." Two other Indians, one for threatening women with a knife and another for breaking and entering, were branded on the shoulder with a *P* for pollution. Brands were not always accessible to the public eye, in which case they served as private reminders of colonial authority, although in the cases of these two Indians, their brands may have been visible, since native people often did not wear shirts or other clothing covering their upper bodies. The records do not always note which letters were burned onto one's body: four colonists were burned on the shoulder with a hot iron for stealing and another for same-sex activities, and one man was "burned in the hand" for mistreating his servant boy and causing his death.[55]

Less severe than a physical branding but serving a similar purpose was the sentence of wearing a lettered badge in a prominent place on one's clothing, such as the letters *AD* for "adulterer" assigned to Thomas Bray and Anne Linceford in 1641, to be worn "vpon the outeside of their vppermost garment, in a most emenent place thereof." Katheren Aines, besides being whipped twice for adultery, had to wear a *B* "cutt out of ridd [red] cloth" on her right sleeve (the court record is not clear, but Aimes may have been a Baptist), and Mary Mendame, who had consorted with the Indian Tinsin, was sentenced to wear a permanent badge on her left sleeve.[56] More women (five) received this punishment than men (three), perhaps because branding was reserved for men. Badges were removable and the penalty for not wearing one when prescribed was a permanent brand burned into the skin, although there is no record of a person refusing to wear a badge and so receiving a brand in Plymouth. As well, signs describing the offender's sin sometimes were worn while doing time in the stocks, a wooden device often attached to the whipping post in which the legs and arms of the accused were anchored for an hour to as long as overnight.[57] Joane Barnes, who slandered the children of two men, sat in the stocks with a paper stating her offense on her hat, as did Hester Rickard in 1660/1 for "laciviouse and vnaturall practices." In 1666 John Williams, convicted of abusing his wife, stood in the market place with an inscription over his head "declar[ing] to the world" his crime.[58]

Particularly heinous crimes drew a combination of corporal punishments. In October of 1681, for example, Thomas Saddeler was hauled into court for bestiality with a "mare of a blackish couller." The court claimed that because Saddeler did not have "the feare of God" nor "the dignity of humaine nature," but rather was "seduced by the instigation of the diuill," he had led the black horse to "a certaine obscure and woodey place, on Mount Hope," tied its head in a bush, and "wickedly and most abominably" committed "buggery." Saddeler's "felonious and carnal" act challenged all divine and human authority, for he did it "to the great dishonor and contempt of Almighty God and of all mankind, and against the peace of our sovereign Kinge, his crowne, and dignity, and against the lawes of God, his majestie, and this jurisdiction." When asked whether he was guilty of the crime, Saddeler denied it and requested "to be tryed by his equalls." With no apparent witnesses to the alleged event nor a confession of guilt from the accused, the jury of twelve men was unable to determine whether he had actually followed through with the crime. For presumed attempted buggery "in the highest nature," however, Saddeler was sentenced "to be seuerly whipt att the post, . . . to sitt on the gallo[w]ss with a rope about his necke during the pleasure of the Court, . . . to be branded in the forehead with a Roman P to signify his abominable pollution," and to be banished from the colony, all of which the constable accordingly performed.[59] Also imposed on Lyford and Oldham, banishment—bodily removal from the colony—was usually a last resort, reserved for the most notoriously polluting elements, virtually all of them men: incorrigible burglars, those with excessively unruly speech, Quakers, a rapist, and seditious persons.[60] Where Saddeler went is unknown, but with his forehead permanently marked by his pollution he could not hide his crime and was certainly ostracized in any town in New England.

Sitting on the scaffold with the gallows hanging rope around the neck was an uncommon punishment, imposed only one other time in Plymouth, but it served as a severe reminder to Saddeler and the spectators of the capital nature of his alleged crime. Although most capital crimes did not result in execution, willful murder always received the death penalty; out of a total of thirteen or fourteen executions—twelve hangings (five Englishmen, one English woman, five male Indians, and one Frenchman), one beheading (an Indian), and one shooting to death of an Indian (whether this was an official execution is questionable)—throughout the colony's seventy-two years, all but one (for bestiality) were punishments for murder.[61] In 1639, for example, three Englishmen confessed to murdering a Narragansett boy for some wampumpeag and three cloth coats. Although some of "the rude and ignorant sort" of the colony complained about an

Englishman being put to death for an Indian, the three men were hanged.[62] In 1648 Allis Bishop, the only woman executed in Plymouth, confessed to the stabbing murder of her sleeping four-year-old daughter, "the frute of her owne body," and was sentenced "to bee hanged by the necke vntell her body is dead."[63] Executions were highly publicized and well-attended events, drawing crowds from outlying towns. While the accused stood upon the gallows, local ministers delivered sermons exhorting the criminal and surrounding observers to repentance. By the 1670s execution sermons had become a critical aspect of the dramatic spectacle of public hangings, for they explicitly linked the civil punishment of the criminal's body with public humiliation and divine purification.[64] After the minister prayed with the convicted, he (or she) was required to confess the sin, "his Cap was pulled over his Eyes," and "he was Turned off [executed]."[65]

"Brought into the Light": Regulating the Self

The performance of an execution, like all corporal punishment, was part of a larger ritual cycle, a thoroughly public process meant not only to reshape the criminal's body, conduct, and, hopefully, soul, but also to mold public feelings and behavior regarding sinful acts. The entire criminalizing process occurred within an extraordinarily public world, in which people watched each other for signs of sin and the spoken confession carried great weight. The high value placed on public purity in Plymouth generated an intense sense of communal responsibility for the actions of each of its members. Individuals were expected to observe each other closely for behavioral indiscretions; personal privacy was minimized for the moral good of the community, and Plymouth's civil leaders depended upon its inhabitants to help maintain public purity. Most of those who witnessed against their neighbors in court were probably more concerned with getting personal satisfaction out of seeing others disciplined than with promoting an abstract notion of social purity. Leaders, however, were exceedingly conscious of the meanings of individual crimes as corporeal sins that arose from unclean hearts and thus caused corporate pollution, both physical and spiritual. True confession purged the souls of both individuals and the social body of dangerous corruption.

In 1642, however, Bradford wondered whether such intensive public "surveillance of the body," as Amanda Porterfield terms it, might, in fact, be *causing* people to behave more sinfully, for unprecedented sexual "uncleanness" seemed to have been running rampant in Plymouth since the summer of 1639.[66] Between mid-1639 and mid-1642 nine fornication cases resulted in one offender being fined, three sitting in the stocks (one of them, Francis West, was also ordered to build the stocks for Duxbury, apparently so he and his wife, Margery, could sit in them), and the rest being whipped.[67] There were two adultery cases, both already mentioned. One was between Mary Mendame, a married English woman, and Tinsin, an Indian man, for which Mary was "whipt at a carts tayle through the townes streets, and [ordered] to weare a badge vpon her left sleeue during her aboad within this government; and if shee shalbe found without it abroad, then to be burned in the face with a hott iron." Tinsin was "well whipt with a halter about his neck at the post"; the halter, court records explained, symbolized his weakness in having allowed Mary to "allure," "entice," and "draw" him into the crime—and, perhaps, wearing the halter also indicated his "savage" animal nature. The other adultery case involved Thomas Bray, a single man of Yarmouth, and Anne Linceford. When Linceford's husband Francis was away on business, she and Bray many times lay in bed together; both confessed to their crime and were sentenced to be whipped and to wear the letters *AD* on their outer garments.[68]

More atrocious to Bradford were the cases of apparent incest and sodomy during this three-year period. Lydia Hatch was publicly whipped for "lying in the same bed with her brother Jonathan," and Edward Michell and Edward Preston (Preston also had "lude carriages" with Lydia Hatch) were whipped for their "lude & sodomiticall practices." Preston apparently tried to seduce John Keene, as well, who "resisted the temptacion" but was surely "in some thing faulty" so was made to watch while Michell and Preston were whipped.[69] The worst among this spate of sexual indiscretions was Plymouth's only other case of bestiality, the incident that finally led Bradford to speculate about the general crime wave. In late June of 1642 in the town of Duxbury, Thomas Granger, a servant sixteen or seventeen years of age and already a husband and father, was observed engaging in "lewd practices" with a horse. The constable immediately arrested Granger and threw him into prison until his trial in September, at which he eventually confessed to committing "buggery" with not only the mare but also "a cowe, two goats, diuerse [five] sheep, two calues, and a turkey." Granger was found guilty and sentenced to death by hanging. On September 8, at his execution ceremony, he stood on the scaffold and again publicly confessed, then several animals were led before him and he pointed out those he had sodomized. In a remarkable public spectacle of blood and noise, "the mare and then the cow and the rest of the lesser cattle [animals] were killed before [Granger's] face, . . . and then he himself was executed." The ritual killing of both Granger and the polluted animals helped to purify the community of his abominable sin, for, according to Bradford, it followed the Old Testament prescription, "If a man lies with a beast, he shall be put to death; and you shall kill the beast" (Lev. 20:15).[70]

Because "many both men and women have been punished sharply enough" for these "sundry notorious sins," Bradford wondered in 1642 why so many were still intent on engaging in them. He knew that people closely watched each others' actions in Plymouth and crimes were handled directly and efficiently: "Wickedness . . . was so much witnessed against and so narrowly looked unto, and severely punished when it was known, as in no place more, or so much, that I have known or heard of." In fact, Plymouth's war against sin was so fierce that authorities were "somewhat censured even by moderate and good men for their severity in punishments." And yet even "all this" could not halt the outbreak of sin in the late 1630s and early 1640s. But Bradford speculated that there were probably, in fact, not more sins being committed at that time, but rather surveillance had become more intense: "Evils . . . are here more discovered and seen and made public by due search, inquisition and due punishment; for the churches look narrowly to their members, and the magistrates over all, more strictly than in other places." Besides, he explained, Plymouth's towns were small, close-knit communities where all inhabitants' activities were on display, even those thought to be done in private. In "other places which are full and populous" people could hide their crimes, "as it were, in a wood or thicket"; thus, "many horrible evils by that means are never seen nor known." In Plymouth, on the other hand, "the people are but few" and sinful behaviors were "brought into the light and set in the plain field, or rather on a hill, made conspicuous to the view of all."[71]

An essential part of bringing private sins into public light was the criminal's confession. Actions done in secret, like the secrets of one's heart, must be made plain, thus eliciting a confession was of prime importance. Separatists' high valuation of individual responsibility required a confession from the accused or the testimonies of at least two witnesses in order to convict.[72] Furthermore, as already noted, speech—the governed or unbridled tongue—was extraordinarily powerful. The ritualized utterance of confession sharpened the double-edged sword of punishment and humiliation. Corporal punishment was of little use if the soul were not also touched in the process and humiliation for one's sins deeply felt. Honest-spoken evidence of a contrite heart—the "naked confession," as

Plymouth's pastor John Reyner termed it—outwardly exposed one's inner sense of humiliation and self-abasement before a just God, his appointed spokesmen the court officers, and the entire community. Indeed, ministers so highly esteemed the confession of criminal sin that upon the arrest of Granger for bestiality, three of them, Reyner and Charles Chauncy of Plymouth and Ralph Partridge of Duxbury, debated at length whether they should allow the court to use torture—"the inflicting of bodily torments"—to elicit Granger's confession. Reyner, in the tradition of Robinson's moderation, hedged his answer and made no definitive statement. Partridge stated outright that a magistrate "may not extract a confession of a capital crime from a suspected person by any violent means," whether inflicted or merely threatened. Chauncy, the strictest of the three, declared that in matters "concern[ing] the safety or ruin of states or countries, magistrates may proceed so far to bodily torments, as racks, hot irons, etc. to extract a confession, especially where presumptions [of a capital crime] are strong."[73]

There are no recorded uses of torture to extract a confession or for any other purpose in Plymouth. But the ministers' debate highlighted the importance of the accused's confession for determining whether a crime had been committed as well as linking the body's punishment with the soul's humiliation and, ideally, producing the reformation of both. Because body and soul were inextricably entwined, as Robinson and other nonconforming ministers argued, spoken confession and corporal punishment worked together to connect the criminal's body with his soul and the self with divine power. As well, the criminal's confession worked publicly in critical ways. It warned those observing the communal spectacle of a whipping, branding, or hanging that they too must strive to exhibit humble attitudes and pure actions, reinforcing the power of divine and civil authority to maintain social order. Furthermore, evil deeds were contagious, Bradford and others believed, and one member's crime infected the entire social body with sin, threatening to call down God's punishment on all. Attempting to come to terms with Granger's especially egregious transgression of multiple acts of bestiality, Bradford noted "how one wicked person may infect many," thus "in 20 years' time it is a question whether the greater part [of the colony] be not grown the worser?" When Rayner, Partridge, and Chauncy debated the appropriateness of torture to extract a confession they also discussed sodomy, arguing that such sins of "unnatural" uncleanness must be punished with death because they were an abomination before God: "The land is defiled by such sins" and such evil must be removed by physically removing the infecting agent. Before executing Granger, however, they wanted to hear his confession, for it would help to purify the social body of sin and return the community to good standing in its covenantal contract with the divine.[74]

Michel Foucault's work on surveillance and punishment of the body investigated eighteenth-century changes in the treatment of criminals in France, from the public spectacle of corporeal mutilation and execution to hidden incarceration in prisons where the soul rather than the body became the focus of transformative discipline. More recent historians of crime and punishment, however, have noted that this transition began at a much earlier period.[75] Foucault nevertheless may have been correct about France, for there were significant differences between French Catholic and English Protestant understandings of the relationship between soul and body. While colonial leaders were firmly committed to the traditional public ritual that inscribed the criminal body with fleshly marks of the state's godly authority, they intended such physical punishment to access the inner heart, or soul, of the individual offender and generate a sense of humiliation for one's actions and thus a purification of the community. Physical pain—whippings, brandings, sitting in the stocks, being tied neck and heels—ideally produced feelings of shame and humiliation, a confession and repentance, and a reformation of conduct. There are only a few inklings of what the experience of corporal punishment might have been like, as in Dorothy Temple's fainting during her first set of whippings. Defendants' voices have been silenced for centuries, and those still audible in court records say nothing at all about bodily pain and what it meant for those who received it. Yet we can surmise that pain carried different meanings for people in seventeenth-century Plymouth from those it holds for people today. Physical pain was a familiar part of everyday life: the corporal discipline children received from an early age to "break" their wills and "tenderize" their hearts, the intense pain of childbirth for women, and the lack of pharmaceuticals for all forms of bodily ailments, for example. Through pain, the body was "brought down" and the soul reminded of its utter dependence upon God.[76]

During Plymouth's first two decades, corporal punishments rose to the century's high of around thirteen per year in the early 1640s, as Bradford himself recognized. Indeed, the colony saw more corporal punishments during the period between 1639 and 1642 than during any other four-year period in its history. But after 1642 there was a sharp drop, and the rest of that decade into the mid-1650s saw a yearly average of less than four sentences imposed. During the 1660s and 1670s, with the arrival of Quakers and growing tensions between Indians and English, the numbers of punishments rose again, averaging around eight per year. After Metacom's Rebellion ended in 1677 corporal punishments dropped to around four per year by the early 1690s, and Plymouth did not participate in the witchcraft mania that absorbed the Bay Colony in 1692. As the population of Plymouth grew and became more heterogeneous, activities not in line with the founders' ideals increased as well, and colonial authorities seemed to recognize that the original impetus of creating a homogeneously godly society had become unrealistic. After 1642 there was a shift in sentencing, as the court began to impose less harsh punishments for such common infractions as fornication. Besides incorrectly locating historical shifts in conceptions of corporal discipline, at least for English Protestants, Foucault also disregarded the possibility of effective resistance to civil authority during public rituals of punishment and execution. In Plymouth the accused was sometimes able to manipulate events through the offering or withholding of a confession, begging for mercy and promising to reform one's "carriage," soliciting the support of friends, or using the courts to achieve satisfaction for a real or imagined offense against oneself. While it is clear that the balance of power in Plymouth was weighted toward civil and church authorities, individuals within this system found means to act with some agency within the disciplinary ritual context.

Plymouth's inhabitants lived their lives as "on a hill," their bodies—clothing, speech, and other aspects of daily conduct—accessible to the sight and hearing of all. Through the ritual cycle of crime and punishment, as in their dress and speech, colonists employed their bodies to achieve some autonomy within the relatively restrictive confines of their particular cultural world. Understanding the ways available for visibly inscribing self-identity upon one's own body, individuals went about fashioning themselves in an exceedingly public social culture. Watching each other at work, in the meetinghouse, at the marketplace, in court, and in the home, they attempted to shape their own and others' bodies in continuously shifting ways as they navigated social relations. The body was the site of this negotiation for it was one's body that revealed the state of one's inner soul—that made "inwardness tangible." The self in Plymouth, as in early modern England according to Michael C. Schoenfeldt, was "in continual need of monitoring from within and without." The correspondence between self-government and "the larger world of political power" rendered external and internal "self-discipline an extension of governmental control." And yet it also invested the individual with an authority to manipulate public expectations to personal advantage. Plymouth authorities hoped to promote a "discourse of self-regulation" by which people constrained their contentious pride and embodied modest plainness for the good of the community, and they held up such eminent community members as godly ministers as examples to follow.[77] Perhaps at least godly church members heeded such examples.

CHAPTER 4

The True and Visible Church

The Body of Christ

I N OCTOBER OF 1627 ISAACK DE RASIERES TRAVELED FROM
Dutch Fort Amsterdam to New Plymouth to discuss trade relations
between the two competing colonies. Rasieres understandably was
interested in the military capabilities of these English religious dissenters,
including the layout of their plantation and particularly their fort, located
at the top of Burial Hill overlooking the village. He described the fort as
"a large square house with a flat roof, built of thick sawn planks stayed with
oak beams, upon the top of which they have six cannon, which shoot iron
balls of four and five pounds, and command the surrounding country."
The room beneath the cannoned roof "they use for their church, where
they preach on Sundays and the usual holidays." On Sunday Rasieres observed the saints' ritual procession to the meethinghouse-fort for Lord's
Day worship, a procession that mirrored the militaristic and religious, civil
and ecclesiastical, meanings built into the structure's architecture and use.
The beating of the sergeant's drum called them to worship as the people gathered outside the door of Captain Myles Standish's house.[1] Wearing
clothing and carrying accoutrements signifying each person's role in the
village—Governor William Bradford in a long robe, teaching elder William Brewster in his cloak, Standish, also in a cloak, wearing his side-arms
and carrying a small cane, and the other men of the village carrying their

muskets—they lined up three abreast in order of rank and status: first the sergeant, followed by Bradford with Brewster on his right and Standish on his left, then the rest of the villagers. His beating drum now silent, the sergeant led them in an orderly fashion up the hill to the meetinghouse-fort. As they entered the building and sat down, each man placed his fire-arm next to him. "Thus," Rasieres concluded, "they are constantly on their guard night and day"—even during their day of worship and rest from worldly labors.[2]

The saints exhibited military-style discipline as they marched to the meetinghouse together, the procession embodying the villagers' cohesive-ness as members of the civil and religious community. But the distribu-tion of individuals within this moving display of corporate unity, which al-lowed the social body to "represent itself to itself" and to God, performed a recognizable hierarchy of authority; those with higher status led the way, while lesser members fell in behind, probably grouped by families.[3] At least by the 1630s the approach to the meetinghouse engaged their senses in ways intended to teach the saints social order and propriety: erected next to the building were stocks, a whipping post, cage, and other "instruments of justice" for the public humiliation and disciplining of miscreants. On one April Sabbath in 1633, for example, worshippers passed John Holmes, "censured for drunkennes," and two couples, John and Joan Hews and John and Alice Thorp, who had conceived children before their marriages, sitting in the stocks.[4] A more gruesome display appeared on the meeting-house itself. Several times throughout the seventeenth century Plymouth magistrates passed laws for trapping wolves and bringing in their heads in return for a bounty payment, and worshippers could see and smell those bloody heads, nailed to the external walls of the building.[5] In 1623 and again in 1677 even more grisly heads—Wituwamat's and Metacom's—oversaw the saints' worship. Such visual displays of polluting bodies and body parts demonstrated the authority of godly civil power to cleanse the community and the New England wilderness of dangerous elements. Pun-ishing or dismembering criminal bodies—constraining English bodies or severing Indian body parts—reinforced the separatists' belief in their own identities as visible saints constituting the true church, the pure body of Christ. Apprehending these sensory signs as they walked to the meeting-house to worship their God surely affected people viscerally, provoking emotional and physical responses, while the constant sense of danger the surrounding wilderness evoked moved the colonists to carry their weapons to worship with them.[6] The saints placed their meetinghouse beneath the fort, a practical decision but also one signifying the complexly interwoven meanings of godly worship, civil military might, and protection against physical and spiritual pollution by dangerous forces.

John Robinson's embodied theology informed the ways Plymouth's civil and religious leaders conceptualized their church community and strove to build and sustain the pure body of Christ made up of members who visibly embodied sainthood and rejected polluting social and spiritual elements. Seeing themselves as radically separate from the "body of the world" and its corrupt religious institutions, they strove to erect communal boundaries that enclosed Christ's pure, visible body and promoted its sanctity. At the same time, the boundaries were to exclude forces they believed undermined its internal order and close-knit social bonds.[7] Motivated by new understandings of sacred space and time, the saints at Plymouth regularly gathered in the meetinghouse to embody their church community and perform rituals intended to engender individual and communal holiness and keep at bay threats to that holiness. Although they rejected the liturgical calendar and elaborate ceremonies of the Anglican and Roman Churches, nonconformists nevertheless developed an efficacious complex of ritual activities intended to sustain the true church, keeping it spiritually pure and in good moral and physical health. Echoing humoral conceptions of human physiology, illness, and health, the saints understood themselves to be "feeding" the body of Christ through nourishment rituals—Sabbath worship, the sacraments of baptism and the Lord's Supper, and days of thanksgiving—that established, regenerated, and preserved participants' physical and spiritual purity. The church body "excreted" dangerous polluting elements through purgation rituals—fast days and admonishment, humiliation, censure, and excommunication—that reformed or, if necessary, expelled from the church members whose sins could infect the entire body.

Separatists' ritual practices performed their basic belief in the corporeality of saintliness in order to support and preserve their community's internal bonds and external boundaries; peoples' "natural bodies," to use anthropologist Mary Douglas's terminology, directly reflected and symbolized the corporate "social body."[8] However, from the beginning over half of those on board the *Mayflower* were nonseparating "strangers," whom company leaders had included in order to "avoid any suspicion of partiality," Bradford explained; yet these ungodly strangers seemed "not well affected to unity and concord, but gave some appearance of faction." Plymouth's elders imagined that one way of imposing godly values and promoting "common affections truly bent upon the general good," as Robinson had requested, was to require all colonists to attend Sabbath worship.[9] However, such an order went against Robinson's separatist principle that only visible saints constituted the true body of Christ. Moreover, church leaders encountered difficulties getting less committed folks into the meetinghouse on Sundays, and within the meetinghouse itself conflicts over ritual practices drew contested lines between saints and sinners. While the Plymouth saints subscribed to Robinson's model of the ideal community and pursued that model with varying degrees of persistence and success, in practice they found it difficult to maintain his standards while establishing an economically and politically viable plantation in America. Robinson's words regarding the social bonds of "common affections" for the "common good" often seemed to echo more loudly in colonists' ears than his words of separatist exclusivity. New Plymouth's church in fact proved to be more liberal in its treatment of sinners and, due to periodic lack of ordained ministers, more lax in its religious worship than were the Massachusetts Bay churches, whose founders were nonseparating.[10]

"The Best Compact of All Bodies": Gathering the Body of Christ

Separatists understood the church to be a spiritual but also a political entity, a "body politic," whose members—visible saints—voluntarily gathered out of the larger corrupt society to bind themselves to each other and God in a "visible" written covenant, or mutual agreement.[11] "We are knit together as a body," wrote Robinson and Brewster, "in a most strict and sacred bond and covenant of the Lord, . . . by virtue whereof we do hold ourselves straitly tied to all care of each other's good and of the whole, by every one and so mutually."[12] Weaving together multiple metaphors of the human body, Robinson argued that individuals' bodies both mirrored and constituted the church body, the "body of Christ." The analogical linkages between the body of Christ, the church body, and the bodies of its members located corporeality at the center of separatist doctrine and practice; the body was the axis upon which all meanings turned. The literal and metaphorical possibilities the human body offered for understanding proper relationships between divine and human and within human communities appeared endless for Robinson and provided the foundation upon which the Plymouth settlers built their religious communal body and engaged the ritual practices that nourished and cleansed it.

Robinson was on the cusp of a larger transition in conceptions of the social body. "Organicist conceptions of society based on bodily metaphors, and referring both to the parts of the body and to the functioning of the human . . . body as a whole," notes Jacques Le Goff, "seem to go back to early Antiquity."[13] However, by the end of the sixteenth century "such a profession of confidence in the ultimate unity of religious and social systems modeled on bodily organization was no longer viable." Instead, the advent of scientific investigation, anatomical dissection of cadavers, and representation in medical texts of the human body dismembered into separate parts, coupled with the rise of individualism brought on by the Protestant Reformation and the end of the feudal state, began to fragment earlier organic conceptions of both human and social bodies.[14] Analogies valorizing the ultimate wholeness of a social body over its individual members were breaking down—becoming dismembered, so to speak. Likewise, nonconformists viewed the individual believer as an independent entity, who pursued and was accountable for his or her personal and immediate relationship with God. Yet Robinson also resisted the new fragmented social model, for individuals must submit "democratically" to each other within a church body in order to function properly as followers of Christ. The private person required public membership: "As the church is a public body, so are they [true believers] members of the body, and parts of the whole, and of the same public nature with it: and not private parts."[15] Separatist doctrine echoed ancient metaphors that described the church as a singular entity, the body of Christ, composed of many individual members, or body parts, functioning together as one cohesive, organic being, in submission to the body's head, Christ. Combining Pauline theology and humoral-faculty theory, Robinson argued that the intimate union between Christ and his church was the "most strait and immediate conjunction, as that between . . . the head and the body; . . . as the body receiveth sense and motion from the head immediately, . . . so hath every true and visible church of Christ [a] direct, an immediate interest in, and title to Christ himself." There must be no "unnatural, monstrous, and adulterous interposition by any person [e.g., the pope, bishops, or priests] whatsoever, betwixt . . . the head and the body . . . which are Christ and his church." When compared with other kinds of social bodies, in fact, "the church, being the body of Christ, is the most entire, and best compact of all bodies."[16]

The old organicist model of human society placed the king or pope at the head of the political body and ascribed various social groups and classes to lesser body parts, such as the clergy (eyes), judges (eyes, ears, and tongue), stewards (belly and intestines), warriors (hands), and peasants (feet).[17] Rather than a pyramid-type model of social relationships, however, Robinson imagined a single hierarchy: the divine Christ, not any human being, was the head; the rest of the body's parts were of equal standing and value in their activities and relationships to each other and to the head. For "this body mystical" to thrive, all of its members—feet, hands, eyes, ears—must work together and help each other.[18] The officers of the church, Robinson argued, were not "above" laypersons; God had endowed ministers, elders, and deacons with certain innate physical and spiritual gifts that seemed to place them in positions of authority, but in fact rendered them servants of Christ's body. Elders were the church's "eyes and mouth for her government, and ministration of spiritual things," and deacons were its "hands . . . for the distribution of her bodily things to them that need." But Robinson "den[ied] the similitude to hold absolutely." For it might be that a church lacked deacons—must the hungry then go without food? Or it might lack a minister—must it be denied spiritual nourishment? In such cases other members, including women, were entitled, indeed obligated, to feed Christ's body.[19]

Robinson intended his vision of the true visible church to undermine the hierarchical structures of the churches of England and Rome and to grant egalitarian rights and duties to all members, lay as well as clerical; his social model embraced the new individualism of the Reformation, but maintained the close-knit cohesion of the traditional organicist social body and members' obedient submission to that body. Yet for Robinson correspondences between the social body and the human body were more than metaphorical; they were concrete and practical. He viewed the Church of England as a polluted body that still looked too much like the Roman church, a "monstrous body" with two heads—Christ and the pope—and "Satan's limbs" as members. He also condemned it as a corrupt, "monstrous" female body: "Your odious commixture of all sorts of people in the body of your church, in whose lap the vilest miscreants are dandled[,] sucking her breasts, as her natural children, . . . is that which advantageth 'Hell.'" Church ceremonies were a "confused heap of dead, defiled, polluted stones . . . fitter for burning than for building": the Roman liturgical calendar and its regularized feast and fast days for saints; sacraments that were all elaborate form but, to "ignorant ministry" and laypeople, "unknown devotions"; the religious ceremonies of marriage and burial of the dead (which dissenters like Robinson replaced with civil ceremonies); the clerical hierarchy with their ornate vestments; and the "proud majesty" of church buildings and cathedrals "furnished with all manner of pompous and superstitious monuments; as carved and painted images . . . chanting and organ music." All these material "corruptions" could "creep into the purest churches in the world" and must, "by divine authority, be purged out."[20]

Indeed, Robinson believed the Church of England was beyond all possible reformation or purification as puritans hoped. True Christians must separate themselves, spiritually and physically, from such corruption and form independent, pure churches—or risk certain contamination through commingling with "vile miscreants." It was not enough simply to hold differing beliefs. A true saint must remove his or her body, whose unstable humors were susceptible to its surroundings, from the corrupt body of the Anglican Church, for sin was transmitted *physically*, by participating in unholy worship. The ceremonies of the church "poison the air which you all draw in, and wherein you breathe"; their "plagu[e]y spiritual leprosy of sin, uncovered, infects all, both persons and things, amongst you."[21] The territorial Church of England embraced all those who lived within its parishes' boundaries, but the "true, visible church of Christ is gathered by separation from the world, and the men of the world visibly." The true church was composed, then, only of visible saints, that is, of individuals who experienced the invisible "inward graces residing in the heart, and known to God alone" and who manifested those hidden graces visibly through their behaviors: "Persons visibly wicked are not visibly Christ's, and so not visibly or in respect of men, true matter of the church, or members of his body."[22] One's faith required a corporeal manifestation if a person were to be counted among those ears, hands, and feet constituting Christ's body. A verbal profession was not enough if one continued in "unclean" behaviors: "idolatry," which Robinson believed the Church of England enacted in its worship services; "covetous[ness]" and meanness toward one's neighbors; "rail[ing]," as in using one's tongue to blaspheme God's law and people and cause contention and division within the body of Christ; as well as more obvious sins, like drunkenness, murder, incest, adultery, and fornication. All such persons and behaviors were "infectious" and "polluting" and must be "purge[d] out." On the other hand, a visible saint carried him- or herself soberly and modestly, behaved with "tender compassion towards the weak," and regularly participated in true Christian worship. One's "carriage," or conduct as a representation of one's inner self, was critical. A visible saint had a "plain" and "upright" carriage—dressed modestly rather than frivolously, spoke kindly rather than contentiously, labored industriously rather than languished idly—and was welcomed as a member of Christ's body.[23]

Recognizing the slipperiness of early modern self-fashioning, however, Robinson acknowledged that it was possible that one could pretend to be a true member of Christ's body by carrying oneself as a good Christian. One could appear externally pure but be internally evil, one's sin invisible to the human eye and visible only to God. These were people who had shaped their bodies to conform outwardly to social expectations; they had "put on the outside an vizard [mask] of sanctity."[24] But eventually, Robinson believed, one's true character would make itself known; the heart's leanings would reveal themselves physically, for soul and body were so conjoined that "the soul . . . inform[s] and quicken[s] the body, and the body [is] quickened and used by it, as an active and lively instrument for her operations and works."[25] Thus, as in the public sphere, it was the job of each and every church member to watch others' behaviors closely. When a sinner's corrupt character became physically visible, the church must respond quickly, employing rituals for reforming or expelling that person who would infect Christ's body with moral sickness and decay, in order to restore the church's health, purity, and right relationship—its covenant—with God.

"No Place Now Is Holy or Unholy": Embodying Sacred Space and Time

The church at Plymouth was not a building made of wood or stone—the meetinghouse-fort described by Rasieres—but a mystical, yet visible, body of flesh and blood members who had withdrawn themselves from the rest of the world and covenanted together. Wherever the church gathered its true members, especially on the Sunday Sabbath, or Lord's Day, and performed proper religious activities or "ordinances"—those rituals of nourishment and purgation God had ordained in the scriptures for pure worship—there existed, for that moment and in that place, the holy body of Christ manifested in the corporeal bodies of his people. Indeed, during their first year in New England Plymouth's inhabitants observed the Lord's Day without the convenience of a meetinghouse and often under unusual circumstances. The first recorded Sabbath, for example, was on December 11, 1620, soon after the *Mayflower* had landed. On Friday an exploratory expedition had been caught in a violent storm that destroyed their mast and almost capsized the shallop while they were traversing the harbor. In the midst of the storm, the men of the expedition were able, by the workings of a generous "Divine Providence," to land on a sandy beach on Clark's Island. Some of them feared they were "amongst the Indians, [but] others were so wet and cold they could not endure, but got on shore, and with much difficulty got fire, and so the whole were refreshed and rested in safety that night." The next day dawned "fair [and] sunshining," and "they found themselves to be on an island secure from the Indians, where they might dry their stuff, fix their pieces [firearms] and rest themselves; and gave God thanks for His mercies in their manifold deliverances. And this being the last day of the week, they prepared there to keep the Sabbath," a day of "rest."[26]

After erecting their meetinghouse-fort in 1622 Plymouth's godly folks were able to perform Sabbath and other religious activities in relative security. Yet religious dissenters had developed new understandings of sacred space and time, which were reflected in the saints' activities during pre-meetinghouse Lord's Days, such as that observed by the expedition party on Clark's Island: they could worship in any place and at any time, as long as it was exclusively with other members of Christ's body, for divine providence was everywhere present.[27] Dismissing the notion that particular times or places, like the holidays of the liturgical calendar or official buildings of worship, were inherently sacred, Robinson argued that "no place now is holy, or unholy." Rather, any place, "natural or civil," could be used "for any lawful work, civil or religious, private or public."[28] By "natural" Robinson meant that human actions were, by nature, constrained by their physicality and so occurred in a finite, concrete location. By "civil" he referred to the fact that people required a place "well and conveniently [to] assemble together." Robinson's view was exceedingly pragmatic, emphasizing human "convenience" and valorizing the bodies of visible saints themselves, not particular places, times, or objects, as the carriers of sacred presence. Proper worship had three elements: 1) "things natural, and simply necessary to the exercise," such as the "natural circumstances of time and place," as well as other "natural" things, like water for baptism and bread and wine for the Lord's Supper; 2) "things civil, and comely," such as "a convenient place [in] which the church may conveniently . . . meet together, not a stable, or swine-stye," as well as the minister's plain, dark clothing, the linen cloth on the Lord's Table, and other "accessories" required to dispense the "things of God" in a simple, straightforward manner; and 3) "things sacred, and holy," that is, the human *actions* (not inanimate ritual objects) of "external Divine worship" commanded by God and performed with heartfelt intentionality by those who submitted themselves "body and soul" to the body of Christ. "God's most gracious precious presence" was manifested in space and time only through the saints' actions; thus, they might employ any "commodious" or "convenient" place or moment to embody Christ.[29]

In the 1650s New Plymouth's church leaders clarified Robinson's teachings when they drafted an argument, in response to criticisms from anabaptists, concerning the differences between holy things and things that were simply useful, or between things sacred and things profane. Something was holy, they argued, if it had been set apart by God's command, and the Sabbath and its ordinances of worship were the only things thus delimited. An object was not made holy by being used during a holy exercise: when a candle and spectacles were used to read the Word, they were not thereby made holy; neither were the "light and aire" nor the "houre to preach in" made holy by being used for "reading and speaking holy things in publick Assemblyes." It was the saints' actions—reading, preaching, singing, praying—performed on a holy day—the Sabbath—that embodied holiness, not the objects used. Sanctification, then, occurred "when any Creature [object] or time is soe sett apart for holy thinges as it must not be vsed in Any thinge but that which is holy." There were, however, gradations of holiness. For example, when holy actions, such as reading Scripture, were done on the Sabbath, they were "more acceptable than if the same things had bin done att another time," such as reading the Bible to one's family on a weekday evening: "Though the same holy actions be don att another time, they shall not be accoumpted soe holy as att this [sanctified] time." Notably, the church leaders further argued that not only God but also human beings had their "owne power" to set apart and "dedicate" time, like a day of fasting, or resources, like a portion of one's estate, for holy use. Although they were not as holy as the things set apart by God—that is, the time and ritual activities of the Sabbath—once people had set apart those days or resources it was a sin to use them for other purposes. Holiness, then, was generated by divine ordination and human intentions and actions; God and humans joined forces to sacralize times, places, and things.[30]

Officially stripped of sacred significance, New Plymouth's meetinghouse was nevertheless a specialized building—a civil and religious structure in which colonists, both saints and sinners, met each other and God. In the meetinghouse on the Sabbath the saints performed the holy ordinances of prayer, psalm-singing, administering the sacraments, and reading, preaching, and hearing the Word of God. Separatists' embodied theology called for the ritual actions they considered to be scriptural and necessary for pure, holy worship; because body and soul were bound together in visible sainthood, an intimate relationship and continuous exchange of qualities inhered among one's "inward" intentions, one's "outward" actions, the corporate body of Christ, and God. Biblically mandated rituals brought soul, body, church, and God into one accord, purifying, or making holy, participants' bodies and souls and the body social and nourishing their covenant with each other and the divine. Rejecting elaborate ceremony, nonconformists' "plain" approach to worship, oriented around divine ordination and human "convenience," radically "re-ritualized religious experience."[31] Rather than the annual liturgical calendar of the Roman church, nonconformists' religious time wove together two ritual cycles. One cycle revolved weekly around the Sabbath, rotating between days of labor and a day of "rest" and worship, during which the saints performed what they understood to be divinely ordained "religious actions" that sustained the health of Christ's body by "feeding" it holy food—preaching, praying, psalm-singing, and administering and receiving the sacraments of baptism and the Lord's Supper—and purging it of pollution—admonishing, censuring, and excommunicating offenders.[32] The other cycle revolved in an irregular, reciprocal movement between the immediate human moral condition revealed in people's sinful or godly actions, on the one hand, and God's anger or pleasure with that condition communicated through divine providences, or events in the natural world, on the other. Church leaders called for days of fasting, humiliation, and prayer in response to divine displeasure in order to purge the social body of outbreaks of sin; when God answered the people's prayers of repentance with merciful providences, days of thanksgiving spiritually and physically nourished the body of Christ as its members expressed gratitude for divine deliverance from danger and shared a meal together.[33]

"The Joint Feast of That Heavenly Repast": Sabbath Worship

Throughout the seventeenth century the "Sabbatarian ideal"—the hallmark of nonconformist religious practice—marked the weekly movement between profane and sacred time, labor and worship, at New Plymouth.[34] One explicit reason the separatists left Leiden for New England was that they found "how little good we did or were like to do to the Dutch in reforming the sabbath."[35] The separatist doctrine of the Lord's Day conflated the biblical stories of God's creating the world in six days and resting on the seventh and of Christ's resurrection on the first day of the week.

Similar to (although not precisely the same as) the Jewish Sabbath, the Lord's Day started late on the last day of the week and extended into the first day of the week. It was a day of abstention from work and participation in public religious activities, while the other six days were dedicated to "worldly labor," unless set apart by human institution as a day of fast or thanksgiving. The Sabbath began on Saturday evening, sometimes as early as three in the afternoon, when individuals and families were expected to withdraw from all worldly labor and prepare themselves for the Lord's Day with family prayers, psalm-singing, and Bible reading. They gave Sunday over to two communal meetings; the morning worship lasted from eight or nine o'clock until noon, including, if scheduled, the Lord's Supper and baptisms, followed by a midday break for a meal. In the afternoon the congregation reassembled for further preaching and prayer, as well as discussion of church business.[36]

Denying that any particular place was holy and yet recognizing the need for a convenient building in which the saints might gather as the body of Christ, the infant congregation had met in Scrooby, England, in William Brewster's manor house, and in Leiden they had gathered at John Robinson's home.[37] When they arrived in New England the saints were free to construct buildings and worship practices thoroughly reflecting their theology of space, time, and human embodiment.[38] For twenty-four years the church at New Plymouth met in the meetinghouse-fort, which was "fitted accordingly for that use." It was spare of interior decoration with minimal furniture — only rows of rough wooden benches and no pulpit — although they likely added a table for the administration of the Lord's Supper at a later date, when the church had a permanent minister. Plymouth completed its second meetinghouse in 1648, though nothing is known of its interior. The third meetinghouse, built in 1683 after a year of debate about whether to repair the old one, was more elaborate than the former two, being forty-five feet long, forty feet wide, and sixteen feet deep, "with seats, Galleryes, &c in every other Respect."[39] It likely incorporated characteristics of other late seventeenth-century New England village meetinghouses: a raised pulpit beneath which sat the table for the Lord's Supper, a central turret for the bell, and boxed seats or pews, in which church members seated themselves according to gender, age, and social rank and status, with more prominent and older saints in front, censured members, children, and servants in back or in the gallery (with deacons located among them to keep order), and men and women seated separately on opposite sides of the building.[40] Like the Lord's Day procession described by Rasieres in 1627, as church members filled the meetinghouse they materialized not so much Robinson's idealized "democratical" body of Christ as they did Plymouth's hierarchically stratified civil body.

Inside the meetinghouse, the physical space in which people worshipped intentionally generated particular sensory experiences. Its stark plainness, without traditional church furniture or ornamentation, concretely displayed to themselves and God the saints' pursuit of pure devotion and transparent correspondence between thought and deed, intentions and behavior, and in turn produced "plain" and modest human bodies that demonstrated godly, humble souls.[41] Quietly seated on hard benches, sometimes in stifling heat or frigid cold, for hours at a time, Plymouth's saints embodied Christ through their rituals of Lord's Day worship. The Sabbath was the one day each week when they intentionally gathered to enact "Christ's kingdom" through the "communion of saints and public worship"; the "administration of the word, sacraments, alms, and the rest" made all the members "one entire body of communion."[42] Each meeting began with the pastor or teaching elder standing to recite the opening prayer. Robinson believed that prayers should be "conceived in the heart," then "brought to the lips" through the outward act of speech. During a prayer "the pastor's voice is only heard, unto which the people . . . are to add their Amen." Rather than kneeling and bowing the head in false humility as did the Anglicans, when a man (or woman) prayed he should, "both in soul and body, be bent upon God, with whom he converseth. The eyes of the mind are lifted to God in prayer; and why not the eyes of the body also?" It was "not that this gesture of body is simply necessary"—Robinson was not about to prescribe an "empty" ritual act—but it was "most convenient . . . both to express and further the intention of a godly heart." So inextricably conjoined were body and soul, that as the heart intended, so the body acted; likewise, as the body gestured appropriately, it furthered the heart's godly intentions. Standing and looking upward, with the eyes open, was the hallmark posture of separatist prayer.[43]

After the opening prayer the entire congregation stood to join their voices in song. Worship and thanksgiving to God in musical form was limited to singing psalms in unison without musical instruments (called psalmody) and it elicited some debate among Plymouth church members throughout the seventeenth century. Rejecting the Anglican style of congregational singing—nonscriptural lyrics set to elaborate, harmonized vocal music accompanied by organs or other musical instruments—nonconformists demanded "simplicitie and gravitie" in "externall worship";

the text, derived from Scripture, took precedence over the music, likely borrowed from secular ballads.[44] The plain human voice, uncorrupted by "artificial" instrumentation, was the proper medium for the expression of heartfelt, "solemn" praise. Sounding in unison, men's, women's, and children's voices became a single vocalization of the body of Christ. New England church leaders debated whether to allow only the saints to participate or to include those who had not become full members when the congregation raised its voice in song. In his introduction to the *Bay Psalm Book*, first published in 1640 in Boston and later adopted by the Plymouth church, John Cotton, father of New Plymouth's pastor John Cotton Jr., asked whether the psalms should be sung by "whole churches together with their voices? or by one man singing alone and the rest joyning in silence, & in the closing saying amen[?]" His answer held that all, both the elect and the ungodly, should join together.[45] Three years earlier, New Plymouth's church leaders had outlined their understanding of the scriptural difference between the two "externall action[s]" of prayer and psalm-singing: "In prayer wee speake to God but in singing wee speake to ourselues and one another by Admonishing our selues and one another." Despite Robinson's vision of the pure, separated church, Plymouth's elders recognized that there were many among them who were not full members of the church body, and yet these "prophane" persons might benefit from mutual admonishment. They were not to be "prohibited from p[e]rforming actes of worshipp. . . . Wee find in the holy Scriptures an Insightment vnto all to singe praises to God . . . and wher God Insights wee see Noe Reason to Prohibite."[46]

During its first six decades, New Plymouth's "mixed Multitude" sang from the 1612 metrical psalter composed by Henry Ainsworth, the teaching elder in Francis Johnson's separatist church in Amsterdam. However, the *Ainsworth Psalter* caused problems for some church members. It contained some rather complex tunes and odd rewordings of the Psalms' texts, which made singing them difficult, especially for new members. In early 1681 a brother of the church at Plymouth complained that he was unable to practice the ordinance of psalm-singing unless someone recited the words before the congregation sang it, and a debate ensued. Some wanted to maintain the custom of singing without first reading the psalm, but apparently others also had problems with the lyrics, for "the body of the ch[urc]h declared for the lawfullnesse of reading," and from thence forward an elder recited the psalm, the pastor "expound[ed]" on it, and then the congregation sang it.[47] A few years later, the elders decided to sing a different version of Psalm 130, for Ainsworth's tune was too difficult. With no instruments to begin songs and hold them to a consistent key and tune, a human voice was depended upon to "set" a tune and lead the singing. However, few were able to do this effectively, often setting a tune too high or low or shifting from one tune to another within one psalm, leading to confusion.[48] Psalm-singing, then, directly linked physiological limitations with the perceived level of spiritual edification of a ritual activity. When the voices of the tune-setter and the congregation could not execute a tune plainly and properly, embarrassment, frustration, and dissonance ensued, rendering the body of Christ unable to function as a harmonious, organic entity. By 1693 the elders acknowledged that many of Ainsworth's psalms had "such difficult tunes that none in the ch[urc]h could sett," and the brethren agreed to use both the Ainsworth and the Bay books. Three years later members decided by universal consent that the Bay's translation was the more "edifying" because its psalms were easier to sing. From that point on the Plymouth church sang exclusively from the *Bay Psalm Book*.[49]

Following the singing of psalms, the teaching elder or pastor delivered his sermon, which could last as long as two or three hours, while the congregation sat silently listening. Teaching and hearing the Word was the central ordinance of the New Plymouth church, for, more than any other ritual act, it was "the means to gather a church" as the body of Christ. Like a physical body, which took medicine, a "physic" or "natural agent," to heal and make itself whole, the church body ingested the "moral agent" of the Word to sustain its health. Robinson described the preacher's spoken words as food—the "joint feast of that heavenly repast, the word of God"—to nourish the body of Christ.[50] When the church at New Plymouth had no other minister, Brewster, their lay preacher, taught twice every Sabbath, morning and evening. He was "well spoken haueing a Graue deliberate vtterance," and he told people "plainly of theire faults and euills both publickly and privately," but he did it in such a manner "as vsually was well taken from him." His speech was "very plaine and distinct" and yet "very stirring and moueing the affections, . . . Rip[p]ing vp the h[e]art and Cons[c]ience be fore God." Brewster believed that it was better for a minister to pray more frequently in shorter prayers than to be "longe and tediouse," except during such solemn occasions as days of fasting and humiliation, for he was aware of his listeners' difficulties in keeping their minds focused when their bodies were fatigued and their spirits flagging.[51] Indeed, nonconformist preachers could be "long-winded" in their prayers and sermons, "guarantee[ing] exhaustion" in their congregations. To keep their listeners' attention and move their hearts, they raised and lowered their voices in dramatic waves and their delivery style was often physically energetic.[52] Authors of popular manuals for lawyers, ministers, and other public speakers employed the epistemology and rhetoric developed by Petrus Ramus, who argued that knowledge, including divine knowledge, entered the human mind through the physical senses. Hearing the minister's voice and seeing his gestures ideally moved the passions and aroused the hearts of his listeners, opening their souls to God's grace and wisdom. Eloquent preaching, as the primary vehicle of grace, fed congregations the Word through "the cooking, that is, the dressing and serving up of an oration." Direct speech was too blunt and dry, unable to sweeten the "bitter pill" of divine truth and make it tasty and digestible for the layperson's consumption. Effective preaching required rhetorical flourishes, the "sugar" that coated the bitter pill.[53]

Sermon delivery—the "garnishing of utterance"—proceeded from the "eloquence of the body." Ministers' bodies were concrete media for the communication of divine truths and the most effective tools for the sensory arousal and manipulation of listeners' passions and affections. A preacher had two corporeal tools at his disposal: *voice*, which involved utterance ("the sweet framing of the voice") and emphasis ("the elevation of some word or words in the sentence, wherein the chief force lies"), and *gesture*, "the comely carriage of the bodie." Voice pertained to the ear and gesture belonged to the eye, and employing both modes simultaneously impacted listeners' two most important senses: hearing and vision. In "plain" preaching the minister should modulate the voice as necessary to express the godly intentions of his heart and true meanings of God's Word and thus to move his listeners. He should "begin with a submisse voice" and then "ascend by degrees as occasion serueth." Effective modulation could produce, for example, "a bitter, angry, cholerike, and furious voyce," "a moderate, temperate, and stayed voice," a "full, sobbing, flexible, interrupted" voice, a "contracted, stammering, trembling" voice of "feare and bashfulnesse," or a "hollow voyce, fetcht from the bottome of the throate, groaning."[54] Gestures included "the turning of the eye, carriage of the hand, setting of the countenance, framing of the voice, &c."[55] Plain but eloquent gestures, the voice's "more excellent and more vniversall" partner, should be "manlike and graue": "Stand vpright & straight as nature hath appointed," English lawyer and rhetorician Abraham Fraunce directed, for "much wauering and ouercurious and nice motion is verie ridiculous." While a minister should avoid frequent gesturing with only the head, it was his face, especially the eyes, that most emphatically revealed the "passion of the mind," and "so the eyes verie diligentlie are to be regarded." Lips, nose, chin, and shoulders, as well, should be "decentlie moderated," and arms, hands, and feet appropriately utilized.[56]

Nonconformist ministers were concerned that too much cooking and saucing of rhetoric might overwhelm and hide the raw meat of the Word. Excessive sermon ornamentation threatened so to entice listeners with exaggerated modulations of voice and gesture that they glorified the minister himself and ignored the purpose of the sermon, which was to pierce through the senses to the soul with the sword of God's truth. The passions were to be moved, but only as a means to penetrate the heart and mind. However, once he had set out the purpose of the sermon in "plain" words, the minister might embellish judiciously with voice and gesture in order to engage listeners' senses according to his personal preference and natural aptitude.[57] Robinson argued for "decorum," "eloquence," and "temperance," echoing the more detailed prescriptions of his friend, William Ames, who believed the teacher's "speech and action should be completely spiritual, flowing from the very heart" and combine "zeal, charity, mildness, freedom, and humility" with "solemn authority." Ames argued, "Pronunciation must be natural, familiar, clear, and distinct so that it can be easily understood. It should fit the matter in such a way that the affections [of listeners] are moved." Two types of voice were "offensive": one "heavy, slow, singing, drowsy," the other "hasty and swift, overwhelming the ears with so much speed that there is no distinct understanding of the subject." Ames disallowed any overly "affected" form of sermon delivery that would be "ridiculous" in a civic setting, such as in a court of law. One should employ only stylistics that "contribute to the spiritual edification of the people."[58]

Plymouth's Brewster embodied such moderated passion in his preaching, and later ministers John Rayner, a former fellow of Cambridge University, and Harvard-trained John Cotton Jr., surely practiced a similar plainstyle. While Brewster's speech was grave, deliberate, plain, and distinct, he was also compassionate; his preaching and praying could "rip up" the hearts and deeply move the affections of his auditors. Preachers hoped to have a powerful impact on their congregations. Wearing the apparel appropriate to his station and calling—a dark, formal woolen suit—imparted a sense of dignity and elicited feelings of awe from his listeners. His bright white linen collar and cuffs highlighted his face and hands as the spoken Word issued from his mouth; his voice moved with inflections, now loud, now soft, his hands gestured, now animated, now gentle, and his eyes flashed with godly anger or softened with compassion. Delivering and listening to a sermon were, ideally, extraordinarily physical experiences in Plymouth, the minister's vocal expressions and bodily gestures the powerful vehicles of God's grace to human beings. Listening to two sermons on the Sabbath, morning and afternoon, was an active undertaking on the part of the congregation, with one's eyes, ears, and heart open to the movings of God's grace. After the sermon, members again stood and joined their voices in song, and the ruling elder raised his eyes to heaven to deliver the final prayer or blessing, while the congregation sat silently until offering in unison the concluding "Amen."[59]

The timing of the blessing for the "closing and finishing of theire Religiouse exercises" caused some conflicts in the New Plymouth church, exposing the line drawn between the true saints and those who were unable or unwilling to attain that status. The standard practice was for the elder or pastor to dispense the blessing at the end of public worship. If, however, the Lord's Supper were to be observed that Sabbath, "noncommunicating" attendees left the meetinghouse after the final psalm, and full communicating church members remained for communion; the closing blessing then occurred after the administration of the sacrament. On June 25, 1684, some noncommunicating members expressed dissatisfaction that "the ch[urc]h never allowed the Blessing to be dispensed at the conclusion of the publick worship on a sacrament morning till after the Lords supper was administred," when they already had left the meeting. The elders asked the congregation to "expresse their mindes about it," and the consensus went against the noncommunicants: the church decided it was not "lawfull" to dispense the blessing before the sacrament, and there was "noe further discourse of that matter." However, "some time after," probably because of further complaints, the elders "consented to & practiced" delivering the concluding blessing before the Lord's Supper was administered.[60]

Regardless of Robinson's ideals of separatism that envisioned the body of Christ as a pure community of visible saints, most colonists never became full, communicating members of the church, although Plymouth churches likely applied the standards of membership (public confession of faith, commitment to the covenant, and an upright carriage) more liberally than did many other New England churches.[61] Tensions nevertheless sparked when separatist doctrine met colonial realities. Understanding that communal cohesion among saints and strangers—inclusiveness rather than exclusivity—was necessary for sustaining the plantation and regulating social order, by 1650 Plymouth had joined other colonies in requiring that all inhabitants attend the weekly "public worship of God." In 1670 the general court passed a law allowing select men to "repaire to any house or place where they may suspect that any slothfully doe lurke att hom[e] or gett together in companies to neglect the publicke worship of God or prophane the Lords day."[62] Getting people into the meetinghouse on the Sabbath, and to behave appropriately when there, remained a perennial problem. Men and women, both Indians and English, appeared in court for "breach of the Sabbath": conducting "common business," such as washing clothing, hunting, fishing, planting, "traveling by horse or foot," "carrying burdens," and "putting out to sea," as well as gathering in homes and taverns to drink with friends and play cards, holding their own religious meetings, "speaking vil[e] and deriding speeches against Gods word and ordinances," stealing, fighting, and otherwise avoiding mandated Sunday church services.[63] Most of the accused were only admonished and fined, but a few who could not pay the fine or whose crimes were especially egregious were whipped or placed in the stocks.

Even more disruptive were those who attended meetings yet failed to exhibit proper decorum. In March of 1652 Nathaniel Bassett and Joseph Prior of Duxbury were sentenced to either pay a fine or be bound to a post for two hours in public "with a paper on theire heades" on which their crime of "disturbing the church of Duxburrow on the Lords day" was to be written so all could read it. In 1660 Quaker Joseph Allin was accused of the same crime in Scituate. Duxbury's meeting was again disrupted in 1666 when three men, Edward Land, John Cooper, and John Simons, exhibited "prophane and abusiue carriages each towards other." The magistrates felt that Cooper, "being most faulty," should received corporal punishment, but he got off with a fine after exhibiting "some manifestation of sorrow." As they left a church service in March of 1669, John Bryant "use[d] reviling speeches" toward Edward Gray and was fined. That same month four men were caught smoking tobacco at the Yarmouth meetinghouse during the Sabbath meeting. Apparently, many loitered outside meetinghouses and disrupted worship, for in 1665 and 1669 the court passed laws prohibiting "sleep[ing] or play[ing] about the meeting house in times of the publicke worship of God on the Lords day," including smoking tobacco within two miles of the meetinghouse while going to or coming from worship services and "vnnecessary violent ryding" on the Sabbath.[64] Although many inhabitants found ways to avoid Lord's Day worship, legislation meant that a large number of those who did attend were not, at least visibly, saints—that is, communicating members who carried themselves as upstanding, godly people and participated in the Lord's Supper. On days when the sacrament was to be administered—which, during John Cotton Jr.'s tenure from 1667 to 1697, occurred approximately once every one or two months—those who were not full members left the meetinghouse (apparently sometimes fighting or smoking tobacco) after the regular service, and communicating members remained to participate in the sacraments. Thus, the true saints plainly displayed their separate social identity as a distinct holy body during their most significant and efficacious rituals, the sacraments.

"A Reall Feeding to the Soule": The Lord's Supper and Baptism

Like the sensory experience of ingesting spiritual food through hearing and seeing the Word preached, it was through the body's senses that the sacraments of the Lord's Supper and baptism worked as vehicles of divine grace to the individual, nourishing relationships among oneself, God, and the church body. E. Brooks Holifield has noted that nonconformists "insisted that [the sacraments] were 'visible Words' that impressed themselves upon the five senses. The Word 'clothed in the sacrament' spoke more fully than the 'stark word.' It was better designed to influence the embodied mind, which could appropriate spiritual truth only by means of the eye and the ear, aided when necessary by the other senses" of taste, touch, and smell.[65] For Robinson, the sacraments were physical and spiritual "seals" of God's covenant with those who submitted themselves, "body and soul," to the church and its ministrations. Those who had received God's grace and displayed it in their daily lives were "fitted for, and made capable of the sacraments" and could then "communicate in the pure use of them." The people, not the sacraments, embodied Christ.[66] In practice, the Lord's Supper and baptism remained primary physical signs of the true church and sensual media by which God's grace entered human bodies; performing the sacraments in a pure manner, using the "natural" elements of water, bread, wine, and active, sensing human bodies, manifested Christ's presence in the world.

In England and the Netherlands John Robinson fed the church body with "the Lord's Supper every Sabbath, and baptism as often as there was occasion of children to baptize."[67] However, the Plymouth company arrived in New England with no ordained minister to provide these important, though not essential, rituals. In fact, for one-third of the colony's seventy-year existence, between 1620 and 1629 and again between 1654 and 1669, saints in the town of New Plymouth were unable to partake in baptism and the Lord's Supper. They struggled to call and retain ministers but regularly encountered difficulties in attracting competent ordained servants for their church body. With his emphasis on preaching and hearing the Word rather than on participating in the sacraments, Robinson argued that teaching required a "special gift," while administering the sacraments required "no special gift" on the part of the minister. However, he fell back on traditional church doctrine in his view that the sacraments could only be administered by an ordained officer.[68] Yet he seemed to provide a way for a true church to ordain ministers for its use: "In America," for example, a gathered church body that did not have an ordained minister could claim the power invested in it by their covenant with God and "choose, and appoint their own ministers from within themselves." Significantly, ordaining power did not descend from God, "through [the bishops'] fingers," to the minister as in the Anglican Church, but rather it "flowed from the 'body,' or church members, to the 'eye,' or minister."[69] However, the church at New Plymouth never did empower someone from among their own to administer the sacraments. Robinson himself, while seemingly liberal in his stance concerning laypeople's authority to select and ordain ministers, in practice held to a more conservative position, accepting for ordination only those who had been formally trained and who undertook ministry as a fulltime position, financially supported by the congregation. He continually expected to immigrate to New England; both he and the Plymouth church assumed it would be pastorless for only a short period of time, yet Robinson, who died in Leiden in 1625, never did arrive as anticipated. Elder Brewster might have served as pastor, and he wrote to Robinson in 1623 to ask if he might, as ruling elder of the church, be allowed to administer the sacraments. Robinson replied that he could not, and the humble Brewster "would never be persuaded to take higher office upon him" without his pastor's consent.[70]

Doing without the sacraments during the first decade of settlement, while less than ideal for the saints at Plymouth, was not a critical matter in their own understanding of themselves as a true visible church body, for they did enjoy regular teaching by Brewster. Robinson comforted them: "The true church of Christ [may] be for a time without [the sacraments], though never without spiritual right unto them. . . . It doth not then cease to be a church, no, nor a visible church neither. It remains visible in itself though it be not actually seen, or open to the eye of all."[71] However, lacking sacraments and the public visibility and authority they bestowed did create problems in Plymouth, as when Anglican minister John Lyford attempted to administer the Anglican sacramental rites without permission in 1624.[72] Hearing that Plymouth's leaders would not allow Lyford to fulfill his role as pastor, their investors wrote to Governor Bradford that "there is something amiss amongst you." The investors accused them of "being contentious, cruel, and hard hearted, among your neighbours, and towards such as in all points, both civil and religious, jump not with you" and admonished them to "let your practices and course in religion, in the church, be made complete and full; . . . and let all the ordinances of God be used completely in the church."[73] Bradford wrote back admitting Plymouth's "want of both the sacraments" and lamenting their lack of an ordained separatist minister: "The more is our grief, that our [own] pastor [Robinson] is kept from us, by whom we might enjoy them."[74] Despite the investors' admonishments, Plymouth's leaders handled their difficulties with Lyford in accordance with their principles of spiritual and social purity and pollution by eventually excommunicating and banishing him from church and town.

Many of New Plymouth's difficulties in acquiring and keeping a decent minister that plagued them throughout the early and middle years of the century were grounded in disagreements about proper administration of the sacraments. In the first sixteen years of settlement the church had and lost four unsatisfactory pastors or potential pastors: Lyford, one Mr. Rogers (who was "Crased in his braine"), Ralph Smith ("very weake" in the ministry and "a poor healp to them"), and Roger Williams (whose teaching they initially "well approued," though he later incited controversy with his "strange opinions" and "practice" and "left them something abruptly").[75] Having "been so bitten by Mr. Lyford" and others, they preferred doing without the sacraments to dealing with the problematic ministers their sacramental rites required. Although they often "Gro[a]n[ed] vnder the want of Gospell ordinances," Nathaniel Morton noted in the church records, they still held "publick worship euery lords day."[76] When Smith resigned his position in 1636 the church recruited John Reyner, "a godly man . . . and of a meek and humble spirit, sound in the truth and every way unreproveable in his life and conversation." After a trial period they chose Reyner for their pastor, who served the community for eighteen years. These were not untroubled years, however, for when Reyner finally left in November of 1654, it was under a cloud of ill content.[77] Part of the problem was Charles Chauncy, who arrived in 1638 with the intention of serving as assistant to Reyner but soon instigated conflicts over correct sacramental practices. Concerning the Lord's Supper, Chauncy claimed it should be administered every Lord's Day in the evening, while most nonconforming churches held it in the morning after the general worship service. The church at Sandwich in Plymouth Colony, influenced by Chauncy, did begin to observe the Lord's Supper in the evening, but generally the dispute over the timing of the Lord's Supper, according to John Winthrop, was "a matter of no great ill consequence, save some outward inconvenience, [so] there was little stir about it."[78] Chauncy, a stauncher separatist than most at Plymouth, apparently believed that holding this separate, exclusive evening meeting for the true saints demarcated a more visible spatial and temporal break between insiders and outsiders.[79]

Discussing the Lord's Supper, John Robinson followed traditional church doctrine in acknowledging that "no unbaptized person may eat of" the bread and wine, but he went further than that. With the Lord's Supper as a definitive public mark of full church membership, only those who had entered into a covenanted relationship with the local body of Christ and lived as visible saints were allowed to ingest the material signs of Christ's body.[80] Emphasizing the corporeality of sacramental actions and their ability to demarcate boundaries around the local church, Robinson wrote, "The holy sacrament of the Lord's Supper . . . is a testimony of that visible communion of love, also of one member with another."[81] Refuting the traditional belief in transubstantiation—that Christ was literally present in the bread and wine—nonconformists transferred divine presence from inanimate ritual materials, the bread and wine, to their own bodies. When they "plainly" performed the Lord's Supper, human bodies materialized sacred power in the physical world.[82]

Descriptions of the Lord's Supper in separatist churches in England and Amsterdam illustrate how the sacramental actions plainly—immediately and accurately—reenacted what participants understood to be Christ's and his disciples' behavior at the Last Supper and intentionally performed the close-knit community of the local church as "one spiritual bodie of Christ." Refusing to "kneel to or before the bread," which implied an "idolatrous" belief in transubstantiation, the saints stood or sat around a table to demonstrate their equal status before Christ, their spiritual head. The table was covered with a plain, white linen cloth on which sat loaves of bread and a cup of wine. The pastor "must take [the] breade and blesse and geue thankes, and then must he breake it and pronounce it to be the body of Christ, which was broken for thee, that by fayth they might feede thereon spirituallie & growe into one spiritual bodie of Christ." After eating some of the bread the pastor "deliuered yt vnto some of them," and the deacons delivered it to the others gathered around the table and "bidd them take and eate it among them, & feede on Christ in their consciences." Then the pastor took the cup of wine and blessed it and gave thanks, "pronounc[ing] it to be the bloud of Christ in the newe Testament, which was shedd for remission of sinnes, that by fayth we might drinke it spirituallie, and so be nourished in one spirituall bodie of Christ, all sinne being clensed away." After drinking some of the wine the pastor "bydd them drinke thereof like-wise and diuide it among them." He "deliuered the Cupp vnto one and he to an other, and soe from one to an other till they had all drunken," each person speaking the words of Christ: "Take, eat: this is my bodie, which is broken for you: this do ye in remembrance of me." The sacrament concluded with a prayer of thanks, asking "for their further profiting in godlines & vowing their obedience."[83] Passing the bread and wine from one saint's hands to the next around the table, rather than receiving the el-ements from a priest's hands, nurtured the egalitarian bonds among mem-bers and the agency of each participant to feed oneself and others Christ's body and blood. In this ritualized setting the ordinary actions of ingesting food became holy actions; the "sacrament of nourishment" fed the body of Christ.[84]

Plymouth's disputes over the performance of the Lord's Supper insti-gated by Charles Chauncy in the late 1630s did not, in fact, generate serious controversy, and the New Plymouth church, when it had an ordained min-ister, continued to observe the rite at the usual time, during the morning meeting. However, Chauncy's views on baptism provoked more far-reaching conflicts. The dispute was possibly an anabaptist one about the propriety of infant baptism; Winslow suggested that Chauncy, "to our great grief, . . . waiveth the administration of baptism to infants," although he did, in fact, baptize them.[85] But it was certainly about the correct practice of the sacra-ment itself. While the church preferred sprinkling water on the individu-al's head, Chauncy held that baptism "ought only to be by dipping, and putting the whole body under water, and that sprinkling was unlawful." The church elders "yielded that immersion or dipping was lawful but in this cold country not so convenient." The physical realities of the harsh New England environment contributed to the shaping of ritual perform-ances, which, in turn, shaped bodies in particular ways. Preferring to be guided by Robinson's principle of human "convenience," the elders (other than Chauncy) saw no need to implement a practice possibly dangerous to one's physical health. The thought of immersing an infant, whose survival during its first year of life was already tenuous, in a vessel of cold water in the frigid, unheated meetinghouse in the middle of January surely sent shivers up the backs of parents. Chauncy's reasoning was that sprinkling was "an human invention," while immersion, apparently, was scriptural. The church, however, would not concede "that sprinkling (which all the churches of Christ do for the most part use at this day) was unlawful and an human invention." They yielded to Chauncy to the extent that they would "suffer him to practice as he was persuaded," but only if those being baptized (or, presumably, their parents) desired it. In return, they expected Chauncy to allow Reyner to use sprinkling or pouring for children whose parents wished the rite performed in that way. The primary goal was to maintain the church body's solidarity through compromise, that "there might be no disturbance in the church hereabout."[86]

The elders' decision regarding the proper or "lawful" method of baptism was characteristically diplomatic, with their ultimate concern the physical and spiritual wellbeing of the church and its members. They already had experienced more confusion and disorder due to problematic ministers than they could justify with their vision of themselves as the pure body of Christ, its members closely bound by mutual affection and support. Regarding the baptismal dispute with Chauncy, they were confident that "the way of God in which we walk and according to which we perform our worship and service to Him" was scriptural. "Nevertheless," Winslow declared, "if any through tenderness of conscience be otherwise minded, to such we never turn a deaf ear, nor become rigorous, though we have the stream of authority on our sides."[87] Willing to yield to Chauncy to an extent, church leaders chose not to impose an authoritative ruling against him, but rather to allow members a choice in how they wanted to be baptized. The mediation of power in this case employed strategies intended to grant individuals the right to negotiate their own actions within certain ritual limits (sprinkling, pouring, or immersion). With the human body itself—its physical comfort and significance as a sacramental medium—at the heart of the controversy, bodies, especially those of infants, became the sites of struggles over theological meanings of the sacraments, the authority of the clergy to perform those rites in particular ways, and the agency of individuals to manipulate how rituals would be enacted upon oneself or one's children.

For Robinson, baptism was a physical and spiritual seal of God's covenant administered only to the children of at least one faithful parent. Like the Jewish rite of circumcision, baptism, although it did not mark the body permanently, was the public rite of initiation into the covenant between

God and his chosen people and "a lively sign of . . . incorporation into, and participation of the washing of his blood and Spirit." Plymouth elders described it as "a Reall feeding to the Soule to haue the seale of Baptisme aplyed to it." There was an immediate correspondence between the corporeal action and its spiritual effect; through one's body, specifically the head or face or, in Chauncy's case, one's entire body, God's grace was administered to the heart. While infants could not yet fulfill the covenant with their actions and understanding, they were included in it by "the outward washing of the body with water signifying, confirming, and applying the inward washing of the soul," which admitted the child "into the family of God." The rite of baptism was both an outward sign of an inward event and an efficacious act by which infants were claimed by God and the covenanted community.[88] In Leiden and Plymouth the saints probably practiced the rite in a plain manner similar to that in the Amsterdam church, described by Daniel Bucke in 1592 at the baptism of seven children by Francis Johnson: "They had neither god fathers nor godmothers, and he [Johnson] tooke water and washed the faces of them that were baptised: . . . sayinge onely in the administracion of this sacrament, 'I doe Baptise thee in the name of the father of the sonne and of the holy g[h]ost,' withoute usinge any other cerimony therein."[89] Bucke described the ritual administration of water on the children's bodies not as sprinkling or pouring but as washing their faces, which might be construed as a gentle, nurturing act; Johnson may have cared about the children's sensory experiences of the ritual, just as Plymouth's leaders were concerned about the physical experience of immersion in cold New England water. One's face immediately reflected one's inner heart; the rite outwardly mirrored the correspondent inward spiritual washing.

Regardless of Plymouth elders' flexibility in negotiating their baptismal practices with Chauncy, he announced he could not back down from his position. The church called in outside help and "procured some other ministers to dispute the point with him publicly." Ralph Partridge, pastor at Duxbury, and other ministers within the colony debated with Chauncy "sundry times, very ably and sufficiently," but he "was not satisfied." At this, Plymouth looked further afield, applying to churches throughout New England. All the ministers concluded against him, yet Chauncy still would not concede. In spite of his contentious nature, the church at Plymouth was "very loath to part with him," probably because of their difficulties in calling and retaining ordained ministers and the status Chauncy, a highly educated divine and former lecturer at Cambridge University, brought to their community. However, Chauncy "removed himself to Scituate," whose church had called him to the ministry.[90] Two years later the Plymouth church might have felt providentially vindicated. At Scituate Chauncy "persevered in his opinion of dipping in baptism," but it caused him some problems. He practiced immersion on two of his own children, one of whom he baptized in "very cold weather" and it "swooned away." Other baptisees panicked in fright; one child, catching hold of Chauncy while being lowered into the water, nearly pulled the minister in with him. The mother of a three-year-old was so afraid of endangering her child that she turned her back on Chauncy and traveled thirty miles to Boston to have the child baptized there.[91]

After Reyner departed Plymouth in 1654, the church was again without an ordained minister until the arrival of John Cotton Jr. in 1667 and his or-dination as their pastor in 1669. Church membership finally began to grow and official records to be kept: in 1667 there were forty-seven church mem-bers; two years later the church body had grown by twenty-seven mem-bers. During Cotton's thirty-year tenure 178 people became full church members, although many not recorded moved away or died, and he bap-tized 574 children.[92] Before and after Cotton's arrival, however, the church continued to experience problems concerning the rite of baptism. In the 1650s and again in the 1670s anabaptists challenged the doctrine of infant baptism; some, like minister John Myles in Swansea, rebaptized adults who had been baptized as infants.[93] Because baptism was a "lively" physical sign that "sealed" the self, body and soul, to the body of Christ, Plymouth or-thodoxy propounded that to rebaptize an individual as an adult was redun-dant and, worse, an explicit rejection of the efficacy of infant baptism; even those baptized as infants in a "false" church, such as the Church of Eng-land, they believed, "retain [their] outward washing without repetition."[94] Given that at least one parent was a communicating member of Christ's body, the child became a permanent member of that body through his or her ritual "washing with water."

Questions arose, however, over whether the child of a censured church member—one who had fallen out of good standing due to sinful behavior—could be baptized. In June of 1692, for example, Susanna Ran-som, a communicating church member, was called before the New Ply-mouth church for "having falling [sic] into scandall by excessive drinking." In July she manifested through speech and writing "some Repentance for her sin of Drunkenesse" and the elders admonished and censured her; that is, they denied her participation in the Lord's Supper and watched her daily behavior to determine whether her repentance were real. Ransom's censure continued for a year until June of 1693, when she desired to have her son John baptized. Pastor Cotton asked the church body to consider whether the child of a censured church member may be "regularly baptized." The following month, however, Cotton had no need for an answer, for Ransom fully repented of her sin before the church and the brethren accepted her confession and released her from censure. Infant John Ransom's name is listed among those of the twenty-nine children Cotton baptized that year.[95]

"Power to Void and Purge Excrements": Admonition, Censure, and Excommunication

The church body at Plymouth strove to sustain its purity and covenantal relationship with God in two ways: by the ongoing observance of proper worship—rituals of nourishment—and by the disciplining of those members who threatened its order, cohesion, and holiness—rituals of purgation. Individuals like Susanna Ransom corrupted the church with their sinful behaviors, and Robinson empowered the church body with rites that allowed it to discipline and expel, temporarily or permanently, polluting members from its midst. Using graphic humoral metaphors of bodily functions—constipation and excretion—Robinson argued that "true churches not using aright the power they have for reformation [are] like true bodies which through some obstructions, or stoppings for a time cannot void things noxious, and hurtful till there be a remedy." A church that did not use its God-given power to expel a sinful member was like "a monstrous body wanting the faculties and instruments of evacuation and expulsion of excrements, or other noisome things, and therefore is never appointed of God to live, but devoted to death and destruction." The "power to void and purge excrements," he continued, "is prodigious in nature," for "neither the natural nor [the] spiritual body" can live without it.[96] Using scatological language to conflate the human body and the body of Christ vividly delineated the categories of purity and pollution for Robinson and church members. These were not simply clever or sensational metaphors but concrete, living principles that literally determined the health and survival or illness and potential death of the church body.

Drawing on ancient Israelite principles of contagion, Robinson argued that the sinful actions of one person "doth so pollute the whole congregation" that, if not dealt with, the other members became equally guilty—

an "accessory to that other man's sin"—and equally polluted by it. The members of a body must all "touch" each other; in touching one who was "spiritually polluted," other members became "defiled." Sinning persons were "infectious," and failing to "censure, sequester, reject, and avoid" them caused other members of Christ's body to become "stained and polluted" themselves. Thus, all members must remain alert to sin's insidious nature, for "this [polluting] strain comes more ways than you are aware." Robinson described three ways Christ's body became contaminated. "First, When a man doth not consider or observe his brother as he ought, nor watch over him in the holy communion of the saints"; a person may, in fact, be ignorant of another's sin yet still guilty by virtue of neglecting to observe each member of the body continuously and diligently. "A second case of pollution is the neglect of admonition for the reformation of the offender." Admonishment, an expression of "true love . . . for the purging, gaining, humbling, and saving of the offender," should occur first in "secret," if the sin were a personal offense of one person toward another; then in "private," with one or two witnesses; and finally in public before the entire church. The third cause of contact pollution arose when the church body failed to expunge an incorrigible offender from its midst, which occurred in two phases.[97] "Censuring" a member, such as Susanna Ransom, meant denying him or her full communicating membership and access to the sacraments, although one still was expected to attend public worship. Censured members who proved to be incorrigible were then excommunicated from the church body. Yet the purpose and end of excommunication was not permanent rejection of the offending member but repentance and return to the church body, which would bring God's blessing to both the penitent and the entire congregation.[98]

The Plymouth church accomplished avoidance or, in some cases, voiding of pollution through the three-step process of observing, admonishing, and expunging outlined by Robinson. The principle of visible sainthood at the heart of Robinson's teaching about the body of Christ and the maintenance of its purity supported "watching"—the continual daily surveillance of members by each other. After Susanna Ransom was admonished for drunkenness, during her period of censure "the church . . . waite[d] upon God for discovery of the truth of her Repentance." Discovering "truth" required more than Ransom's verbal confession. Rather, members observed Ransom's daily behavior, for a contrite heart must be made visible in reformed actions. While everyday communal surveillance was a commonly accepted and expected practice, there were times when church elders explicitly called upon the body to watch and listen. On January 28, 1676/7, for example, they asked members to stay after public worship to discuss "rumors as if some of the bretheren walked disorderly, in sitting too long together in publick houses & with vaine company & drinking." The members unanimously agreed, for the "healing of that evill," that if "they saw or heard of any such carriage . . . to demand a reason of the party why he soe did." If the offender "did not give satisfying answers to such sober, christian demands, it should be accounted Just matter of offence."[99] Metacom's Rebellion had just ended successfully for the colonists, and the church was concerned about keeping itself in God's providential good graces. Each member bound him- or herself not only to watch other members for signs of sinful behavior, but also to admonish them—"to demand a reason." If an acceptable reason for socializing and drinking were not forthcoming, the offender would be brought before the church to answer to the body of Christ so that it might be "healed."

Robinson always described the rituals of purgation in terms of communal power; the authority "to cut off any member is given to the whole body," not to any one member, such as the pope or pastor, or to an elite group, such as bishops or elders. "The power of excommunication is an essential property" of the church body and must be exercised "when they meet together in open assembly . . . on the Sabbath." Unlike the ordinances of preaching and prayer, where one man "prepareth in secret," the ordinances of admonition, censure, and excommunication could be instigated by anyone: "The sin must be told to the church, and they upon knowledge of it, must admonish the sinner, and so the excommunication is publicly to be prepared, with the foreknowledge and foreconsent of the body." The offending member stood before the church and his or her sin was described, either by the one offended, by the one who had observed the offense, or by an elder of the church. In response, the sinner might deny the accusation, but ideally the person read or spoke *ad lib* his or her statement of confession and repentance or another member read it for him or her, and then male church members debated the veracity and sincerity of the offender's words.[100] In the case of Susanna Ransom, the church followed Robinson's order of public censure: after she confessed, the elders spoke, then the men of the church openly discussed and decided how to handle her situation, and finally "the women lastly by silent consent" agreed. At least for adult male members Ransom's censure was relatively democratic, as well as very public.[101] Public surveillance coupled with public admonishment were intended to humiliate the sinning member, elicit a repentant heart and reformed behavior, and, ideally, reconnect the now purified member to Christ's body. Censure and excommunication were, in fact, like surgery: the diseased member must be "cut off," lest he or she cause sickness in the whole body, until the member could be healed—in humoral-medical terms purged of pollution—and properly reattached.

During Cotton's tenure as pastor, the church admonished, censured, or excommunicated eighteen men and sixteen women (a few repeat offenders appeared more than once) and eleven whose genders were not noted.[102] The largest number stood before the church body for unspecified sins, described as "inordinate walking," "some failings," or "irregular actings"—four men, five women, and seven of unknown gender. Fornication or "moral scandal" was the most prevalent specified problem; four men, eight women, and one person of unknown gender were caught in sexual "uncleanness," usually because their infants were born six months or less after their marriages. "Intemperance" or "excessive drinking" was the third category of sin that brought individual members before the public meeting: five men, one woman (Susanna Ransom), and two unnamed persons. The other offenses were selling alcohol to Indians (three people); "carnal fellowship," which might refer to fornication or to loitering with unchurched friends (one man); and "scandalous words" or a "passionate and evil carriage" (two men and one woman). Notably, the church preferred dealing with sinning members themselves, rather than bringing them before the civil authorities, for virtually no individuals described as drinking excessively, fornicating, or committing other sinful crimes appear in the court records. Thus, with each censure and excommunication the body of Christ reinscribed the boundaries around itself, maintaining a separation between its members and the larger civil body.

The church brethren greatly preferred to censure offenders and retain them as attending members, rather than to excommunicate them outright from any participation whatsoever in the church body; only five church members required excommunication.[103] Indeed, excommunication was a last resort, used only when the offending member was repeatedly unrepentant. For example, in 1681 the elders ordered Samuel Dunham Sr., an elderly church member and "a poor old drunkard," to appear before the church. At first he failed to appear, and when he finally presented himself before the church he was "not humbled" but exhibited rude "expressions & behaviors," although the church was "patient" with him for two more Sabbaths. Finally, however, "God gave the church strength to purge him out." Dunham eventually repented and was reconciled to the church two years later. However, he continued to exhibit drunken and disorderly behavior and, between 1684 and 1690, was periodically admonished, censured, watched, reconciled, and again admonished and censured by the church body—although he was not again excommunicated.[104] As for a human body, severing a church member was a radical move that inherently weakened Christ's body, although retaining the polluting member also threatened its health. As well, a thoroughgoing excommunication might have lessened the chances of an individual reforming his or her behavior and eventually returning to the church, for the ultimate purpose of excommunication was repentance and readmittance. In fact, this usually worked. Of the five church members who were excommunicated, all but one were readmitted within one to two years after their ritual expulsions.

At the literal and figurative heart of the church body during purgation rites stood the individual sinner, who, like all members, embodied great power to bring spiritual illness or health, God's anger or mercy, upon the body of Christ. Admonition, censure, and excommunication continuously cycled members like Samuel Dunham through the individual performance of polluting actions and the communal performance of purgation rites, allowing these members to develop a "ritual mastery," to use Catherine Bell's term, that enabled them to utilize the rites to their own ends.[105] Dunham likely understood that he was a social outcast, the "town drunk," an elderly man who was treated with pity at best and disgust, even physical abuse, at worst. When he became drunk and disorderly he attracted the watchful attention of church members as they went about their daily activities, guaranteeing him access to a more formal public display. Standing before his neighbors assembled as Christ's physical presence on earth afforded Dunham the opportunity to be scrutinized by God and fellow human beings and to speak his mind to both in return; he was allowed a moment of recognition that he, too, was a valued member of the body of Christ with the potential to pollute or purify that sacred body through his speech and actions. Within the highly structured boundaries of the church community, individual bodies retained a subversive power to undermine or support that structure at will. While public humiliation and censure may have dissuaded most members from attracting unpleasant attention to themselves, there were others, especially those of lower social status, who might have found the rituals of purgation potent modes of public self-fashioning. Indeed, one egregiously sinning member could provoke the entire church body to turn inward and repent of personal and communal sins through another purgation ritual, a day of fasting, humiliation, and prayer.

"Pinched with Hunger . . . Partakers of Plenty": Days of Fasting and Thanksgiving

With the excommunications in early 1682 of Samuel Dunham for drunkenness and George Watson and his wife for "morall scandall," Pastor Cotton became deeply concerned about the ongoing purity of the church at Plymouth—the contagion of sinful behavior seemed to be seriously threatening the health of Christ's body. Dissenting doctrine, however, offered Cotton an effective ritual response, which he was quick to employ. The pastor called the church to a day of fasting, to be held at his house on February 8, "to humble ourselves for outbreaking of sins among us." He wrote to his friend at Barnstable, Thomas Hinckley, that the day of humiliation was appointed "on the account of such sad outbreakings. Pity, good sir, and pray for this poor church, that upon it may be engraven, 'Holiness to the Lord.'" During the daylong fast the church met as a body to pray and hear preaching by Cotton and church elders Samuel Fuller and Nathaniel Morton. They also discussed taking practical action for the "suppression of sensuality" and agreed to present a petition to the civil court "to suppresse soe much selling of strong drinke" and reduce the number of ordinaries, or drinking establishments, in the town. The following month Samuel Dunham appeared before the magistrates who fined him five shillings "for being much ouertaken with drinke." The incorrigible Dunham's appearance in civil court followed from the church's lack of success in reforming one of its own; in excommunicating him from the church body, they handed him over to civil surveillance and authority.[106]

Recognizing that pollution must be voided and further "sensuality" suppressed in order for "holiness" to be engraved upon Christ's body, the church turned to a familiar ritual of communal purification. While they regularized sacred time around the weekly Sabbath, especially problematic events required an immediate reaction on the part of the congregation. Calling for spontaneous days of fasting, humiliation, and prayer allowed the church, as a unified, intentional body, to respond directly to crises that threatened its physical and spiritual health. Although there is no record of Cotton calling for a day of thanksgiving to follow the fast day on February 8, the ritual cycle loosely fluctuated between days of humiliation and days of gratitude to God for answering their fast-day prayers.[107] The meager spring of 1623, for example, had required Indians and English alike to scavenge for food, and then they were hit with a two-month drought from mid-May to mid-July. Believing the drought was a providential punishment for some unknown sin—God "seemed in his anger to arm himself against us"—the saints observed a day of fasting and humiliation. They gathered in the meetinghouse-fort for nine hours, fervently confessing their sins and praying for the Lord's mercy. God seemed to hear their heartfelt supplications, for as they returned to their homes "it began to be overcast, and shortly after to rain, with such sweet and gentle showers" that "the earth was thoroughly wet and soaked therewith, which did so apparently revive and quicken the decayed corn and other fruits, as was wonderful." Even the Indians were "astonished to behold" this answer to prayer; Hobbamock, who lived at Plymouth as a translator, declared, "The Englishman's God is a good God, for he hath heard you, and sent you rain." For fourteen days it rained, and throughout the rest of the summer the weather alternated between showers and warm weather; by autumn the colonists were able to gather in a "fruitful and liberal harvest." Rather than "smother[ing]" their gratitude, they agreed that the proper response to God's merciful care for his people was a public "day of thanksgiving unto the Lord."[108]

Throughout the seventeenth century Plymouth's church and court called for numerous days of fasting and humiliation in response to both external and internal threats to the integrity and health of the social body.[109] As a covenanted body in a contractual relationship with the divine, they believed that God indicated his anger with human sin through ominous divine providences: events in the physical world that threatened the community's survival, such as sickness, death, war, religious persecution, and agricultural problems like drought, flooding, and insect infestation. Dangers could arise from within the social body itself, as well, such as the sinful behavior of individual members—like Dunham and the Watsons—and internal conflicts that divided the church body. The appropriate response to such divine providences was to call for a day of fasting, humiliation, and prayer to purge personal and communal sin and restore physical, moral, and spiritual health. Ideally, God recognized the heartfelt desires of his people to repent and purify themselves through their fast-day activities, and he responded accordingly by answering their prayers and sending merciful divine providences: healing of physical illness and of divisions within the church, success in war, rain during a drought, or a good harvest. In turn, the community called for a day of thanksgiving to express their gratitude to God for his "wonderful favor and mercy," which indicated that they remained his covenanted people.

Purging and nourishing the body of Christ with these spontaneous rituals required the intentional participation of all members. The Plymouth church drew upon a rich history of fasting and thanksgiving that extended from ancient Israelite practices, through elaborate medieval Roman Catholic fast and feast days, to English puritans' instigation of civil fasts and thanksgivings, when the first Protestant treatises on "the Holie exercise of a true Fast" appeared.[110] These treatises condemned the "Popish Fast," which did not require total abstinence from all food, and linked "outward" and "inward exercises," or bodily and spiritual activities. The authors declared that physical self-denial produced a strong sense of one's "unworthinesse." The body was to be "brought down" so that the mind, likewise, might be humiliated. Nicholas Bownde's *Holy Exercise of Fasting* (1604) had the greatest influence on dissenters' views, and Thomas Thacher at Boston's Third Church reiterated Bownde's principles in a fast-day sermon seventy years later, when church practices in Massachusetts and Plymouth were virtually the same.[111] Both Bownde and Thacher explicitly directed their teachings to lay practitioners and both paid close attention to the human body and its role in connecting one's inner soul, the church body, and God. Thatcher linked divine providential afflictions of the community to the proper human response of corresponding afflictions imposed on one's body during fasting, which in turn afflicted the soul. For Bownde, body and soul were directly linked through "inward" and "outward" activities: "The outward appertaineth to the body, and is called a Bodily exercise, as to abstaine from meat, drinke, sleepe, and such like." Inward activities belonged to the "soule, and consisteth in the inward vertues and graces of the minde," which were "holpen forward by this bodily exercise." Recognizing pollution in the social body, a member imposed want on his or her own body so that he or she felt the insufficiency of the soul.[112]

The outward activities of a fast ordained by God were fivefold. For a twenty-four-hour period, from one evening to the next, one must: abstain from all meat and drink, although children and those who were ill may take some sustenance; deny oneself ordinary sleep and spend that time in prayer; avoid "costly apparell and trimming up of our selves, which might puffe up the body with pride," and wear instead "our woorst clothes, rather than our best, or our second [best]"; abstain from sexual activity; and avoid all worldly labors and recreations and dedicate that time to God's worship and service, although one may respond to a sudden casualty, such as fire, flood, or thieves.[113] Performing these acts of self-denial focused attention on one's sensory experiences by suppressing "natural" or "ordinary" desires for food, sleep, fine apparel, sex, and physical activity. Shunning expensive clothing and withdrawing from physical contact with the secular world purged the outer body of worldly pollution; abstaining from food, drink, and sex closed the body's openings to external pollution; and limiting sleep weakened one's defenses against spiritual promptings. Purifying the body's boundaries and orifices in these ways expressed a fundamental concern with the maintenance of individual and corporate boundaries, expunging pollution and reinstating purity.[114]

Seemingly paradoxically, in order to withdraw from the outer world of sensory fulfillment and promote inner spiritual experience, a person utilized the vehicle of sense, the body. Without a full belly, when the body was "pinched with hunger," a person was "more fit" for fervent prayer and supplication. Denying oneself corporeal comforts humbled the soul and broke "our harde and stonie hearts," while it "outwardly declare[d]" the intentions of the inner broken heart. Although church members might hold private fasts for personal difficulties and conflicts, the most effective kind of fasting occurred when members acted as a corporate body. Bownde believed that each person should be deeply moved to humility by the problems of the entire community and "succour [others] with our praiers as much as we can." Likewise, Thacher understood fasting to be the answer to spiritual and physical "great sickness": "Thy health shall spring forth speedily," for fasting brought "healing to your Souls, of your Families, of your Churches of your commonwealths, healing of your affairs inward and outward spiritual and worldly."[115] Ritually denying one's natural desires brought the human heart, the community, and the divine will into proper alignment with each other; one's body was the critical link connecting the inner self, the outer social body, and God. Self-abasement, in fact, became ritual mastery investing each member with the power to affect the health and survival of the body of Christ.[116]

In Leiden the separatist congregation observed many days of humiliation and prayer as they sought God for guidance in their migration to America. They not only abstained from food and other sensory comforts; physical gestures—kneeling, weeping, and fervent praying—also expressed the intensity of their concerns, and these emotional expressions bound them together as a single body.[117] Plymouth church and court records frequently note fast days and the reasons for their observance, yet they say little about the actual activities occurring on those days, perhaps because their authors assumed these were common knowledge. It appears that Cotton denied himself at least food, drink, and sleep while fasting. On March 8, 1687/8, the day after a fast at Plymouth "for the awfull hand of God in the measles this winter, that God would in mercy recover us[,] blesse our labours by sea & land, our seed time & harvest & continue the meanes of grace & give us the grace of the meanes," he penned a short note to his brother-in-law Increase Mather: "This day past our congregation kept a fast, with reference to the present visitation [of measles], so that I am too weary now to write."[118] Cotton, revealing a rare moment of lethargy, assumed Mather would understand his lack of energy after a day of fasting from food, sleep, and other sustaining activities. The rigors of a fast day altered one's physical being, which, if done with heartfelt intentionality, altered one's mental and emotional being as well. The body was brought down so that the spirit might be humbled and divine mercy engaged.

Ministers discussed fasting in far more detail than they did thanksgiving, and the church at Plymouth observed at least three times as many fast days as it did days of thanksgiving. But expressing gratitude to God for his benevolent mercies was a critical turn in the ritual cycle. Alternating between anxiety and relief, humiliation and exultation, purgation and nourishment, the body of Christ continuously generated its covenant with God in a cyclical exchange of spiritual and physical activities. Bownde declared that at times of rejoicing, when God had answered their prayers, "feasting were more fit for them then [*sic*] fasting."[119] The Plymouth church held days of thanksgiving in response to God's merciful providences: for civil and religious "liberties," bodily health, an ordained ministry, victory in wars against Indians and European powers, and good harvests. Although they did not necessarily link thanksgiving days with harvest festivals, fourteen of Plymouth's twenty-six recorded thanksgivings were observed in the autumn, usually in November but sometimes in late October or early December. Among other mercies, these autumn rituals expressed gratitude to God for "the fruits of the earth." The one (now well-known) thanksgiving harvest festival described in any detail occurred after the first settlers had been at Plymouth for a year; although many had not survived that initial year, the remaining souls were deeply thankful for what they understood to be God's benevolent support of their undertaking, providentially confirmed in a plentiful harvest: "They found the Lord to be with them in all their ways, and to bless their outgoings and incomings," Governor Bradford exulted at the time, "for which let His holy name have the praise forever, to all posterity."[120] To celebrate, Bradford sent four men hunting, who brought back enough fowl (turkeys and other wild game birds) to feed the company for "almost a week." Massasoit and ninety of his men arrived with five deer, and the English and Indians "feasted" and recreated together for three days—the colonists demonstrating their weaponry and the Indians no doubt performing in dancing and singing. "And although it be not always so plentiful as it was at this time with us," Winslow, writing to friends in England, concluded, "yet by the goodness of God, we are so far from want that we often wish you partakers of our plenty."[121]

Although not all thanksgiving days included harvest festivals, they apparently always involved sharing food at communal "feasts." Generally, after morning worship in the meetinghouse, members gathered in each others' homes for a festive meal.[122] On a "very cold" December 22, 1636, for example, the church at Scituate gathered in the meetinghouse at half past eight in the morning to observe a day of thanksgiving. They began with "a short prayer, then a psalme sang, then more large in prayer, after that an other Psalme, & then the Word taught, after that prayer—& the[n] a psalme" until after the noon hour. Then they gathered in members' homes to "mak[e] merry to the creatures, the poorer sort beeing invited of the richer." Three years later, on another cold December morning, the Barnstable church kept a thanksgiving "for God's exceeding mercye in bringing us hither Safely keeping us healthy & well in o[u]r weake beginnings & in our church Estate." They did not yet have a meetinghouse so met instead "att Mr. Hulls house." After public "praises to God," they "devided into 3 companies to feast togeather, some att Mr Hulls, some att Mr Maos, some att Brother Lumberds senior."[123] Feasting of this sort, in the homes of early colonists who were often on the edge of survival, was certainly not the English upper classes' "gluttonous" feasting condemned by moralists who abhorred the carousing and overindulgence they observed on Anglican feast days, nor was it like the feasting colonists enjoyed during thanksgiving harvest festivals.[124] And yet the use of food to draw the community together, to redistribute resources and provide a generous meal to those less prosperous, and to acknowledge gratitude to God for abundant blessings remained a powerful ritual gesture, both symbolic and practical. While they ate and "made merry" together, they fed the body of Christ, nourishing its health, strengthening its identity, and weaving more tightly the bonds of common affection among its members.[125]

Abstaining from bodily pleasures on days of fasting, humiliation, and prayer, and celebrating together with food and recreation on days of thanksgiving placed individuals' bodies at the center of religious life in Plymouth churches. Likewise, the other rituals of nourishment and purgation—Sabbath worship, the sacraments of the Lord's Supper and baptism, and admonishment, censure, and excommunication—which took place within a particular formulation of sacred space and time, invested individual human bodies with a ritual mastery that continuously knit together or, at times, threatened to unravel the ligaments of the social body. Focusing on the visibility of sainthood, the church at New Plymouth watched the bodies of its members closely in order to deal immediately with dangers to its health and purity. Corresponding to the church body was the institution of the family, in which individuals' bodies and souls first received molding and shaping to become godly members of the community.

CHAPTER 5

As in a Mirror

Domestic Bodies

W
HEN FIFTY-YEAR-OLD NEW PLYMOUTH RESIDENT
Mary Ring died in July 1631, she left behind two daughters
in their twenties, an eleven-year-old son, and a one-year-old
granddaughter. Mary and her husband William had been devout members
of John Robinson's separatist congregation in Leiden and were among
those who had hoped to sail to North America with the first company in
1620. However, the ship they were on, the *Mayflower*'s sister ship the *Speed-
well*, sprang a leak when leaving England, forcing most of its passengers
to return to the Netherlands. When William died, Mary and her children
set sail with a company of Leiden separatists bound for Plymouth in 1629.
The newcomers were joyfully greeted by the colonists, who immediately
set about helping to clear land for planting and to build houses. Mary's
daughters soon married Plymouth residents, Elizabeth to Stephen Deane
and Susanna to Thomas Clarke. For two years Mary led an active public life
in the village of New Plymouth. She likely rejoiced with Governor William
Bradford and the other saints at the arrival of New Plymouth church's first
(at least initially) acceptable pastor, Ralph Smith, who had made the transatlantic crossing with her. She traded timber, furs, and other goods with
Bradford, Edward Winslow, and others, and she was probably well aware of
the enormous challenges the plantation faced in establishing its fish and fur

trades during that time. She counted among her good friends Plymouth's physician and church deacon Samuel Fuller and saw the return of unwanted scoundrel Thomas Morton from England in 1630 and his eventual second arrest and imprisonment.[1]

As Mary walked about the village, renewing friendships with people she had not seen for nine years, visiting with new neighbors and purchasing items from them, attending worship services, joining the crowd gathered to watch Plymouth's first execution (the hanging of John Billington for the murder of John Newcomen), her colorful clothing displayed the status of a godly middle-class woman recently arrived from Holland.[2] Gathering in the meetinghouse for worship or court proceedings and going about their daily activities in towns and on their farms, Plymouth's inhabitants lived exceedingly public lives, conforming to and resisting expectations that shaped their bodies in various ways, which they in turn used to fashion visible self-identities. When they returned to their homes, however, they entered more intimate spaces in which family members pursued domestic activities—performing housekeeping and income-producing labors, praying, eating, and sleeping together, disciplining and being disciplined—that also explicitly and implicitly generated particular corporealities.

We can determine something about the modest, godly domestic life of the widow Mary Ring from her will and probate inventory, which list a number of household goods. Mary and her three children—and after a year only Mary and her young son Andrew—likely lived in a typical one-room dwelling, in which all domestic activities occurred within a small, dark, and crowded fifteen- or twenty-foot-square space, lit only by the open fireplace and one lamp and a candlestick. Mary's home was well stocked with cooking implements: three brass pots, a quart pot, and three kettles; two skillets and a frying pan; two sieves; a fire-iron for lighting the fire, bellows, two pothooks and a trammel for hanging kettles over the fire, a spit for roasting meat, and a gridiron; and cooking utensils—a flat slice, a ladle, a skimmer, a chopping knife, and an iron fork. She also owned two basins for washing and a full complement of serving implements: a chafing dish, a dozen trenchers, six platters of earthenware, wood, or pewter, two trays, a fruit dish, three saucers, a salt cellar, three cups (one of them a wooden goblet), one bowl, and three porringers, most of it perhaps stored in Mary's one cupboard. She owned no spoons, indicating that she and her children ate with their fingers, a common practice at the time. The home boasted only one chair and, although she had a tablecloth and two dozen table napkins, no table. For meals Mary likely sat in the chair and her children on the chest and trunk in which Mary stored their clothing, linens, and bedding, with their food placed on the cupboard covered with the tablecloth, or they may have held porringers in their laps to eat. The family members shared two beds, or perhaps even one, for Mary indicated in her will that her "new bed & bolster" had not yet been stuffed with feathers and that she still slept in her older (and far less comfortable) flock bed. Notably, Mary owned no bedstead or other frame on which a "bed," or bag containing feathers or flocking, could be raised off of the earthen floor of the house. She did own curtains for a "hanging" bed frame but apparently did not use them, a warming pan to heat the bed in winter, and plenty of bedding: pillows and bolsters, linen sheets and pillow cases, blankets and coverlets. Another important item was a chamber pot, which allowed Mary and her children to avoid having to go outdoors to relieve themselves during the night. She also owned one precious trinket, a silver whistle.[3]

It appears that Mary spent most of her time when at home cooking and sewing, for her inventory lists several pieces of wool and linen cloth, including one piece of green say, a fine textured wool, with which she intended to make a coat for her young grandchild Elizabeth Deane. A godly woman, she was concerned about the moral upbringing of her children; in her will she requested that her "two loving friends" from Leiden, Samuel Fuller and Thomas Blossom, counsel and advise her young son Andrew "in anything they shall see good & convenient for him." As well, she asked that her son-in-law Stephen Deane raise Andrew "in the knowledge & feare of God," directing Deane not to "oppresse" Andrew "by any burthens" but teach him to have a tender heart, "as he will answere to God." She apparently hoped Fuller, Blossom, and Deane would continue the godly training she had provided her children from the Bible and seven other Christian books she owned.[4]

One of these books, listed simply as "dod" in her inventory, may have been John Dod and Robert Cleaver's *Godly Forme of Hovshold Gouernment*, an extremely popular English household manual providing guidelines for properly managing the home and family. Samuel Fuller and William Brewster each owned copies of Dod and Cleaver, and Alice and William Bradford owned an equally popular household manual, William Gouge's *Of Domesticall Duties*. The manuals precisely detailed and standardized the ways husband and wife, mother and father, children and servants should appear—their demeanor, facial expressions, dress, and other forms of self-fashioning—and behave—their speech, treatment of each other, and other forms of conduct—in the godly home, for it was there that individuals learned the principles of modesty and plainness, authority and submission, and how to embody them in society, or, as Edmund S. Morgan put it, how to live "a smooth, honest, civil life." Even those who did not own or read these well-known household manuals understood how the family and its members should be formed, for the ideals the manuals promoted thoroughly pervaded the cultural ethos of early New England.[5] In fact, the boundaries between domestic and public spheres were fluid, for family organization, government, and activities corresponded to larger social institutions, and the lessons learned at home, the social values continuously inscribed on family members' bodies, ideally produced good community citizens. "The Houshold," wrote Cleaver and Dod, "is as it were a little Commonwealth"; when it was governed properly, it furthered God's kingdom to benefit the larger community. Gouge expanded on the theme: "A familie is a little Church, and a little common-wealth. . . . Or rather it is a schoole wherein the first principles and ground of Gouernment and subiection are learned: whereby men are fitted to greater matters in Church or common-wealth."[6] The home was the locus in which the biological and moral self was conceived and birthed, nourished and nurtured, disciplined and educated for the greater public good.

Discovering whether and how Plymouth families like that of Mary Ring actually followed the manuals' guidelines, as well as how they experienced and pursued their daily lives within their homes, is difficult, however. As John Demos observed, a basic barrier to gaining entrance into a "typical" Plymouth home is the lack of descriptive sources; no one left diaries, journals, or letters describing their everyday domestic lives as did some residents in other colonies.[7] Plymouth's court records deal with familial conflicts, but they point to moments when family members *ignored* the prescriptions for proper household government, which relatively few families did, or at least not egregiously enough to take their problems to court. It was the duty of mothers and fathers to discipline family members privately within the home—"within the secret of our owne walles," as Cleaver and Dod put it—and avoid the public court system if at all possible.[8] However, bringing together a variety of primary sources—court records, prescriptive literature by Cleaver and Dod, Gouge, and Robinson, and probate inventories that note domestic material culture like cooking utensils and bedding—and work already done by such scholars as Demos, archaeologist James Deetz, and architectural and food historians offers glimpses of bodies and the ways their domestic environments and family relationships might have produced particular physical experiences and expressions and invested them with religious meanings.

Colonists' descriptions of the homes and domestic lives of southern New England native people are another fruitful source of information about the saints' ideals of domesticated bodies. Relationships between Plymouth colonists, especially Edward Winslow and Reverend John Cotton Jr., and many Indians were quite intimate. During the early years colonists and Wampanoags frequently visited and entertained each other in their homes, and Winslow described much of what he observed during these encounters. Although he was little involved in evangelizing Indians himself, Winslow published one of the Eliot Tracts on Indian missions, reflecting his close contact with and interest in native people. Cotton was a missionary to the Wampanoags on Martha's Vineyard before he moved to Plymouth in 1667, and he continued his missionary activities as an extension of his pastoral duties at Plymouth. Meanwhile, Richard Bourne of Sandwich, "a pious, sober, and active person," and later Cotton's son Josiah also preached among the Plymouth Indians.[9] Massachusetts's overseer of Indian missions, Daniel Gookin, articulated the common view of Indian bodies as "mirrors" reflecting godly colonists' images of, in a sense, their own shadows—of what they might become if they abandoned "civilized" and "moral" practices.[10] Gookin visualized Indians as negative or "corrupted" reflections of moral civility, a harsher attitude than that of Plymouth missionaries to the Indians, but his mirror trope suggests observing English and Indian domestic bodies in a comparative mode, allowing them to reflect information about each other. Where the historical record tells us little about colonists' foodways and sleepways, for example, it attends to the ways native people ate and slept. English observers accentuated what they did about Indians primarily because of its seeming exoticism, but the types of activities colonists chose to highlight reveal much about what they deemed important about daily life, both the Indians' and their own.[11] Thus, the details of native life on which observers focused and the ways they responded to and interpreted those details provide information, in contrast, about English life; indeed, authors mentioned some aspects of colonial home life only in conjunction with particular Indian activities. Furthermore, some missionaries attempted to reconfigure the domestic spaces and living bodies of Indians who converted to Christianity—the "praying Indians"—according to English notions of civility and godliness. Notably, Plymouth's missionaries tended to treat Indian converts less rigorously than did Gookin,

John Elliot, and other Massachusetts Bay missionaries, allowing them to retain more autonomy and maintain many aspects of a traditional native lifestyle.[12] Such differences among missionaries' approaches reveal both differences and similarities among Indian and English understandings of the proper shaping of moral bodies within the home.

The family dwelling enclosed its members in a physical environment that provided particular sensory experiences and produced particular domestic conduct, as well as reflecting distinctive social and cultural values. Indians generated more fluid boundaries around their families—two or more families might share a dwelling, for example, and some native men had more than one wife—while the English drew comparatively distinct lines around what they thought of as the "private" household, at the center of which were its two "governors": a married man and woman who each fulfilled three distinct roles of husband, father, and master, or wife, mother, and mistress, and together were divinely ordained to hold authority over other family members, namely, children and servants.[13] Widows like Mary Ring looked to godly men in the community to provide male authority. Among both Indians and English, each family member embodied his or her identity, duties, and interpersonal relations in particular ways. Colonial authors paid special attention to four aspects of Indians' domestic life—household dwellings, family organization and relations, sleeping arrangements, and foodways—suggesting the importance of these for the English and their understandings of how godly modesty and civility should be practiced in the home. Viewing colonial and colonized bodies in their domesticated aspects reveals a growing sense of individualism and privatization of the self over the course of the seventeenth century in Plymouth.

"Artists in Building and Finishing": Domestic Dwellings

A family's dwelling in Plymouth Colony, whether Indian or English, was the center of human activity and cultural production. As James Deetz noted, "People are conceived, are born, and die in houses. . . . The form of a house can be a strong reflection of the needs and minds of those who built it; in addition, it shapes and directs their behavior."[14] Like clothing did for its wearer, the shape, size, layout, and sensory qualities (such as lighting, temperature, and odors) of domestic spaces molded inhabitants' embodied knowledges (to use Robert Orsi's term), experiences, and behaviors, which reflected social values. Both native and English dwellings provided basic protection from the elements, but beyond that they demonstrated a range of cultural meanings and generated a spectrum of sensory experiences, activities, and forms of family organization. The two converged, in some ways, in praying Indians' homes; Massachusetts missionaries' expectations for reshaping Indian lives through altered domestic environments illustrate what it meant for bodies, both Indian and English, to be domesticated, "civilized," and thus Christianized, while Plymouth missionaries seemed less concerned with civilizing the Indians in order to convert them.

Edward Winslow described his first sight of traditional Indian dwellings—*wetu*s, or wigwams—in 1620:

> The houses were made with young sapling trees, bended and both ends stuck into the ground. They were made round, like unto an arbor, and covered down to the ground with thick and well wrought mats, and the door was not over a yard high, made of a mat to open. The chimney was a wide open hole in the top, for which they had a mat to cover it close when they pleased. One might stand and go upright in them. In the midst of them were four little trunches [stakes] knocked into the ground, and small sticks laid over, on which they hung their pots, and what they had to seethe [boil]. . . . The houses were double matted, for as they were matted without, so were they within, with newer and fairer mats.[15]

William Wood noted that the mats covering a wetu were so tightly woven that they "deny entrance to any drop of rain . . . neither can the piercing north wind find a cranny through which he can convey his cooling breath." In fact, Wood believed, Indian wetus were "warmer than our English houses"; Gookin found them "as warm as the best English houses." The open central fire, however, often produced "such smokey dwellings that when there is good fires they are not able to stand upright, but lie all along under the smoke, never using any stools or chairs, it being as rare to see an Indian sit on a stool at home as it is strange to see an Englishman sit on his heels abroad." Wigwams had no internal walls partitioning domestic space into rooms for specific uses, and they were lightweight and transportable, summer homes being smaller than winter homes. In the summer "families [are] dispersed by reason of heat and occasions." In the winter extended families lived together in larger dwellings, fifty to sixty or even 100 feet long by thirty feet wide, in which "forty or fifty men [are] inmates under one roof," with two to four fires at intervals inside. Rounded walls with no corners or internal partitions enclosed families and larger groups around the central hearth in a way that created a sense of intimacy—the self identified as a member of a larger familial body rather than as an independent individual—while the impermanence of the dwelling generated a sense of connectedness with the larger community and the natural environment.[16]

Although Wood and Gookin both thought Indian dwellings were cleverly constructed and Gookin found them comfortable for lodging during his overnight visits in native homes, such domestic spaces were vastly different from those they considered appropriate for "civilized" bodies. The dense smokiness and lack of technology for supporting one's body off the ground reflected Indians' lack of civility—Indian bodies squatted closer to the earth than did English bodies, raised up on chairs or stools. And colonists viewed the impermanence of native houses, which allowed Indian populations to follow migratory game patterns and changes in the growing season, as a significant characteristic of Indian "savagery." Such an "unfixed, confused, and ungoverned a life, uncivilized and unsubdued to labor and order" had to be altered for Indians to become "settled," civilized, and Christianized.[17] Missionaries expected those Indians who hoped to convert to Christianity to pursue lives embodying English practices as closely as possible; the foundation of that life was "fixed cohabitation," that is, living in permanent houses arranged on an Anglicized, gridded town plan populated exclusively by praying Indians.[18] In Massachusetts they directed Indians who chose to live in "praying towns" to build houses "after the English form." However, native converts discovered that English homes were less comfortable than their wetus, "not so warm," and more expensive to build, requiring lumber, nails, and other specialized materials. Despite the expectation that they were to dwell permanently in one location, planting kitchen gardens enclosed by fences and establishing other elements of civilized domestic life, Plymouth's praying Indians continued to live in wigwams and likely continued to move their portable dwellings regularly in order "to avoid annoyance by fleas" as did some at Natick in the Bay Colony. As well, Gookin acknowledged, Indians carried an embodied knowledge of wetu construction, for they were "generally artists in building and finishing their own wigwams," a sense they apparently did not have for English forms of building.[19]

Within their wetus, however, some praying Indians in Massachusetts and perhaps in Plymouth organized domestic space in ways that reflected the growing English privatization of individual bodies and their activities. They built their wigwams larger in order "that they may have their partitions in them for husbands and wives togeather, and their children and

servants in their places also, who formerly were never private in what nature is ashamed of, either for the sun or any man to see."[20] Massachusetts
minister Thomas Shepard viewed this Anglicized wigwam as the intermediary structure between a traditional native dwelling and the square English
home with permanently walled rooms. Partitions helped to segregate activities, especially those it would be "shameful" for others to observe (like
husband-wife sexual relations), and to differentiate familial roles according
to gender, age, and status, as in English dwellings. "A place for everyone,
and everyone in his or her place," John Holstun has noted; "this is the
[missionaries'] spatial ideal ruling distribution of bodies."[21] The remaking
of praying Indians' embodied sense of domestic space reflected a sense with
which English colonists were already viscerally familiar, or at least to which
they aspired. In fact, colonists' homes were more similar to Indian dwellings than they were to modern domestic spaces.

Plymouth's earliest permanent dwellings, like that of Mary Ring, were
simple single-cell (one-room) woodframe "cottages," as Bradford called
them, approximately sixteen- to twenty-foot-square buildings each with a
large open stone fireplace dominating one wall and a packed earthen floor.
One-room dwellings sometimes had a small loft, reached by a ladder or
steep, narrow staircase, above half or more of the lower room that the family used for storing seed corn, books, and farm supplies and sometimes for
sleeping. Throughout the seventeenth century some families continued to
live in one-room homes, while most eventually lived in two-celled "hall and
parlor" structures with a central, double-sided fireplace in the partitioning
wall. These larger homes typically began as single-cell homes, with rooms
added as the family's economic situation allowed.[22] New England's two-
room woodframe houses with a central fireplace and chimney contrasted to
Chesapeake Bay–area brick homes with fireplaces and tall chimneys at either end of the house. By the second half of the seventeenth century many
New Englanders had the economic resources to build more ostentatious
brick homes with several prominent chimneys as did Virginia's Anglicans,
but they apparently believed that a wood frame and siding with a single
central chimney, even if this "simpler," more rustic house were larger and
more expensive to build than a brick Chesapeake-style house, demonstrated
their guiding principle of modesty and plainness.[23] Home architecture
shaped and directed its inhabitants' sensory experiences and behavior; as a
physical extension of the male householder—the family's "governor"—it
also intentionally displayed the family's godliness, wealth, and social status.
Moreover, Robert Blair St. George argues, a New England house, like the

little commonwealth it contained, explicitly corresponded to both human body and social body: its timbers were the skeleton, wooden siding the skin, the fireplace its heart. All "functioned as signs of Christ's perfect body as a model of a 'loving' social order." As a human face, which reflected the divine image, had eyes, mouth, and nose, the countenance of a good house had "well-placed" windows and door. Like a modest human body, a godly home was "dressed" and "ornamented" in plain fashion; it was the wife's duty to "order the decking and trimming of the house," Gouge explained. But she must do so with "honest thriftinesse, or frugalitie," warned Cleaver and Dod, rather than "prank[ing] up . . . her house, and chambers in brau-eries [ostentatious display]." As a person fashioned his or her public image with clothing, so did the outward appearance of one's house contribute to public self-fashioning.[24]

This modest "organic house form" typically was solidly square or, with additions, rectangular, distinguishing it from Indians' round wigwams. In New England, with its seemingly limitless resources, particularly stone and wood, colonists theoretically were free to construct any form of dwelling of which they were technologically capable. However, Deetz has specu-lated that "each builder carried with him . . . an unconscious, implicit" sense—that is, an embodied knowledge—of the "fundamental unit" of spatial dimension "in which an Anglo-American feels most comfortable": the square. Colonists enlarged their square houses with square additions. The missionaries' impulse to replace roundness with squareness in Indian homes in the Bay Colony reflected this sense that a civilized space had equal-length sides and four corners and was firmly rooted in the ground. Colonists apparently felt the greatest sensory and psychological comfort in solid, small, square, dim domestic spaces. When Bradford's assistant Isaac Allerton and his second wife Fear, daughter of William Brewster, and their five children moved three miles outside of New Plymouth in 1629, he built an almost-square (twenty by twenty-two feet) one-room dwell-ing with a fireplace in one wall, similar to the first building erected at Ply-mouth, the communal storehouse. In such homes window openings were few in number—single-cell homes had only one or two windows—and small in size, generally one or two feet square. They were either unglazed with wooden shutters that completely blocked the light when closed or covered with linseed-oiled paper or cloth that allowed only filtered light into the room. Some colonists later imported expensive leaded glass panes from England, which improved interior lighting and displayed elevated so-cial status. Artificial lighting—candles or small pottery oil lamps like those

Mary Ring owned—provided poor illumination, so even during daylight hours the corners of rooms were cast in shadow. The fireplace with chimney produced less smoky interiors than those of wigwams and allowed for the construction of an upper loft, but it did not heat the room as efficiently as central open fires did in Indian dwellings. During the winter ink could freeze in inkwells as one was writing, and inhabitants clustered around the hearth for warmth and light.[25]

In spite of Gookin's complaints regarding the lack of privacy in an Indian wetu, colonists' one-room dwellings were no different. All domestic activities, including those associated with basic body functions (eating, elimination, sleeping, sexual relations, birth, and death) as well as social and work-related activities (entertaining guests, preparing food, sewing clothing, repairing farm equipment, reading books, and writing letters) took place in one small, unpartitioned space. Even in two-celled homes personal privacy was minimal and rooms "cluttered" with the diverse, specialized implements considered necessary for civilized life: cooking, eating, and other food processing equipment; furniture for sleeping and storage; craft tools for spinning, weaving, woodworking; and hunting, fishing, and farm equipment.[26] Native domestic spaces also were filled with various household implements. Winslow described the first wigwam interior he encountered:

> Round about the fire [were] mats, which are their beds. . . . In the houses we found wooden bowls, trays and dishes, earthen pots, handbaskets made of crabshells wrought together, also an English pail or bucket; it wanted a bail, but it had two iron ears. There was also baskets of sundry sorts, bigger and some lesser, finer and some coarser; some were curiously wrought with black and white in pretty works, and sundry other of their household stuff. . . . There was also a company of deer's feet stuck up in the houses, harts' horns, and eagles' claws, and sundry such like things there was, also two or three baskets full of parched acorns, pieces of fish, and a piece of a broiled herring. We found also a little silk grass, and a little tobacco seed, with some other seeds which we knew not.[27]

Nevertheless, Gookin believed that natives' "household stuff is but little and mean"; Indians used one kind of item for several purposes, such as woven rush mats "for covering their houses and doors, and to sleep and sit upon." There was less distinctiveness, to English eyes, among various native implements and their uses, which colonists believed indicated a generally less differentiated and thus less civilized domestic culture.[28]

Colonists' dwellings were filled with furniture, equipment, and other goods—and people. Mary Ring's family was small compared to the majority of those living in one- and two-room houses; Plymouth families averaged nine members plus servants, apprentices, or, occasionally, extended family members. In spaces typically four to eight hundred square feet in size, crowded with bedsteads, storage chests, a table, and one or more chairs, as well as all the tools needed for survival, several people lived out the most intimate details of their lives within sight and sound of each other. In the 1640s James and Mary Lindale lived with their children in a two-room house in Duxbury. The "fire room" with the open hearth contained pieces of farming and hunting equipment, cooking, eating, and other domestic implements, a Bible and some other books, and three chairs and a table. The chamber contained four beds, bedding and other household linen, clothing, a table, two chests, four bushels of corn, and thirty-three pounds of whalebone. During the mid-1600s Thomas and Jane Gilbert raised a family of three children in a one-room house in Taunton that contained two beds, three chests, four chairs, a table board and two stools, and all the implements of domestic life.[29] Tasks flowed into each other, as a mother perched upon a stool, nursed her infant, rocked another youngster in the cradle with her foot, and tended the cooking pot at the hearth. Nearby her husband sat in what might have been the family's only chair and repaired a harness, explained the details of beer-making to his apprentice, or read the Bible aloud to his family. Older children played, washed dishes, cut out pieces of wool for clothing, or oiled a firearm. The dimly lit space was filled with artifacts, sounds of talking and laughter or an infant's crying, and the smells of cooking food, hot candle wax or lamp oil, and body odors. To modern sensibilities it might have generated an oppressive sense of confinement and confusion. But colonists carried a vastly different embodied sense of comfort and safety and a vastly "different way of ordering the physical world." Richard L. Bushman notes, "There seems to have been no sense of shame or undue confinement associated with the one-room house."[30]

Not all Plymouth homes were so small, of course, and over time some became larger—perhaps three square rooms in a "long-house" style, like Myles Standish's fifteen-by-sixty-foot home in Duxbury, with a root cellar, an upper loft, and lean-to built onto the back for cooking. John and Priscilla Alden also built their much smaller ten-by-forty-foot dwelling in the long-house style when they moved to Duxbury around 1630; in it they raised ten children. When former Governor Bradford's wife Alice died in 1670/1, her home in New Plymouth was unusually large, with seven rooms, whose names indicated they had been added onto the house over the years: "the New Parlour Chamber," in which was a bed, chairs, stools, a table, and a carved chest; "the outward Parlour Chamber" with a curtained bed; "the old parlour Chamber," which appears to have been for servant sleeping and for storage; "the studdy," with its dozens of books; "the old Parlour," which appears to have been the primary living space with its two beds, cupboards containing eating utensils, linens, and clothing, a table, stools and chairs, and a desk; "the great Parlour" for entertaining, with six "great Chaires," a table and "form" (bench), cushions, and plates, glasses, and knives; and the kitchen, with a plethora of cooking and eating implements, including four dozen trenchers, as well as a spinning wheel and two beer barrels.[31] Colonial dwellings demonstrated a continuum of civility; wealthier families could build homes that were larger and lighter, allowing opportunities for more individual privacy and such civilized pursuits as reading, writing, and entertaining, and filled with a greater variety of useful and decorative artifacts. Poorer families lived in smaller, darker, earthen floored, one-room homes, without window glazing and with little artificial lighting and fewer and cruder furnishings and tools, something like Indian families who lived in small, smoky dwellings with simple domestic implements. When very poor William Zoanes of Scituate died in 1671 he owned no furniture or even a bed, only some iron, brass, and pewter cooking implements, a "hetchell" for combing flax, and bedding.[32] The bodies inhabiting each home were shaped by its size and visual clarity and by the diversity and number of objects it contained; each family member experienced and reflected the dwelling's social rank and level of godly civility or heathen savagery. For most Plymouth families, Indian and English, the close contact with others' bodies and activities, even in larger homes, apparently produced a sense of comforting reassurance and connectedness. However, the unrelenting physical closeness of a disliked spouse or other family member might generate tense discomfort and conflicts.

"Pruned, Erected, Ordered, and Watered": Family Roles and Relationships

Although the ideal was for family members to work out their disagreements privately, serious conflicts could end up in court. In 1654/5 Joane Miller of Taunton was presented in the Plymouth General Court "for beating and reviling her husband [Obadiah], and egging her children to healp her, bid[d]ing them knock him in the head, and wishing his victuals might choake him." At the same court, John Pecke of Rehoboth was fined for attempting for many years to have sex with his father's maidservant "to satisfy his fleshly, beastly lust . . . without any intent to marry her." An extended family appeared in court in early 1662; the court officers severely reproved Sandwich's George Barlow and his wife "for theire most vngodly liueing in contension one with the other, and admonished [them] to liue otherwise." George's daughters-in-law, Anna, Dorcas, and Mary, were convicted of "crewell and vnaturall practice" toward their father-in-law, which had degenerated into physical violence: Anna had "chopped" George in the back. The following year John Dunhame was presented for "abusiue and unciuil carriage towards his wife" in continually "tyrannizing" over her, especially attempting to beat her in a "debased" manner. Dunhame had even drawn a sword and threatened to take his own life in front of her. The court sentenced him to be whipped, but his wife begged the court's mercy so it simply fined him the huge sum of twenty pounds, admonished him to "reform his former abusiue carriage towards her both in word and deed," and warned it would be taking notice of his behavior in the future.[33] Such incidents are dramatic examples of how familial relationships could become physically abusive, as family members took out their frustrations or attempted to alter each others' attitudes and behaviors within the home. That few such cases ended up in court does not mean that few families experienced difficulties within their domestic lives but only that they were able to resolve their conflicts without the aid of civil authorities. Perhaps many, if not most, families generally lived together in godly "peace and love," as the court admonished them to do. The court cases, however, expose the ways family tensions might erupt in gendered and generational conflicts that Plymouth's saints hoped to avoid by following the clearly defined ideals of godly family government detailed in household manuals.

John Robinson had proclaimed, "God hath ordained marriage . . . for the benefit of man's natural and spiritual life, in an individual society . . . between one man and one woman."[34] Within the domestic space of the household individuals' bodies and souls were shaped and molded, nurtured and disciplined, "bred and brought up," wrote Gouge, "and out of families are they sent into the Church and common-wealth." To produce well-formed citizens the family was structured, or "ordered," in three interrelated, homologous hierarchies: the husband was over the wife; together they were parents over their children and master and mistress over their servants. As the institution of the family corresponded to other social institutions, the hierarchical relationship between husband and wife corresponded to that between Christ and his body, the church: the husband was the wife's head and she was his body, together they were "one flesh." Thus, he must love her "as his owne flesh" and "gouerne her in all duties" as the head guides the body; she, in turn, must "submit and subiect" herself to him, as the body must obey the head's directions. The husband and father carried ultimate authority and responsibility in the family, which was like a physiological body made ill by humoral imbalance: "When the head is well and sound, and also the stomacke pure from hurtfull humours, the bodie is commonly well affected." Likewise, when the head of the family faithfully feared God, all was right within the household. However, when its head was "empty" due to "idle-mindednesse, and carelesse letting passe of matters," the family went astray.[35] As members of a church closely observed each other for signs of sin, husbands and wives were to "watch ouer the manners and behauiour" of their children and servants for any indication they were shirking their duties or falling into immorality. According to nonconformists' theology of the body and visible sainthood, the goal of domestic corporeal care and discipline was "to shape and frame the soule vnto virtue." Although "the soule is more precious then the body," a family member's body was the mediator between his or her soul and other members. Authors of household manuals forefronted the body and its senses as the media through which husbands, wives, children, and servants accessed and shaped their own and others' minds and hearts and by which—in facial, gestural, vocal, and other physical expressions—one's inner thoughts, attitudes, and feelings became visible.[36]

Like the wife to her husband, children were to submit "dutifully" and with "reverent love" to both parents, and servants were to obey their masters and mistresses. Parents, in return, had specific corporeal "duties" toward their children: to govern them well by loving them, providing for their "bodily" needs, and disciplining them with speech and the rod when necessary but without "too much austeritie and seueritie." Likewise, masters and mistresses must provide their servants with appropriate lodging, food, clothing, recreation, and rest, keep them on task, and correct them as needed with corporal discipline, but not unmercifully. The Plymouth General Court attempted to ensure that masters treated their servants properly. In 1655, for example, John Hall of Yarmouth accused Francis Baker of kicking and "vnreasonably stricking" Hall's son Samuel, whom he had placed as a servant with Baker. The court allowed Samuel to return to his father. In June of 1657 young Joseph Gray of Taunton complained that he was being ill used by his master, Thomas Gilbert Jr. Gilbert had not provided

Gray with winter clothing, and the boy's foot had frozen, making him lame. The court ordered that Gilbert provide Gray with competent clothing, especially shoes and stockings, and take "some speedy course . . . for the curing of the boyes foot, being in danger of perishing." But the court also admonished Gray to "carry towards his mistris as a seruant ought to doe, with all due respect and obedience."[37] More gruesome ongoing abuse culminated on January 15, 1654/5, in Marshfield, when fourteen-year-old servant John Walker died due to exposure and being forced to carry a heavy log, which fell on him, when he was lame and weak from lack of adequate food and clothing and regular whippings by his master and mistress, Robert and Susanna Latham. Walker's body was black and blue all over, his hands and feet were frozen, there were three deep festering sores in his buttocks, his nose was bleeding, and perhaps saddest of all, he had "constantly wett his bedd and his cloathes, lying in them, and soe [he] suffered by it, his clothes being frozen about him." The court found Latham guilty of manslaughter but he begged for mercy, which the court granted, and instead of execution Latham was burned (branded) in the hand and all of his goods confiscated.[38]

With principles of civil, godly family life in mind, Winslow and others observed the ways Indians formed their families and embodied familial relations, recording far more information about natives' domestic lives than about colonists'. But the things colonists noticed about Indians revealed the categories of family life the English considered fundamental and universal: gender roles, marital relations, and childrearing. Like the English, Indian men and women formed marital alliances, and a sachem, Winslow noted, only married a woman who was "equal to him in birth," also one of the directives English household manuals gave for selecting a spouse.[39] Manuals mentioned the need for potential spouses' "meetness," that is, to have similar "riches in temporall substance," such as estates and education, and "riches of the mind," or proper religious convictions and their corresponding inward virtues (soberness, chastity, humility, honesty, frugality, and so on). However, they discussed far more "riches of the body," for the temporal and mental riches were disclosed and confirmed by the visible and audible characteristics of potential spouses: "lookes" (the face, especially the eyes, which were "the glasses of the mind"), speech, apparel, manners, age, sexual potency, and physical health.[40] For example, "the outward composition of the countenance doth soonest and best declare the inward disposition of the heart"; as "godlinesse is in the face of a man or of a woman," so "follie and wickenesse may many times be seene and discerned by the face." Thus, a husband's face should be amiable, pleasant, and gracious, rather than exhibiting a "loftie proud countenance," a "grim sterne countenance," a "fierce fiery countenance," or "a frowning and lowring face, by hanging downe the head, putting out the lips, with the like," for such visible expressions exposed the "anger, malice, griefe, with other like affections of heart." When a wife beheld "mildnesse and amiablenesse in her husbands face," she beheld "it as the face of God, and therein as in a looking glasse beholds the kindnesse and loue of his heart." Furthermore, a person's inner characteristics could not be determined by meeting him or her only three or four times; thus, potential spouses needed to see each other "eating, and walking, working, and playing, talking and laughing, and chiding too" over a period of time in order to come to know the other's true nature before marrying.[41]

Native people may have followed somewhat similar methods for selecting a spouse, and both the Indians and English disdained incest and adultery. There were also important differences in marital patterns, however, such as the Indians' apparent freedom to engage in premarital sexual relations and a sachem's freedom to marry more than one wife as a marker of status. Godly household manuals condemned both of these and the Plymouth General Court criminalized such actions. Colonists wrote little about the Indians' marital sex; it likely occurred discreetly in the wetu while other family members were present but sleeping. James Rosier reported that native men "lie with their wives secretly," but did not elaborate on when or where.[42] Because most colonial families also lived in one- or two-room dwellings, most English husbands and wives likely pursued their sexual activities as openly or as discreetly as did Indians. In a godly marriage husband and wife became "one flesh" in both mind and body, explained Cleaver and Dod; it was both their mutual duty and their delight to perform "that neare coniunction . . . in regard of their bodies." During sex the husband conceded "power ouer his owne body" to his wife. He, in turn, "used" her body, not only for pleasure but to "possess . . . her will and affections" also.[43] As in all behavior, a godly husband and wife enjoyed their sex life in moderation—neither too little nor too much—to nurture mutual love and hopefully, but not necessarily, produce children. Spouses should not regularly avoid sexual relations, as did John Williams Jr. of Scituate whose wife Elizabeth repeatedly took him to court for "sequestration of himselfe from the marriage bed" and his "insufficiency for converse [sexual relations] with weomen," as well as his "abusiue and harsh carriages towards her both in words and actions" in 1665.[44] But neither should they express "immoderate, intemperate, or excessiue lust" for each other. "As a man may surfeit at his own table or be drunken with his own drink," warned Robinson, "so may he play the adulterer with his own wife, both by inordinate affection and action." Although the "marriage bed cover[s] much inordinateness this way: yet must modesty be observed by the married."[45]

One indicator of marital modesty was the avoidance of sexual relations while the wife was menstruating. Winslow noted that Indians took it a step further: during a woman's menstrual period "she separateth herself from all other company, and liveth certain days in a house alone; after which, she washeth herself, and all that she hath touched or used, and is again received to her husband's bed or family." Indians believed that while a woman was bleeding, Ann Marie Plane explains, she was embodying "special powers which could effect good or ill," and her isolation from the rest of the community regulated and contained those powers. Using menstrual huts also allowed Indian women a reprieve from their domestic duties and, perhaps, an opportunity to socialize with other menstruating women in the ritual wetu. The English did not require menstruating women to sequester themselves from the home, and praying Indians who wanted to reproduce a "civil" English lifestyle as closely as possible forbade the use of menstrual huts in 1648, abolishing "the old Ceremony of the Maide walking alone and living apart so many dayes." Housewives should not enjoy such monthly periods of rest from their labors, for a godly lifestyle required ongoing, diligent attention to one's duties.[46]

Although English women did not leave the home during their monthly periods, godly husbands and wives were not to engage in sexual relations while the woman was menstruating; Gouge believed that marital sex during this period was a "polluted copulation," and Cleaver and Dod likewise forbade it. Authors based their views on two sources: biblical injunctions, which prohibited a man lying with a menstruating woman because she was "unclean" and anything she touched became polluted, and humoral medical texts, which described menstruation as a means for women to expel bodily impurities (men sweated to purify the blood) and discharge the natural excess of blood in female bodies. Menstruation ceased during pregnancy because the mother's body diverted the excess blood to the fetus to nourish it.[47] After childbirth God converted the mother's blood into milk and "bringeth it into the breasts furnished with nipples." This made it "conuenient to minister the warme milke vnto the child," whom God endowed with "industrie to draw out the milke." Indeed, breastfeeding was a woman's primary duty to God, husband, and children, and Roger Williams praised native women for "keep[ing] their children long at the breast," often for over a year. Apparently many mothers in England, although probably not in Plymouth, placed their infants with wet nurses, which was "both against the law of nature, and also against the will of God." Moreover, explained Gouge, not breastfeeding one's own infant was "hurtfull both for the childs body, and also for his wit," for "with the milke passeth some smacke of the affection and disposition of the mother"; infants, as Cleaver and Dod noted and Robinson also believed, "suck in godlinesse together with their mothers milke." God gave a woman "two breasts" to "employ . . . in the seruice of God, and to be a helpe to her husband in suckling the child common to them both." A mother who refused to perform this duty revealed an egregious lack of gratitude to God.[48]

Such unthankfulness and a fear that nursing might wrinkle the skin revealed pride, a woman's "natural" vice. A godly wife, in contrast, embodied modesty, for she taught her children by example and demonstrated her love for her husband through subjection—helping and obeying him. A wife shaped her "countenance, gesture, and whole cariage before her husband" with modesty in order to be pleasing to him and express her contented willingness to be ruled by him. Her face and body should not display "a frowning brow, a lowring eie, a sullen looke, a powting lip, a swelling face, a deriding mouth, a scornefull cast of the armes and hands, a disdainfull turning of this side and that side of the body, and a fretfull flinging out of her husbands presence." Her apparel should be plain rather than proud, costly, or "light and garish"; her hairstyle should be simple, rather than "plaited, cri[m]ped, broyded, curled, and curiously laid out"; and her spoken "words must be few, reuerend and meeke," rather than "loquacities, talkatiuenesse, [or] ouer-much tatling."[49] This widespread emphasis on female modesty led Winslow and others to notice and comment on whether Indian women embodied this virtue. Some were so "modest, as they will scarce talk one with another in the company of men, being very chaste also," yet others were "light, lascivious and wanton"—"common strumpets" just like some English women. Wood exclaimed that Indian women's "carriage it is very civil": "These women's modesty drives them to wear more clothes than their men, having always a coat of cloth or skins wrapped like a blanket about their loins, reaching down to their hams, which they never put off in company." Winslow observed such modesty in 1621, when he visited an Indian village and the women removed the furs they were wearing to sell them to the colonists. The women immediately replaced their fur coats with boughs, which they tied around their bodies "with great shamefacedness (for indeed they are more modest than some of our English women are)." Women's breasts, proclaimed Cleaver and Dod, were for nursing their infants in the service of God and their husbands, not for "show" or "ostentation." Apparently not all native women modestly covered their breasts, however, for the praying Indians' civil code prohibited them "go[ing] with naked breasts."[50]

Winslow believed Indian women "live a most slavish life," for they performed the domestic and agricultural labor (which was a man's job according to colonists) for the family and community. Apparently native men had little to do with domestic life, for they "employ themselves wholly in hunting, and other exercises of the bow, except at some times they take some pains in fishing"; they also led and participated in religious ceremonies and negotiated with colonial authorities.[51] Native men, in fact, sounded something like Cleaver and Dod's description of the godly husband as "Lord of all": his duties were to travel abroad, "deale with many men," and "be skilfull in talke" in order to acquire money and goods. The wife's duties were within the home where she oversaw and ordered all things, saving the money and goods her husband provided and avoiding conversations with men. But such apparently separate spheres certainly did not constrain many Plymouth women, such as Mary Ring, and in most Plymouth households the home was as much a man's sphere as it was a woman's, where husband and wife labored together for the family's physical survival and godly upbringing.[52]

Household manuals' childrearing techniques echoed John Robinson's when they explained how parents trained their children's souls, especially their wills, by training their bodies. As a godly mother shaped her infant's body by tightly swaddling it to "lay their lim[b]s right, each in his place," she "shape[d] and frame[d] [the child's] soul vnto virtue." As children grew, parents physically repressed their natural willfulness through moderate diet, modest clothing, and verbal and corporal discipline. To generate humoral balance and moral godliness, parents must not "pamper children with too much meate or that which is delicate, but . . . giue them that which is wholesome and sufficient, and no more." Excess bred both physical and mental disease and led to "a thousand more" vices. Parents also must not adorn their children with "costly apparel" or "new fashions," for it stirred up pride and "youthful nature will soone be inflamed with this vice." Finally, parents must discipline their children, first verbally by "chiding and reprehension" then, if words proved ineffective, physically with "the rod," for "great is the godlinesse in that seueritie by which the power of sinning is taken away." But striking a child was "a strong and bitter pill" that must only be used as a last resort, for, household manuals recognized, it could cause a child to become either sad and discouraged or angry and obstinate.[53]

Though a child's "body be but small," said Cleaver and Dod, his heart was "great" and inclined to evil, therefore parents must teach him virtue and a godly life. Some colonists believed Indians "spoiled" their children with overmuch tenderness, but both native and English parents taught their children to revere their superiors: "The younger [Indians] reverence the elder," noted Winslow, "and do all mean offices, whilst they be together, although they be strangers."[54] Likewise, godly children should "frame their gestures" in ways that expressed the reverent love they felt toward their elders by demonstrating "a certaine honest and modest shamefa[ced]ness" through good manners. They should remain silent before their elders and "use faire speech" when they did speak; they should stand, remove their hats, and bow or curtsey in the presence of their superiors; and they should treat their peers with courtesy and their inferiors with gentleness. All should be done with the proper attitude, or "active obedience," that is, sincerely, cheerfully, thankfully, and "without murmuring or grudging." Simultaneously performing these outward and inward "duties" fused body and soul, behavior and intentions, eventually producing an adult man or woman who felt a deep submission to God's authoritative will and who knew his or her place in society and how to embody that role properly: like plants, "they that are pruned, erected, ordered, and watered . . . are made straight, fertile and fruitfull."[55]

It is impossible to determine how closely Plymouth's saints and other colonists followed household manuals' prescriptions, but colonial leaders certainly were concerned that contentious families like those that ended up in court learn to live together in domestic harmony. Most court cases of familial discord revolved around marital sexual tensions: adultery or a lack of ability to perform. In June of 1686, for example, two extreme cases of sexual discord came to court. The first was brought by John Glover of Barnstable, who requested a divorce from his wife Mary, who, he claimed, had "violated the marriage covenant by entertaining some other man or men into bed fellowship with her," which resulted in Mary infecting John with "the pox, to his great sorrow and paine." The court granted John's petition. The second case was more extenuated and resulted in a unique resolution regarding the couple's physical living situation within their home.

Dorothy Clarke of New Plymouth was summoned to court for leaving her husband Nathaniel and taking with her some "money, rings, & treasure" without his consent. She brought the goods to court with her, as well as a petition for divorce, stating, "Mr Nathaniel Clarke hath not performed the duty of a husband to me, for he is misformed, and is always unable to perform the act of generation." Nathaniel's alleged inability to perform sexually, according to Dorothy, caused their "lives [to be] very uncomfortable in the sight of God." Nathaniel denied his wife's accusation that he "(by reason of some deformity or infirmity of body, as she saith,) is uncapable to performe the conjugall duty of an husband towards her." The court ordered "that his body be viewed by some persons skilfull and judicious," and Nathaniel "showed himself" to three physicians, who determined his genitalia were not malformed and did function properly. Officers denied Dorothy's petition for a divorce; indeed, they ordered her to remain living in her husband's house, though they recognized "an uncomfortable difference" between the two and feared "least they should ruine each other in their estates." The court hoped to solve the problem by granting Dorothy, if she wished, the "liberty to live in part of the said house to the quantity of half"; Nathaniel was to live in the other half of their home.[56]

Apparently the arrangement satisfied both Elizabeth and Nathaniel, for she never again took him to court for impotence. But their marital woes, like those of John and Elizabeth Williams, demonstrate the importance of one's body being able to perform sexually, so that a husband and wife might comfortably live together in godly union. For any husband and wife, however, achieving sexual compatibility might be complicated by the lack of privacy in a one- or two-room home containing several family members. Despite the apparent rigors of godly domestic life propounded by household manuals, colonists increasingly wanted privacy and bodily comfort while in bed.

"Lightheaded for Want of Sleep": Beds and Bedding

While the first generation of Plymouth families typically built and lived in small one-room homes, most established colonists eventually replaced or added onto their dwellings to live in two-room hall-and-parlor houses, with a cramped upstairs loft for storage and sleeping space for servants and children. The hall was used primarily for cooking and other domestic and work related activities, but also sleeping; parents and their youngest children slept in the status-invested parlor, or chamber, where homeowners displayed their most valuable objects (finer furniture, books, silver and pewter, ceramics) and entertained.[57] It seems likely the Clarkes lived in a two-room home, for the court's concern about protecting their individual estates led it to assign one-half of the house to each. Nathaniel probably took over the parlor, which "literally represented the household's material wealth, a husband's legal prerogative," and Elizabeth the hall, "where domestic work took place—the women's realm." Creating a sleeping chamber separate from the hall, "first for parents and then for others," Bushman notes, "was the most significant alteration in ordinary houses . . . before 1660." Jack Goody, likewise, argues that the early modern "privatisation [of the self] is most marked in changes in sleeping arrangements."[58] The partitioning of living spaces in both English and Indian dwellings demonstrated this increasing privatization of sleeping bodies.

Although by modern standards colonists' sleeping arrangements throughout the seventeenth century were hardly private, they strove to segregate bodies according to age and status. Parents with some means might sleep in the parlor or chamber in a bed on a bedstead with curtains to provide some privacy, with an infant in bed with them or in a cradle nearby, convenient for breastfeeding, and young children in a trundle bed on the floor. Older children, servants, and extended family members might sleep in the hall or the loft, sharing pallets or small flock beds on the floor or perhaps on a simple bed frame or in a built-in settle bed. Josiah Winslow, brother of Edward, and his wife Margaret raised their five children, for example, in a two-room house in Marshfield that had one bedstead, a trundle bed, and a settle bed in one room for the older children and one bed with valance and curtains, in which Edward and Margaret likely slept, in the kitchen. William and Tamasin Lumpkin of Yarmouth raised their three daughters in a three-room house that had one bed and bedstead in the parlor, one bed and bedding in the kitchen, and one bed and bedding in the "inner room" between the parlor and the kitchen. Duxbury's Henry and Mary Howland raised eight children in a house that had one feather bed and one flock bed in the "new room" (apparently an addition to the original house), one bed in the "middle room," and three beds "above in the Chambers" (probably two lofts, one over the middle room and one over the new room). Even at the end of the seventeenth century, few people slept alone—beds were always shared: husband, wife, and infant together; older children, including teenagers and unmarried adult family members, together; and servants together, sometimes sharing a bed with the children of the household. Such arrangements could result in an infant's or young child's death through being "overlayed," or smothered by a larger bedmate. In Scituate in 1680, the six-month-old son of Thomas and Sarah Hatch was found dead in the morning, lying on his face with one side of his head and part of his body "very blacke." His parents being "absent," probably traveling, the infant had shared a bed with two women: his sister Sarah and twenty-year-old Waitstill Elmes. Both women testified that the baby had gone to sleep the evening before with a head cold. The court found that either he had smothered from lying on his face or he had been "accidentally ouer layed in the bed" by Sarah or Waitstill.[59]

An Indian or an English household's arrangement of its sleeping environments—especially whether and how it separated sleeping bodies and created bodily comfort during rest—expressed gradations of civility. When Edward Winslow and Stephen Hopkins had paid their first visit to Sowams, in the summer of 1621, Massasoit, sachem of the Wampanoags, "kindly welcomed" them. After sharing tobacco and conversation, the Englishmen "desired to go to rest." Despite the fact that it was common in England and New England for travelers to share beds, even with strangers, Winslow and Hopkins were appalled to discover that Massasoit expected them to share his bed: "He laid us on the bed with himself and his wife, they at the one end and we at the other, it being only planks laid a foot from the ground, and a thin mat upon them." To make matters worse, "two more of his chief men, for want of room, pressed by and upon us, so that we were worse weary of our lodging than of our journey." The next day Massasoit begged them to stay longer, but Winslow and Hopkins "feared that we should either be light-headed for want of sleep, for what with bad lodging, the savages' barbarous singing (for they used to sing themselves asleep), lice and fleas within doors, and mosquitoes without, we could hardly sleep all the time of our being there." Indians built sleeping platforms, raised one or two feet off the ground and six to eight feet wide, around the inside wall of the wigwam. Covered with rush mats and animal skins, the platforms were shared by various household members. "The undivided interiors of the wigwams," according to Kathleen Bragdon, "imparted a sense of sociability, even as they lay sleepy in the darkness; one, then another, would sing to themselves." However, Winslow and Hopkins likely would not have agreed with Roger Williams's assessment that two Indian families would sleep "comfortably and lovingly in a little round house."[60] The visceral experience of lying on a hard mat, Indian men's greased bodies pressed against their own, "barbarous singing," biting lice, fleas, and mosquitoes, and lack of sleep made them thoroughly aware of their discomforted bodies.

Before reaching Sowams Winslow and Hopkins had slept "in the open fields" while lodging with the Namascheuck Indians, "for houses they had none, though they spent the most of the summer there." If their wetu had been assembled, the Namascheucks surely would have invited the English in, for Indians typically were extraordinarily hospitable, often giving up their own beds to visitors and sleeping outdoors, or sharing their beds as did Massasoit. Because the central fire rendered their wigwams warmer than English homes, Indians used few "bedcloaths. And so, themselves and any that have occasion to lodge with them, must be content to turne often to the Fire, if the night be cold." Williams highlighted natives' and colonists' different cultures of sleep; in defense of natives' "hard lodgings" he argued, "Nature and Custom gives sound sleep to these Americans on the Earth, on a Boord or Mat." While Winslow experienced Indian accommodations as far less desirable than English ones, indeed as savage, Williams composed a ditty that employed the figure of hospitable Indians at sleep to criticize Englishmen's overblown notions of their own civility and godliness:

> God gives them [Indians] sleep on Ground, on Straw,
> on Sedgie Mats or Boord:
> When English softest Beds of Downe,
> sometimes no sleep affoord.

> I have knowne them leave their House and Mat
> to lodge a Friend or stranger,
> When Jewes and Christians oft have sent
> Christ Jesus to the Manger.

Williams echoed popular attitudes in England that "the soundest slumber . . . belonged to those with simple minds and callused hands," while the educated classes were "'round behem'd with cares and woes'": soft English bodies contained troubled minds and hearts lacking in godly warmth and generosity, while Indian bodies, hardened by exposure to the elements and rough bedding, slept peacefully in their Christ-like hospitality.[61]

Most English beds, meaning the stuffed bag on which one slept, in fact were not filled with the softest down, particularly early in Plymouth's history. Nevertheless, even the poorest colonist aspired to own a feather bed, a large cloth sack filled with feathers. Within a household the finest beds were reserved for parents, while children and servants (and poorer adults) slept on flock beds—bags of coarse linen stuffed with odds and ends of fabric or straw. Nathaniel and Lucy Tilden of Scituate slept themselves and seven children in five beds, three of them flock, in three rooms and two servants on two flock beds in the "servants chamber." Beds were placed directly on the floor or on bedsteads—wooden frames that varied in quality from rough wooden planks with ropes strung across to hold the bed, to bedsteads with headboards, to more elaborate hanging bedsteads, which had upper frames on which hung valances and long curtains. The latter, like feather beds, were reserved for adult members of wealthier families; curtains kept out chilly drafts and created privacy. As well, sleeping further from the ground signified higher status; thus, Winslow and Hopkins noted that Massasoit's bed planks were a foot off the ground, while they slept outdoors on the ground with the Namascheucks. The poorest colonists, who owned no feather beds or bedsteads, placed their flock beds or simple mats directly on the earthen floor. As space-savers, trundle or "truckle" bedsteads were stored underneath larger beds and pulled out for children to sleep close to the floor and a settle bed might be built into a corner of a room. Seventeenth-century bedsteads slept two or more people in a relatively small space—in Leiden, for example, the separatists' beds measured five and a half feet long by three and a half feet wide—their bodies certainly touching as they slept. On the feather or flock bed went its "furniture," or bedding. Closest to the sleeper's body were linen sheets, which usually came in pairs and gradations of quality, determining softness and comfort against the sleeper's skin: finest Holland linen, "new hempen" linen, "flaxen" linen, or "worne," "course," and "thinn" sheets. On top of the sheets went woolen blankets, "ruggs" (often dyed green or blue), and "coverlids" or coverlets. Bedding also included bolsters, which may have been used to support the head during sleep or might refer to a mattress firmer than a normal bed; down, feather, or flock pillows; and "pillowbeeres" or "pillow coates," that is, pillow cases usually matching the sheets' grade of linen.[62]

From the varieties of bedsteads, beds, and bedding in Plymouth probate inventories, it is apparent that most Plymouth colonists took their sleeping environments seriously and, if they followed Cleaver and Dod's directives, further prepared themselves for comfortable sleeping with bedtime prayers: "For seeing that it is Gods good hand ouer vs, that doth defend vs and all our familie in the night from outward dangers, and giueth vs freedome from feares and terrors, and from Sathans rage, and also giueth vs rest & comfortable sleepe, for the refreshing of our fraile bodies, is it not meete we should begge it at his hand by prayer, before we prepare our selues to rest, and praise him for it when we rise from it?"[63] Although the poorest colonists slept on the meanest of flock beds laid directly on the earthen floors of their dwellings, many rested their "fraile bodies" on soft beds and pillows with smooth, clean linen sheets. Beds and bedding, John E. Crowley explains, "provided psychological and physical satisfactions: they asserted status, displayed wealth, and provided protection from the elements." Their houses colder than Indians' dwellings, in the winter colonists' bodies during sleep were enclosed and weighted down by heavy woolen blankets, rugs, and coverlets; between the sheets a housewife might slip a covered warming pan filled with hot coals to heat the bed before entering it, as did Mary Ring. Like distinctions in dress, the privacy, height, comfort, warmth, and smoothness of the bed in which one slept signified one's status in the family. But bedding's "display of fabrics" also "crucially communicated status" and civility to the larger community as well, for householders received guests and entertained in the parlor, using the bed as a place to sit or recline and discuss business or community affairs.[64]

Beds and bedding were standard items in a woman's dowry and typically moved with her from one home to the next. Mary Ring may have brought a feather bed and bedstead with her from Leiden that she gave to one of her daughters when Susanna or Elizabeth married, explaining why when Mary died she had a "new bed & bolster" for which she had feathers that were not yet "put in it" and no bedstead. The extraordinarily wealthy Governor Thomas Prence's fifteen-hundred-pound estate in 1673 separately listed the items brought by his wife to their marriage. Among a wide variety of household goods, including cooking and eating utensils, chairs, chests, scales, a "smoothing Iron," and candlesticks, the most valuable items Mary Prence owned were her "1 bedsted 2 featherbeds and bolsters 1 paire of blanketts 2 suites of Curtaines and vallence and Curtaine rodds and Coards," valued at fifteen pounds, and "1 bed two bolsters 1 rugg," valued at four pounds. In fact, sleeping equipment constituted 41 percent of the total value of Mary Prence's property. Mary Ring's feather bed and bolster, at two pounds, ten shillings, were the most expensive items she owned. Together with her flock bed, two flock bolsters, five pairs of sheets and one half-sheet, three feather pillows, two "fine" pillow cases and two "little" pillow cases, a pillowcase full of feathers, three blankets, two curtains, two coverlets, and "1 peece [of fabric] to make a case for a bolster," they constituted one-third of Mary's property when it was inventoried in 1633. When widow Margaret Howland died in 1683, her two bedsteads, old feather bed, old flock bed, and bedding also totaled about one-third of her moveable property.[65]

Even for men, bedsteads, beds, and bedding were often their most valuable property, from approximately 8 percent to over one-third of the value of one's movable estate in Plymouth. While there were significant variations, poorer individuals generally invested a larger proportion of their resources in sleeping equipment; in 1671 the very poor William Zoanes's estate, valued at nineteen pounds, included his "beding and bed linine," which was worth four and a half pounds (34 percent of his estate), twice as much as his clothing. Zoanes's next most valuable possession was his cow, worth three pounds. On the other hand, Myles Standish, who raised six sons and one daughter with his wife Barbara in Duxbury, invested a comparatively small portion of his large estate of 358 pounds (much of it in books) in sleeping equipment. His five bedsteads (including one settle bed), four feather beds, three bolsters (one of them feather), three blankets, four rugs, one coverlet, three pillows (one of them "great" and probably shared by those sleeping in a bed), and five pairs of sheets (including one "fine" pair) were valued at around twenty-one pounds, five times the value of William Zoanes's bedding, but only 8 percent of Standish's estate. The items required to create an appropriate sleeping environment were often worth more than one's clothing or livestock and sometimes worth almost as much as the house itself. By 1672 John Sutton of Rehoboth, for example, had invested seven pounds in his "featherbed a bolster 3 pillowes 2 blanketts 1 Rugg & a paire of sheets" and eight pounds in building his "dwelling house." Reverend Thomas Walley's sleeping equipment (valued at twenty-four pounds) was worth five pounds more than all his livestock: two mares, two horses, four cows and calves, and a heifer. Walley's "2 bedds bolster pillowes blanketts and Ruggs curtaines & vallence . . . bed linen . . . child bed linnine and a blankett . . . bedsteads feathers & a little woole" constituted 22 percent of his 110-pound estate in Barnstable in 1678.[66]

Such expenditures highlight the extreme value colonists placed on physical comfort during sleep, as well as their growing desire for personal privacy as it reflected wealth, status, and civility. Perhaps colonists also hoped that spending a large amount on their sleeping environments would engender more civil relations among family members, especially those who shared a bed. Linking civility with godliness, John Eliot and other missionaries imposed English-style sleeping arrangements on New England natives as one of the first and most significant steps in bringing them to Christianity. Altering the body's activities and experiences in the most intimate of spaces—the bed—prepared and shaped it to receive God's grace. It becomes clearer why Edward Winslow and Stephen Hopkins were appalled at the sleeping arrangements they encountered in Massasoit's wetu. And yet Massasoit was enacting the important native cultural practice of hospitality when he invited the Englishmen into his wigwam to share his bed. Sharing food with visitors, as well, helped to forge social and political connections.

"In Our Houses Eating and Drinking": Food and Foodways

Especially during the early years of settlement, when the saints had not yet adapted to the new environment or had time to establish a successful corn crop, when their "hungry bellies" craved more than fish and water, and corn was "more precious than silver," food was the most powerful commodity of social exchange between Indians and Plymouth colonists, who refused to trade in firearms.[67] When Samoset walked into the infant plantation in March of 1620/1, the first thing he asked for was some beer; the colonists "gave him strong water and biscuit, and butter, and cheese, and pudding, and a piece of mallard, all which he liked well." Soon after, a visiting group of Wampanoags "did eat liberally of our English victuals," and when Massasoit himself arrived in state, "our governor [Bradford] kissing his hand, the king [Massasoit] kissed him, and so they sat down. The governor called for some strong water, and drunk to him, and [Massasoit] drunk a great draught that made him sweat all the while after." Then Bradford "called for a little fresh meat, which the king did eat willingly, and did give his followers." Only after physically sharing kisses, drink, and food did the English governor and the Wampanoag sachem establish a peace treaty, which they concluded with a mutual embrace. The next day Massasoit's brother, Quadequina, welcomed Myles Standish and Isaac Allerton with "three or four ground-nuts [a tuber that grew in moist areas], and some tobacco." The English thought of tobacco as a foodstuff—people "drank" it—and Indians smoked it as a primary means of generating social bonds and tribal alliances. Wherever colonists traveled during these early years, native people fed them generously and in return the English shared what victuals they had. Winslow made a point of recording the foods Indians offered the colonists as they many times sat down and ate together: "roasted crab, fishes, and other dried shell fish," boiled cod, squirrel meat, oysters, parched cornmeal "very precious at that time of year [spring]," and tobacco. Indeed, he never "doubt[ed] but we should have enough where'er we came [among the Indians]."[68] Likewise, when Indians visited Plymouth, colonists "entertained" them with food and drink: "Wee . . . haue them in our houses eating and drinking, and warming themselues," wrote Robert Cushman.[69]

Besides the thanksgiving harvest festival of 1621—a three-day feast of shared food and recreation among Indians and English—another feast of commensality occurred two years later at the wedding of William Bradford and Alice Southworth in August, when foodstuffs were plentiful. Emmanuel Altham, who attended the wedding, wrote to his brother in England that Massasoit, his five wives, and about 130 more natives arrived, bringing "four bucks and a turkey." Indians and colonists feasted on "twelve pasty venisons" and other savory pies, "pieces of roasted venison, and other such good cheer in such quantity that I could wish you some of our share."[70] Despite language barriers, sitting down to nourish one's own and others' bodies was a social practice recognized by both Indians and English as a powerful form of communication that helped to erase cultural differences. Bradford described exchanges of precious foodstuffs—notably cheeses and sugar—as signs of peace and friendship among the colonists, their English investors, and Dutch visitors.[71] "Commensalism—the sharing of food—establishes communion and connection in all cultures," notes Carol M. Counihan; eating together in a communal meal grounded social exchanges in participants' bodies, more effectively cementing relationships than through words representing abstract notions of friendship. Conversely, refusing to share food, as did some Plymouth men when they confronted Corbitant whom they believed had slain Tisquantum, "represent[s] a severe rupture of connection."[72]

While colonists expected to enjoy three meals each day, Indians ate according to their immediate food supplies, causing their body shapes, English observers believed, to fluctuate. New England natives experienced alternating periods of plentiful and scant resources, depending upon the season and the success of the hunt, and their food culture reflected those shifts; they sometimes gorged at communal feasts and other times survived on nothing more than parched corn and water. Wood observed this pattern, imagining it as another characteristically "wild" practice that shaped Indian bodies in uncivilized ways:

> [The Indians] be great eaters and yet little meat-men. When they visit our English, being invited to eat, they are very moderate, whether it be to show their manners or for shamefacedness I know not. But at home they will eat till their bellies stand forth, ready to split with fullness, it being their fashion to eat all at some times and sometimes nothing at all in two or three days, wise providence being a stranger to their wilder ways.[73]

John Smith observed, "It is strange to see how [Indians'] bodies alter with their diet; euen as the deare and wilde beastes, they seeme fat and leane, strong and weak."[74] Such extreme fluctuations between prodigality and want, colonists thought, were neither physically nor spiritually healthy. Moderation at all times was the providential way of nourishing the body and generating balance among the humors. Robinson admonished the saints to "restrain their appetite[s]," especially at meals "where there is a variety of delicates . . . to provoke" one to gluttony.[75] Colonists ritually abstained from food on fast days to enhance their sense of humiliation and godliness and they feasted on thanksgiving days, but on all other days food intake was ideally modest but regular and the foods "plain."

The early years of frequent want, however, required colonists to eat more like the Indians than the saints would have liked, making them fundamentally aware of their bodies' needs.[76] At least some of them engaged the experience of hunger as a sign of godliness. Robert Cushman believed a significant threat to the saints' venture in New England was their leaving behind "the satiety of bodily delights." But, he argued, "nature is content with little, and health is much endangered by mixtures upon the stomach. The delights of the palate do often inflame the vital parts."[77] Linking these humoral principles with his theology of the body, Cushman warned that colonists' "self-love"—that is, being more concerned with "serving their bellies" than serving the common good—was a "disease" that "will infect both soul and body, yea, and the contagion of it is such . . . as will even hazard the welfare of that society." Grounding self-love literally in bodily satiation, Cushman believed people exposed their self-love when they sought "their own bellies" and he differentiated between "a temperate good man" and "a belly-god" who craved "belly-cheer." Filling the belly with a surfeit of rich foods caused an "over-flowing of blood" and thus a "dangerous disease." Physiological disease implied spiritual disease, for God could "feel our pulses" and determine whether one carried the disease of self-love. Indeed, corporeal deprivation could enhance one's godliness: "See whether thine heart cannot be as merry, and thy mind as joyful, and thy countenance as cheerful, with co[a]rse fare, with pulse [beans], with bread and water (if God offer thee no butter, nor the times afford other) as if thou had the greatest dainties." When all were in want was "no time for men to look to get riches, brave [proud] cloth[e]s, dainty fare . . . no time to pamper the flesh, live at ease, snatch, catch, scrape, and pil[e], and hoard up." It was a time to act as a spiritual and communal "body," to "open the doors, the chests, and vessels, and say, brother, neighbor, friend, what want

ye, any thing that I have? . . . Let . . . his hunger [be] thy hunger."[78] Cushman connected the physical and moral health of the social body with that
of its individual members, and food was both the literal and the metaphorical link. Feeding one's own belly when others went hungry would cause
the downfall of the plantation's entire enterprise; the egalitarian sharing
of food, in contrast, promoted the common affections and generated individual and corporate health.

After the early lean years harvests became more dependable, English
grains and vegetables took root, shipments from England were more frequent, cows arrived to provide dairy products, and settlement of the Bay
Colony encouraged increased trade in English foods. Colonists were able
to indulge more predictably in such familiar domesticated foods as wheat
and rye, fruits and vegetables like apples and spinach, pork, beef, chicken,
and dairy products. At Plymouth colonists reproduced as closely as possible the English foodways with which their yeoman tastes were familiar.
While the wealthiest colonists could eat a variety of English foodstuffs fairly
dependably and so embody greater domestic civility, the poorest farmers,
especially those living far from settlements, survived on a diet of mostly indigenous products: corn porridge, fish, and wild game. But the majority of
households ate quite similarly in terms of quantity and variety, combining
indigenous and domesticated products, and even the poorest inhabitants
ate more meat than did their counterparts in England.[79]

Like the Indians, the colonists' nourishment fluctuated, though for
most not with such extremes, according to the seasons; indulging in the
"dainty fare" Cushman so abhorred was rarely an option. Alternating between an abundance of a wide variety of fresh foods between mid-summer
and late fall and a repetitious diet of "pork and peas, bread and pudding,
all washed down with beer" during winter and spring, colonists strove to
moderate such fluctuations by preserving and storing foods to take them
through the lean months. Sacks of corn and barrels of meat were significant items in the probate inventories of those who died during the winter
and early spring, signifying the high value householders placed on their
ability to generate adequate stores that would carry their families through
late spring; wealthier families clearly had an advantage. John Howland apparently took great care to provide for his family at New Plymouth, for
when he died in early March of 1672/3, in his storage chamber were twenty
bushels of corn, four bushels of malt and four of rye, six bushels of wheat,
two and a half bushels of barley, two fliches of bacon, one-third barrel of
pork, a half barrel of beef, thirty-four pounds of butter and lard, fourteen

pounds of sugar, six pounds of tobacco, and a peck of beans. For most, stored supplies could be depleted by early summer, however, and some survived simply on corn porridge, ground nuts, and shellfish.[80] Colonists were viscerally familiar with seasonal and status-based patterns of food consumption, which were the norm in England. Stephen Mennell has linked "the physiological effects of inadequate and irregular feeding" to the "psychological volatility" and "superstitious" beliefs and behaviors characteristic of English people during this period. However, the Plymouth saints' apparent "superstitions" must be understood as a critical sense of their dependence on divine providence. Significantly, they literally and symbolically ritualized that dependence with food, tending to hold their fast days in the spring, when food supplies were low and their need for divine support greater, and their thanksgiving days in the autumn, to express gratitude for the harvest and enjoy a feast.[81]

During the first years the colonists ate together in communal meals until they constructed individual dwellings. Once established as independent families, food preparation and consumption occurred within homes, and the sense of communal commensality, of nourishing the social body by sharing communal meals, diminished. Families became responsible for feeding themselves, for creating a domestic community within the "little commonwealth" of the household. Feeding her family was the most important daily duty of the adult woman. The housewife was expected to be "of an upright and sincere religion, . . . a godly, constant, and religious woman . . . of great modesty and temperance." According to popular cookery book author Gervase Markham, a housewife was to embody godliness: her clothing was to "be comely, cleanly and strong, made as well to preserve the health as adorn the person," and "her diet [should] be wholesome and cleanly, prepared at due hours, and cooked with care and diligence." In a nutshell, the goodwife "must be of chaste thought, stout courage, patient, untired, watchful, diligent, witty, pleasant, . . . and generally skilful in all the worthy knowledges which do belong to her vocation." Feeding her family was, indeed, a physically demanding job, requiring patience, diligence, and skill. An adult woman in Plymouth, like Mary Ring, tended the kitchen garden, harvested and preserved plant foods, cleaned fish, slaughtered chickens, churned butter, and prepared meals over the hot fire in heavy iron pots, blackened with soot. Nevertheless, while cooking she should "be cleanly both in body and garments." She must also have "a quick eye, a curious [fastidious; sensitive] nose, a perfect taste, and a ready ear (she must not be butter-fingered, sweet-toothed, nor faint-hearted; for the first will let everything fall, the second will consume what it should increase, and the last will lose time with too much niceness)." A Plymouth housewife surely employed all her bodily strength, sensory perceptions, and wit to combine indigenous and domestic foods and produce palatable meals that nourished her family, both corporeally and spiritually, for modest, godly meals were "rather to satisfy nature than our affections, and apter to kill hunger than revive new appetites."[82]

During the first thirteen years food preparation was especially laborious, for maize, or Indian corn, the colonists' staple food, had to be pounded by hand with mortar and pestle into grits, meal, and flour—a practice learned from the Indians—until the first grist mill was erected in 1633. Native people, according to John Winthrop Jr., generally boiled their corn whole and ate it "in stead of Breade." Or they parched it in the fire and "beate it in their wooden Morters with a long Stone for a pestle, into fine meale" called *nokake*, "a sweet, toothsome, and hearty" foodstuff they carried on journeys and ate dry or mixed with water. Unlike the Indians, who could wash down dry cornmeal with a mouthful of cold water, however, English tastes and stomachs preferred a more refined corn product: finely ground, carefully sifted of chaff and other impurities, and thoroughly softened and cooked. They mixed the ground and sifted meal with water and sometimes English rye or wheat flour, poured the batter in the bottom of an iron pot, and baked it over the fire to make a dense bread. A stiffer cornmeal batter, mixed with suet or butter and dried fruits like strawberries or cranberries, wrapped in a cloth, and boiled in broth, produced a "bag-pudding." Winthrop, however, preferred "sampe," a soft, "very well boyled" cornmeal porridge sweetened with milk or butter and sugar, for its taste and humorally healthful qualities: "Easy of Digestion, [sampe] is of a nature Divertical and Clensing and hath no Quality of binding in the Body [causing constipation] . . . but rather to keepe [the body] in a fitt temperature."[83]

Cushman had proclaimed that plain and simple foods reflected modest godliness, yet both colonists and Indians prepared food in similar ways. Plymouth housewives boiled ground corn with water to make a "water pottage" or with beer to produce a "drinked pottage" for breakfast and supper. The basic dinner porridge, or pottage, eaten in the middle of the day, was cornmeal boiled with dried peas. The cook might add a joint of meat, a wild fowl or chicken, fish, eel, or shellfish, onions, and "sallet herbs" or garden greens to produce a one-pot meal, the standard daily fare. Often, day after day, the pot continuously simmered over the fire, the housewife adding more foods as needed, to produce a soft, liquid mess of undifferentiated foodstuffs typical of English yeoman cookery. Raw foods—fruits and vegetables—were suspect; colonists preferred to eat food that had been well processed by substantial cooking.[84] Indian pottages were similar in composition and content, though they used only indigenous foods: maize boiled with kidney beans, to which they frequently added "fish and flesh of all sorts," like "shads, eels, alewives . . . venison, beaver, bear's flesh, moose, otters, rackoons, . . . cutting this flesh in small pieces and boiling it." They also mixed into the pottage "several sorts of roots, . . . Jerusalem artichokes, and ground nuts, . . . and pompions [pumpkins], and squashes, and also several sorts of nuts." Because Indians, apparently unlike the English, boiled whole pieces of fish, bones and all, in their stews, Gookin "wondered many times that they were not in danger of being choaked with fish bones; but they are so dexterous to separate the bones from the fish in their eating thereof, that they are in no hazard."[85]

Unlike in England, colonists generally had sufficient animal protein, both wild and domesticated; they prepared raw carcasses by hacking them into large chunks with an ax. During harvest festivals and other communal celebrations, such as the thanksgiving harvest festival of 1621 and the Bradford-Southworth wedding in 1623, they roasted whole venison carcasses or large joints over an open fire. For special occasions, such as the meal ending a day of thanksgiving, a wealthier housewife, especially later in the seventeenth century, might tempt family members' and guests' palates and demonstrate her sophistication by adding precious spices—ginger, nutmeg, cloves—to savory pies filled with minced meat. Normally, however, housewives boiled chunks of meat in the cooking pot until the meat fell off the bone and blended with the other ingredients.[86] Dairy foods provided an important source of seasonal protein and the comforting taste and feel of fat. Deetz has noted Plymouth's more careful division of cows and goats than of swine to various households in 1627, the abundance of ceramics used in dairy processing, and the general high valuing of dairy products, especially cheese or "white meat," in England.[87] Until the arrival of dairy cows in 1624, the colonists' diet, like the Indians' diet, was exceedingly low in fat, which was perhaps the greatest alteration in nourishment and taste to which their bodies had to adjust, having come from Holland, where butter and cheese were plentiful. In a 1621 letter Winslow recommended to those who would venture to New England, "If you bring anything for comfort in the country, butter or sallet oil, or both is very good."[88] By the 1630s even the poorest husbandman usually owned a cow, and families consumed dairy products in abundance during the summer months;

housewives stirred butter into puddings and pottages and spread it on corn bread and served soft cheeses with bread.

Mealtimes gathered household members together and, more than any other activity, displayed the hierarchical ordering within the little commonwealth, as individuals embodied their places and roles and learned appropriate conduct. Family members, sometimes including servants, ate meals together at a table, if they owned one. Because space in one-and two-roomed dwellings was limited, some families set up a "table boarde," a large piece of lumber placed on barrels, at mealtimes. Many families, like that of Mary Ring, did not have a table or table board and many did not own chairs, so they sat where they could, on trunks, chests, stools, kegs, or bedsteads; in the poorest homes, as in Indian wigwams, people squatted or sat on the floor in front of the fire. In wealthier families a carpet covered the table between meals, replaced with a table cloth and individual linen napkins during mealtimes.[89] More refined families raised their members' bodies off the floor onto chairs or forms (long benches) and seated them around the table according to their rank and status. At the head of the table sat the husband, father, and master—the household's "governor"—perhaps in the only chair, while other family members sat around the table on stools, boxes, and forms. The father recited blessings before and after the meal, an important means of instructing households in godliness, household manuals noted, for such prayers reminded the family of their utter dependence upon divine providence for their bodily sustenance.[90] In 1623 Winslow explained why the English "crave[d] a blessing on our meat before we did eat, and after to give thanks for the same." He was eating a meal with Conbatant, sachem of Mattapuyst, who asked "what was the meaning of that . . . custom." Winslow went into a lengthy explanation of the Christian God and his laws, concluding that because everything they had came from God, they asked God to bless the food they "were about to eat, that it might nourish and strengthen our bodies; and having eaten sufficient, being satisfied therewith, we again returned thanks to the same our God, for that our refreshing, &c." In a moment of intercultural connection over food, Conbatant and his men apparently "liked" Winslow's explanation "very well; and said, they believed almost all the same things."[91]

The housewife served the meal of pottage in trenchers (shallow wooden bowls), trays, pewter porringers, or wooden or earthenware bowls, which were shared between two or more family members eating simultaneously out of the same dish. Such undifferentiated foods as pottage, eaten out of a communal trencher, or a whole roasted pig, from which one cut off pieces of flesh to consume during a community celebration, evoked a sense of identity as a member of a larger corporate body, rather than as a private individual. Family members often shared drinking vessels as well; leather, pottery, or, in wealthier families, pewter or silver cups held beer or water. After 1660 smoother ceramic cups and mugs became more common. As with clothing and bedding, the utilitarian roughness and plainness of eating utensils corresponded to lower economic and social status, while those who could afford finer, smoother, decorated ceramics represented the wealthier, more "civilized" end of the social spectrum.[92] The sensory look and feel of coarse or smooth utensils generated an embodied knowledge of one's position in the family and in society. As with garments and bed linens, higher economic and social status allowed a family to invest in a greater number of trenchers, plates, and cups, which encouraged privatization of the self within the family during eating as well as sleeping.

Family members were to wash their hands and clean their fingernails before sitting down to a meal and after eating, for, as in Mary Ring's family, the fingers were the primary eating utensils, with perhaps a knife to cut and spear pieces of meat or cheese and, less frequently, a spoon. Indians made "very smooth and artificial [artful] . . . dishes, spoons, and ladles" out of wood, and spoons had become common in England during the sixteenth century. But they were itemized in few inventories in seventeenth-century Plymouth. Some wealthier inhabitants, like William Kemp, Nathaniel Tilden, and governors William Bradford Thomas Prence, owned sets of silver spoons, but many families owned no eating utensils at all or at most one or two wooden or pewter spoons, indicating that they ate primarily with their hands. When upper middle-class Thomas Gilbert died in 1671, he left behind three brass kettles, two iron pots, and a silver cup, and in 1672 lower middle-class John Sutton owned two pewter platters, two porringers, a drinking cup, and some wooden dishes, platters, and trays; neither man owned a spoon.[93] Colonists likely followed a common code of table manners that disallowed lower-ranked family members from putting their fingers into a dish of food before the male and female householders had taken their first portions.[94] Using spoons allowed one to avoid bodily contact with foods and signified greater gentility, a quality the upper classes began to embrace toward the end of the seventeenth century. Gentility "regulated dining as it did the body, including the wish to keep the food clean, separated from dirt and fingers." However, by the middle of the eighteenth century one-third to one-half of Plymouth's population still ate as most

had during the mid-seventeenth century. Bushman describes the correspondences among foods, dining practices, and bodies by the mid-1700s:

> [They ate] with spoons or fingers, though likely sitting up at tables. They
> had no finishes on their tables or tablewares. Their skin had likely been
> roughened by weather, fireplace heat, and work. They bent over their
> bowls unconcerned about posture or manners. . . . A common diet of
> simply prepared cereals and meat brought people together, but the modes
> of presenting food and the manner of eating it divided the politer classes
> of society from the vulgar and coarse.[95]

Missionaries hoped to educate native people in civil English ways in
order to bring them to Christ, and they began in the home, where individuals' souls, missionaries believed, were first constrained, nurtured, and
molded, preparing one to perform his or her duties properly in the social
world. Missionaries educated Indians' souls by educating their bodies in
extraordinarily concrete ways. They hoped to domesticate natives' bodies
according to English notions and thus access their souls and prepare them
for God's grace.[96] Although Plymouth missionaries were less rigorous than
Bay missionaries in their demands that Indians alter central aspects of their
personal and domestic lives, Plymouth's saints usually imagined their own
corporeal understandings and practices as more civilized and godly than
those of New England's native people. Indians often, though not always,
served as mirrors in which colonists saw reflected both their beliefs about
their own superior abilities to shape and display moral bodies and their
own potential to slip into beastly, savage ways. Colonists themselves, however, exhibited gradations of civility in various types of household dwellings
and ways they rendered bodies and constructed family relations—through
such activities as sex, sleeping, and eating—toward less or more privatization, cleanliness, and morality. Beginning with the parents and extending
through children and servants, households were to mold their members'
bodies with civility and godliness in order to educate their souls, producing
individuals who visibly demonstrated in saintly countenance, gestures, and
carriage their godly souls.

"In the American incarnation," writes Myra Jehlen, "the Protestant soul
acquired a newly powerful body."[97] Surely this is true. The saints at Plymouth encountered an unfamiliar world that threatened to alter their physiological and moral constitutions, and yet New England also promised to

be a place where they might fully pursue, engage, and activate their theology of the body. The colonists brought with them implicit and explicit aesthetic, philosophical, medical, and theological models of human corporeality that impelled them to shape their own, each others', and others' bodies as they generated new meanings regarding their physical relationships to the land, its native inhabitants, each other, and the self. Ultimately they physically and, they believed, spiritually thrived as they established households, churches, and towns that, for the most part, materialized their principles of godly life.

Some recent scholars, echoing Perry Miller, have argued that the fundamental shift from medieval to Protestant notions of embodiment produced a detachment of soul from body and a hierarchical ordering of the two, conflating rational intellect with the soul and elevating it above the body. This shift, they claim, presaged the later Cartesian split between mind and body, which located individual subjectivity in the disembodied consciousness of thinking self-awareness. Such arguments, however, depend in part on Weberian ideas about puritan "worldly asceticism" deduced from the Calvinist doctrine of predestination. Max Weber incorrectly argued that New England puritans experienced an "unprecedented inner loneliness of the single individual" that produced an "entirely negative attitude . . . to all the sensuous and emotional elements in culture and in religion, because they are of no use toward salvation." Pasi Falk is a bit more accurate in his claim that English puritanism articulated the most "pointed expression" of the sovereignty of reason over corporeality; reason's "task was to curb and instrumentalize the body into part of the dynamics of culture." Yet all these arguments suggest a more teleological than historical perspective, looking backward from a Cartesian and capitalist modern world and attempting with the advantage of hindsight to read more into seventeenth-century dissenting Protestant ideas than was actually there. They might accurately describe some later developments, but Calvin, like Robinson and many of his cohorts, valued the volitional affections equally with, and more often above, the rational mind and maintained an intimate bond between the feeling soul and corporeal experience, locating true Christianity in its embodied expression. And they were hardly averse to enjoying corporeal pleasures in moderation.[98]

Important shifts in conceptions of embodiment did occur with the Reformation, but it is less appropriate to characterize these shifts as instigating a split between embodied and rational, material and spiritual, or profane and sacred and, rather, more accurate to see them as a redefining of spirituality and materiality, a shifting of the grounds of sacredness, or divine presence, from carved statues to living bodies, from "empty" ritual gestures to actions motivated by heart intentionality. While medieval Catholicism spatially and temporally contained or funneled the divine only through particular images, objects, and actions, Protestants imagined a new and different valuing of materiality and human embodiment. The sacred transgressed the medieval structures, to be dispersed throughout every aspect of daily human life. Just as the natural, everyday world reflected the goodness of God and revealed the hand of divine providence at work, so also did the natural human being, as a unity of body and soul, reflect the glory of God as a person's inner heart and outer actions coincided in daily moral practices. The human body—individual living bodies—took on a radically heightened significance. Certainly the Plymouth separatists, as we have seen, lived a thoroughly embodied existence, exhibiting no split among the head's "cold" rationality, the heart's "warm" emotions and intentions, and the body's actions.

Yet there existed no single, homogeneous, unchanging human body in seventeenth-century Plymouth; colonial bodies, both English and Indian, sinful and godly, and their experiences were continuously being shaped and reshaped over time. As in England and the rest of New England, a shift in ideas about corporeality took place in Plymouth during the 1600s. With the rise of the middle class and increased wealth among colonists, they began to replace their earlier understanding of their bodies as members of an organic community with a greater individualization of the self and privatization of individual bodies. In the beginning they had viewed several things—physically separating themselves from corrupt English society and the savage American environment, the leveling of social differences, and the enhancing of social bonds by mutual care for each others' physical needs—as critical for the maintenance of godliness and civilization. By the time Plymouth Colony joined Massachusetts Province in 1691, ending Plymouth's seventy-year existence as an independent colony, they had transposed the earlier separatist communal bondedness into an interactive exchange with the larger social world that developed simultaneously with a stronger sense of individuality. Indeed, the ideal tightly interwoven community of common affections never did exist in Plymouth in the ways John Robinson and William Bradford had envisioned, as encounters with non-separatists and native people pushed the saints to reflect on meanings of their material existence. Indeed, the human body at any point in history is never a static, reified entity; it is always problematic, a shifting site of exchanges between self and world that is continuously shaping and being shaped by immediate natural and cultural forces.

Introduction

1. Sociologist of religion Dawne Moon has coined the term *everyday theologies,* the individual and collective process of "seeking to make sense of the world" that reproduces shifting "hierarchies of power and privilege" (*God, Sex, and Politics: Homosexuality and Everyday Theologies* [Chicago: University of Chicago Press, 2004], 12–16, quotes p. 15).

2. Trudy Eden also has pointed out the similarities between early modern and recent understandings of the body as manipulable, continuously being altered and shaped by "the many contingencies of life" ("Food, Assimilation, and the Malleability of the Human Body in Early Virginia," in *A Centre of Wonders: The Body in Early America,* ed. Janet Moore Lindman and Michele Lise Tarter [Ithaca, N.Y.: Cornell University Press, 2001], 30).

3. Emphasis in original. Pierre Bourdieu, *Outline of a Theory of Practice,* trans. Richard Nice (Cambridge: Cambridge University Press, 1977), 95, 94.

4. John Robinson, *New Essays; or Observations Divine and Moral,* in *The Works of John Robinson, Pastor of the Pilgrim Fathers,* ed. Robert Ashton, 3 vols. (Boston: Doctrinal Tract and Book Society, 1851) 1:243–44. Excerpts from sixteenth- and seventeenth-century English sources are quoted verbatim throughout this work, using spelling, punctuation, and grammatical structure as they were written. Where the language is unclear, letters, words, and punctuation are added within brackets in order to clarify the writer's meaning.

5. Robinson, *New Essays,* 1:246–48. On childrearing, see Gloria L. Main, *Peoples of a Spacious Land: Families and Cultures in Colonial New England* (Cambridge, Mass.:

Harvard University Press, 2001), 117–55. On mothers' and fathers' roles in raising their sons, see Anne S. Lombard, *Making Manhood: Growing Up Male in Colonial New England* (Cambridge, Mass.: Harvard University Press, 2003), 1–45.

6. Edmund S. Morgan, *Visible Saints: The History of a Puritan Idea* (repr., Ithaca, N.Y.: Cornell University Press, 1965), 34–35.

7. Perry Miller, *The New England Mind: The Seventeenth Century* (1939; repr., Cambridge, Mass.: Belknap Press, 1954), 49, 51, 173. Miller defined *eupraxia* as "conduct not only good but appropriate to the circumstance, tactful and efficient, [and] it became one of the principal catchwords of New England thought, freighted with both a cosmological and an ethical significance" (164). For puritans, rational divine order permeated the universe and impelled good conduct; "the service which God designed man to perform was simply 'eupraxia'" (182).

8. Miller, *New England Mind*, 32; Amanda Porterfield, *Female Piety in Puritan New England: The Emergence of Religious Humanism* (New York: Oxford University Press, 1992), 31. Arguing against Miller, Porterfield claims that "in fact, the closing of that division [between spirit and body] was precisely the engine of Puritan piety enabling the felt coincidence of faith in divine righteousness and commitment to personal humility that led Puritan men and women to challenge earthly monarchs and establish themselves as a new elite" (31).

9. William Ames, *The Marrow of Theology: William Ames, 1576–1633* (*The Marrow of Sacred Divinity*, 1629), trans. and ed. John D. Eusden (Durham, N.C.: Labyrinth Press, 1983), 2:3, "Good Works"; 1:8, "The Creation."

10. Robinson, *New Essays*, 1:62–65. Emphasis added.

11. Porterfield, *Female Piety in Puritan New England*, 21, 25–36, quote p. 31.

12. Miller, *New England Mind*, 41, 54.

13. See Mary Potter Engel, *John Calvin's Perspectival Anthropology* (Atlanta: Scholars Press, 1988).

14. John Calvin, *Institutes of the Christian Religion*, trans. Henry Beveridge (Grand Rapids, Mich.: Wm. B. Eerdmans, 1989), 1.5.3–4.

15. Ames, *Marrow of Sacred Divinity*, 1:8, "The Creation"; Robinson, *New Essays*, 1:17–18; John Robinson, *Justification of Separation from the Church of England* (1610), in *Works* 2:339; Thomas Cartwright, *A Treatise of Christian Religion* (London: by Felix Kyngston for Thomas Man, 1616), 34.

16. Cartwright, *Treatise of Christian Religion*, 35; Engel, *Calvin's Perspectival Anthropology*, 169.

17. "The statement of our Lord is, that a man must be born again, because he is flesh. He requires not to be born again, with reference to the body . . . [but his mind] must be totally renewed" (Calvin, *Institutes*, 2.3.1).

18. Calvin, *Institutes*, 4.12.15–16; William J. Bouwsma, *John Calvin: A Sixteenth-Century Portrait* (New York: Oxford University Press, 1988), 134–37; Margaret R. Miles, "Theology, Anthropology, and the Human Body in Calvin's *Institutes of the Christian Religion*," *Harvard Theological Review* 74 (1981): 319.

19. Eamon Duffy, *The Stripping of the Altars: Traditional Religion in England* (New Haven, Conn.: Yale University Press, 1992); Lee Palmer Wandel, *Voracious Idols*

and Violent Hands: Iconoclasm in Reformation Zurich, Strasbourg, and Basel (Cambridge: Cambridge University Press, 1995); Carlos N. M. Eire, *War Against the Idols: The Reformation of Worship from Erasmus to Calvin* (Cambridge: Cambridge University Press, 1986); Margaret Aston, *England's Iconoclasts*, vol. 1 (Oxford: Clarendon Press, 1988).

20. Ann Kibbey, *The Interpretation of Material Shapes in Puritanism: A Study of Rhetoric, Prejudice, and Violence* (Cambridge: Cambridge University Press, 1986), 49.

21. Leon Howard, "In Rightly Dividing the Word of Truth: Ramean Hermeneutics and the Commandment Against Adultery," in *Essays on Puritans and Puritanism by Leon Howard*, ed. James Barbour and Thomas Quirk (Albuquerque: University of New Mexico Press, 1986), 135. On Ramus, his theories, and their influence on English puritans, see Miller, *New England Mind*, 150–60, 346–54; Walter J. Ong, *Ramus, Method, and the Decay of Dialogue* (Cambridge, Mass.: Harvard University Press, 1958); Wilbur Samuel Howell, *Logic and Rhetoric in England, 1500–1700* (Princeton, N.J.: Princeton University Press, 1956); Keith L. Sprunger, "Ames, Ramus, and the Method of Puritan Theology," *Harvard Theological Review* 59 (1966): 133–51.

22. Cartwright, *Treatise of Christian Religion*, 42, 51; Robinson, *New Essays*, 1:67.

23. William Bradford, "A Dialogue, or the Sum of a Conference between Some Young Men Born in New England and Sundry Ancient Men that came out of Holland and Old England, anno domini 1648," in *Chronicles of the Pilgrim Fathers of the Colony of Plymouth, from 1602–1625*, ed. Alexander Young (Boston: Charles C. Little, 1841), 423–24, 439; Timothy George, *John Robinson and the English Separatist Tradition* (Macon, Ga.: Mercer University Press, 1982), 93 n. 2, 111, 161–66; Philip F. Gura, *A Glimpse of Sion's Glory: Puritan Radicalism in New England, 1620–1660* (Middletown, Conn.: Wesleyan University Press, 1984), 33–35; Morgan, *Visible Saints*.

24. John Robinson, *An Answer to a Censorious Epistle*, in *Works*, 3:416.

25. John Robinson, *Of Religious Communion, Private and Public* (1614), in *Works*, 3:274.

26. Emphasis added. Robinson, *Of Religious Communion*, 3:243.

27. Robinson, *Justification of Separation*, 2:105; George, *John Robinson*, 136–39; Edmund S. Morgan, *Visible Saints: The History of a Puritan Idea* (New York: New York University Press, 1965), 33–63.

28. William Bradford, *Of Plymouth Plantation, 1620–1647*, ed. Samuel Eliot Morison (New York: Alfred A. Knopf, 1994), 16; Christopher Lawne, *The Prophane Schisme of the Brownists or Separatists* (London: W. Stansby for W. Burke, 1612), 87. On separatism in England and the Netherlands, see: Edward Arber, *The Story of the Pilgrim Fathers, 1606–1623 A.D.* (Boston: Houghton Mifflin, 1897); Henry Martyn Dexter, *The England and Holland of the Pilgrims* (Boston: Houghton Mifflin, 1905); Champlin Burrage, *The Early English Dissenters in the Light of Recent Research (1550–1641)* (Cambridge: Cambridge University Press, 1912); B. R. White, *The English Separatist Tradition: From the Marian Martyrs to the Pilgrim Fathers* (London: Oxford University Press, 1971); Keith L. Sprunger, *Dutch Puritanism: A History of English and Scottish Churches of the Netherlands in the Sixteenth and Seventeenth Centuries* (Leiden:

E. J. Brill, 1982); J. W. Martin, *Religious Radicals in Tudor England* (Ronceverte, W.V.: Hambledon Press, 1989); R. J. Acheson, *Radical Puritans in England, 1550–1660* (London: Longman, 1990); Meic Pearse, *The Great Restoration: The Religious Radicals of the 16th and 17th Centuries* (Cumbria, U.K.: Paternoster Press, 1998).

29. Bradford, *Of Plymouth Plantation*, 24–25, 27.

30. Edward Winslow, *Hypocrisie Unmasked* (1646), in *Chronicles of the Pilgrim Fathers of the Colony of Plymouth, 1602–1625*, ed. Alexander Young (New York: Da Capo Press, 1971), 381; Nathaniel Morton, *New Englands Memoriall* (1669) (New York: Scholars' Facsimiles & Reprints, 1937), 3.

31. Susan Vincent, *Dressing the Elite: Clothes in Early Modern England* (Oxford: Berg, 2003), 129, 158.

32. Allan Hunt, *Governance of the Consuming Passions: A History of Sumptuary Regulation* (London: Macmillan, 1996); Anthony Fletcher, *Gender, Sex, and Subordination in England, 1500–1800* (New Haven, Conn.: Yale University Press, 1995); Steve Hindle, *The State and Social Change in Early Modern England, 1550–1640* (New York: Palgrave, 2000, 2002); Susan Dwyer Amussen, *An Ordered Society: Gender and Class in Early Modern England* (New York: Columbia University Press, 1988).

33. Stephen Greenblatt, *Renaissance Self-Fashioning: From More to Shakepeare* (Chicago: University of Chicago Press, 1980), 2–3.

34. Robinson, *Justification of Separation*, 2:118.

35. Peter Lake, "'A Charitable Christian Hatred': The Godly and their Enemies in the 1630s," in *The Culture of English Puritanism, 1560–1700*, ed. Christopher Durston and Jacqueline Eales (London: Macmillan, 1996), 161.

36. Bradford, *Of Plymouth Plantation*, 17, 11; Michelle Burnham, "Merchants, Money, and the Economics of 'Plain Style' in William Bradford's *Of Plymouth Plantation*," *American Literature* 72 (2000): 699. Cf. David S. Lovejoy, "Plain Englishmen at Plymouth," *New England Quarterly* 63 (1990): 240.

37. Nancy G. Sirasi, *Medieval and Early Renaissance Medicine: An Introduction to Knowledge and Practice* (Chicago: University of Chicago Press, 1990), 97–106; Herbert Leventhal, *In the Shadow of the Enlightenment: Occultism and Renaissance Science in Eighteenth-Century America* (New York: New York University Press, 1976), 9; Arthur O. Lovejoy, *The Great Chain of Being: A Study of the History of an Idea* (New York: Harper & Row, 1960); Carolyn Merchant, *The Death of Nature* (New York: HarperCollins, 1980), 100–101; Lawrence Babb, *The Elizabethan Malady: A Study of Melancholia in English Literature from 1580 to 1642* (East Lansing, Mich.: State College Press), vii, 175–80, 195; Robert Burton, *The Anatomy of Melancholy*, 6th ed. (1651), ed. Floyd Dell and Paul Jordan-Smith (London: George Routledge, 1931); Trudy Eden, *The Early American Table: Food and Society in the New World* (DeKalb: Northern Illinois University Press, 2008), 9–22.

38. Burton, *Anatomy of Melancholy*, 1.1.2.5–11; Miller, *Seventeenth Century*, 239–79; Babb, *Elizabethan Malady*, 2–5, 19; E. Ruth Harvey, *The Inward Wits: Psychological Theory in the Middle Ages and the Renaissance* (London: The Warburg Institute, 1975), 34; Sirasi, *Medieval and Early Renaissance Medicine*, 107–9; Charles Lloyd Cohen, *God's Caress: The Psychology of Puritan Religious Experience* (New York: Oxford University Press, 1986), 27–30; J. Rodney Fulcher, "Puritans and the Passions: The

Faculty Psychology in American Puritanism," *Journal of the History of Behavioral Sciences* 9 (1973): 123–39.

39. Michael C. Schoenfeldt, *Bodies and Selves in Early Modern England: Physiology and Inwardness in Spenser, Shakespeare, Herbert, and Milton* (Cambridge: Cambridge University Press, 1999), 20.

40. Karen Ordahl Kupperman, *Indians and English: Facing Off in America* (Ithaca, N.Y.: Cornell University Press, 2000), 20. Other recent histories also penetrate the complex exchanges between Europeans and Indians; see, for example, Daniel K. Richter, *Facing East from Indian County: A Native History of Early America* (Cambridge, Mass.: Harvard University Press, 2001); and Joyce E. Chaplin, *Subject Matter: Technology, the Body, and Science on the Anglo-American Frontier, 1500–1676* (Cambridge, Mass.: Harvard University Press, 2001).

41. Daniel Gookin, "Historical Collections of the Indians in New England" (1674), Massachusetts Historical Society, *Collections* 1 (1792): 223.

42. Bradford, *Of Plymouth Plantation*, 25–27, quote from p. 25.

43. Groundbreaking work by Caroline Walker Bynum and Peter Brown in the 1980s has led to more recent studies by, for example, Amy Hollywood, Suzannah Biernoff, and R. Marie Griffith: Bynum, *Holy Feast and Holy Fast: The Religious Significance of Food to Medieval Women* (Berkeley: University of California Press, 1987) and *Fragmentation and Redemption: Essays on Gender and the Human Body in Medieval Religion* (repr., New York: Zone Books, 1992); Brown, *The Body and Society: Men, Women, and Sexual Renunciation in Early Christianity* (New York: Columbia University Press, 1988); Hollywood, *Sensible Ecstasy: Mysticism, Sexual Difference, and the Demands of History* (Chicago: University of Chicago Press, 2002); Biernoff, *Sight and Embodiment in the Middle Ages: Ocular Desires* (New York: Palgrave Macmillan, 2002); Griffith, *Born Again Bodies: Flesh and Spirit in American Christianity* (Berkeley: University of California Press, 2004).

44. Michel Feher, ed., *Fragments for a History of the Human Body*, 3 vols. (New York: Zone Books, 1989), 1:11.

45. Susan Bordo, "The Body and the Reproduction of Femininity: A Feminist Appropriation of Foucault," in *Gender/Body/Knowledge: Feminist Reconstructions of Being and Knowing*, ed. Alison M. Jaggar and Susan R. Bordo (New Brunswick: Rutgers University Press, 1989): 13–33.

46. Bourdieu, *Outline of a Theory of Practice*, 10–22, esp. 18–19.

47. Anthony Fletcher, *Gender, Sex, and Subordination in England, 1500–1800* (New Haven, Conn.: Yale University Press, 1995), 98.

48. See Clifford Geertz's discussion of the identical movements of an eye twitch, a wink, and a parody of a wink, which nevertheless have vastly different meanings within a particular culture ("Thick Description: Toward an Interpretive Theory of Culture," in *The Interpretation of Cultures: Selected Essays by Clifford Geertz* [New York: Basic Books, 1973], 6–7).

49. Bostonian Samuel Sewall's diary is one well-known exception; in it he notes daily events, often quite tersely but with remarkable candidness, although he still says little about the most commonplace physiological activities (M. Halsey Thomas, ed., *The Diary of Samuel Sewall, 1674–1729*, 2 vols. [New York: 1973]).

50. Gary B. Nash, "Social Development," in *Colonial British America: Essays in the New History of the Early Modern Era*, ed. Jack P. Green and J. R. Pole (Baltimore: Johns Hopkins University Press, 1984), 235.

51. David D. Hall, *Worlds of Wonder, Days of Judgment: Popular Religious Belief in Early New England* (New York: Alfred A. Knopf, 1989). On writing cultural history, see Lynn Hunt, "History, Culture, and Text," in *The New Cultural History*, ed. Lynn Hunt (Berkeley: University of California Press, 1989), 1–22.

52. For example, the work of Karen Ordahl Kupperman on colonists' "readings" of Indian bodies; Ann Kibbey on violence against Indian and female bodies during the Pequot War and antinomian controversy; Amanda Porterfield on puritans' theological understandings of embodiment; Robert Blair St. George on yeoman farmers' use of the human body as a model for house architecture; Jane Kamensky on the tongue; Richard Godbeer on sex, hair, and periwigs; Elizabeth Reis on beliefs about female bodies that contributed to witchcraft accusations; and Joyce E. Chaplin on the colonial racialization of Indians' bodies. Kupperman, *Indians and English*; Kibbey, *Interpretation of Material Shapes in Puritanism*; Porterfield, *Female Piety in Puritan New England*; Robert Blair St. George, "'Set Thine House in Order': The Domestication of the Yeomanry in Seventeenth-Century New England," in *New England Begins: The Seventeenth Century*, vol. 2, *Mentality and Environment* (Boston: Museum of Fine Arts, 1982), 159–88; Jane Kamensky, *Governing the Tongue: The Politics of Speech in Early New England* (New York: Oxford University Press, 1997); Richard Godbeer, "Perversions of Anatomy, Anatomies of Perversion: The Periwig Controversy in Colonial Massachusetts," Massachusetts Historical Society, *Proceedings* 109 (1998): 1–23; Elizabeth Reis, "The Devil, the Body, and the Feminine Soul in Puritan New England," *Journal of American History* 82 (1995): 15–36; and Chaplin, *Subject Matter*.

53. There are many correspondences between Chaplin's work and my own, for both of us sustain an explicit focus on corporeality; mine, however, is more temporally and geographically restricted and more fully investigates the religious aspects of the body's practices and meanings. I earlier took up some of the same issues (which I also explore in greater detail in chapter 2) Chaplin addresses regarding nature, technology, and English and Indian bodies in "'Civilized' Bodies and the 'Savage' Environment of Early New Plymouth," in *A Centre of Wonders: The Body in Early America*, ed. Janet Moore Lindman and Michele Lise Tarter (Ithaca, N.Y.: Cornell University Press, 2001), 43–59.

54. Robert Orsi, "Everyday Miracles: The Study of Lived Religion," in *Lived Religion in America: Toward a History of Practice*, ed. David D. Hall (Princeton, N.J.: Princeton University Press, 1997), 7.

55. Mark A. Petersen discusses the scholarly treatment of Plymouth as "something of a backwater" in "The Plymouth Church and the Evolution of Puritan Religious Culture," *New England Quarterly* 66 (1993): 570–93, quote p. 572.

56. For example, George F. Willison, *Saints and Strangers: Being the Lives of the Pilgrim Fathers & Their Families, with Their Friends & Foes* (Orleans, Mass.: Parnassus Imprints, 1945); J. M. Bumsted, *The Pilgrims' Progress: The Ecclesiastical History of the Old Colony, 1620–1775* (1965); George D. Langdon, *Pilgrim Colony: A History of New*

Plymouth, 1620–1691 (New Haven, Conn.: Yale University Press, 1966); Eugene Aubrey Stratton, *Plymouth Colony: Its History and People, 1620–1691* (Salt Lake City: Ancestry Publications, 1986). More recently, H. Roger King has explored the history of Cape Cod and its contributions to Plymouth's religious tolerance and economic growth in *Cape Cod and Plymouth Colony in the Seventeenth Century* (Lanham, Md.: University Press of America, 1993).

57. John Demos, *A Little Commonwealth: Family Life in Plymouth Colony* (London: Oxford University Press, 1970; new ed. 2000); John Demos, "Notes on Life in Plymouth Colony," *William and Mary Quarterly* 22 (1965): 264–86.

58. James Deetz and Patricia Scott Deetz, *The Times of Their Lives: Life, Love, and Death in Plymouth Colony* (New York: Anchor Books, 2000).

59. John Winthrop, "A Modell of Christian Charity," in *The Puritans*, ed. Perry Miller and Thomas Johnson, 2nd ed. (New York: Harper Torchbooks, 1963), 195.

60. On differences between Plymouth and the other New England colonies, see J. M. Bumsted, "A Well-Bounded Toleration: Church and State in the Plymouth Colony," *Journal of Church and State* 10 (1968): 265–79; David S. Lovejoy, "Plain Englishmen at Plymouth," *New England Quarterly* 63 (1990): 232–48; Petersen, "The Plymouth Church."

61. Second ellipses in original. Robert Blair St. George, *Conversing by Signs: Poetics of Implication in Colonial New England Culture* (Chapel Hill: University of North Carolina Press, 1998), 3.

1. Massasoit's Stool and Wituwamat's Head

1. Sowams, or Pokanoket, was located at present-day Barrington, Rhode Island, on Narraganset Bay.

2. Edward Winslow, *Good Newes from New England* (1624), in *Chronicles of the Pilgrim Fathers of the Colony of Plymouth, from 1602 to 1625*, ed. Alexander Young (New York: Da Capo Press, 1971), 317–23. William Bradford briefly noted, "The Governor [Bradford] and people here had notice that Massasoit their friend was sick and near unto death. They sent to visit him, and withal sent him such comfortable things as gave him great content and was a means of his recovery" (William Bradford, *Of Plymouth Plantation, 1620–1647*, ed. Samuel Eliot Morison [New York: Alfred A. Knopf, 1994], 117).

3. Wessagusset eventually became the town of Weymouth, Massachusetts.

4. Winslow, *Good Newes*, 296–302; Phineas Pratt, "A Declaration of the Affairs of the English People that First Inhabited New England," Massachusetts Historical Society, *Collections* 34 (1857): 478. See chapter 2 for a discussion of Thomas Morton of Ma-re Mount.

5. Bradford, *Of Plymouth Plantation*, 99, 103, 105–10, 116; Sir Ferdinando Gorges, *A Briefe Narration of the Original Undertakings of the Advancement of Plantations into the Parts of America* (London, 1658), in Gorges, *America Painted to the Life* (London, 1659), 28; Winslow, *Good Newes*, 332–33.

6. Bradford, *Of Plymouth Plantation*, 116; Gorges, *Briefe Narration*, 28; Winslow, *Good Newes*, 340, 273, 327, 329, 332–33; Pratt, "Declaration," 478.

7. "A Letter of William Bradford and Isaac Allerton, 1623," *American Historical Review* 8 (1902): 298; Gorges, *Briefe Narration*, 28; Winslow, *Good Newes*, 331–38; Pratt, "Declaration," 485.

8. Winslow, *Good Newes*, 338–41.

9. Winslow, *Good Newes*, 343; Bradford, *Of Plymouth Plantation*, 118; Pratt, "Declaration," 486; "Letter of William Bradford and Isaac Allerton," 299.

10. Emmanuel Altham to Sir Edward Altham (1623), in *Three Visitors to Early Plymouth*, ed. Sydney V. James Jr. (Bedford, Mass.: Applewood Books, 1997), 31.

11. John Robinson, "His Letter to the Governor (Dec. 19, 1623)," in Bradford, *Of Plymouth Plantation*, 374–75.

12. Perry Miller, *The New England Mind: The Seventeenth Century* (Cambridge, Mass.: Harvard University Press, 1982). See the introduction for a discussion of Miller's views and the models of embodiment outlined in the following paragraph.

13. Miller, *New England Mind*, 3–34, 92–97, 116–95; Perry Miller, introduction to *The Puritans*, rev. ed., 2 vols., ed. Perry Miller and Thomas H. Johnson (New York: Harper and Row, 1963), 1:28–41, 56–58.

14. On colonists "reading" Indian bodies, see Karen Ordahl Kupperman, *Indians and English: Facing Off in Early America* (Ithaca, N.Y.: Cornell University Press, 2000), 41–76; and Joyce E. Chaplin, *Subject Matter: Technology, the Body, and Science on the Anglo-American Frontier, 1500–1676* (Cambridge, Mass.: Harvard University Press, 2001), 36–75.

15. [Edward Winslow], *A Relation or Iournall of the beginning and proceedings of the English Plantation setled at Plimoth in New England* (1622), in *Mourt's Relation: A Journal of the Pilgrims at Plymouth*, ed. Dwight B. Heath (Bedford, Mass.: Applewood Books, 1963), 55–57, quote p. 57. After Massasoit (or Osamequin) and Governor William Bradford concluded this treaty between the Wampanoags (or Pokanokets) and Plymouth in 1621, the two groups maintained friendly relations until Massasoit's death in 1660 (Bradford, *Of Plymouth Plantation*, 80–81; *Records of the Colony of New Plymouth in New England*, ed. Nathaniel B. Shurtleff, 12 vols. [Boston: William White, 1855–61] 3:192, hereafter cited as *Plymouth Colony Records*).

16. Karen Ordahl Kupperman, *Settling with the Indians: The Meeting of English and Indian Cultures in America, 1580–1640* (Totowa, N.J.: Rowman and Littlefield, 1980), 33–44, quote p. 34; [Winslow], *Relation*, 49; Kupperman, *Indians and English*, 42–43, 49–52; Lawrence Babb, *The Elizabethan Malady: A Study of Melancholia in English Literature from 1580 to 1642* (East Lansing: Michigan State College Press, 1951), 9–10. On sachems' speechways as signs of status and power, see Kathleen J. Bragdon, *Native People of Southern New England, 1500–1650* (Norman: University of Oklahoma Press, 1996), 173–74.

17. Winslow, *Good Newes*, 362.

18. Ibid., 323.

19. See Bragdon's discussion of native ritual practices and the significance of "the sensory dimensions of scent, sound, and motion" (*Native People of Southern New England*, 217–30, quote p. 224). Cf. Winslow, *Good Newes*, 356; Kupperman, *Indians and English*, 132–35.

20. William Wood, *New England's Prospect* (1634), ed. Alden T. Vaughan (Amherst: University of Massachusetts Press, 1977), 101.

21. Winslow, *Good Newes*, 357–58. Cf. Bragdon, *Native People of Southern New England*, 205; James Axtell, *The Invasion Within: The Contest of Cultures in Colonial North America* (New York: Oxford University Press, 1985), 17, 227–28.

22. Winslow, *Good Newes*, 317–18; John Robinson, *New Essays; or, Observations Divine and Moral* (1628), in *The Works of John Robinson*, ed. Robert Ashton, 3 vols. (Boston: Doctrinal Tract and Book Society, 1851), 1:127–30; Nancy G. Sirasi, *Medieval and Early Renaissance Medicine: An Introduction to Knowledge and Practice* (Chicago: University of Chicago Press, 1990), 97–106.

23. Sirasi, *Medieval and Early Renaissance Medicine*, 115–52; Anthony Fletcher, *Gender, Sex, and Subordination in England, 1500–1800* (New Haven, Conn.: Yale University Press, 1995), 30–31; Patricia Ann Watson, *The Angelical Conjunction: The Preacher-Physicians of Colonial New England* (Knoxville: University of Tennessee Press, 1991), 74–96. For example, Plymouth's John Atwood owned a copy of James Hart's *KAINIKH, or the Diet of the Diseased* (London, 1633) and William Bradford's wife Alice owned *Phillip Barough's Method of Physick* (London, 1617), which discuss such concerns as nutrition, the effects of the seasons on the body, the cutting of a sick person's hair, the purging of humors by bloodletting with leaches, and the preparation of herbal remedies to balance the humors.

24. Winslow, *Good Newes*, 319–20; Andrew Boord[e], *The Breuiarie of Health* (London: 1598), 8 verso, 17 verso. For a description of conserve, see Gervase Markham, *The English Housewife* (*The English Hus-wife* [1615]), ed. Michael R. Best (repr., Montreal: McGill-Queen's University Press, 1998), 116–17. Roger Williams (incorrectly) recorded that when they were very ill, Indians "have not (but what sometimes they get from the English) a raisin or currant or any physick, Fruit or spice, or any Comfort more than their Corne and Water, &c" (*A Key into the Language of America* [London, 1643], facsimile reprint [Menston, U.K.: Scholar Press, 1971], 186).

25. Boord[e], *Breuiarie of Health*, 14 and verso, 28 verso, 71 verso.

26. Hart, *Diet of the Diseased*, 41–43.

27. Hart, *Diet of the Diseased*, 60; Nicholas Culpepper, *English Physitian, or An Astrologo-Physical Discourse of the Vulgar Herbs of this Nation* (London, 1652), 223, 216. Like Hart, Culpepper claimed that the boiled leaves of strawberries produced a drink that would "cool the Liver and Blood, and asswage all Inflamations in the Reins [kidneys] and bladder, provoketh Urine, and allayeth the heat and sharpness thereof" (223). Although Hart, Culpepper, and Boorde did not mention it, strawberries leaves and sassafras also have laxative properties. It is difficult to determine the illness that affected Massasoit and other Wampanoag villagers; perhaps their very limited early spring diet, lacking fresh fruits or vegetables, had created a vitamin C deficiency, which can cause mouth sores and difficulty swallowing, and a fiber deficiency, which causes constipation.

28. Physician Andrew Boorde explained that vomiting was caused by excessive eating and drinking, "malice of the stomack," or "lubrication of the intestinesse of intrayles" (*Breuiarie of Health*, 13). See Hart, *Diet of the Diseased*, pt. 3, chap. 10 on

"Purgation or evacuation of corrupted humors in generall" and chap. 13 on "Vomits, Glisters, Suppositories."

29. Winslow, *Good Newes*, 322, 320.

30. [Winslow], *Relation*, 74; Joyce E. Chaplin, *Subject Matter: Technology, the Body, and Science on the Anglo-American Frontier, 1500–1676* (Cambridge, Mass.: Harvard University Press, 2001), 185, 183; Bradford, *Of Plymouth Plantation*, 270–71.

31. Bradford, *Of Plymouth Plantation*, 77, 223, 235, 260; Winslow, *Good Newes*, 297; "Governour Bradford's Letter Book," Massachusetts Historical Society, *Collections* 3 (1974): 66, 74–76.

32. Winslow, *Good Newes*, 321, 323.

33. Williams, *Key in the Language of America*, 190; Winslow, *Good Newes*, 358. Cf. Neal Salisbury, *Manitou and Providence: Indians, Europeans, and the Making of New England, 1500–1643* (New York: Oxford University Press, 1982), 137. For comparisons of Indian and English medicine, see Francis Jennings, *The Invasion of America: Indians, Colonialism, and the Cant of Conquest* (New York: W. W. Norton, 1975), 51–53; Micaela Sullivan-Fowler and Norman Gevitz, "Angelica Roots to Defend the Heart, Coltsfoot for the Measles: Indigenous and Naturalized Remedies in a 1696 Vade Mecum," in *Plants and People*, ed. Peter Benes (Boston: Boston University, 1996), 66–77; Sandra M. Narva, "'A Most Surprising Worm-Killer': A History of the Use and Cultivation of Wormseed (*Chenopodium ambroisides*, var. *anthelminticum*) in Early America," in *Plants and People*, ed. Peter Benes (Boston: Boston University, 1996), 78–91; Axtell, *The Invasion Within*, 227–32; Richard W. Cogley, *John Eliot's Mission to the Indians before King Philip's War* (Cambridge, Mass.: Harvard University Press, 1999), 172–76.

34. David Harley, "Spiritual Physic, Providence, and English Medicine, 1560–1640," in *Medicine and the Reformation*, ed. Ole Peter Grell and Andrew Cunningham (London: Routledge, 1993), 101–17, esp. 107. See also Andrew Wear, "Puritan Perceptions of Illness in Seventeenth Century England," in *Patients and Practitioners: Lay Perceptions of Medicine in Pre-Industrial Society*, ed. Roy Porter (Cambridge: Cambridge University Press, 1985), 55–99; Watson, *Angelical Conjunction*, 7–35.

35. Bragdon, *Native People of Southern New England*, 104–93, 201–8, quote p. 206.

36. Herbert Leventhal, *In the Shadow of the Enlightenment: Occultism and Renaissance Science in Eighteenth-Century America* (New York: New York University Press, 1976), 9. Cf. Arthur O. Lovejoy, *The Great Chain of Being: A Study of the History of an Idea* (New York: Harper & Row, 1960); Carolyn Merchant, *The Death of Nature* (New York: HarperCollins, 1980), 100–101.

37. Robinson, *New Essays*, 1:67. Robinson described the extent to which humans shared qualities with the nonhuman world: "being with the elements, life with the plants, sense with the beasts, and with the angels reason" (*Justification of Separation from the Church of England* [1610], in *Works*, 2:140).

38. Robert Cushman, *A Sermon Preached at Plimmoth in New-England*, December 9, 1621 (London, 1622), 14; Robinson, *New Essays*, 1:19–21.

39. John Robinson, *Of Religious Communion, Private and Public* (1614), in *Works*, 3:245–46; Robinson, *New Essays*, 1:17–18; Robinson, *Justification of Separation*, 2:339;

John Robinson, *A Treatise of the Lawfulnes of Hearing of the Ministers of the Church of England* (1634), in *Works*, 3:376.

40. Robert Cushman, "Cushman's Discourse," in *Chronicles of the Pilgrim Fathers of the Colony of Plymouth, from 1602–1625*, ed. Alexander Young (New York: Da Capo Press, 1971), 256.

41. Robinson, *New Essays*, 1:114.

42. Bradford, *Of Plymouth Plantation*, 118.

43. Robinson, *New Essays*, 1:25, 115; Gorges, *Briefe Narrative*, 28. On Englishmen "going native," see chapter 2.

44. Winslow, *Good Newes*, 273–74; Robinson, *New Essays*, 1:91–95, quote p. 94; Isaack de Rasieres to Samuel Blommaert (ca. 1628), *Three Visitors*, 78; Gorges, *Briefe Narration*, 28.

45. John Billington, who in 1630 was the first person executed for murder in Plymouth, was perhaps the most notorious of the "profane" strangers who sailed with the saints on the *Mayflower* in 1620 (Bradford, *Of Plymouth Plantation*, 156–57, 234; Bradford, "Letter Book," 37).

46. Robinson, *New Essays*, 1:225–26.

47. Ibid., 1:147–48.

48. Ibid., 1:148; Cushman, *Sermon*, 15–16.

49. William Ames, *The Marrow of Theology: William Ames, 1576–1633* (*The Marrow of Sacred Divinity*, 1629), trans. and ed. John D. Eusden (Durham, N.C.: Labyrinth Press, 1983), 2:3, "Good Works."

50. See Robinson's letter of instruction to the separatists aboard the *Mayflower*, in [Winslow], *Relation*, 9–14; also in Bradford, *Of Plymouth Plantation*, 368–71.

51. On the frequently condemned though common practice of manipulating one's appearance in early modern England, see Susan Vincent, *Dressing the Elite: Clothes in Early Modern England* (Oxford: Berg, 2003); Adrian Streete, "Reforming Signs: Semiotics, Calvinism, and Clothing in Sixteenth-Century England," *Literature and History* 12 (2003): 1–18; Martha L. Finch, "'Fashions of Worldly Dames': Separatist Discourses of Dress in Early Modern London, Amsterdam, and Plymouth Colony," *Church History* 74 (2005): 494–533. Robinson discussed "outward appearances" and deception in *New Essays*, 1:183–86.

52. On the importance of sight (over hearing) and sacred images in medieval Christianity, see Eamon Duffy, *The Stripping of the Altars: Traditional Religion in England* (New Haven, Conn.: Yale University Press, 1992), 392, 413, 421, 429, 531, 533; John Phillips, *The Reformation of Images: Destruction of Art in England, 1535–1660* (Berkeley: University of California Press, 1973), 14–17; Lee Palmer Wandel, *Voracious Idols and Violent Hands: Iconoclasm in Reformation Zurich, Strasbourg, and Basel* (Cambridge: Cambridge University Press, 1995), 26–51. On the continuing importance of the visual and public self-presentation and display in early New England, see Robert Blair St. George, *Conversing by Signs: Poetics of Implication in Colonial New England Culture* (Chapel Hill: University of North Carolina Press, 1998), esp. 3–4.

53. See the introduction and chapter 4 for detailed discussions of visible sainthood.

54. Winslow, *Journal*, 77–80; Bradford, *Of Plymouth Plantation*, 98–99; Winslow, *Good Newes*, 302.

55. Winslow, *Good Newes*, 309–11.

56. Winslow, *Good Newes*, 311–12; Karen Ordahl Kupperman, "English Perceptions of Treachery, 1583–1640: The Case of the American 'Savages,'" *Historical Journal* 20 (1977): 263–87.

57. Winslow, *Good Newes*, 331, 339; Thomas Morton, *New English Canaan* (1632), in *Tracts and Other Papers*, vol. 2, ed. Peter Force (Gloucester, Mass.: Peter Smith, 1963), 94, 75–76, 78. For an analysis of the conspiratorial nature, on the parts of both Indians and English, of the Massachusetts-Plymouth conflict, see Salisbury, *Manitou and Providence*, 125–34.

58. Thomas Laqueur, *Making Sex: Body and Gender from the Greeks to Freud* (Cambridge, Mass.: Harvard University Press, 1990), 98; Fletcher, *Gender, Sex, and Subordination*, 33, 87.

59. Robinson, *New Essays*, 1:92–93.

60. Fletcher, *Gender, Sex, and Subordination*, 61–71, 12–15, quote from Levinus Lemnius, *Touchstone of Complexions* (1633), 69, cited in Fletcher, 61; Laura Gowing, *Domestic Dangers: Women, Words, and Sex in Early Modern London* (Oxford: Oxford University Press, 1996), 1–8.

61. Winslow, *Good Newes*, 339, 341. On the gendered language of insult and men as "effeminate," see Gowing, *Domestic Dangers*, 59–110; and Anne S. Lombard, *Making Manhood: Growing Up Male in Colonial New England* (Cambridge, Mass.: Harvard University Press, 2003), 10–11.

62. Winslow, *Good Newes*, 359; Wood, *New England's Prospect*, 103.

63. Ann Kibbey, *The Interpretation of Material Shapes in Puritanism: A Study of Rhetoric, Prejudice, and Violence* (Cambridge: Cambridge University Press, 1986), 102.

64. Bradford, *Plymouth Plantation*, 118; "A Letter of William Bradford and Isaac Allerton," 298–99; Altham, *Three Visitors*, 31; Winslow, *Good Newes*, 335.

65. *Plymouth Colony Records*, 5:205–6.

66. Cotton Mather, *Magnalia Christi Americana; Or, The Ecclesiastical History of New-England* (London, 1702), 54; Thomas Church, *The History of King Philip's War* (1716, repr. 1772), 2nd ed. (Exeter, N.H.: J. & B. Williams, 1829), 125–26. Thomas Church was the son of Captain Benjamin Church.

67. *Plymouth Church Records, 1620–1859*, 2 vols. (New York: New England Society, 1920), 1:152–53. Metacom, or Philip, was actually killed on Aug. 12; the day of thanksgiving was held on Aug. 17.

68. Increase Mather, *A Brief History of the War with the Indians in New England* (London, 1676), 47, 45.

69. William Hubbard, *A Narrative of the Indian Wars in New-England* (Boston, 1775), 180.

70. Francis Dillon has claimed that Wituwamat's head remained on the fort "for many years," but he cites no supporting documentation for this (*A Place for Habitation: The Pilgrim Fathers and Their Quest* [London: Hutchinson, 1973], 184).

71. Regina Janes, "Beheadings," *Representations* 35 (Summer 1991): 31. Janes writes, "The [severed and publicly displayed] head tells all. It identifies itself, and it speaks, to

the extent of its previous owner's ability, a silent narrative of fallen greatness and mastery transferred. On its face, the head carries our social identity: the lineaments that enable us to recognize members of our species and to tell one of us from the next" (29). See also: Stephen Greenblatt, "Mutilation and Meaning," in *The Body in Parts: Fantasies of Corporeality in Early Modern Europe*, ed. David Hillman and Carla Mazzio (New York: Routledge, 1997), 221–41, esp. 232–34; Elizabeth Hanson, "Torture and Truth in Renaissance England," *Representations* 34 (Spring 1991): 53–84; Paula Sampson Preston, "The Severed Head of Charles I of England: Its Use as a Political Stimulus, *Winterthur Portfolio* 6 (1970): 1–13; Nancy Klein Maguire, "The Theatrical Mack/Masque of Politics: The Case of Charles I," *Journal of British Studies* 28 (1989): 1–22.

72. Mather, *Magnalia Christi Americana*, 199; Jill Lepore, *The Name of War: King Philip's War and the Origins of American Identity* (New York: Vintage Books, 1999), 174; Cotton Mather, *The Life and Death of the Renown'd Mr. John Eliot* (London, 1691), 95.

73. Winslow, *Good Newes*, 343; Altham, *Three Visitors*, 31.

2. A Banquet in the Wilderness

1. William Bradford, *Of Plymouth Plantation, 1620–1647*, ed. Samuel Eliot Morison (New York: Alfred A. Knopf, 1994), 61–62, 25, 64. An earlier version of this chapter appears as "'Civilized' Bodies and the 'Savage' Environment of Early New Plymouth," in *A Centre of Wonders: The Body in Early America*, ed. Janet Moore Lindman and Michele Lise Tarter (Ithaca, N.Y.: Cornell University Press, 2001), 43–74.

2. [Edward Winslow], *A Relation or Iournall of the beginning and proceedings of the English Plantation setled at* Plimoth *in New England* (London: 1622), in *Mourt's Relation: A Journal of the Pilgrims at Plymouth*, ed. Dwight B. Heath (Bedford, Mass.: Applewood Books, 1963), 15–16.

3. The women likely were washing their families' linen undergarments (see chapter 3). During their voyage to New England Francis Higginson noted that his wife and daughter went on shore "to wash our linens" ("Letter to His Friends in England" [July 24, 1629], in *Letters From New England: The Massachusetts Bay Colony, 1629–1638*, ed. Everett Emerson [Amherst: University of Massachusetts Press, 1976], 14).

4. [Winslow], *Relation*, 19–22. English travelers to America were suspicious of drinking the water they found there, unsure of its humoral effects; they were also accustomed to water in England being polluted and unsafe to drink. See Dean Albertson, "Puritan Liquor in the Planting of New England," *New England Quarterly* 23 (1950): 477–90.

5. [Winslow], *Relation*, 12–24, 35–37; Bradford, *Of Plymouth Plantation*, 64–66, 68–70. Cf. William Wood, *New England's Prospect* (1634), ed. Alden T. Vaughan (Amherst: University of Massachusetts Press, 1977), 108.

6. The settlers learned the name of the former Wampanoag village, whose inhabitants had died four years earlier from disease, from Samoset, who first visited them in March 1621 ([Winslow], *Relation*, 51; Bradford, *Of Plymouth Plantation*, 79–80).

7. [Winslow], *Relation*, 55, 58, 61; Bradford, *Of Plymouth Plantation*, 77–79, 81, 447; Eugene Aubrey Stratton, *Plymouth Colony: Its History and People, 1620–1691* (Salt Lake City: Ancestry Publishing, 1986), 21.

8. On the separatists' occupations in Leiden and their communal living arrangement, see Marshall W. S. Swan, *The Pilgrims in Holland* (Amsterdam: Veldhuizen and Boxman, 1953), 10–11.

9. See J. S. Wood and M. Steinitz, "The World We Have Gained: House, Common, and Village in New England," *Journal of Historical Geography* 18 (1992): 111; John Frederick Martin, *Profits in the Wilderness: Entrepreneurship and the Founding of New England in the Seventeenth Century* (Chapel Hill: University of North Carolina Press, 1991), 113–17; Cecilia Tichi, *New World, New Earth: Environmental Reform in American Literature from the Puritans through Whitman* (New Haven, Conn.: Yale University Press, 1979), 47–54; Yi-Fu Tuan, *Landscapes of Fear* (New York: Pantheon Books, 1979), 55. On this transformative process in Ohio's Western Reserve during the early 1800s, see Amy DeRogatis, *Moral Geography: Maps, Missionaries, and the American Frontier* (New York: Columbia University Press, 2003).

10. Chris Shilling, *The Body and Social Theory* (London: Sage Publications, 1996), 103; Edward S. Casey, *The Fate of Place: A Philosophical History* (Berkeley: University of California Press, 1997), 202–42; Yi-Fu Tuan, *Space and Place: The Perspective of Experience* (Minneapolis: University of Minnesota Press, 1977), 43–50; Arnold Berleant, *Living in the Landscape: Toward an Aesthetics of Environment* (Lawrence: University of Kansas Press, 1997), 97–111; Jonathan Z. Smith, *To Take Place: Toward Theory in Ritual* (Chicago: University of Chicago Press, 1987), 24–46; J. Douglas Porteous, *Landscapes of the Mind: Worlds of Sense and Metaphor* (Toronto: University of Toronto Press, 1990), 70.

11. Bradford, *Of Plymouth Plantation*, 62.

12. Bryan S. Turner, *The Body and Society: Explorations in Social Theory*, 2nd ed. (London: Sage, 1996), 66, 230.

13. Berleant, *Living in the Landscape*, 106.

14. Joyce E. Chaplin, *Subject Matter: Technology, the Body, and Science on the Anglo-American Frontier, 1500–1676* (Cambridge, Mass.: Harvard University Press, 2001), 117; Stephen Greenblatt, *Marvelous Possessions: The Wonder of the New World* (Chicago: University of Chicago Press, 1991).

15. [Winslow], *Relation*, 41; Bradford, *Of Plymouth Plantation*, xxiv; George D. Langdon Jr., *Pilgrim Colony: A History of New Plymouth, 1620–1691* (New Haven, Conn.: Yale University Press, 1966), 12.

16. Wood, *New England's Prospect*, 28.

17. Rhys Isaac, *The Transformation of Virginia, 1740–1790* (Chapel Hill: University of North Carolina Press, 1982), 51. Hippocrates wrote the classic text describing the direct influence of the environment on human physiology, character, and health: *Airs, Waters, and Places* (London: Wyman and Sons, 1881).

18. Bradford, *Of Plymouth Plantation*, 26 (emphasis added).

19. William Cronon, *Changes in the Land: Indians, Colonists, and the Ecology of New England* (New York: Hill and Wang, 1983), 159–70.

20. John Robinson, *New Essays; or, Observations Divine and Moral* (1628), in *The Works of John Robinson* (Boston: Doctrinal Tract and Book Society, 1851), 1:14–15.

21. John Josselyn, *Two Voyages to New-England* (1674), in *John Josselyn, Colonial Traveler: A Critical Edition of* Two Voyages to New-England, ed. Paul J. Lindholdt (Hanover, N.H.: University Press of New England, 1988), 64; Clarence J. Glacken, *Traces on the Rhodian Shore: Nature and Culture in Western Thought from Ancient Times to the End of the Eighteenth Century* (Berkeley: University of California Press, 1967), 438–59, quote pp. 445–46; Trudy Eden, "Food, Assimilation, and the Malleability of the Human Body in Early Virginia," in *A Centre of Wonders: The Body in Early America*, ed. Janet Moore Lindman and Michele Lise Tarter (Ithaca, N.Y.: Cornell University Press, 2001), 29–42; Joyce E. Chaplin, "Natural Philosophy and an Early Racial Idiom in North America: Comparing English and Indian Bodies," *William and Mary Quarterly* 54 (1997): 234–35.

22. Karen Ordahl Kupperman, "Climate and Mastery of the Wilderness in Seventeenth-Century New England," in *Seventeenth-Century New England*, ed. David D. Hall and David Grayson Allen (Boston: The Colonial Society of Massachusetts), *Publications* 63 (1984): 13; John Canup, *Out of the Wilderness: The Emergence of an American Identity in Colonial New England* (Middletown, Conn.: Wesleyan University Press, 1990), 8–28; John Smith, *A Description of New England* (London, 1616) in *Works*, ed. Edward Arber, 2 vols. (Westminster: Archibald Constable, 1895), 1:13; Francis Higginson, *New-Englands Plantation* (London, 1630), 5, 9; Thomas Morton, *New English Canaan* (London, 1632), in *Tracts and Other Papers*, ed. Peter Force (Gloucester, Mass.: Peter Smith, 1963), 2:64; Wood, *New England's Prospect*, 32;

23. Josselyn, *Two Voyages*, 35.

24. John White, *The Planters Plea* (London, 1630), 23.

25. Bradford, *Of Plymouth Plantation*, 28. Those who settled further south required a "seasoning" period of about two years, during which one's body adapted to a climate warmer than that of England; see William Hubbard, *A General History of New England* (1680), Massachusetts Historical Society, *Collections* 15–16 (1815–1818): 324–25; John Smith, *A Map of Virginia* (1612), in *Works*, ed. Edward Arber (Westminster, U.K.: Archibald Constable, 1895), 1:47. Cf. Karen Ordahl Kupperman, "Fear of Hot Climates in the Anglo-American Colonial Experience," *William and Mary Quarterly* 41 (1984): 215–16; Canup, *Out of the Wilderness*, 11–12; Earle Carville, "Environment, Disease, and Mortality in Early Virginia," *Journal of American Geography* 5 (1979): 365–90.

26. Canup, *Out of the Wilderness*, 5, 10; Bradford, *Of Plymouth Plantation*, 26.

27. John Smith, *New Englands Trials* (1622), in *Chronicles of the Pilgrim Fathers*, ed. John Masefield (London: J. M. Dent and Sons, n.d.), 252. Cf. David Cressy, *Coming Over: Migration and Communication between England and New England in the Seventeenth Century* (Cambridge: Cambridge University Press, 1987), 159.

28. Bradford, *Of Plymouth Plantation*, 26, 329, 57, 58–59.

29. Bradford, *Of Plymouth Plantation*, 58–59. Cf. W. Sears Nickerson, *Land Ho! 1620: A Seaman's Story of the* Mayflower, *Her Construction, Her Navigation, and Her First Landfall* (ca. 1930), ed. Delores Bird Carpenter (East Lansing: Michigan State University Press, 1997), 25–28.

30. William Strachey, *A True Reportory of the Wreck and Redemption of Sir Thomas Gates, Knight, upon and from the Islands of Bermudas*, in *A Voyage to Virginia in 1609*, ed. Louis Wright (Charlottesville: University Press of Virginia, 1964), 4, 5, quoted in Richard Cullen Rath, *How Early America Sounded* (Ithaca, N.Y.: Cornell University Press, 2003), 14–15.

31. Wood, *New England's Prospect*, 28.

32. Edward Winslow, "A Letter Sent from New England to a Friend," in *Mourt's Relation*, 86; Bradford, *Of Plymouth Plantation*, 223. For a description of shipboard illnesses and diet, see Cressy, *Coming Over*, 169–72.

33. Bradford, *Of Plymouth Plantation*, 58, 77–79, 84; Sir Ferdinando Gorges, *A Briefe Narration of the Original Undertakings of the Advancement of Plantations into the Parts of America* (London, 1658), 32, in Gorges, *America Painted to the Life* (London, 1659).

34. Bradford, *Of Plymouth Plantation*, 130.

35. Nathaniel B. Shurtlieff, ed., *Records of the Colony of New Plymouth in New England*, 12 vols. (Boston: William White, 1855–61), 3:195–96, hereafter cited as *Plymouth Colony Records*.

36. Seventeenth-century New England church and court records and other documents that included dates used both the "Old Style" Julian and the "New Style" Gregorian calendars. Thus, a double-dating system for recording dates occurring between January 1 and March 25 indicated both the old-style and the new-style years with a slash, e.g., February 13, 1642/3, or March 2, 1679/80. I follow the same dating system in this book.

37. *Plymouth Colony Records*, 3:158; 6:8, 75–76; 2:174; Bradford, *Of Plymouth Plantation*, 87. For the other coroner inquests of deaths by environmental factors, see *Plymouth Colony Records*, 1:39, 88; 2:151, 175; 3:15, 16, 28, 70, 92–93, 148, 159–60, 208; 4:12, 83–84, 170–71, 176, 177; 5:7, 29, 94–95, 101, 122–23, 225–27, 262–63; 6:7.

38. Canup, *Out of the Wilderness*, 41.

39. Morton, *New English Canaan*, 10.

40. Mount Wollaston was located on the former Indian site of Pasonagessit, near present-day Quincy on the Massachusetts Bay, thirty miles north of Plymouth. It was first named for Morton's partner Captain Wollaston, "a man of pretty parts," and then renamed Ma-re Mount, or "mountain by the sea," when Wollaston left New England for Virginia (Bradford, *Of Plymouth Plantation*, 204).

41. Bradford, *Of Plymouth Plantation*, 205; Morton, *New English Canaan*, 41. A "pettifogger" was a lawyer who handled petty cases; the term implied trickery and cheating. On Morton's and Plymouth's opposing views of the wilderness, see Michael Zuckerman, "Pilgrims in the Wilderness: Community, Modernity, and the Maypole at Merry Mount," *New England Quarterly* 50 (1977): 261–63; Richard Drinnon, "The Maypole of Merry Mount: Thomas Morton and the Puritan Patriarchs," *Massachusetts Review* 21 (1980): 393–95.

42. Bradford, *Of Plymouth Plantation*, 207; Karen Ordahl Kupperman, "Thomas Morton, Historian," *New England Quarterly* 50 (1977): 663–64; Chaplin, *Subject Matter*, 79–115; Harold L. Peterson, "The Military Equipment of the Plymouth and Bay Colonies, 1620–1690," *New England Quarterly* 20 (1947): 197–208; Harold L. Peterson,

Arms and Armor of the Pilgrims, 1620–1692 (Plymouth, Mass.: Plimoth Plantation, 1957); Douglas Edward Leach, "The Military System of Plymouth Colony," *New England Quarterly* 24 (1951): 342–64.

43. Nathaniel Morton, *New England's Memorial* (1687), in *Chronicles of the Pilgrim Fathers*, ed. John Masefield (New York: E. P. Dutton, n.d.), 92; William Bradford, "Governor Bradford's Letter Book," Massachusetts Historical Society, *Collections* 3 (1794): 62, 63–64; Bradford, *Of Plymouth Plantation*, 208.

44. Bradford, *Of Plymouth Plantation*, 205–7; Morton, *New England Canaan*, 89, 10; Zuckerman, "Pilgrims in the Wilderness," 263. Cf. Edith Murphy, "'A Rich Widow, Now to Be Tane Down or Laid Downe': Solving the Riddle of Thomas Morton's 'Rise Oedipus,'" *William and Mary Quarterly* 53 (1996): 755–68. On May Day celebrations in early modern England, see David Cressy, *Bonfires and Bells: National Memory and the Protestant Calendar in Elizabethan and Stuart England* (Berkeley: University of California Press, 1989), 21–23.

45. Bradford, *Of Plymouth Plantation*, 208, 206, 205; Bradford, "Governor Bradford's Letter Book," 61–62. Some scholars have taken Bradford's word that Morton's men had sexual relations with Indian women (Zuckerman, "Pilgrims in the Wilderness," 263; Richard Slotkin, *Regeneration Through Violence: The Mythology of the American Frontier, 1600-1860* (Norman: University of Oklahoma Press, 2000), 60–64), while others note there is "no conclusive evidence" of this (John P. McWilliams Jr., "Fictions of Merry Mount," *American Quarterly* 29 [1977]: 12).

46. David D. Smits, "'We Are Not to Grow Wild': Seventeenth-Century New England's Repudiation of Anglo-Indian Intermarriage," *American Indian Culture and Research Journal* 11, no. 4 (1987): 6, 9.

47. *Plymouth Colony Records*, 1:132; 2:4; 5:31, 107, 163; 6:92.

48. Neal Salisbury, *Manitou and Providence: Indians, Europeans, and the Making of New England, 1500–1643* (New York: Oxford University Press, 1982), 160; Kathleen J. Bragdon, *Native People of Southern New England, 1500–1650* (Norman: University of Oklahoma Press, 1996), 178; Smits, "'We Are Not to Grow Wild,'" 4–5, 16–17, 15. On native women's modesty, see Morton, *New English Canaan*, 23; [Winslow], *Relation*, 79; Wood, *New England's Prospect*, 114, 115; Edward Winslow, *Good Newes from New England* (1624), in *Chronicles of the Pilgrim Fathers of the Colony of New Plymouth, 1602–1625*, ed. Alexander Young (New York: Da Capo Press, 1971), 364.

49. Penobscot was located near the present site of Castine, Maine.

50. Bradford, *Of Plymouth Plantation*, 219–20, 226, 232–33.

51. John W. Adams and Alice Bee Kasakoff, "Migration and the Family in Colonial New England: The View from Genealogies," *Journal of Family History* 9 (1984): 30.

52. *Plymouth Colony Records*, 5:169; 4:104; 6:178.

53. Bradford, "Governor Bradford's Letter Book," 61, 63; Emmanuel Altham to Sir Edward Altham, March 1623/4, in *Three Visitors to Early Plymouth*, ed. Sydney V. James Jr. (Bedford, Mass.: Applewood Books, 1997), 38; Bradford, *Of Plymouth Plantation*, 127.

54. John Winthrop to Margaret Winthrop, July 23, 1630, *Winthrop Papers*, 2:303, quoted in Karen Ordahl Kupperman, "The Beehive as a Model for Colonial Design,"

in *America in European Consciousness, 1493–1750*, ed. Kupperman (Chapel Hill: University of North Carolina Press, 1995), 282; Bradford, *Of Plymouth Plantation*, 316–22, quotes pp. 316, 321; Canup, *Out of the Wilderness*, 29–54, quotes pp. 41, 42; Isaac, *Transformation of Virginia*, 49, 368 n. 13; Carolyn Merchant, *Ecological Revolutions: Nature, Gender, and Science in New England* (Chapel Hill: University of North Carolina Press, 1989), 65. See chapter 3 for a discussion of the sexual crime wave in Plymouth in 1642.

55. Gorges, *Briefe Narration*, 32; Winslow, *Good Newes*, 345, 370; John Wiswall to George Rigby (September 27, 1638), in *Letters From New England: The Massachusetts Bay Colony, 1629–1638*, ed. Everett Emerson (Amherst: University of Massachusetts Press, 1976), 232; John Winthrop Jr., "Indian Corne" (ca. 1662), in Fulmer Mood, "John Winthrop, Jr., on Indian Corn," *New England Quarterly* 10 (1937): 131, 127–28. On corn as the colonists' single most important crop, see Cronon, *Changes in the Land*, 127; Jonathan Beecher Field, "'Peculiar Manuerance': Puritans, Indians, and the Rhetoric of Agriculture, 1629–1654," in *Plants and People*, ed. Peter Benes (Boston: Boston University, 1996), 20.

56. Wood, *New England's Prospect*, 33.

57. Like Massasoit and his men described in chapter 1, Tisquantum was a "tall, straight man" who brought "tall, proper men" to meet the English, and Quadequina was a "tall, proper young man" ([Winslow], *Relation*, 51, 53, 57).

58. Carolyn Freeman Travers, "Were They Shorter Back Then?" (1998), Plimoth-on-Web (Plymouth, Mass.: Plimoth Plantation, 2000), 1–4, www.plimoth.org/Library/l-short.htm. Travers based her analysis on a comparison of studies of human skeletal remains in England and New England.

59. Carolyn Freeman Travers, "Did They All Die Young?" (1998), Plimoth-on-Web (Plymouth, Mass.: Plimoth Plantation, 2000), 1–5, www.plimoth.org/Library/l-young.htm; John Demos, *A Little Commonwealth: Family Life in Plymouth Colony* (London: Oxford University Press, 1970), 192, table II.

60. Robert Blair St. George, "'Set Thine House in Order': The Domestication of the Yeomanry in Seventeenth-Century New England," in *New England Begins: The Seventeenth Century*, vol. 2, *Mentality and Environment* (Boston: Museum of Fine Arts, 1982), 180; John Demos, "Notes on Life in Plymouth Colony," *William and Mary Quarterly* 22 (1965): 271; Demos, *A Little Commonwealth*, 192–93; Kupperman, "Climate and Mastery of the Wilderness," 16–17; Wood, *New England's Prospect*, 33; Richard Archer, "New England Mosaic: A Demographic Analysis for the Seventeenth Century," *William and Mary Quarterly* 47 (1990): 477–502; Thomas R. Cole, "Family, Settlement, and Migration in Southeastern Massachusetts, 1650–1805: The Case for Regional Analysis," *New England Historical and Genealogical Register* 132 (1978): 171–85; Cressy, *Coming Over*, 69.

61. Morton, *New English Canaan*, 82, 64; George Gardyner, *A Description of the New World* (London, 1651), 90–92, cited in Cressy, *Coming Over*, 33; Wood, *New England's Prospect*, 33; Edward Winslow, *Good Newes*, 369–70.

62. Bradford, *Of Plymouth Plantation*, 328–29.

63. Theano S. Terkenli has defined "rootedness": "The word describes a state of mind or being in which a person's whole life and pursuits are centered around a

broadly defined home. The core meaning of rootedness is found in the sense of literally belonging somewhere" ("Home as Region," *The Geographical Review* 85 [1995]: 329).

64. Bradford, *Of Plymouth Plantation*, 23–24.

65. Field, "'Peculiar Manuerance,'" 22. For a lengthy discussion of reasons for emigration, see Cressy, *Coming Over*, 74–106.

66. R[obert] C[ushman], "Reasons and Considerations touching the lawfulness of removing out of England into the parts of America" (1622), in *Mourt's Relation: A Journal of the Pilgrims at Plymouth*, ed. Dwight B. Heath (Bedford, Mass.: Applewood Books, 1963), 91–92. Cf. John Winthrop, "General Considerations for the Plantation in New-England; with an Answer to Several Objections," in *Chronicles of the First Planters of the Colony of Massachusetts Bay, from 1623 to 1636*, ed. Alexander Young (Boston: Charles C. Little and James Brown, 1846), 271–72; John Cotton, "God's Promise to His Plantations" (London: 1630), *Old South Leaflets*, 3, no. 53 (Boston: Directors of the Old South Work, n.d.), 1–16.

67. On the decimation of the New England native population due to disease, see Francis Jennings, *The Invasion of America: Indians, Colonialism, and the Cant of Conquest* (New York: W. W. Norton, 1975), 15–31; Cronon, *Changes in the Land*, 84–89, 161–62; Karen Ordahl Kupperman, *Settling with the Indians: The Meeting of English and Indian Cultures in America, 1580–1640* (Totowa, N.J.: Rowman and Littlefield, 1980), 5–6.

68. Emmanuel Altham to Sir Edward Altham, September 1623, *Three Visitors*, 29; [Winslow], *Relation*, 51, 63; Robert Cushman, "Cushman's Discourse" (1621), in *Chronicles of the Pilgrim Fathers of the Colony of Plymouth, 1602–1625*, ed. Alexander Young (New York: Da Capo Press, 1971), 258–59; Bradford, *Of Plymouth Plantation*, 25.

69. [Winslow], *Relation*, 18, 46; Bragdon, *Native People of Southern New England*, 16.

70. [Winslow], *Relation*, 25, 35, 37, 41; Richard M. Candee, "A Documentary History of Plymouth Colony Architecture, 1620–1700," pt. 1, *Old-Time New England* 59 (1969): 61; Abbott Lowell Cummings, *The Framed Houses of Massachusetts Bay, 1625–1725* (Cambridge, Mass.: Harvard University Press, 1979), 18–21. For a humorous account of Plymouth's first shelters, see Edward Ward, *A Trip to New-England* (1699), in *Boston in 1682 and 1699*, ed. George Parker Winship (New York: Burt Franklin, 1970), 49–50.

71. [Winslow], *Relation*, 41–44, 48; Bradford, *Of Plymouth Plantation*, 72, 85.

72. Winslow, "A Letter Sent From New England," 81, 82, 86; Bradford, *Of Plymouth Plantation*, 76, 94, 97, 111; Winslow, *Good Newes*, 295; John Pory to the Earl of Southampton, Jan. 13, 1622/23 and later, *Three Visitors*, 11; Altham, Sept. 1623, *Three Visitors*, 24.

73. Isaack de Rasieres to Samuel Blommaert, ca. 1628, *Three Visitors*, 76; Candee, "Documentary History," 62–63; John Smith, *Advertisement For the inexperienced Planters of New-England, or anywhere* (1623), in *The Puritans*, rev. ed., 2 vols., ed. Perry Miller and Thomas H. Johnson (New York: Harper Torchbooks, 1963), 2:397. On "palisado" houses, see Cummings, *Framed Houses*, 21; James Deetz, "Plymouth

Colony Architecture: Archaeological Evidence from the Seventeenth Century," in *Architecture in Colonial Massachusetts*, Colonial Society of Massachusetts, *Publications* 51 (1979): 43–59; St. George, "'Set Thine House in Order,'" 161–62.

74. Darrett B. Rutman, *Husbandmen of Plymouth: Farms and Villages in the Old Colony, 1620–1692* (Boston: Beacon Press, 1967), 4; Demos, *Little Commonwealth*, 13–14.

75. Bradford, *Of Plymouth Plantation*, 121.

76. Ibid., 120.

77. John J. Waters, "The Traditional World of the New England Peasants: A View from Seventeenth-Century Barnstable," *New England Historical and Genealogical Register* 130 (1976): 5.

78. John R. Stilgoe, *Common Landscape of America, 1580 to 1845* (New Haven, Conn.: Yale University Press, 1982), 12–17, 141; David Hackett Fischer, *Albion's Seed: Four British Folkways in America* (New York: Oxford University Press, 1989), 181–88.

79. See, e.g., *Records of the Town of Plymouth* (Plymouth, Mass.: Avery and Doten, 1889), 1:26–27, 55, 57–58, 84–85, 92–93.

80. Bradford, *Of Plymouth Plantation*, 145.

81. Field, "'Peculiar Manuerance,'" 12–24. Discussing "spatial practices," Michel de Certeau writes that moving around in a particular environment generates "lived space," which has order, shape, and, over time, a familiarity that becomes "encysted" in the body (*The Practice of Everyday Life*, trans. Steven Rendall [Berkeley: University of California Press, 1984], 92–93, 108, 117–18).

82. Winslow, "A Letter," 83–85; Winslow, *Good Newes*, 355.

83. Cushman, "Reasons and Considerations," 91–91.

84. See, e.g., David Grayson Allen, "*Vacuum Domicilum*: The Social and Cultural Landscape of Seventeenth-Century New England," in *New England Begins: The Seventeenth Century*, vol. 1, *Introduction: Migration and Settlement* (Boston: Museum of Fine Arts, 1982); Jennings, *The Invasion of America*, 82–83; Martin, *Profits in the Wilderness*, 111–20; Kupperman, *Settling with the Indians*, 89–90.

85. Robinson, *New Essays*, 1:113–16.

86. Yi-Fu Tuan writes, "Villagers everywhere create a humanized landscape out of an original wilderness, knowing that they can maintain their creation only through sweat and constant vigilance" (*Landscapes of Fear*, 55).

87. Cronon, *Changes in the Land*, 21.

88. Winslow, *Good Newes*, 372–74.

89. Rasieres, *Three Visitors*, 77; Robert Child, "Letter," Colonial Society of Massachusetts, *Publications* 38 (1947–51): 51; Bradford, *Of Plymouth Plantation*, 315, 333.

90. Bradford, *Of Plymouth Plantation.*, 129.

91. *Ibid.*, 143–44, 315.

92. Cushman, "Cushman's Discourse," 256, 265; Kupperman, *Settling with the Indians*, 172–76.

93. Bradford, *Of Plymouth Plantation*, 25; Morton, *New English Canaan*, 31, 33–34; Winslow, *Good Newes*, 365–66; Phineas Pratt, "A Declaration of the Affairs of the English People that First Inhabited New England," Massachusetts Historical Society, *Collections* 34 (1857): 477; [Winslow], *Relation*, 59. Carolyn Merchant argues that Indians'

"mimetic consciousness" integrated all the sensory perceptions to sustain their lives through hunting and agriculture, while puritans' emphasis on vision over the other senses distanced humans from nature; see *Ecological Revolutions*, 20–23, 47–48, 58.

94. Peter A. Thomas, "Contrastive Subsistence Strategies and Land Use as Factors for Understanding Indian-White Relations in New England," *Ethnohistory* 23 (1976): 1–18; Bragdon, *Native People of Southern New England*, 14–20; James T. Lemon, "Early Americans and their Social Environment," *Journal of Historical Geography* 6 (1980): 115–31.

95. Higginson, *New-Englands Plantation*, 12.

96. Morton, *New English Canaan*, 20; Cronon, *Changes in the Land*, 54–58; Jennings, *Invasion of America*, 58–61; Bragdon, *Native People of Southern New England*, 80–101; James Axtell, *The Invasion Within: The Contest of Cultures in Colonial North America* (New York: Oxford University Press, 1985), 136–38, 148–59.

97. Wood, *New England's Prospect*, 96.

98. Wood, *New England's Prospect*, 83–84; Winslow, *Good Newes*, 355; Bradford, *Of Plymouth Plantation*, 111–12. For a debate about whether using fish as fertilizer was an Indian or an English invention, see Lynn Ceci, "Fish Fertilizer: A Native North American Practice?" *Science* 188 (1975): 26–30; and Nanepashemet, "It Smells Fishy to Me: An Argument Supporting the Use of Fish Fertilizer by the Native People of Southern New England," in *Algonkians of New England: Past and Present*, ed. Peter Benes (Boston: Boston University Press, 1993), 42–50. On Plymouth's cultivation of maize, see Rutman, *Husbandmen of Plymouth*, 7–12, 17, 46, 50.

99. Cronon, *Changes in the Land*, 128; Jennings, *Invasion of America*, 63.

100. Axtell, *Invasion Within*, 155. See also Daniel A. Romani Jr., "'Our *English Clover-grass* sowen thrives very well': The Importation of English Grasses and Forages into Seventeenth-Century New England," in *Plants and People*, ed. Peter Benes (Boston: Boston University, 1996), 25–37; Peter W. Cook, "Domestic Livestock of Massachusetts Bay, 1620–1725," in *The Farm*, ed. Peter Benes (Boston: Boston University Press, 1988), 109–25; Peter W. Cook, "To Graze the Common: The Cattle and Sheep of Seventeenth-Century Massachusetts," *Essex Institute Historical Collections* 121 (1985): 91–106. On theories of fertilizer and the use of animal manure, see Merchant, *Ecological Revolutions*, 119–22; Carolyn Merchant, *The Death of Nature* (New York: HarperCollins, 1980), 51–53.

101. Bradford, *Of Plymouth Plantation*, 141; Winslow, *Good Newes*, 370–71; [Winslow], *Relation*, 63.

102. Axtell, *Invasion Within*, 157. For a further description of plows and other farm tools, see Rutman, *Husbandmen of Plymouth*, 33–36; Robert W. Walcott, "Husbandry in Colonial New England," *New England Quarterly* 9 (1936): 218–52.

103. Cronon, *Changes in the Land*, 149–50.

104. Rutman, *Husbandmen of Plymouth*, 53–62.

105. Winslow, *Good Newes*, 362–63.

106. Bradford, *Of Plymouth Plantation*, 294–97; Jennings, *Invasion of America*, 202–27; Cotton, "God's Promise," 5–6; Ann Kibbey, *The Interpretation of Material Shapes in Puritanism: A Study of Rhetoric, Prejudice, and Violence* (Cambridge: Cambridge University Press, 1986), 92–105.

107. Ronald Dale Karr, "'Why Should You Be So Furious?': The Violence of the Pequot War, *Journal of American History* 85 (1998): 906; Bradford, *Of Plymouth Plantation*, 292, 296.

108. Morton, *New England's Memorial*, 133.

109. Bradford, *Of Plymouth Plantation*, 145.

110. *Plymouth Colony Records*, 1:17, 11:18; Martin, *Profits in the Wilderness*, 120–21.

111. Bradford, *Of Plymouth Plantation*, 315, 334; H. Roger King, *Cape Cod and Plymouth Colony in the Seventeenth Century* (Lanham, Md.: University Press of America, 1994), 51–52. For a complete history of town settlement in Plymouth Colony, see Langdon, *Pilgrim Colony*, 38–57.

112. Bradford, *Of Plymouth Plantation*, 253–54.

113. On Indian and English population shifts throughout the seventeenth century, see Merchant, *Ecological Revolutions*, 90; Jennings, *Invasion of America*, 30–31; Demos, "Notes," 264–70; Adams and Kasakoff, "Migration and the Family," 28–29; Cole, "Family, Settlement, and Migration," 174–75.

114. William Bradford, "A Descriptive and Historical Account of New England in Verse," in "Governor Bradford's Letter Book," Massachusetts Historical Society, *Collections* 3 (1794): 79.

115. For lengthy descriptions of New England's material abundance, see Josselyn, *Two Voyages*, 43–59; Morton, *New English Canaan*, 50–56; Wood, *New England's Prospect*, 53–57; Smith, *New Englands Trials*, 264. For banquet descriptions, see Gervase Markham, *The English Housewife* (1615), ed. Michael R. Best (Montreal and Kingston: McGill-Queen's University Press, 1998), 123–24; Thomas Dawson, *The Good Huswifes Iewell* (London, 1587), A2-A3; John Murrell, *A New Booke of Cookerie* (London, 1615), 16–17.

116. Cronon, *Changes in the Land*, 169. See also Jack Goody, *Cooking, Cuisine, and Class: A Study in Comparative Sociology* (Cambridge: Cambridge University Press, 1982), 133–39; Martin, *Profits in the Wilderness*; Merchant, *Death of Nature*, 51–56.

117. Lemon, "Early Americans and their Social Environment," 122.

3. As on a Hill

1. William Bradford, *Of Plymouth Plantation, 1620–1647*, ed. Samuel Eliot Morison (New York: Alfred A. Knopf, 1994), 75–76; "The Rev. John Robinson's Farewell Letters to John Carver, July 1620," in Bradford, *Of Plymouth Plantation*, 369–70; John Robinson, *New Essays; Or Observations, Divine and Moral*, in *The Works of John Robinson, Pastor of the Pilgrim Fathers*, ed. Robert Ashton, 3 vols. (Boston: Doctrinal Tract and Book Society, 1851), 1:157–58; David Hillman and Carla Mazzio, introduction to *The Body in Parts: Fantasies of Corporeality in Early Modern Europe*, ed. Hillman and Mazzio (New York: Routledge, 1997), xi-xxix.

2. Robert Cushman, *A Sermon Preached at Plimmoth in New-England, December 9, 1621* (London, 1622), 1, 10, 13, 18; Robinson, *New Essays*, 1:232–33, 210.

3. Robinson, *New Essays*, 1:206–9, 193, 184–85.

4. Robinson, "Farewell Letters," 369–70.

5. Nathaniel Morton, *New England's Memorial* (1687), in *Chronicles of the Pilgrim Fathers*, ed. Ernest Rhys (New York: E. P. Dutton and Co., n.d.), 11–13; Bradford, *Of Plymouth Plantation*, 47–48; Robinson, *New Essays*, 1:172. For a eulogistic poem written at the death of Robinson, see *Plymouth Church Records, 1620–1859*, 2 vols. (New York: New England Society, 1920), 1:62–63, 138–39.

6. Morton, *New England's Memorial*, 146–47; *Plymouth Church Records*, 1:80–81.

7. Bradford, *Of Plymouth Plantation*, 147–63, quotes pp. 147–48, 149, 157, 158; *Plymouth Church Records*, 1:55.

8. Bradford, *Of Plymouth Plantation*, 165–66; Thomas Morton, *New English Canaan* (London, 1632), in *Tracts and Other Papers*, ed. Peter Force, vol. 2, no. 5 (Gloucester, Mass.: Peter Smith, 1963), 81.

9. Bradford, *Of Plymouth Plantation*, 166–69, quotes from p. 166–67, 168.

10. Len Travers, ed., "The Missionary Journal of John Cotton, Jr., 1666–1678," Massachusetts Historical Society, *Proceedings* 109 (1997): 52–53; Richard D. Pierce, ed., *The Records of the First Church at Boston, 1630–1868*, Colonial Society of Massachusetts, *Collections* 39 (1961): 60–61; Mark A. Petersen, "The Plymouth Church and the Evolution of Puritan Religious Culture," *New England Quarterly* 66 (1993): 582–84; David J. Silverman, "Indians, Missionaries, and Religious Translation: Creating Wampanoag Christianity in Seventeenth-Century Martha's Vineyard," *William and Mary Quarterly* 62 (2005): 141–42. Cotton's call to Plymouth is recorded in *Records of the Town of Plymouth*, vol. 1, 1636–1705 (Plymouth, Mass.: Avery and Doten, 1889), 91–92.

11. George D. Langdon Jr., *Pilgrim Colony: A History of New Plymouth, 1620–1691* (New Haven, Conn.: Yale University Press, 1966), 100. Cotton was personally present or his maintenance was discussed in court twenty-five times over the course of his tenure in Plymouth (*Records of the Town of Plymouth*, 98–190).

12. Phillip Stubbes, *The Second Part of the Anatomy of Abuses, containing the display of corruptions* (1583), ed. Frederick J. Furnivall (London: N. Trubner, 1882), 108; Aileen Ribeiro, *Dress and Morality* (Oxford: Berg, 2003), 68, 85; Diana de Marly, *Dress in North America*, vol. 1, *The New World, 1492–1800* (New York: Holmes and Meier, 1900), 28; Anne Hollander, *Seeing Through Clothes* (Berkeley: University of California Press, 1993), 370–71; Robinson, *New Essays*, 1:82; Thomas Prence, "Selected Probates, 1628–1672," *Plymouth Colony Archive Project*, http://etext.lib.virginia.edu/users/deetz/.

13. William Bradford, *A Dialogue, or the Sum of a Conference between Some Young Men Born in New England and Sundry Ancient Men that Came Out of Holland and Old England, Anno Domini 1648*, in *Chronicles of the Pilgrim Fathers of the Colony of Plymouth, from 1602 to 1625*, ed. Alexander Young (Baltimore: Genealogical Publishing, 1974), 445–47. For a full investigation of the controversy over Thomasine Johnson's dress, see Martha L. Finch, "'Fashions of Worldly Dames': Separatist Discourses of Dress in Early Modern London, Amsterdam, and Plymouth Colony," *Church History* 74 (2005): 494–533.

14. N. B. Harte, "State Control of Dress and Social Change in Pre-Industrial England," in *Trade, Government, and Economy in Pre-Industrial England: Essays Presented to F. J. Fisher*, ed. D.C. Coleman and A. H. Johns (London: Weidenfeld and Nicolson,

1976), 132–65; Susan Vincent, *Dressing the Elite: Clothes in Early Modern England* (Oxford: Berg, 2003), 117–43; Paul Raffield, "Reformation, Regulation, and the Image: Sumptuary Legislation and the Subject of Law," *Law and Critique* 13 (2002): 127–50; Alan Hunt, "The Governance of Consumption: Sumptuary Laws and Shifting Forms of Regulation," *Economy and Society* 25 (1996): 410–27; Bradford, *Dialogue*, 447.

15. Bradford, *Of Plymouth Plantation*, 17, 11, 45, 50, 92, 130, 182, 192, 200; Michelle Burnham, "Merchants, Money, and the Economics of 'Plain Style' in William Bradford's *Of Plymouth Plantation*," *American Literature* 72 (2000): 699; David S. Lovejoy, "Plain Englishmen at Plymouth," *New England Quarterly* 63 (1990): 240; Keith L. Sprunger, *Dutch Puritanism: A History of English and Scottish Churches of the Netherlands in the Sixteenth and Seventeenth Centuries* (Leiden: E. J. Brill, 1982), 43–45; Robinson, "Farewell Letters," 370; Jane Ashelford, *The Art of Dress: Clothes and Society, 1500–1914* (London: National Trust Enterprises, 1996), 50.

16. Bradford, *Of Plymouth Plantation*, 44; Lovejoy, "Plain Englishmen at Plymouth," 232–48.

17. For example, *Records of the Governor and Company of the Massachusetts Bay in New England*, ed. Nathaniel B. Shurtleff (Boston: William White, 1853), 1:126. For a discussion of sumptuary laws in early New England, see Patricia Trautman, "When Gentlemen Wore Lace: Sumptuary Legislation and Dress in Seventeenth-Century New England," *Journal of Regional Cultures* 2, no. 3 (1983): 9–21.

18. Plymouth's apparel legislation occurred in 1645, 1658, 1671, and 1685. See *Records of the Colony of New Plymouth in New England*, ed. Nathaniel B. Shurtleff, 12 vols. (Boston: William White, 1855–61), 11:48, 96–97, 173–74 (hereafter cited as *Plymouth Colony Records*); *The General Laws and Liberties of New-Plimouth Colony* (June 1671), 9; *The Book of the General Laws of the Inhabitants of New-Plimouth* (June 2, 1685), 25.

19. George C. Homans, "The Puritans and the Clothing Industry in England," *New England Quarterly* 13 (1940): 519–29; Roze Hentschell, "Treasonous Textiles: Foreign Cloth and the Construction of Englishness," *Journal of Medieval and Early Modern Studies* 32 (2002): 543–70; Vincent, *Dressing the Elite*, 158, 166–67; George Johnson, *A Discourse of Some Troubles and Excommunications in the Banished English Church at Amsterdam* (Amsterdam, 1603), 13, 35, 54; Christopher Breward, *The Culture of Fashion* (Manchester, U.K.: Manchester University Press, 1995), 70; Ribeiro, *Dress and Morality*, 73.

20. John Demos, *A Little Commonwealth: Family Life in Plymouth Colony* (London: Oxford University Press, 1970), 53; *Plymouth Church Records*, 1:81; John Robinson, *A Treatise of the Lawfulnes of Hearing of the Ministers in the Church of England* (1634), in *Works*, 3:365; Maija Jansson, "'The Hat is No Expression of Honor,'" *Proceedings of the American Philosophical Society* 133 (1989): 26.

21. For clothing inventories, see "Selected Probates, 1628–1672," *Plymouth Colony Archive Project*. Cf. De Marly, *Dress in North America*, 28; Pat Poppy, "Mary Ring: The Clothing of an Early American Settler," *Costume* 37 (2003): 33–40.

22. Patricia Trautman, "Dress in Seventeenth-Century Cambridge, Massachusetts: An Inventory-Based Reconstruction," in *Early American Probate Inventories*,

ed. Peter Benes (Boston: Boston University Press, 1989), 55–56, 59–60, 72; Bushman, *Refinement in America*, 71; Jill M. Hall, Wardrobe Curator, Plimoth Plantation, personal email correspondence, March 4, 2000; Maureen Richard, "Washing Household Linens and Linen Clothing in 1627 Plymouth," in *Women's Work in New England, 1620–1920*, ed. Peter Benes (Boston: Boston University, 2003): 10–21; Philip Stubbes, *A perfect pathway to Felicitie, containing godly meditations and prayers, for all times, and necessarie to be practiced of all good Christians* (London: 1610), 215; Keith Thomas, "Cleanliness and Godliness in Early Modern England," in *Religion, Culture, and Society in Early Modern Britain: Essays in Honor of Patrick Collinson*, ed. Anthony Fletcher and Peter Roberts (Cambridge: Cambridge University Press, 1994), 57–59; Richard L. Bushman and Claudia L. Bushman, "The Early History of Cleanliness in America," *Journal of American History* 74 (1988): 1219.

23. Stubbes, *Perfect Pathway*, 215; Thomas, "Cleanliness and Godliness," 59–67; Norbert Elias, *The History of Manners*, vol. 1, *The Civilizing Process*, trans. Edmund Jephcott (New York: Pantheon Books, 1978), 70. On garbage disposal, see James Deetz, *In Small Things Forgotten: The Archaeology of Early American Life* (New York: Doubleday, 1977), 125–26.

24. Richard L. Bushman, *The Refinement of America: Persons, Houses, Cities* (New York: Vintage Books, 1993), 71–72.

25. Jill M. Hall, "'I shall Cut my cote after my cloth': Reproducing the Dress of the Pilgrims," in *Textiles in New England II: Four Centuries of Material Life*, ed. Peter Benes (Boston: Boston University, 2001): 239.

26. Trautman, "Dress," 60–61; Demos, *Little Commonwealth*, 55.

27. John Robinson, *A Letter to the Congregational Church in London* (1624), in *Works*, 3:383; Robinson, *New Essays*, 1:103–4.

28. Robert St. George, "'Heated' Speech and Literacy in Seventeenth-Century New England," in *Seventeenth-Century New England*, ed. David D. Hall and David G. Allen, The Colonial Society of Massachusetts, *Publications* 63 (1984): 278–79; Jane Kamensky, *Governing the Tongue: The Politics of Speech in Early New England* (New York: Oxford University Press, 1997), 18.

29. Robinson, *New Essays*, 1:100–101, 103, 244, 246–48.

30. Demos, *Little Commonwealth*, 137; *Plymouth Colony Records*, 1:8; 11:33–34, 63; St. George, "'Heated Speech,'" 281. Cf. *Plymouth Colony Records*, 11:95, 96, 101, 128, 138, 172, 173, 175, 177.

31. *Plymouth Colony Records*, 2:70, 98; 3:50. Fifty shillings equaled two and a half pounds; for livestock values in 1652, see James Lindale, "Selected Probates, 1628–1672."

32. *Plymouth Colony Records*, 1:35; St. George, "'Heated Speech,'" 281.

33. *Plymouth Colony Records*, 2:146, 148; 4:11; 6:152.

34. *Plymouth Colony Records*, 1:12; 4:11; 3:23, 96, 97, 159; St. George, "'Heated Speech,'" 295–96.

35. St. George, "'Heated Speech,'" 311–14. On the involvement of women in slander cases in seventeenth-century Connecticut courts, see Cornelia Hughes Dayton, *Women Before the Bar: Gender, Law, and Society in Connecticut, 1639–1789* (Chapel Hill: University of North Carolina Press, 1995), 285–303.

36. Kamensky, *Governing the Tongue*, 19–22; St. George, "'Heated Speech,'" 310–16; Laura Gowing, "Gender and the Language of Insult in Early Modern London," *History Workshop Journal* 35 (1993): 1–21; Anthony Fletcher, *Gender, Sex, and Subordination in England, 1500–1800* (New Haven, Conn.: Yale University Press, 1995), 12–16; John Robinson, *Justification of Separation from the Church of England* (1610), in *Works*, 2:248, 228, 215–16; John Robinson, *The People's Plea for the Exercise of Prophecy, against Mr. John Yates his Monopolie* (1618), in *Works*, 3:281–341, esp. 289, 306, 324–29.

37. For a discussion of Hutchinson, who "in the end [Massachusetts authorities] condemned for her independence of both speech and spirit" (31), see Sandra M. Gustafson, *Eloquence is Power: Oratory and Performance in Early America* (Chapel Hill: University of North Carolina Press, 2000), 19–33.

38. *Plymouth Colony Records*, 5:9.

39. Robinson, *New Essays*, 1:215.

40. Edwin Powers, *Crime and Punishment in Early Massachusetts, 1620–1692: A Documentary History* (Boston: Beacon Press, 1966), 100–151; J. A. Sharpe, *Crime in Early Modern England, 1550–1750* (London: Longham, 1984).

41. Lisa M. Lauria, "Sexual Misconduct in Plymouth Colony," Plymouth Colony Archive Project, Department of Anthropology, University of Virginia, 1998, http://etext.virginia.edu/users/deetz/Plymouth/Laurai.html; Bradford, *Of Plymouth Plantation*, 234. See Powers, *Crime and Punishment*, 96–98; Edgar J. McManus, *Law and Liberty in Early New England: Criminal Justice and Due Process, 1620-1692* (Amherst: University of Massachusetts Press, 1993), 24; John D. Cushing, ed., *The Laws of the Pilgrims: A Facsimile Edition of The Book of the General Laws of the Inhabitants of the Jurisdiction of New-Plimouth 1672 & 1685* (Delaware: Michael Glazier, 1977), xiii–xiv. The 1636 body of laws was not printed at the time; it is now contained in *Plymouth Colony Records*, 11:6–26.

42. *Plymouth Colony Records*, 11:11, 12, 126. Interestingly enough, there is no order in the court records for the erecting of a scaffold, although scaffolds were used for both hangings and punishments of humiliation. For the four-year difficulties the court had in getting a prison built, see ibid., 1:75, 115, 142; 2:23. The first recorded imprisonment (for "disorderly living") was in March of 1641/2 (ibid., 2:36).

43. McManus, *Law and Liberty*, 16–17; *Laws of the Inhabitants of the Jurisdiction of New-Plimouth* (1672), 3–5; *Laws of the Inhabitants of the Jurisdiction of New-Plimouth* (1685), 9–10.

44. *Plymouth Colony Records*, 4:211.

45. Ibid., 2:73.

46. Ibid., 2:137, 163; 5:29, 31–32.

47. Ibid., 4:10.

48. Ibid., 4:175, 199.

49. Ibid., 6:20; *Laws of the Inhabitants of the Jurisdiction of New-Plimouth* (1672), 4–5.

50. For studies of the punishment of Quakers in Massachusetts Bay and Plymouth colonies, see Carla Gardina Pestana, *Quakers and Baptists in Colonial Massachusetts* (Cambridge: Cambridge University Press, 1991), esp. 25–43; Gura, *Glimpse of Sion's Glory*, 146–48; Powers, *Crime and Punishment*, 321–66.

51. *Plymouth Colony Records*, 3:11–12; 5:32, 42. Eighty-eight men and twenty-two women were whipped in Plymouth Colony between 1633 and 1692.

52. Ibid., 6:176–77; 5:163.

53. Ibid., 1:132.

54. Ibid., 127.

55. Ibid., 1:64, 74, 143; 3:73; 4:136–37; 6:166; 7:308–9. Cf. McManus, *Law and Liberty*, 166; Powers, *Crime and Punishment*, 201–2. According to the general court records, no women were ever branded in Plymouth.

56. *Plymouth Colony Records*, 2:28; 1:132; 3:23, 112.

57. In Plymouth Colony, fifty men and thirteen women were sentenced to sit in the stocks over a period of sixty years.

58. Ibid., 3:210; 4:125.

59. Ibid., 6:74–75.

60. Fifteen men and three women were banished from Plymouth; several were Indians who, after the end Metacom's Rebellion in 1677, were enslaved and sold out of the colony.

61. *Plymouth Colony Records*, 1:97; 2:132–4; 5:167–68, 205–6; 7:305–7.

62. Bradford, *Of Plymouth Plantation*, 299–301; *Plymouth Colony Records*, 1:96–97.

63. *Plymouth Colony Records*, 2:132–35.

64. Ronald A. Bosco, introduction to *Sermons for Days of Fast, Prayer, and Humiliation and Execution Sermons*, ed. Ronald A. Bosco (Delmar, N.Y.: Scholars' Facsimiles and Reprints, 1978), lxxiv–lxxvii.

65. See description of the execution of James Morgan for murder, in Boston, 1686 (John Dunton to Mr. George Larkin, March 25, 1686, in *The Puritans: A Sourcebook of Their Writings*, rev. ed., ed. Perry Miller and Thomas H. Johnson [New York: Harper Torchbooks, 1963], 2:414–20, quotes p. 420).

66. Amanda Porterfield, *Female Piety in Puritan New England: The Emergence of Religious Humanism* (New York: Oxford University Press, 1992), 26.

67. *Plymouth Colony Records*, 1:93–94, 103, 127, 132, 162, 164; 2:42.

68. Ibid., 1:132; 2:28.

69. Ibid., 2:35–36.

70. Bradford, *Of Plymouth Plantation*, 320–21; *Plymouth Colony Records*, 2:44, 51.

71. Bradford, *Of Plymouth Plantation*, 316–17.

72. See Powers, *Crime and Punishment*, 202–4; Elizabeth Reis, *Damned Women: Sinners and Witches in Puritan New England* (Ithaca: Cornell University Press, 1997), 121–63, esp. 128–31.

73. "Opinions of Three Ministers on Unnatural Vice, 1642," in Bradford, *Of Plymouth Plantation*, appendix X, 404–13, quotes pp. 405, 407, 413.

74. Bradford, *Of Plymouth Plantation*, 321–22; "Opinions of Three Ministers," 410. For a discussion of the ministers' debate, see Richard Godbeer, "'The Cry of Sodom': Discourse, Intercourse, and Desire in Colonial New England," *William and Mary Quarterly* 52 (1995):259–86. In this case, social purification was accomplished through the execution of Granger, but it was more often achieved by banishing the offender from the colony.

75. Michel Foucault, *Discipline and Punish: The Birth of the Prison*, trans. Alan Sheridan (New York: Vintage Books, 1979); David Garland, *Punishment in Modern Society: A Study in Social Theory* (Oxford: Clarendon Press, 1990), 131–75; Richard J. Evans, *Rituals of Retribution: Capital Punishment in Germany, 1600–1987* (Oxford: Oxford University Press, 1996), 880–91.

76. Cf. McManus, *Law and Liberty*, 183–84.

77. Michael C. Schoenfeldt, *Bodies and Selves in Early Modern England: Physiology and Inwardness in Spenser, Shakespeare, Herbert, and Milton* (Cambridge: Cambridge University Press, 1999), 38–39.

4. The True and Visible Church

1. Distinctive *sounds*—the beating of a drum, blowing of a conch shell, or, later, ringing of a bell—gathered the social body in early New England. Plymouth acquired a bell for their meetinghouse in 1679, which also sounded an alarm in case of fire, Indian threat, or other dangers and signaled evening curfew. See *Records of the Town of Plymouth*, 2 vols. (Plymouth, Mass.: Avery and Doten, 1889), 1:161, 188, 190 (hereafter cited as *Plymouth Town Records*); Elbridge H. Goss, "Early Bells of Massachusetts," *New England Historical and Genealogical Register* 37 (1883): 46–52; Richard Cullen Rath, *How Early America Sounded* (Ithaca, N.Y.: Cornell University Press, 2003), 43–53, 61–68.

2. Isaack de Rasieres to Samuel Blommaert (1628), in *Three Visitors to Early Plymouth*, ed. Sydney V. James Jr. (Plymouth, Mass.: Plimoth Plantation, 1963), 76.

3. Robert Darnton, *The Great Cat Massacre and Other Episodes in French Cultural History* (New York: Vintage Books, 1985), 116–24, quote p. 120.

4. *Records of the Colony of New Plymouth in New England*, ed. Nathaniel B. Shurtleff, 12 vols. (Boston: William White, 1855–61), 1:12, hereafter cited as *Plymouth Colony Records*.

5. *Plymouth Colony Records*, 11:17, 38, 58, 117, 131, 140, 206, 214, 234; Alice Earle Morse, *The Sabbath in Puritan New England* (New York: Charles Scribner's Sons, 1902), 11; James P. Walsh, "Holy Time and Sacred Space in Puritan New England," *American Quarterly* 32 (1980): 86; Brian Wilson, "The New World's Jerusalems: Franciscans, Puritans, and Sacred Space in the Colonial Americas, 1519–1820," PhD dissertation (University of California, Santa Barbara, 1996), 194; David Hackett Fischer, *Albion's Seed: Four British Folkways in America* (New York: Oxford University Press, 1989), 118.

6. New England courts periodically passed laws requiring inhabitants to carry their firearms to worship; in October of 1675, for example, Plymouth's magistrates ordered that "every one that comes to the meeting on the Lords day bring his armes with him, and furnished with att least six charges of powder and shott" (*Plymouth Colony Records*, 5:176).

7. John Robinson, *A Justification of Separation from the Church of England* (1610), in *The Works of John Robinson, Pastor of the Pilgrim Fathers*, ed. Robert Ashton, 3 vols. (Boston: Doctrinal Tract and Book Society, 1851), 2:351.

8. Mary Douglas, *Purity and Danger: An Analysis of the Concepts of Pollution and Taboo* (1966; repr., New York: Routledge, 1994), esp. 115–40; Douglas, *Natural Symbols: Explorations in Cosmology* (London: Barrie and Jenkins, 1973), esp. 93, 99–100, 178–80.

9. William Bradford, *Of Plymouth Plantation, 1640–1647*, ed. Samuel Eliot Morison (New York: Alfred A. Knopf, 1994), 44, 369–70.

10. See J. M. Bumsted, "A Well-Bounded Toleration: Church and State in the Plymouth Colony," *Journal of Church and State* 10 (1968): 265–79; David S. Lovejoy, "Plain Englishmen at Plymouth," *New England Quarterly* 63 (1990): 232–48.

11. The concrete visibility of one's commitment to the church covenant, unlike the "mere fiction" of "a Popish implicit faith," was critical: it was by "the visible hand of man [that] he on his part contracts with God, and enters covenant with him visibly." William Bradford, *A Dialogue . . . Between Some Young Men . . . and Sundry Ancient Men*, in *Chronicles of the Pilgrim Fathers of Plymouth Colony, from 1602 to 1625*, ed. Alexander Young, 2nd ed., (Baltimore: Genealogical Publishing, 1974), 416; Robinson, *Justification*, 2:332). Cf. Edmund S. Morgan, *Visible Saints: The History of a Puritan Idea* (repr., New York: New York University Press, 1963), 29; Perry Miller, *The New England Mind: The Seventeenth Century* (1939; repr., Cambridge, Mass.: Belknap Press, 1954), 365–472.

12. Letter to Edwin Sandys (Dec. 15, 1617), in Bradford, *Of Plymouth Plantation*, 33.

13. Jacques Le Goff, "Head or Heart? The Political Use of Body Metaphors in the Middle Ages," in *Fragments for a History of the Human Body, Part Three*, ed. Michel Feher (New York: Zone, 1989), 13–26, quote p. 13.

14. David Hillman and Carla Mazzio, introduction to *The Body in Parts: Fantasies of Corporeality in Early Modern Europe* (New York: Routledge, 1997), xiii xiv. See also Alan E. Bernstein, "Political Anatomy," *University Publishing* (Winter 1978): 8–9; Natalie Zemon Davis, "The Sacred and the Body Social in Sixteenth-Century Lyon," *Past and Present* 90 (1981): 40–70.

15. Robinson, *Justification*, 2:449.

16. Ibid., 138–39, 245, 463.

17. Le Goff, "Head or Heart?," 16–18.

18. Robinson, *Justification*, 2:267.

19. Ibid., 2:167–70.

20. Robinson, *Justification*, 2:274; John Robinson, *An Answer to a Censorious Epistle* (1642), in *Works*, 3:412–17.

21. Robinson, *Justification*, 2:274, 342; Robinson, *Censorious Epistle*, 3:418–19. Bradford described it as "secession from the corruptions found amongst them" (*A Dialogue*, 417; *Of Plymouth Plantation*, 8).

22. Bradford, *Of Plymouth Plantation*, 350, 284, 282. Cf. Morgan, *Visible Saints*; Horton Davies, *The Worship of the American Puritans, 1629–1730* (New York: Peter Land, 1990), 12–13.

23. Robinson, *Justification*, 2:122, 223, 265, 271, 345–46.

24. Ibid., 2:118.

25. John Robinson, *Of Religious Communion, Private and Public* (1614), in *Works*, 3:243.

26. [Edward Winslow], *A Relation or Iournall of the beginning and proceedings of the English Plantation setled at Plimoth in New England* (1622), in *Mourt's Relation: A Journal of the Pilgrims at Plymouth*, ed. Dwight B. Heath (Bedford, Mass.: Applewood Books, 1963), 38; Bradford, *Of Plymouth Plantation*, 72; Nathaniel Morton, *New Englands Memoriall* (1669) (New York: Scholars' Facsimiles & Reprints, 1937), 32–33.

27. On sacred space and time, see Mircea Eliade, *The Sacred and the Profane: The Nature of Religion* (1957), trans. Willard R. Trask (San Diego: Harcourt Brace Jovanovich, 1987), chaps. 1 and 2; Jonathan Z. Smith, *To Take Place: Toward Theory in Ritual* (Chicago: University of Chicago Press, 1987), chap. 5.

28. John Robinson, *A Treatise of the Lawfulness of Hearing the Ministers in the Church of England* (1634), in *Works*, 3:373. David D. Hall has observed, "Protestants rejected the assumption—crucial to most ritual practice—that certain zones of time and space were sacred. For them, all of time and space was holy (or equally profane)" (*Worlds of Wonder, Days of Judgment: Popular Religious Belief in Early New England* [New York: Alfred A. Knopf, 1989], 166–67). James P. Walsh has termed the puritan New England construction of time and space as one of "homogeneous sanctity" ("Holy Time and Sacred Space," 79–95, quote p. 79).

29. John Robinson, *A Just and Necessary Apology of Certain Christians, no less contumeliously than commonly called Brownists or Barrowists* (1625), in *Works*, 3:59–61; Robinson, *Lawfulness of Hearing the Ministers*, 3:374–76. On the early modern meaning of "convenience" as "suitability 'to the performance of some action or to the satisfying of requirements,'" see John E. Crowley, "The Sensibility of Comfort," *American Historical Review* 104 (1999): 761–62.

30. *Plymouth Church Records, 1620–1859*, 2 vols. (New York: New England Society, 1920), 1:105–7.

31. Charles E. Hambrick-Stowe, *The Practice of Piety: Puritan Devotional Disciplines in Seventeenth-Century New England* (Chapel Hill: University of North Carolina Press, 1982), 43, 51.

32. Robinson, *Lawfulness of Hearing the Ministers*, 3:361–62; Robinson, *Justification*, 2:450.

33. See Hall, *Worlds of Wonder*, 166–69; Richard Godbeer, *The Devil's Dominion: Magic and Religion in Early New England* (Cambridge: Cambridge University Press, 1992), 10–11, 27–28.

34. Winton U. Solberg, *Redeem the Time: The Puritan Sabbath in Early America* (Cambridge, Mass.: Harvard University Press, 1977), 117.

35. Edward Winslow, *Hypocrisie Unmasked* (1646), in *Chronicles of the Pilgrim Fathers of the Colony of Plymouth, 1602–1625*, ed. Alexander Young (New York: Da Capo Press, 1971), 381. Also noted by Nathaniel Morton, in *New Englands Memoriall*, 9.

36. *Plymouth Church Records*, 1:101–5; Bownde, *Doctrine of the Sabbath*, 45, 46, quoted in John H. Primus, *Holy Time: Moderate Puritanism and the Sabbath* (Macon, Ga.: Mercer University Press, 1989), 154; John Cotton, "A Short Discourse . . . touchinge the time when the Lordes day beginneth," in Winton U. Solberg, "John Cotton's Treatise on the Duration of the Lord's Day," in *Sibley's Heir*, Colonial Society

of Massachusetts, *Publications* 59 (1982): 505–22; Davies, *Worship of the American Puritans*, 52–58.

37. *Plymouth Church Records*, 1:79; Robert Ashton, "Memoir of Rev. John Robinson," Massachusetts Historical Society, *Collections* 31 (1852): 111–64, 125.

38. Amir H. Ameri, "Housing Ideologies in the New England and Chesapeake Bay Colonies, c. 1650–1700," *Journal of the Society of Architectural Historians* 56 (1997): 12–13; Walsh, "Holy Time and Sacred Space"; Hall, *Worlds of Wonder*, 117–18; Davies, *Worship of the American Puritans*, 233–54; Anthony Garvan, "The New England Plain Style," *Comparative Studies in Society and History* 3 (1960): 106–22; Fischer, *Albion's Seed*, 117–18.

39. Morton, *New Englands Memoriall*, 53; *Plymouth Town Records*, 1:169, 170–71, 173; *Plymouth Church Records*, 1:253.

40. Robert J. Dinkin, "Seating the Meetinghouse in Early Massachusetts," *New England Quarterly* 43 (1970): 450–64; Darrett B. Rutman, *Winthrop's Boston: Portrait of a Puritan Town, 1630–1649* (New York: W. W. Norton, 1965), 127.

41. See Garvan, "New England Plain Style."

42. Robinson, *Justification*, 2:241.

43. Robinson, *Justification*, 2:451–55; Robinson, *Just and Necessary Apology*, 3:21, 26

44. John Cotton, "Singing of Psalmes a Gospel Ordinance," cited in Davies, *Worship of the American Puritans*, 118. See Davies's discussion of psalm-singing (115–32). For an analysis of early eighteenth-century church music in the Bay Colony, see David W. Music, "Cotton Mather and Congregational Singing in Puritan New England," *Studies in Puritan American Spirituality* 2 (1992): 1–30; Patrick Collinson, *From Iconoclasm to Iconophobia: The Cultural Impact of the Second English Reformation Stenton Lectures* (Berkshire, U.K.: University of Reading, 1986), 21.

45. John Cotton, "Preface to the Bay Psalm Book," in *The Puritans*, rev. ed., ed. Perry Miller and Thomas H. Johnson (New York: Harper and Row, 1963), 2 vols., 2:669–72, 670; Davies, *Worship of the American Puritans*, 123. On the authorship of the Bay Psalm Book's preface, see Zoltan Haraszti, *The Enigma of the Bay Psalm Book* (Chicago: University of Chicago Press, 1950).

46. *Plymouth Church Records*, 1:95–97.

47. Ibid., 156–57. This form of psalmody was called "lining out."

48. Boston's Samuel Sewall recorded in his diary on Dec. 28, 1705, that in the meeting that day he had intended to set the Windsor tune but "fell into" High-Dutch, and then, when trying to set another tune, he "went into a key much too high" (cited in Davies, *Worship of the American Puritans*, 126).

49. *Plymouth Church Records*, 1:160, 171–72, 178, 257, 277–78, 282.

50. Robinson, *Justification*, 2:383–413, 475; *The People's Plea for the Exercise of Prophecy* (1618), in *Works*, 3:286.

51. *Plymouth Church Records*, 1:80–81. Cf. Bradford, *Of Plymouth Plantation*, 324–28.

52. Davies, *Worship and Theology in England*, 2:173; Francis J. Bremer, *Shaping New Englands: Puritan Clergymen in Seventeenth-Century England and New England* (New York: Twayne Publishers, 1994), 25–32. Church of England supporters often ridiculed

nonconformist preachers for their overdramatic "squeeking and roaring" and "strange new Postures" (Davies, *Worship and Theology in England*, 2:169, 174–75).

53. John Barton, *The Art of Rhetorick Concisely and Compleatly Handled* (London, 1634), A3, 1; John Charles Adams, "Linguistic Values and Religious Experience: An Analysis of the Clothing Metaphors in Alexander Richardson's Ramist-Puritan Lectures on Speech 'Speech is a Garment to Cloath Our Reason,'" *Quarterly Journal of Speech* 9 (1990): 58–68; John C. Adams, "Alexander Richardson and the Ramist Poetics of Michael Wigglesworth," *Early American Literature* 25 (1990): 271–88; Miller, *New England Mind*, 300–30, 350–56.

54. Abraham Fraunce, *The Arcadian Rhetorike* (London, 1588), ed. Ethel Seaton (Oxford: Basil Blackwell, 1950), 106–20.

55. Barton, *Art of Rhetorick*, 35, sig. A7.

56. Fraunce, *Arcadian Rhetorike*, 120–29.

57. Miller, *Seventeenth Century*, 346–54.

58. John Robinson, *New Essays; or Observations Divine and Moral* (1628), in *Works*, 1:103–4; William Ames, *The Marrow of Theology: William Ames, 1576–1633 (The Marrow of Sacred Divinity*, 1629), trans. and ed. John D. Eusden (Durham, N.C.: Labyrinth Press, 1983), 1:35:60–67, pp.195–96.

59. *Plymouth Church Records*, 1:148.

60. Ibid., 1:99–100, 159, 255–56.

61. John Demos, *A Little Commonwealth: Family Life in Plymouth Colony* (London: Oxford University Press, 1970), 8.

62. *Plymouth Colony Records*, 11:57, 58, 99, 217–18, 122, 176; quote from 11:228.

63. *Plymouth Colony Records*, 1:87, 92; 2: 140, 156, 173, 174; 3:4, 5, 10, 47, 111, 124, 212, 224; 4:5, 28, 29; 5:27, 51, 53, 61, 99, 152, 156, 157, 162, 238–39, 253, 254; 6:82, 94, 172, 178; 11:258.

64. Ibid., 3: 4, 191; 4:133; 5:16; 11:258, 224–25.

65. E. Brooks Holifield, *The Covenant Sealed: The Development of Puritan Sacramental Theology in Old and New England, 1570–1720* (New Haven, Conn.: Yale University Press, 1974), 71. Cf. Davies, *Worship and Theology in England*, 1:36, 48–50.

66. Robinson, *Justification*, 2:334, 316. Cf. Holifield, *Covenant Sealed*, 64.

67. Bradford, *Of Plymouth Plantation*, 142.

68. Robinson, *Justification*, 2:383; Holifield, *Covenant Sealed*, 71; Davies, *Worship and Theology in England*, 1:341.

69. Robinson, *Justification*, 2:130, 233, 445; David D. Hall, *The Faithful Shepherd: A History of the New England Ministry in the Seventeenth Century* (Chapel Hill: University of North Carolina Press, 1972), 40.

70. John Robinson to William Brewster (Dec. 20, 1623), appendix V, in Bradford, *Of Plymouth Plantation*, 377; Bradford, *Of Plymouth Plantation*, 162.

71. Robinson, *Justification*, 2:362.

72. Bradford, *Of Plymouth Plantation*, 147–63, quote p. 157; *Plymouth Church Records*, 1:54–60. On the Lyford controversy, see chapter 3.

73. Letters from James Sherley et al. to William Bradford et al. (Apr., 1624; Dec., 1624), in "Governor Bradford's Letter Book," Massachusetts Historical Society, *Collections* 3 (1794): 27, 29, 33.

74. Bradford, *Of Plymouth Plantation*, 142.

75. *Plymouth Church Records*, 1:63–65; Bradford, *Of Plymouth Plantation*, 210–11, 257. On Ralph Smith, see his letters to Hugh Goodyear in D. Plooij, *The Pilgrim Fathers from a Dutch Point of View* (New York: New York University Press, 1932), 92, 100–101, 111–13, 114. Unlike Boston, Plymouth happily embraced the "Godly and Zealous" Roger Williams, though the later controversy over his more rigorous separatism provoked Williams's leaving Plymouth for Salem and eventually Rhode Island. On Plymouth's "minister troubles" between 1620 and 1669, see George F. Willison, *Saints and Strangers* (Orleans, Mass.: Parnassus Imprints, 1945), 343–72; Mark A. Petersen, "The Plymouth Church and the Evolution of Puritan Religious Culture," *New England Quarterly* 66 (1993): 573–79.

76. Bradford, *Of Plymouth Plantation*, 210, 222; *Plymouth Church Records*, 1:109. On separatists' willingness to do without the sacraments, see Stephen Mayor, *The Lord's Supper in Early English Dissent* (London: Epworth Press, 1972), 60–61; and Geoffrey F. Nuttall, *The Holy Spirit in Puritan Faith and Experience* (1946; repr. Chicago: University of Chicago Press, 1992), 93–95.

77. Bradford, *Of Plymouth Plantation*, 293, 334; *Plymouth Church Records*, 1:107–10. Cf. H. Roger King, *Cape Cod and Plymouth Colony in the Seventeenth Century* (Lanham, Md.: University Press of America, 1994), 53; George D. Langdon, *Pilgrim Colony: A History of New Plymouth, 1620–1691* (New Haven, Conn.: Yale University Press, 1966), 118.

78. *The Journal of John Winthrop, 1630–1649*, ed. Richard S. Dunn, James Savage, Laetitia Yeandle (Cambridge, Mass.: Harvard University Press, 1996), 322.

79. For more on Chauncy's controversial opinions regarding the sacraments, see Philip. F. Gura, *A Glimpse of Sion's Glory: Puritan Radicalism in New England, 1620–1660* (Middletown, Conn.: Wesleyan University Press, 1984), 106 8.

80. Mayor, *The Lord's Supper*, 41.

81. Robinson, *Religious Communion*, 3:188; Robinson, *Censorious Epistle*, 3:411; Robinson, *Justification*, 2:360, 504.

82. Ann Kibbey, *The Interpretation of Material Shapes in Puritanism: A Study of Rhetoric, Prejudice, and Violence* (Cambridge: Cambridge University Press, 1986), 42–64, esp. 44–46.

83. Daniel Bucke and Robert Browne, quoted in Mayor, *The Lord's Supper*, 33–34. Cf. Davies, *Worship and Theology in England*, 1:331; Holifield, *The Covenant Sealed*, 72.

84. Davies, *Worship of the American Puritans*, 163.

85. Winslow, *Hypocrisie Unmasked*, 405.

86. Bradford, *Of Plymouth Plantation*, 313–14. Cf. *Plymouth Church Records*, 1:74–75.

87. Winslow, *Hypocrisie Unmasked*, 405–6.

88. *Plymouth Church Records*, 1:96–97; Robinson, *Just and Necessary Apology*, 3:17–19; Robinson, *Religious Communion*, 3:166, 183, 200–201; Robinson, *Justification*, 2:360.

89. Quoted in Davies, *Worship and Theology in England*, 1:331.

90. Bradford, *Of Plymouth Plantation*, 314; Winthrop, *Journal*, 322.

91. Winthrop, *Journal*, 398–99.

92. *Plymouth Church Records*, 1:111, 143, 145, 146, 147, 148, 153, 154, 155, 156, 158, 159, 160, 162, 163, 165, 166, 172, 173, 176, 178, 180.

93. *Plymouth Church Records*, 1:92, 146, 155. Cf. Stratton, *Plymouth Colony*, 100–101; Langdon, *Pilgrim Colony*, 81–82.

94. Robinson, *Religious Communion*, 3:169. John Cotton Jr. baptized new adult members who had not been previously baptized as infants or children; in 1696, he noted that of the 178 adults admitted to the church during his thirty-year tenure as pastor at Plymouth, fifteen received baptism (*Plymouth Church Records*, 1:180).

95. *Plymouth Church Records*, 1:277, 280, 281. In early February of 1693/4, the issue came up again; some men argued that the children of censured members should be allowed to be baptized and others were indifferent, so the matter was left undecided (ibid., 1:282).

96. Robinson, *Justification*, 2:89, 368.

97. Ibid., 2:257–58, 352, 271, 265.

98. John Robinson, *An Appeal on Truth's Behalf: A Letter . . . to the Church at Amsterdam* (1624), in *Works*, 3:391.

99. *Plymouth Church Records*, 1:153.

100. Robinson, *Justification*, 2:130, 166, 238, 246.

101. Ibid., 2:254; *Plymouth Church Records*, 1:278. On June 25, 1684, elder Thomas Cushman asked the Plymouth church to consider dealing with offending church members "in private," by which he meant before those in full membership only, rather than before all who attended public worship. The men's answer was that "those whose sin was publick should be publickly dealt with for it," and they desired to continue their "ancient practice" of admonishing sinning members before the entire church. The records do not explain why Cushman brought up this issue at this time (*Plymouth Church Records*, 1:255).

102. Cotton's personal notes, which he used to compose the more terse official church records, are available only for the period from 1682 to 1693; they provide the names of offenders and descriptions of their sins and interactions with the church (ibid., 1:249–82). The official church records tend simply to describe a nameless offender as a "ch[urc]h-child" (an adult member who had been baptized as a child in the Plymouth church) or a "brother" or "sister" (presumably one who had been admitted into the church as an adult).

103. One unnamed member was "cut off" for unspecified "sinning" and not repenting, another member (Samuel Dunham Sr.) was excommunicated for drunkenness, and two (George Watson and his wife) for "moral scandal," probably fornication. Nathaniel Clarke, whose story is told in chapter five, appears to have voluntarily severed himself from the church, for "he had not nothing [*sic*] to say to us, nor would have anything to doe with us" (*Plymouth Church Records*, 1:153, 157, 267).

104. Ibid., 1:157, 160, 252, 267, 270; John Cotton to Thomas Hinckley (Jan. 13, 1681/2), in "The Hinckley Papers," Massachusetts Historical Society, *Collections* 35 (1861): 56–57.

105. See Catherine Bell, *Ritual Theory, Ritual Practice* (New York: Oxford University Press, 1992), 94–117. The saints' ritual practices inscribed individual bodies with

"schema" that shaped one's sense of his or her relationship to the social body and to divine powers beyond the community, while simultaneously investing one with an agency—a "ritual mastery"—to reproduce, resist, and revise those schema.

106. *Plymouth Church Records*, 1:157–58; John Cotton to Thomas Hinckley, "Hinckley Papers," 56–57; *Plymouth Colony Records*, 6:82.

107. See Richard P. Gildrie, "The Ceremonial Puritan: Days of Humiliation and Thanksgiving," *New England Historical and Genealogical Register* 136 (1982): 3–16; W. DeLoss Love Jr., *The Fast and Thanksgiving Days of New England* (New York: Houghton, Mifflin, 1895); Martha L. Finch, "Pinched with Hunger, Partaking of Plenty: Fasts and Thanksgivings in Early New England," in *Eating in Eden: Food and American Utopias*, ed. Etta M. Madden and Martha L. Finch (Lincoln: University of Nebraska Press, 2006), 35–53; Hall, *Worlds of Wonder*, 166–72; Amanda Porterfield, *Female Piety in Puritan New England: The Emergence of Religious Humanism* (New York: Oxford University Press, 1992), 124–27; Davies, *Worship of the American Puritans*, 58–67.

108. Morton, *New Englands Memoriall*, 63–64; John Smith, *Advertisment For the unexperienced Planters of New-England, or anywhere, in The Puritans*, rev. ed., 2 vols., ed. Perry Miller and Thomas H. Johnson (New York: Harper Torchbooks, 1963), 2:396; Edward Winslow, *Good Newes from New England*, in *Chronicles of the Pilgrim Fathers of the Colony of Plymouth, 1602–1625*, ed. Alexander Young (New York: Da Capo Press, 1971), 346–50.

109. At least sixty-nine fast days occurred between 1620 and 1697, which does not include the "frequent fasts" observed between 1654 and 1667 when the church was "groaning" for a pastor and numerous other fasts simply not recorded. Regular records of church fasts and thanksgivings did not commence until 1667 when Cotton arrived. He noted in 1697 that over the preceding thirty years there had been many civil fasts and thanksgivings he did not record (*Plymouth Church Records*, 1:181); the court records note some of them. Church and court records mention twenty-six thanksgiving days.

110. See Patricia Curran, *Grace Before Meals: Food Ritual and Body Discipline in Convent Culture* (Urbana: University of Illinois Press, 1989), 51, 103–4; Susan Hardman, "Puritan Asceticism and the Type of Sacrifice," in *Monks, Hermits, and the Ascetic Tradition: Papers Read at the 1984 Summer Meeting and the 1985 Winter Meeting of the Ecclesiastical History Society*, ed. W. J. Sheils (Oxford: Basil Blackwell, 1985), 288–89; Winthrop S. Hudson, "Fast Days and Civil Religion," in *Theology in Sixteenth- and Seventeenth-Century England: Papers Read at a Clark Library Seminar, February 6, 1971*, ed. Winthrop S. Hudson and Leonard J. Trinterud (Los Angeles: University of California, 1971); C. J. Kitching, "'Prayers Fit for the Time': Fasting and Prayer in Response to National Crises in the Reign of Elizabeth I," in *Monks, Hermits, and the Ascetic Tradition*, 241–50. Earliest treatises include Thomas Becon, *A Fruitful Treatise of Fasting* (London, [1551?]); William Wilkinson, *The Holie exercise of a true Fast* (London, 1580).

111. Nic[h]olas Bownde, *The Holy Exercise of Fasting* (Cambridge, 1604); Thomas Thacher, "A Fast of Gods Chusing" [sermon preached on Mar. 2, 1674] (Boston, 1678). Bownde had great influence in the development of nonconformist religious

practice; his doctrine of the Sabbath established the standard for Sabbatarianism and his Holy Exercise of Fasting can be read as the standard for fast and thanksgiving theory and practice (see Solberg, *Redeem the Time*, 27, 55–58).

112. Thacher, *Fast of Gods Chusing*, 16; Bownde, *Holy Exercise of Fasting*, 28.

113. Bownde, *Holy Exercise of Fasting*, 40–47, 50–57, 199–201; Thatcher, *Fast of Gods Chusing*, 4.

114. Mary Douglas has argued that social structures are vulnerable at their margins, symbolized in rituals concerning margins of the human body, especially orifices through which potentially polluting elements enter and exit the body (*Purity and Danger*, 115, 121, 126–27).

115. Bownde, *Holy Exercise of Fasting*, 225–26, 337–49; Thacher, *Fast of Gods Chusing*, 6, 12.

116. Fast days are an example of Amanda Porterfield's general argument regarding New Englanders' use of self-denial as self-empowerment: "Rather than experiencing power as an enemy against which their humility flourished, Puritans internalized the theological coincidence between God's strength and human weakness to make self-effacement a means of exercising temporal power" (*Female Piety*, 29).

117. Bradford, *Of Plymouth Plantation*, 36, 47; Morton, *New Englands Memoriall*, 11, 12.

118. *Plymouth Church Records*, 1:260; John Cotton to Increase Mather (Mar. 8, 1687/88), "Letters of John Cotton," in "The Mather Papers," Massachusetts Historical Society, *Collections*, 38 (1868): 254.

119. Bownde, *Holy Exercise of Fasting*, 190.

120. Bradford, *Of Plymouth Plantation*, 89–90. Some scholars have argued that this "First Thanksgiving" was not a religious day of thanksgiving but a secular harvest festival (see, e.g., Andrew F. Smith, "The First Thanksgiving," *Gastronomica* 3 [4]: 79–85). However, I agree with those who have noted the tendency of nonconformists to reject all traditional celebrations unless invested with religious meanings and practices, making harvest festivals also days of thanksgiving (see, e.g., Gildrie, "The Ceremonial Puritan"; Ann Blue Wills, "Pilgrims and Progress: How Magazines Made Thanksgiving," *Church History* 72 [2003]: 138–58).

121. Winslow, "A Letter Sent from New England to a Friend," in *Mourt's Relation*, 82.

122. As for fast days, there are almost no extant descriptions of thanksgiving rituals in any early New England sources; these from the towns of Scituate and Barnstable are the only ones from Plymouth, other than Winslow's thanksgiving harvest festival description.

123. John Lathrop, "Scituate and Barnstable Church Records," *New England Historical and Genealogical Register* 10 (1856): 39.

124. For example, Philip Stubbes, *The Anatomy of Abuses* (London: 1583), 1:141–45, 148–49, 183. For two views on English puritan attitudes toward feast days and food consumption, see Bryan S. Turner, *The Body and Society: Explorations in Social Theory*, (Oxford: Basil Blackwell, 1984), 166–67; and Stephen Mennell, *All Manners of Food: Eating and Taste in England and France from the Middle Ages to the Present*, 2nd ed. (Urbana: University of Illinois Press, 1996), 103–8.

125. See Hortense Powdermaker, "Feasts in New Ireland: The Social Function of Eating," *American Anthropologist* 34 (1932): 236–47; Janet Theophano, "Feast, Fast, and Time," *Pennsylvania Life* 27 (1978): 25–32; Anna Meigs, "Food as a Cultural Construction," in *Food and Culture: A Reader*, ed. Carole Counihan and Penny Van Esterik (New York: Routledge, 1997), 95, 103.

5. As in a Mirror

1. John Insley Coddington, "The Widow Mary Ring, of Plymouth, Mass., and Her Children," *The American Genealogist* 42 (1966): 193–205; William Bradford, *Of Plymouth Plantation, 1620–1647*, ed. Samuel Eliot Morison (New York: Alfred A. Knopf, 1994), 213–49; "The Last Will and Testament of Mary Ring," Pilgrim Hall Museum, www.pilgrimhall.org/willmring.htm.

2. See chapter 3 and Pat Poppy, "Mary Ring: The Clothing of an Early American Settler," *Costume* 37 (2003): 33–40.

3. "Last Will and Testament of Mary Ring."

4. Ibid.

5. Edmund S. Morgan, *The Puritan Family: Religion and Domestic Relations in Seventeenth-Century New England*, rev. ed. (New York: Harper and Row, 1966), 10; John Demos, *A Little Commonwealth: Family Life in Plymouth Colony* (London: Oxford University Press, 1970), xvii-xviii, 82–83; Anne S. Lombard, *Making Manhood: Growing Up Male in Colonial New England* (Cambridge, Mass.: Harvard University Press, 2003), 12–13; Richard P. Gildrie, *The Profane, the Civil, and the Godly: The Reformation of Manners in Orthodox New England, 1679–1749* (University Park: Pennsylvania State University Press, 1994), 85–109.

6. Robert Cleaver and John Dod, *A Godly Forme of Hovshold Government. For the Ordering of Private Families, according to the direction of Gods Word* (London, 1621), A recto; William Gouge, *Of Domesticall Duties* (London, 1622), 18. John Demos highlighted this reference when he titled his study of family life in Plymouth Colony *A Little Commonwealth*.

7. For example, Samuel Sewall and John Hull of Boston (Samuel Sewall, *The Diary of Samuel Sewall, 1674–1729*, ed. M. Halsey Thomas, 2 vols. [New York: Farrar, Straus, Giroux, 1973]; John Hull, "The Diaries of John Hull, Mint-master and Treasurer of the Colony of Massachusetts Bay," *American Antiquarian Society, Transactions and Collections* 3 [1857]: 108–316).

8. Cleaver and Dod, *Godly Form of Household Government*, A8.

9. Edward Winslow (publisher), *The Glorious Progress of the Gospel, Amongst the Indians in New England* (1649), Massachusetts Historical Society, *Collections* 24 (1834): 69–98; Len Travers, ed., "The Missionary Journal of John Cotton, Jr., 1666–1678," Massachusetts Historical Society, *Proceedings* 109 (1997): 52–101; Daniel Gookin, "Historical Collections of the Indians in New England" (1674), Massachusetts Historical Society, *Collections* 1 (1792): 196–200.

10. Gookin, "Historical Collections," 223.

11. Karen Ordahl Kupperman discusses Indians and English as "mirror images" primarily to explore native village life; I do so to uncover colonists' domestic life. See

Kupperman, *Indians and English: Facing Off in Early America* (Ithaca, N.Y.: Cornell University Press, 2000), 19, 142–73.

12. Daniel R. Mandell, *Behind the Frontier: Indians in Eighteenth-Century Eastern Massachusetts* (Lincoln: University of Nebraska Press, 1996), 18–23.

13. Cleaver and Dod, *Godly Forme of Hovshold Government*, [A8 recto].

14. James Deetz, *In Small Things Forgotten: The Archaeology of Early American Life* (New York: Doubleday, 1977), 92.

15. [Edward Winslow], *A Relation or Iournall of the beginning and proceedings of the English Plantation setled at Plimoth in New England* (London, 1622), in *Mourt's Relation: A Journal of the Pilgrims at Plymouth*, ed. Dwight B. Heath (Bedford, Mass.: Applewood Books, 1963), 28.

16. William Wood, *New England's Prospect* (1634), ed. Alden T. Vaughan (Amherst: University of Massachusetts Press, 1977), 112–13; Gookin, "Historical Collections," 150. See also Kathleen J. Bragdon, *Native People of Southern New England, 1500–1650* (Norman: University of Oklahoma Press, 1996), 105–6.

17. Letter from John Eliot, in Winslow, *Glorious Progress of the Gospel*, 90. See chapter 2.

18. Letter from John Eliot, in Henry Whitfeld (publisher), *The Light Appearing More and More Towards the Perfect Day* (1651), Massachusetts Historical Society, *Collections* 24 (1843): 142–43. See Brian Wilson, "The New World's Jerusalems: Franciscans, Puritans, and Sacred Space in the Colonial Americas, 1519–1820," PhD diss. (University of California, Santa Barbara, 1996), 215–18; John Holstun, *A Rational Millennium: Puritan Utopias of Seventeenth-Century England and America* (New York: Oxford University Press, 1987), 102–65.

19. Gookin, *Historical Collections*, 181.

20. Thomas Shepard, *The Clear Sun-Shine of the Gospel Breaking Forth Upon the Indians in New-England* (1648), Massachusetts Historical Society, *Collections* 24 (1843): 62.

21. Holstun, *Rational Millennium*, 124.

22. Bradford, *Of Plymouth Plantation*, 76; Deetz, *Small Things Forgotten*, 92–117; James Deetz and Patricia Scott Deetz, *The Times of Their Lives: Life, Love, and Death in Plymouth Colony* (New York: Anchor Books, 2000), 211–71; Patricia E. Scott Deetz and James Deetz, "Vernacular House Forms in Seventeenth-Century Plymouth Colony: An Analysis of Evidence from the Plymouth Colony Room-by-Room Probate Inventories, 1633–1685," Plymouth Colony Archive Project (Department of Anthropology, University of Virginia, 1998), http://etext.virginia.edu/users/deetz/Plymouth/folkhouse.htm; John E. Crowley, *The Invention of Comfort: Sensibilities and Design in Early Modern Britain and America* (Baltimore: Johns Hopkins University Press, 2001), 96–98. Jeremy D. Bangs describes the homes of Robinson's congregation in Leiden, in "A Real Leiden Pilgrim House," in *The Pilgrims in the Netherlands: Recent Research*, ed. Jeremy D. Bangs (Leiden: Leiden Pilgrim Documents Center of the Leiden Municipal Archives, 1985), 45–49.

23. Amir H. Ameri, "Housing Ideologies in the New England and Chesapeake Bay Colonies, c. 1650–1700," *Journal of the Society of Architectural Historians* 56 (1997): 6–15.

24. Robert Blair St. George, *Conversing by Signs: Poetics of Implication in Colonial New England Culture* (Chapel Hill: University of North Carolina Press, 1998), 126–45, quote p. 126; Gouge, *Domesticall Duties*, 367; Cleaver and Dod, *Godly Forme*, [E6 verso–7 verso,] F4 recto; Maurice Howard, "Self-Fashioning and the Classical Moment in Mid-Sixteenth-Century English Architecture," in *Renaissance Bodies: The Human Figure in English Culture, c. 1540–1660*, ed. Lucy Gent and Nigel Llewellyn (repr., London: Reaktion Books, 1995), 199. On clothing, see chapter 3.

25. Deetz, *Small Things Forgotten*, 92–117, quote p. 109; Deetz and Deetz, "Vernacular House Forms"; Richard L. Bushman, *The Refinement of America: Persons, Houses, Cities* (New York: Vintage Books, 1993), 103–10, 122–23; Demos, *Little Commonwealth*, 28–29.

26. For the great variety of "active" (used indoors) and "passive" (used outdoors or for display) artifacts found in Plymouth homes, see Deetz and Deetz, "Vernacular House Forms," 12.

27. [Winslow], *Relation*, 28–29.

28. Gookin, *Historical Collections*, 151.

29. Demos, *Little Commonwealth*, 192; James Lindale, Thomas Gilbert, "Analysis of Selected Probate Inventories," Plymouth Colony Archive Project (Department of Anthropology, University of Virginia, 1998), http://etext.virginia.edu/users/deetz/Plymouth/probates.html. On the crowdedness of living space, in which "physical privacy was at a premium," see David T. Courtwright, "New England Families in Historical Perspective," in *Families and Children*, ed. Peter Benes (Boston: Boston University, 1987), 16–17.

30. Bushman, *Refinement of America*, 106.

31. Alice Bradford, "Selected Probate Inventories."

32. William Zoanes, "Selected Probate Inventories."

33. *Records of the Colony of New Plymouth in New England*, ed. Nathaniel B. Shurtleff, 12 vols. (Boston: William White, 1855), 3:75; 4:10, 103–4 (hereafter cited as *Plymouth Colony Records*).

34. John Robinson, *New Essays; Or Observations Divine and Moral* (1628), in *The Works of John Robinson, Pastor of the Pilgrim Fathers*, ed. Robert Ashton, 3 vols. (Boston: Doctrinal Tract and Book Society, 1851), 1:236.

35. Cleaver and Dod, *Godly Forme*, [A8 verso], H3 verso, [M5 recto], R verso, E3 recto; Gouge, *Domesticall Duties*, 17, 29–30, 343–44.

36. Gouge, *Domesticall Duties*, 155, 656–61, 669–75, quote p. 660; Cleaver and Dod, *Godly Forme*, [D6 recto], [Q5 verso-recto].

37. *Plymouth Colony Records*, 3:83, 88, 119, 132.

38. *Plymouth Colony Records*, 3:71–72, 73, 82.

39. Edward Winslow, *Good Newes from New England* (1624), in *Chronicles of the Pilgrim Fathers of the Colony of New Plymouth, 1602–1625*, ed. Alexander Young (New York: Da Capo Press, 1971), 361.

40. Cleaver and Dod, *Godly Forme*, G3 verso–[G7 verso], I verso-recto; Gouge, *Domesticall Duties*, 179–97. Cf. Robinson, *New Essays*, 1:239.

41. Gouge, *Domesticall Duties*, 386–88; Cleaver and Dod, *Godly Forme*, [G7 verso], G verso-recto.

42. Winslow, *Good Newes*, 361, 364; Bragdon, *Native People*, 178–79; Kupperman, *Indians and English*, 144–48; Gouge, *Domesticall Duties*, 186; Cleaver and Dod, *Godly Forme*, [K6 recto]; Robinson, *New Essays*, 1:241; James Rosier, *A True Relation* (1605), quoted in Kupperman, *Indians and English*, 147.

43. Cleaver and Dod, *Godly Forme*, M2, [L5 recto], L3 recto; Gouge, *Domesticall Duties*, 391. See Richard Godbeer, *Sexual Revolution in Early America* (Baltimore: Johns Hopkins University Press, 2002), 56–62.

44. *Plymouth Colony Records*, 4:93, 106, 107, 125–26, 153, 167, 191.

45. Cleaver and Dod, *Godly Forme*, [K6 verso]; Robinson, *New Essays*, 1:242. Cf. Gouge, *Domesticall Duties*, 221–24.

46. Winslow, *Good Newes*, 364; Ann Marie Plane, "Childbirth Practices Among Native American Women, 1600–1800," in *Medicine and Healing*, ed. Peter Benes (Boston: Boston University, 1992), 20; Concord Code (1646), in Shepard, *Clear Sun-Shine*, 40. See also Bragdon, *Native People*, 196–97.

47. Gouge, *Domesticall Duties*, 223–24; Cleaver and Dod, *Godly Forme*, [K6 recto], M2 recto; Patricia Crawford, "Attitudes to Menstruation in Seventeenth-Century England," *Past and Present* 91 (1981): 49–52.

48. Cleaver and Dod, *Godly Forme*, P4 verso-recto, [P5 recto–P6 verso], Q3 recto; Roger Williams, *A Key into the Language of America* (1643) (Bedford, Mass.: Applewood Books, n.d.), 147; Gouge, *Domesticall Duties*, 507–19, quote p. 512; Gloria L. Main, *Peoples of a Spacious Land: Families and Cultures in Colonial New England* (Cambridge, Mass.: Harvard University Press, 2001), 104–5.

49. Gouge, *Domesticall Duties*, 343, 278–82; Cleaver and Dod, *Godly Forme*, N7 verso, [P8 recto].

50. Winslow, *Good Newes*, 114–15; Winslow, *A Relation*, 79; Cleaver and Dod, *Godly Forme*, [P5 recto]; Noonanetum Code, in John Eliot, *The Day-Breaking if not the Sun-Rising of the Gospell with the Indians in New-England* (1647), Massachusetts Historical Society, *Collections* 24 (1843): 20.

51. Winslow, *Good Newes*, 363.

52. Cleaver and Dod, *Godly Forme*, L4 verso-recto; Gouge, *Domesticall Duties*, 245–46; Lisa Wilson, *Ye Heart of a Man: The Domestic Life of Men in Colonial New England* (New Haven, Conn.: Yale University Press, 1999), 1–5.

53. Cleaver and Dod, *Godly Forme*, Q4 recto–[Q5 verso], [S5 verso–S8 recto]. Cf. Gouge, *Domesticall Duties*, 456, 497–99. See the introduction for Robinson's principles of childrearing.

54. Cleaver and Dod, *Godly Forme*, [S8 recto], [S5 recto]; Winslow, *Good Newes*, 363.

55. Cleaver and Dod, *Godly Forme*, Z verso, [R8 verso]–S3 verso, T recto–T2 verso. Gouge, *Domesticall Duties*, 482–83 Cf. Gouge, 148–59, 436–37.

56. *Plymouth Colony Records*, 6:190–92, 203, 155, 158–60, 187, 207–8, quotes pp. 190–91, 207–8. On male impotence, see Thomas A. Foster, "Deficient Husbands: Manhood, Sexual Incapacity, and Male Marital Sexuality in Seventeenth-Century New England," *William and Mary Quarterly* 56 (1999): 723–44.

57. Deetz and Deetz, "Vernacular House Forms," 13.

58. Crowley, *Invention of Comfort*, 53; Bushman, *Refinement of America*, 109; Jack Goody, *Cooking, Cuisine, and Class: A Study in Comparative Sociology* (Cambridge: Cambridge University Press, 1982), 143.

59. Josiah Winslow, William Lumpkin, Henry Howland, "Selected Probate Inventories"; Peter Benes, "Sleeping Arrangements in Early Massachusetts: The Newbury Household of Henry Lunt, Hatter," *Early American Probate Inventories*, The Dublin Seminar for New England Folklife Annual Proceedings 1987 (Boston: Boston University, 1989), 140–52; *Plymouth Colony Records*, 6: 45.

60. [Winslow], *Relation*, 66–67; Gookin, *Historical Collections*, 150; Bragdon, *Native People*, 106; Williams, *Key into the Language of America*, 33.

61. [Winslow], *Relation*, 63; Williams, *Key into the Language of America.*, 19, 21; A. Roger Ekirch, "Sleep We Have Lost: Pre-industrial Slumber in the British Isles," *American Historical Review* 106 (2001): 346.

62. Demos, *Little Commonwealth*, 44; Nathaniel Tilden, "Selected Probate Inventories"; Bangs, "Real Leiden Pilgrim House," 45–49. I have derived bed, bedstead, and bedding terms and descriptions from probate inventories. See "Selected Probate Inventories."

63. Cleaver and Dod, *Godly Forme*, [C6 verso-recto].

64. Crowley, *Invention of Comfort*, 7.

65. "Last Will and Testament of Mary Ring"; Thomas Prence, Margaret Howland, "Selected Probate Inventories."

66. These inventories are listed by the deceased's name in "Selected Probate Inventories." On the similar high value of bedding in early modern England, see Ekirch, "Sleep We Have Lost," 352; Carole Shammas, "The Domestic Environment in Early Modern England and America," *Journal of Social History* 14 (1980): 7–10. On the continuation of the same in New England during the 1700s, see M. Michelle Jarrett Morris, "'A Bed and Curtains and all Things Thereto Belonging': Context, Value, and Scarcity in Eighteenth-Century Massachusetts," *Textiles in New England II: Four Centuries of Material Life*, ed. Peter Benes (Boston: Boston University, 2001), 43–57.

67. Bradford, *Of Plymouth Plantation*, 101, 144; *Plymouth Church Records*, 1:80.

68. [Winslow], *Relation*, 51, 53, 56, 58, 63, 66, 65, 67, 68, 79.

69. Robert Cushman, *A Sermon Preached at Plimmoth in New-England, December 9, 1621* (London, 1622), [A4 verso-recto].

70. Emmanuel Altham to Sir Edward Altham, September 1623, in *Three Visitors to Early Plymouth*, ed. Sydney V. James Jr. (Plymouth: Plimoth Plantation, 1963), 29. On the thanksgiving harvest festival of 1621, see chapter 4.

71. See William Bradford, "Governor Bradford's Letter Book," Massachusetts Historical Society, *Collections* 3 (1794): 35, 53, 55.

72. Carole M. Counihan, *The Anthropology of Food and Body: Gender, Meaning, and Power* (New York: Routledge, 1999), 95–96; [Winslow], *Relation*, 74–75. On English shifts in hospitality practices during the seventeenth century, see Felicity Heal, "Hospitality and Honor in Early Modern England," *Food and Foodways* 1 (1987): 321–50.

73. Wood, *New England's Prospect*, 87.

74. Smith, *A Map of Virginia* (1612), in *Works, 1608–1631*, ed. Edward Arber (Westminster, U.K.: Archibald Constable, 1895), 68, 74. On Indian "prodigality," feasting, and fasting, see Bragdon, *Native People*, 134, 220; Kupperman, *Indians and English*, 161–65.

75. Robinson, *New Essays*, 1:130.

76. See Bradford, *Of Plymouth Plantation*, 77–79, 111, 121–23, 130–32.

77. Robert Cushman, "Reasons and Considerations Touching the Lawfulness of Removing Out of England into the Parts of America," in *Mourt's Relation: A Journal of the Pilgrims at Plymouth*, ed. Dwight B. Heath (Bedford, Mass.: Applewood Books, 1963), 95.

78. Cushman, *Sermon*, 2, 6–7, 11.

79. Sarah F. McMahon, "A Comfortable Subsistence: The Changing Composition of Diet in Rural New England, 1620–1840," *William and Mary Quarterly* 42 (1985): 44; Bushman, *Refinement of America*, 74.

80. McMahon, "Comfortable Subsistence," 34–45, quote p. 45; James W. Baker, "Seventeenth-Century English Yeoman Foodways at Plimoth Plantation," in *Foodways in the Northeast*, ed. Peter Benes (Boston: Boston University Press, 1984), 109–10; Sarah F. McMahon, "Provisions Laid Up for the Family: Toward a History of Diet in New England, 1650–1850," *Historical Methods* 14 (1981): 7; John Howland, "Selected Probate Inventories."

81. Stephen Mennell, *All Manners of Food: Eating and Taste in England and France from the Middle Ages to the Present*, 2nd ed. (Urbana: University of Illinois Press, 1996), 22–24. On fasts in spring and thanksgivings in autumn, see chapter 4.

82. Gervase Markham, *The English Housewife* (*The English Hus-wife*, 1615), ed. Michael R. Best (Montreal: McGill-Queen's University Press, 1986), 5, 7–8, 64.

83. Bradford, *Of Plymouth Plantation*, 145; John Winthrop Jr., "Indian Corne" (ca. 1662), in Fulmer Mood, "John Winthrop, Jr., on Indian Corn," *New England Quarterly* 10 (1937): 129–30. For a description of *nokake*, see Gookin, *Historical Collections*, 150–51.

84. Richard J. Hooker, *Food and Drink in America* (Indianapolis: Bobs-Merrill, 1981), 5.

85. Gookin, *Historical Collections*, 150.

86. Sara Paston-Williams, *The Art of Dining: A History of Cooking and Eating* (London: National Trust Enterprises, 1993), 169; Deetz, *Small Things Forgotten*, 124–25. For numerous recipes for stewed meats, poultry, and fish, see Markham, *English Housewife*, 74–83.

87. Bradford, *Of Plymouth Plantation*, 187; Deetz, *Small Things Forgotten*, 53–55.

88. Edward Winslow, "A Letter Sent from New England to a Friend," in *Mourt's Relation*, 86.

89. Tables, chairs, and "table linens" tend to appear only in the probate inventories of estates valued at around one hundred pounds or more. Moses Symons, who died in 1676/7 with an estate worth fifty-seven pounds, owned only "4 leggs of a Table," but no table board ("Selected Probate Inventories").

90. Cleaver and Dod, *Godly Forme of Hovhold Gouernment*, [C6 verso].

91. Winslow, *Good Newes*, 325–26.

92. Deetz, *Small Things Forgotten*, 50–56; Paston-Williams, *Art of Dining*, 184, 190; Bushman, *Refinement of America*, 74–75. Not until late in the eighteenth century were foods, or dishes, commonly cooked and served separately upon individual plates, reflecting the growing sense of individualism and privatization.

93. Gookin, *Historical Collections*, 151; William Kemp, Thomas Prence, Thomas Gilbert, John Sutton, "Selected Probate Inventories."

94. Norbert Elias, *The History of Manners*, vol. 1, *The Civilizing Process*, trans. Edmund Jephcott (New York: Pantheon Books, 1978), 89, 92.

95. Bushman, *Refinement of America*, 76, 78. On the use of forks, still rare even by the 1670s in wealthy Boston, see Paston-Williams, *Art of Dining*, 188–89; Elias, *History of Manners*, 1:69, 126–29; Deetz, *Small Things Forgotten*, 60; Gloria L. Main, "The Standard of Living in Southern New England, 1640–1773," *William and Mary Quarterly* 45 (1988): 129.

96. In Massachusetts two civil law codes developed by praying Indians at Noonanetum in 1647 and Concord in 1648 established missionary directives for reshaping Indian bodies through their dwellings and household activities, menstrual regulations, hairstyles, clothing, and other corporeal activities like not picking and eating lice off one's body and not greasing the body. However, such codes were not established by Plymouth's praying Indians (Gookin, *Historical Collections*, 151; Noonanetum Code, in Eliot, *Day-Breaking*, 20–21; Concord Code, in Shepard, *Clear Sun-Shine*, 39–40).

97. Myra Jehlen, *American Incarnation: The Individual, The Nation, and the Continent* (Cambridge, Mass.: Harvard University Press, 1986), 13.

98. See, e.g., Philip A. Mellor and Chris Shilling, "Reflexive Modernity and the Religious Body," *Religion* 24 (1994): 23–42; Max Weber, *The Protestant Ethic and the Spirit of Capitalism*, trans. Talcott Parsons (London: Routledge, 1992), 104–5; Perry Miller, *The New England Mind: The Seventeenth Century* (repr., Cambridge: Belknap Press, Harvard University Press, 1982), 154, 183, 263; Pasi Falk, *The Consuming Body* (London: Sage Publications, 1994), 49–51.